The Medieval Church

The Medieval Church: A Brief History argues for the pervasiveness of the Church in every aspect of life in medieval Europe. It shows how the institution of the Church attempted to control the lives and behaviour of medieval people, for example, through canon law, while at the same time being influenced by popular movements like the friars and heresy.

This fully updated and illustrated second edition offers a new introductory chapter on 'the basics of Christianity', for students who might be unfamiliar with this territory. The book now has new material on some of the key individuals in Church history – Benedict of Nursia, Hildegard of Bingen, Bernard of Clairvaux and Francis of Assisi – as well as a more comprehensive study throughout of the role of women in the medieval Church.

Lynch and Adamo seek to explain the history of the Church as an institution, and to explore its all-pervasive role in medieval life. In the course of the thousand years covered in this book, we see the members and leaders of the western Church struggle with questions that are still relevant today: What is the nature of God? How does a Church keep beliefs from becoming diluted in a diverse society? What role should the state play in religion?

The book is now accompanied by a website (www.routledge.com/cw/lynch) with textual, visual and musical primary sources making it a fantastic resource for students of medieval history.

Joseph H. Lynch earned his Ph.D. from Harvard University in 1971. He was the Joe & Elizabeth Engle Chair in the History of Christianity at The Ohio State University, where he taught from 1976 until 2008. Throughout his career, he earned many teaching awards, held numerous distinguished fellowships, and authored several books on Church history.

Phillip C. Adamo studied medieval history under Joseph Lynch at The Ohio State University. He earned his Ph.D. in 2000. Adamo is currently Associate Professor of History and Director of Medieval Studies at Augsburg College in Minneapolis. In 2006, he was awarded Augsburg's Teaching Award for Outstanding Contributions to Teaching and Learning.

The Medieval Church

A Brief History

2nd Edition

Joseph H. Lynch
Phillip C. Adamo

Routledge
Taylor & Francis Group

LONDON AND NEW YORK

Second edition published 2014
by Routledge
2 Park Square, Milton Park, Abingdon, Oxon OX14 4RN

and by Routledge
711 Third Avenue, New York, NY 10017

Routledge is an imprint of the Taylor & Francis Group, an informa business

First edition published by Longman 1992

British Library Cataloguing in Publication Data
A catalogue record for this book is available from the British Library

Library of Congress Cataloging in Publication Data
A catalog record for this book has been requested

ISBN: 978-0-415-73685-5 (hbk)
ISBN: 978-0-582-77298-4 (pbk)
ISBN: 978-1-315-73522-1 (ebk)

Typeset in 11/13pt Legacy Serif ITC Std
by Graphicraft Limited, Hong Kong

Contents

List of figures

List of maps

Preface to the first edition

Christianity is a religion in which historical events (or what are believed to be historical events) are important. One source of that conviction was the Old Testament, which told of God's dealings with humanity and with his chosen people, the Jews. A second source was the deeply held conviction, which Catholic Christians defended against Gnostic Christians, that Jesus had really been born of a woman, had really lived as a human being, had really died on a cross and had really risen from the dead. From the first generation, Christians understood themselves in a historical way. The presentation of Jesus's life and teachings was not in philosophical treatises (as it might well have been) but in narratives – the gospels – that included place, time, circumstances and other elements of history. The history of the movement that claimed Jesus as its founder – church history proper – was already being written in the late first century with Luke's *Acts of the Apostles*. Luke had no immediate successors. No church writer in the second or third century composed a history in the strict sense of that term, but many of them recorded historical details, including the successions of bishops, the disputes within the group over belief, the spread of their religion and the persecutions by the Roman authorities. Church history received its first full expression in the *Ecclesiastical History* of Bishop Eusebius of Caesarea (*c*.260–339), who was aware that he was a pioneer in his effort to record the historical growth of the church.[1]

Eusebius had several successors in the fourth and fifth centuries, including Socrates, Sozomen, Theodoret and Evagrius, all of whom wrote in Greek.[2] Between the eighth and the fifteenth centuries church histories of many kinds – those of monasteries, bishoprics, the papacy, religious orders – proliferated. Those historians did not think of themselves as living in what we classify as 'the Middle Ages'. Usually, they thought they lived in the sixth and final age of human history, which was connected by God's plan to earlier ages and was moving more or less rapidly toward the end of time.[3]

It was in the fifteenth century, when Renaissance humanists divided European history into three parts – ancient, middle and modern – that a history of the church in its middle or medieval age (*media aetas*) could be conceptualised. The humanists' notion of a middle age was generally a negative one. They saw the *media aetas* as a period of darkness and barbarism separating them from their beloved Rome and Greece. The church of that barbaric age shared, in their view, in the crudeness and corruption of the times. The debate over the character of the church in the middle period grew hotter during the sixteenth century as Catholics, Lutherans, Calvinists, Anglicans and others quarrelled about the nature of the church and used historical arguments to support their respective views.

The study of the medieval church was born in the sixteenth century and has been an enterprise of huge proportions and long duration. It has always been and continues to be a multilingual pursuit: the main language of intellectual life and religion in the medieval west was Latin and that of the Christian east was Greek. Modern scholarship of high quality is produced in virtually every European language and some non-European languages as well. In an annual bibliography published by the *Revue d'histoire ecclésiastique*, there has been an average of 7,524 entries for the last five years, about 40 per cent of which touch on the medieval church.

In view of the mountains of sources and modern scholarship, it may be thought presumptuous to write a history of the medieval church in a single medium-sized volume. The chief justification I can offer is that I have experienced the need for such a work in my own teaching. Also, I am often asked by interested people for something both reliable and manageable to read on the medieval church. This book is intended to be an introduction for beginners and, to be frank, beginners with neither Latin nor extensive knowledge of modern foreign languages. With considerable regret, I have purposely restricted footnotes and suggested reading almost entirely to works in English, since I wanted to provide interested students with sources and secondary works that they could read with profit. In almost every instance, I chose to cite works that would be useful to a beginner who wished to pursue a particular topic. If students were to read what I included in the 'Suggested Reading' and in the notes, they would learn a great deal about the medieval church. Some readers will miss a more extensive treatment of eastern Christianity or of important historical figures. I understand their view, but I had to be selective in my choice of topics. I have concentrated on the western church and I have emphasised ideas and trends over personalities.

For readers who want different treatments of the history of the medieval church, there is no shortage of choices in all sorts of formats and approaches. I shall suggest only a few. Williston Walker, Richard Norris, David W. Lotz and Robert T. Handy, *A History of the Christian Church*, 4th edn (New York, 1985), cover the entire history of the church in about 750 densely printed pages, of which about 200 pages cover the Middle Ages. Generations of students have profited from Margaret Deanesly's *The Medieval Church, 590–1500*, originally published in 1925 and reissued in a ninth edition, reprinted with corrections

(London, 1972). David Knowles and Dimitri Obolensky, *The Middle Ages*, The Christian Centuries, 3 (London and New York, 1969) provide a chronological treatment with considerable attention to eastern Christianity. Bernard Hamilton, *Religion in the Medieval West* (London, 1986), approaches the subject topically. R. W. Southern's *Western Society and the Church in the Middle Ages*, The Pelican History of the Church, 3 (Harmondsworth, Middlesex, 1970) is partly chronological and partly topical in approach. Southern's book is brilliant, but presupposes a great deal of knowledge on the part of the reader.

The history of theology is not identical to the history of the church, but a knowledge of the history of theology is very useful to the student of church history. A detailed presentation of the history of ancient, western medieval and eastern medieval theology can be found in Jaroslav Pelikan, *The Christian Tradition: A History of the Development of Doctrine*, vol. 1: *The Emergence of the Catholic Tradition (100–600)* (Chicago, IL, 1971); vol. 2: *The Spirit of Eastern Christendom (600–1700)* (Chicago, IL, 1974); vol. 3: *The Growth of Medieval Theology (600–1300)* (Chicago, IL, 1978); and vol. 4: *Reformation of Church and Dogma (1300–1700)* (Chicago, IL, 1981). For the very ambitious reader with French, there is Augustin Fliche and Victor Martin, *Histoire de l'Eglise depuis les origines jusqu'à nos jours* (1934–) in 21 large volumes, of which vols 3 to 15 cover the medieval church. There is unfortunately no English translation of those volumes. The multivolume *Handbuch der Kirchengeschichte*, edited by Hubert Jedin, has been translated into English as *History of the Church*, 10 vols, edited by Hubert Jedin and John Dolan (London, 1980–1). Vols 2 to 4 cover the Middle Ages.

The beginner sometimes needs a good reference work to fill in gaps and define terms. An excellent resource in about 1,500 pages is the *Oxford Dictionary of the Christian Church*, edited by F. L. Cross, 2nd edn reprinted with corrections and edited by F. L. Cross and E. A. Livingstone (Oxford, 1977). There are also numerous learned encyclopedias in many languages which can summarise a topic and lead the interested reader to the sources and modern treatments of it. Especially useful for English-speaking readers are the *Dictionary of the Middle Ages*, 13 vols (New York, 1982–9) and the *New Catholic Encyclopedia*, 15 vols and 3 supplements (New York, 1967–87). One crucial way to deepen knowledge is to read original sources. A useful sample of the sources is translated in Marshall W. Baldwin, *Christianity Through the Thirteenth Century* (New York, 1970). *Readings in Church History*, vol. 1, edited by Colman Barry (Paramus, NJ, 1960), has a considerable number of translated sources from the first to the fifteenth centuries. *Documents of the Christian Church*, 2nd edn by Henry Bettenson (Oxford, 1963), pp. 1–182, has an important selection of ancient and medieval sources, with some attention to the history of theology. *The Library of the Christian Classics*, 26 vols (Philadelphia, PA, 1953–66), has modern translations of many important ancient, medieval and early modern works touching on church history and theology. Unless otherwise noted, translations of sources in this book are my own. The longer biblical quotations are from *The Jerusalem Bible, Reader's Edition*, copyright by Doubleday & Co. (Garden City, NY, 1968).

I have many people to thank for their advice and support. Some of the work on this book was completed in 1987–8 with support from the National Endowment for the Humanities and the Institute for Advanced Study in Princeton, NJ. I am grateful to the Department of History and the College of Humanities at the Ohio State University, which have generously supported my work for many years. I want to thank Lawrence Duggan, John Van Engen and Thomas F. X. Noble for advice and helpful criticism. I am also grateful to the undergraduates and graduate students at the Ohio State University who have listened to – and critiqued – my lectures on the medieval church for almost twenty years. I want to thank the Longman Academic Department for the opportunity to write such a work. The choice of subjects, the interpretations – and the errors – are mine alone.

Joseph H. Lynch

Notes

1 Eusebius of Caesarea, *The History of the Church*, translated by G. A. Williamson (London, 1965; reprinted 1988).

2 Glenn F. Chesnut, *The First Christian Histories: Eusebius, Socrates, Sozomen, Theodoret, and Evagrius*, 2nd edition (Macon, Georgia, 1986).

3 Beryl Smalley, *Historians in the Middle Ages* (London, 1974) is a brief, well-illustrated account of the types of medieval historical writing and the intellectual framework within which medieval historians wrote.

Preface to the second edition

I first read Joe Lynch's *The Medieval Church: A Brief History* in 1992, the year it was published. I was an undergraduate senior with an interest in medieval monks, and a professor of mine recommended the book, thinking that Lynch might be a good person for me to study under in graduate school. In 1993, I became Lynch's student at The Ohio State University. After 37 years of teaching there Joe died in 2008. I was deeply saddened – as were all of his students, colleagues and friends. He had been a wonderful teacher and remained a supportive mentor.

In 2009, when I was asked to undertake the second edition of *The Medieval Church*, it was at once a great honour and an occasion for some terror. The book had been very successful since its first publication. It was popular with teachers and students, continued to have good sales, even after 17 years on the market, and had even been translated into Polish and Korean. How could I possibly revise a work that would live up to that!? Joe himself had been working on the second edition off and on for several years, but other scholarly projects and his untimely death kept him from finishing. Now it was on me to try to make a good book even better.

As it turned out, there was some room for improvement. At the very least, there had been almost two decades of new scholarship since the book's first publication, so there was a fair amount of 'updating' to be done. Some of the topics in the book could also be broadened. As just one example, this new edition has much more on women in the medieval church, woven throughout the book. There is also a bit more coverage of the historiographic and scholarly debates concerning various topics. Lynch had a thorough listing of recommended readings, both in his preface and for each chapter at the end of the book. I have updated these lists with primary sources and secondary scholarship at the end of each chapter. A number of practical improvements make the book more accessible and (hopefully) more appealing to its intended audience, including images and better maps that are placed in the text (rather than being clumped at the back of the book). Finally, there is an online primary source reader, with texts chosen and edited specifically for *The Medieval Church*. References to these sources appear at the end of each chapter under the heading 'Companion website'. Readers can go online as they are reading the history to see what the primary sources have to say.

Concerning footnotes: in the preface to the first edition, Lynch wrote 'with considerable regret', that he had 'purposely restricted footnotes'. Yet in his preface for the second edition (not published here), he changed 'restricted' to 'avoided', with the same considerable regret. In drafts of chapters I inherited, it was clear that Lynch did not intend to have footnotes or endnotes. I struggled with this 'restricting vs. avoiding' issue of notes for some time. Lynch himself had trained me always to cite my sources and acknowledge the scholarship of others. What to do? In the end, I opted for endnotes, mostly restricted to direct quotations. Many of the footnotes in the first edition were more about further reading anyway, and these have been adapted into a 'Suggested Reading' section at the end of each chapter. In spite of the paucity of citations, this book is a synthesis based on the scholarly work of generations of historians. While the absence of footnotes may streamline the student's reading experience, I hope the debt owed to those historians is adequately expressed in the 'Suggested Reading' section.

On the subject of debt, I have received a lot of support to make this book happen. First and foremost, I must thank Ann Lynch, Joe's wife, and Daniel Hobbins, Joe's colleague at OSU, who recommended me for the project. Thanks to the office for Undergraduate Research and Graduate Opportunities (URGO), the Center for Teaching and Learning, the Dean's Office, and my colleagues at Augsburg College, especially John Harkness, Tim Jones, Martha Stortz and Han Wiesma, who read early drafts. Thanks to Elle Davis, Andrew Fox, Luke Mueller and Aidan Nancarrow, undergraduates at Augsburg, who helped in researching parts of the book and the companion website. Thanks also to the students of HIS 348, my course on the medieval church, for test-driving the early draft of this edition. Special thanks to the anonymous readers, who provided invaluable feedback. Thanks also to Laura Mothersole, Sarah May, and the team at Routledge. Also to Kathy Auger at Graphicraft, who ably oversaw the book's production. Last but not least, my deep thanks to Mari Shullaw, my editor and a wonderful collaborator. Her best advice to me: 'It's not easy trying to revise the work of a much-loved mentor, but remember that the greatest tribute you can pay him is to trust your own judgment, even when it goes against him!'

I've tried to follow that advice. If the book has gotten better, it's because Joe Lynch was its first author, and my teacher. Yet, by trusting my own judgement, I have also made his work my own. Any errors, therefore, are my own as well.

Phillip C. Adamo

Publisher's acknowledgements

The publisher would like to thank the following copyright holders for their kind permission to reproduce the images in this book: the Bodleian Library; the British Library; Princeton University Library; Pierpont Morgan Library; Biblioteca Capitolare; Kunst Historisches Museum; Musée de Picardie; Biblioteca Apostolica Vaticana; Bibliothèque Nationale de France; the Viking Ship Museum, Oslo; Aachen Cathedral Treasury; Musée du Louvre; and the Staatliche Museen.

Whilst every effort has been made to trace copyright holders, this has not been possible in all cases. Any omissions brought to our attention will be remedied in future editions.

Glossary

Abbot/abbess: Superior of a monastery or nunnery; derived from Syriac word *abba*, 'father'.

Albigensians: Name for dualist heretics of the twelfth and thirteenth centuries; derived from the city of Albi in southern France, one of their centres of influence; also called Cathars (see below).

Apostolic life: The way of life of the apostles, emphasising their poverty and preaching; a powerful religious ideal, particularly in the twelfth and thirteenth centuries.

Apostolic succession: The doctrine that the authority of Jesus was passed down in an unbroken line from the apostles to their successors, the bishops.

Arianism: View defended by Arius, a fourth-century priest in Alexandria, that Jesus was not the same as God, but was the greatest of all creatures; Arianism was the version of Christianity held by important Germanic kingdoms, including the Visigoths and the Lombards, between the fifth and seventh centuries.

Baptism: The first sacrament; the gateway to membership both in the church and in medieval Christian society. The ritual of baptism was thought to wash away the original sin inherited from Adam; the overwhelming majority of those baptised were infants.

Beguines/beghards: Since the twelfth century, a name for pious women who lived in small voluntary groups for religious purposes, but did not take religious vows. They were free to own property, to leave the group and to marry. Beghards were men who lived the same sort of life. They were prominent in the Low Countries and the Rhineland; sometimes suspected by church authorities of heresy.

Benefice: An endowed church office.

Bishop: A church officer consecrated to the highest of the holy orders; usually the head of a diocese with spiritual authority over the other clergy and laity in that diocese; believed to be a successor to the apostles; word derived from the Greek *episcopos*, 'overseer'.

Black Death: Bubonic plague that ravaged Europe and Asia in the mid-fourteenth century and reappeared periodically in Europe for generations.

Byzantine Empire: The eastern Roman Empire with its capital at Constantinople; it was closely intertwined with the Greek Orthodox Church; the empire's long history of advance and retreat ended in 1453 when Constantinople fell to the Ottoman Turks.

Canon: A clergyman who belonged to a cathedral chapter or collegiate church. Those who observed a written rule, often the Rule of St Augustine, were called regular canons. Those who held personal property and lived in their own houses were called secular canons.

Canon law: The body of rules governing the faith, morals and organisation of the church.

Canon (New Testament): The list of books accepted by the church as scripture; the accepted list of 27 items in the New Testament was worked out between the second and the fourth centuries.

Catechumen: a person receiving instruction on the Christian religion in preparation for baptism.

Cathars: Dualist heretics active in the twelfth and thirteenth centuries, mostly in southern Europe; the word derives from the Greek word *catharos*, 'pure'; also called Albigensians.

Catholic Church: Derived from the Greek word *catholicos*, 'universal'; adopted in the second century by one group of Christians to distinguish themselves from their rivals, particularly the gnostic Christians; more generally, 'Catholic' describes those Christian groups which accept the ancient creeds, including Eastern Orthodox, Roman Catholics and Anglicans.

Celibacy: The state of being unmarried; required of western clergy in the major orders (bishop, priest, deacon, subdeacon) since the twelfth century.

Christendom: The collective name for those territories inhabited primarily by Christians.

Cistercians: A variety of Benedictine monks, who appeared as a reform movement in 1098 and flourished in the twelfth and thirteenth centuries; they advocated a return to the strict, literal observance of Benedict's Rule; name derives from Cîteaux, the first monastery of the order; also called white monks because of the undyed wool in their garments.

Clergy: A collective term for men having any of the holy orders (see below) of the Christian church, as distinguished from the unordained members of the church, who were called the laity.

Cluny: A monastery in Burgundy founded in 909; famous for its magnificent liturgy; during the eleventh century Cluny became the head of the first monastic order, with hundreds of monasteries all over Europe.

Conciliarism: The doctrine that the supreme authority in the church is vested in a general or ecumenical council; conciliarism was extremely influential during and after the Great Schism (1378–1414), especially at the Councils of Constance (1414–18) and Basel (1431–49).

Confirmation: A sacrament that confirmed the ritual of baptism through an anointing with holy oils; in the later church confirmation became associated with adolescence.

Conversus: a) A person who entered a monastery as an adult, in contrast to an oblate who entered as a child; or b) a lay brother in a monastery.

Councils: Ecclesiastical meetings of several sorts, including a) a meeting of bishops with their archbishop or metropolitan, called a provincial council; b) a meeting of a bishop with his diocesan clergy, called a diocesan synod; c) a meeting of all (at least in theory) bishops under the emperor or the pope, called an ecumenical council; almost a synonym for 'synod'.

Creed: A brief formal statement of belief; the most famous were the Apostles' Creed, the Athanasian Creed and the Nicene Creed.

Crusades: Military expeditions, traditionally eight in number, undertaken between 1095 and 1271 to win or hold the Holy Land against Muslim rulers; term extended to other military expeditions undertaken to defend or spread Christianity. The word 'crusade' was derived from the cross (*crux*) which crusaders sewed on their clothing.

Deacon: A clergyman holding the holy order just below the priesthood.

Decretal: A papal letter or an excerpt from one that rules on a point of canon law.

Decretum: A major collection of canon law texts arranged topically by the monk Gratian in the 1140s; used in church courts and law schools from the twelfth century onward. The formal title of the book was the Concordance of Discordant Canons.

Diocese: An ecclesiastical division of territory under the supervision of a bishop; there were more than 500 dioceses in the western church by the fourteenth century.

Divine Office: The religious services sung or recited by priests and religious at the canonical hours, i.e. seven fixed times during each day and once during the night.

Dualism: The theological view that the universe is divided between two radically different powers, one good and one evil; groups holding dualistic views included Gnostics in the ancient church and Cathars during the Middle Ages.

Easter: The religious celebration of Christ's resurrection held on the first Sunday after the first full moon on or after 21 March. It was the oldest and greatest annual Christian religious feast.

Ecumenical: An adjective meaning 'universal', derived from the Greek word *oikoumene*, 'the inhabited world' or 'the whole world'.

Eucharist: The sacrament of the Lord's Supper; the mass; or the consecrated bread and wine; derived from a Greek word meaning 'to give thanks'.

Evangelical: Adjective meaning 'pertaining to the gospels'; derived from the Greek word *euangelion*, 'good news', which was an early Christian description of their message and a term for the books – gospels – in which that message was recorded.

Excommunication: The formal suspension or expulsion of a person from the communion of the church; in the Middle Ages excommunication had serious social and legal consequences.

Extreme unction: A sacrament by which members were prepared for death through prayer and the anointing of oil; sometimes called 'last rites'.

Flagellants: During the fourteenth century, some believed the plague to be punishment from God; they organised great processions of flagellants (from Latin *flagellare*, to whip), who inflicted wounds on themselves to make satisfaction for human sin.

Friars: Term for members of the mendicant (begging) orders founded in the thirteenth century, especially Franciscans, Dominicans and Carmelites; derived from the Latin word *frater*, 'brother'.

Gospel: Originally, the 'good news' of Jesus; then a word for certain documents telling of Jesus's life and teachings; there were numerous early Christian gospels of which four – those attributed to Matthew, Mark, Luke and John – were regarded as canonical by the second century.

Heretic: A person who obstinately holds to a view that is contrary to one or more of the fundamental beliefs of the church; it is not mere error, but obstinate holding to the error when instructed by a properly constituted authority.

Hermit: A person who leaves society for religious motives; a solitary religious often contrasted to monks who lived in a community of some sort; the word is derived from the Greek word *eremos*, 'desert', which was a favoured place for the withdrawal of eastern Mediterranean hermits.

Holy orders: A sacrament reserved for the clergy (as opposed to the laity), by which certain members of society were set apart for God's service by becoming priests, monks, friars, etc.

Icon: A sacred image or picture of Christ or a saint; venerated with particular fervour in the Greek Orthodox tradition.

Iconoclasm: The destruction of icons; iconoclasm was a policy of some Byzantine emperors between 725 and 842; eventually repudiated by the Christian churches of the medieval east and west.

Immaculate Conception: The doctrine that Mary had been born free from Eve's original sin, thus making her worthy to be the virgin mother of Jesus; not to be confused with the virginal conception of Jesus through the Holy Spirit in Mary's womb (see below).

Incarnation: The manifestation of God's son, Jesus Christ, becoming a human being on Earth; it derives from a Latin word meaning 'to be put into flesh'. The doctrine of the incarnation claims that Jesus became human so that he could be sacrificed for human salvation.

Investiture: The act of formally putting someone into an office or a landholding; it was a major occasion of dispute in the eleventh and twelfth centuries when reformers opposed lay rulers who invested clergy with the symbols of their positions.

Islam: The religion founded by the Arab prophet Mohammed (570-632); an Arabic word meaning 'submission to the will of God'.

Laity: The unordained people of the church, as distinct from the clergy; derived from the Greek word *laos*, 'the people'.

Last Judgement: The doctrine that Jesus would return to Earth in a 'Second Coming', during which time dead bodies would rise and be reunited with their souls, and all would be judged by Jesus, receiving what they deserved.

Legate: A representative or ambassador, usually a cardinal, sent by the pope to represent him in a particular territory or for a particular purpose.

Liturgy: The formal prayers and rituals in the church, including such things as the mass, the divine office and the anointing of kings.

Mendicants: Beggars; the term referred to members of religious orders who were forbidden to own personal or community property and were required to live on charity; they sometimes sought their income by begging; mendicant is another term for such friars as the Franciscans, Dominicans and Carmelites.

Monk: Generally, a man who joined a religious house, called a monastery, where he took vows of poverty, chastity and obedience; the commonest form of monk was a man living under the provisions of the Rule of St Benedict.

Muslim: A follower of the religion of Islam; also spelled Moslem.

National monarchy: A form of government that arose in the thirteenth century in western Europe; a king and his bureaucracy gained effective control over the loyalty and taxes of their subjects, often at the expense of the church;

the most successful medieval national monarchies were those of England and France.

Oblate: A child who was offered to a monastery by his/her parents; the practice was already recognised in the sixth-century Rule of St Benedict, and was legislated out of existence in the late twelfth century by the popes; often contrasted to a *conversus*, one who entered monastic life as an adult.

Original sin: A doctrine by which Adam and Eve lost their privileged status in paradise, after which this punishment was passed on to all of their human descendants, causing human life ever since to be filled with troubles.

Orders (minor/major): The grades or steps of the Christian ministry; the so-called minor orders were acolyte, lector, exorcist and doorkeeper; the so-called major orders, which bound their holders to celibacy, were bishop, priest, deacon and subdeacon.

Orthodox Church: The dominant form of Christianity in the Byzantine Empire and in the Slavic lands converted from that empire. Its leaders were the patriarchs of Constantinople, Alexandria, Jerusalem and Antioch; after 1054 the Orthodox churches broke with the fifth patriarch, the bishop of Rome and refused to recognise his authority. *Orthodoxos* is a Greek word meaning 'right belief'.

Paradise: The home of Adam and Eve; a place posited in the book of Genesis, free from pain, toil and hunger; the metaphoric image of human life as it could have been.

Parish: Generally a subdivision of a diocese; administered by a resident priest who might have other clergy as his assistants; it was the basic unit of ordinary church life in western Europe.

Peace of God: A movement that arose in southern France in the tenth and eleventh centuries to place limits on fighting; it placed certain classes of people – non-combatants, women, clergy and the poor – under the protection of the church and threatened those who used violence against them with excommunication; see Truce of God.

Penance: The sacrament though which sin could be remedied, through heart-felt regret (contrition), confession and a reparation to the person wronged as well as to God (satisfaction).

Pilgrimage: A journey to a holy place for the purpose of worship or thanksgiving or doing penance; there were many local, regional and universal sites that drew pilgrims in the Middle Ages; among the greatest pilgrim destinations were the places connected with Jesus's life in the Holy Land, the city of Rome and the shrine of St James at Compostela.

Pluralism: The holding by one person of more than one church office or benefice at the same time; it was a favourite way for secular and church officials to support their bureaucrats; in the later Middle Ages it was a widespread abuse.

Pope: Derived from *papa*, 'father'; originally a term for any bishop; in the west it came to be restricted to the bishop of Rome, who, as successor of St Peter, was regarded as the chief bishop of the church; in the west, the pope became the dominant figure in the governance of the church; in the Orthodox churches that position of dominance was rejected.

Priest/presbyter: A man who held the second highest of the holy orders, after that of bishop and above that of deacon; term derived from the Greek word *presbuteros*, 'elder'.

Prior: In Benedictine monasteries, the second in command after the abbot; also a term for the head of a religious house that did not have the legal status of a monastery.

Private church: A church owned by a landlord or a monastery; most rural churches were founded by the owner of the land on which they stood and remained under the control of his family; sometimes called a proprietary church.

Provision: Nomination or appointment to a church office; in the fourteenth century the papacy gained the right of provision over thousands of church offices all over Europe.

Quadrivium: Arithmetic, geometry, astronomy and music; the scientific subjects in the seven liberal arts; the three literary subjects were called the *trivium* (see below).

Regular clergy: Monks, canons, friars and other clergy who lived in communities under a rule; word derived from the Latin word *regula*, 'rule'; often contrasted with the secular clergy, the bishops and priests who worked in the world.

Relic: An object venerated by believers because it was associated with a saint; a relic could be something owned by the saint, such as a piece of clothing or a book, but more often was a part of the saint's body.

Religious: When used as a noun, it is a general term to encompass any person bound to monastic life by vows; it could be used to describe a monk, a canon, a friar or a nun.

Reliquary: A chest, box or shrine, often elaborately decorated, in which a saint's relics were kept. Reliquaries were often the focal point of pilgrimages.

Sacrament: A ritual by which the church mediates God's grace to its members; the medieval church developed seven sacraments, which are generally associated with various stages of life: baptism, confirmation, penance, communion (Eucharist), holy orders (entering religious life), marriage, extreme unction (last rites).

Schism: A formal split in the church over a disagreement about a matter of practice; distinct from heresy because the split is not over belief; the schism of 1054 marked the formal break between Roman Catholicism and the Greek Orthodox Church; the Great Schism (1378–1414) was the split in the western church between those loyal to the pope at Rome and those loyal to the pope at Avignon; derived from the Greek word *schisma*, 'split or tear'.

Secular clergy: The clergy who were not separated from the world by a written rule or by life in a monastic community; it included the bishops and priests who worked with the laity; often contrasted to the regular clergy who lived under a rule; word derived from *saeculum*, 'world'.

Simony: The buying or selling of sacred things, such as sacraments and ecclesiastical positions; word derived from Simon the Magician (Acts 8:18–24), who tried to buy spiritual power from St Peter.

Synod: An ecclesiastical meeting; see definitions under 'council'; word derived from Greek *synodos*, 'a coming together'.

Tithe: The payment of a tenth of one's income to support the church and the clergy; based on texts in the Old Testament books of Leviticus, Numbers and Deuteronomy, and made mandatory in the eighth century by the Carolingian kings Pepin and Charlemagne.

Tonsure: A clipping of hair or shaving the top of the head; tonsure was the ceremony that dedicated a person to God.

Translation: a) To move a bishop from one diocese to another; b) to move a saint's relics from one place to another, often from the original burial place to a reliquary.

Trinity: The doctrine of one God in three persons: Father, Son and Spirit.

Trivium: Grammar, rhetoric and logic, the literary components of the seven liberal arts; the other four subjects were called the *quadrivium* (see above).

Truce of God: A movement that began in the eleventh century which sought to forbid fighting on Sundays and the chief religious seasons and feasts; see Peace of God.

Utraquism: (From the Latin *sub utraque specie*, 'in both kinds'), was a doctrine which maintained that the Eucharist should be administered 'in both kinds', bread *and* wine, to everyone, even laypeople. Standard church practice only allowed the wine to priests. Utraquism began with the followers of Jan Hus in Prague in the early fifteenth century. In 1415, the Council of Constance banned the practice, condemned Hus and burned him at the stake.

Vicar: In the basic meaning, a person who substitutes for another; in many medieval parishes the resident priest was not the legal holder of the parish; the legal holder was a non-resident person or was a monastery and the resident priest was the vicar for the legal holder, who carried out the latter's duties in return for a portion of the parochial income.

Virgin conception/birth: The doctrine that Jesus was miraculously conceived in Mary's womb through the presence of the Holy Spirit, rather than through sexual intercourse with her husband Joseph.

Vows: Formal, voluntary promises to God. Any adult could make a vow, and it was common practice in medieval religion. However, vows are usually associated with those who entered religious houses. By the central Middle Ages, the vows of monks, nuns, regular canons and friars usually involved promises of poverty, chastity and obedience.

Waldensian: A follower of Peter Waldo (Valdes), a twelfth-century advocate of the apostolic life, who eventually broke with the church over his claim to the right to preach without authorisation.

1

The basics of Christianity

In spite of this chapter's title, the 'basics of Christianity' were not and are not eternal and unchanging, at least not historically speaking. Christian believers, both medieval and modern, might claim otherwise, but there is a difference between belief in a doctrine of faith and what the historical narrative tells us. One is not necessarily better than the other; they are simply two different things. Our goal in this chapter is to introduce some basic concepts of historical Christianity as they developed in the medieval church, and to place those 'basics' in their historical context. Grasping these concepts will help the reader to understand what follows in the rest of this book. Whether these next few pages serve as review, or as a first introduction to Christianity, keep in mind as you read that historical Christianity developed and changed throughout the Middle Ages, and continued to change, subject to constant amendment by various groups of Christians up to the present day.

The 'basics' of Christianity include its doctrines on the creation of the universe, the creation and fall of humankind, Satan, the angels, heaven and hell, redemption, the **incarnation** of Christ, the nature of the **Trinity**, the nature of Eve and Mary, and the **Last Judgement**.

I. The creation of the universe

Christianity borrows many of its doctrines from the Hebrew Scripture, what Christians call the Old Testament. According to the first book of the Old Testament, Genesis 1:1 (chapter 1, verse 1), 'In the beginning God created the heavens and the earth'. This idea seems simple enough, but the earliest Christian theologians questioned it. Did God create everything in the universe out of something else? Or was everything created out of nothing? Even in pre-Christian times, Greek and Jewish philosophers had struggled with the concept of creation. The Greek philosopher Plato (429–347 BC) suggested that nothing comes into existence without a cause. He posited a 'demiurge' – from a Greek word meaning artisan or craftsman – who had not necessarily created everything out of nothing, but took what existed in a state of chaos and created order from it. Philo of Alexandria (20 BC–AD 50), a Hellenistic Jew, saw Plato's 'first cause' as the creator God in Genesis. The

Christian theologian Clement of Alexandria (*c.*150–*c.*215) tried to keep the biblical idea of creation from initial chaos, citing the book of Wisdom 11:17: 'Your all-powerful hand, which created the world out of formless matter.' In the late second century, Theophilus of Antioch was arguably the first Christian thinker to deny the existence of the chaotic state of matter before creation, arguing instead that God had created the universe *ex nihilo*, from a Latin phrase meaning 'out of nothing'. Augustine of Hippo (354–430) – whose influence as a Christian writer spanned the Middle Ages and beyond – borrowed from these earlier thinkers and created a doctrine of creation that would have a long hold on the medieval church. Augustine supported the idea of creation *ex nihilo*, even claiming that God had created time itself, which meant that there was no such thing as 'before creation'. God had always been. He summoned *ex nihilo* all that existed. He was not compelled to create the world, but the created world was still sustained by him for every instant of its existence.[1] Augustine's concept of creation stuck, and was even confirmed in 1215 by the church's Fourth Lateran Council.

II. The creation and fall of humankind

The book of Genesis goes on to include the origin of humans. This fascinating tale of creation – of the universe, of Adam and Eve – has been complicated by a learned tradition of explaining or even explaining away some of its stories. For example, there are two biblical accounts of creation (Gen. 1 and 2:1–4, and Gen. 2:5–23), which became harmonised into a single narrative. According to this narrative, God created the visible universe during six 'days', though Augustine and other early thinkers did not believe these could have been the 24-hour days experienced by humans. On the sixth day God said, 'Let us make man in our own image, in the likeness of ourselves.' The first man, Adam, was created from dust and received life from God's breath. He was placed in a wonderful garden, a **paradise**, where he had control over the rest of creation and enjoyed a sort of human perfection, free from suffering and death, though he was lonely since he was the only one of his kind. In response to his need, God created a companion, Eve, from Adam's rib. The paradise of Adam and Eve, with its innocent nakedness and its freedom from pain, toil and hunger, was the image of human life as it could have been.

Genesis 3:1–21 explains why humans no longer live in a paradise, and why they must suffer and die. God had instructed Adam and Eve not to eat the fruit of a certain tree, but, tempted by a serpent, they disobeyed God and ate the fruit. Because of their disobedience, Adam and Eve lost their health and immortality. Whether or not there had been sexual activity in paradise, there certainly was after the expulsion, and it was so shameful that Adam and Eve covered their nakedness, which had not troubled them before their sin of disobedience. Eve bore children in physical pain and Adam gained food by hard physical work. God expelled them from the garden and condemned them to suffer pain, hard work, death and the other ills that are so prominent in the lives of their descendants. The consequences of their sinful rebellion were summed up in the notion of a 'Fall' from God's grace, which led theologians to develop two related doctrines: one on **original sin**, and one on free will.

According to the doctrine on original sin, when Adam lost his privileged status in paradise, this punishment was passed on to all of his descendants, meaning the entire family of humankind. In short, human life, with all its troubles, was the way it was because of the first parents' sin of disobedience, which damaged all succeeding generations. Augustine was one of the main promoters of this doctrine, but he was opposed by a group of theologians collectively known as Pelagians. A **monk** named Pelagius (c.354–c.430) and his followers posited that the human descendants of Adam and Eve were not affected by original sin. They argued that even if Adam had not sinned, he still would have died, and that Adam's sin only affected himself, not the whole human race. Augustine's ideas won out, however, when the **Councils** of Carthage (418) and Ephesus (431) condemned the Pelagian teachings as heresy.

Connected to the doctrine of original sin is the doctrine of free will. If God is omniscient, then he must have known what decision Adam and Eve were going to make regarding the forbidden fruit. If that were true, then how freely did Adam and Eve make their decision? Were they simply predestined to act out some divine plan? If the latter is true, then how could Adam and Eve, and subsequent generations, be held accountable for their actions? Here again, Augustine was the theologian who exercised the greatest influence on this doctrine, though his writings can seem contradictory. He claimed that humans absolutely have free will, but also that God, because he is omnipotent, has power over human will. A theologian named Thomas Aquinas (1225–74) attempted to reconcile some of Augustine's teachings. Concerning God's omniscience – which would give him foreknowledge of all human actions – Aquinas argued that God existed outside of time, making past, present and future all equal in God's view. God sees everything at once, in a single comprehensive act, like a person looking down from a high mountain at a traveller below, who can see the inevitable path the traveller will take, even though the traveller maintains her free will to make choices.

III. Satan, the angels, heaven and hell

In the events leading to the Fall of Adam, one of the indispensable players in the Christian story made his debut. Even though Adam and Eve had chosen to disobey, that was not the entire story of the world's evils. The Christian tradition traces evil not only to human psychology and choice, but also to a person, a bitter enemy of humans: Satan (from a Hebrew word meaning 'the adversary'), or the devil (from a Greek word meaning 'the slanderer'). Satan had taken the form of a serpent in paradise. He had tempted Eve with the promise that eating the fruit of the forbidden tree would make her and Adam like gods, who could differentiate between good and evil.

Satan became a central character in the Christian understanding of the moral universe, yet his appearance in Genesis was abrupt and seemed to require an explanation. In fact, the name Satan does not appear in the book of Genesis (the first appearance of the name is in 1 Chronicles 21:1). Genesis simply describes a serpent; later theologians interpreted the serpent to be Satan. Out of other bits and pieces in the Bible, medieval theologians gradually accounted for Satan's existence in the following way. In addition to the visible world, God had created an invisible world populated by spiritual beings, called seraphim, cherubim, thrones, dominations, virtues, powers, principalities, archangels and angels. These were eventually regarded as the nine choirs who sang God's praises. Christian tradition has a great deal to say about the lowest spirit beings, the archangels and angels, because their activities were described in both the Old and New Testaments, where they appeared as messengers from God to human beings. Indeed, the Greek word for a messenger was *angelos*. A few of the angels had names known to humans (Michael, Gabriel, Raphael), but the overwhelming majority were anonymous. Before the creation of the visible world, some angels rebelled against God, led by a highly placed angel named Lucifer, which meant 'the bearer of light'. The usual explanation for their sin was their pride and unwillingness to serve their creator. After a tremendous battle in heaven, the forces of loyal angels led by the archangel Michael defeated the rebels and cast them out. Thus there was a Fall in the heavenly realm that paralleled Adam's Fall in the world of material creation. The defeated angels were transformed into devils and their leader Lucifer became Satan, the adversary of God and of humans.

Each kind of being – angel, human, devil – had its natural place in the created universe, with three interrelated zones to accommodate them, arranged like a three-storey building. The top floor was heaven, where God lived with the choirs of angels and holy, deceased human beings, known as saints. The middle floor was the earth, where humans lived. The lowest floor was hell, the underworld, where Satan, the devils, and the damned human beings lived. There was a constant flow of traffic between the middle zone and the other two. While this idea is supported biblically, over time, theologians also debated and developed doctrines concerning heaven and hell. For example, twelfth-century theologians reading Aristotle's works on the make-up of the universe attempted to figure out where, exactly, heaven was located. They also developed doctrine on a place called purgatory – whose biblical roots are still a matter of debate – where sinners who were not quite bad enough to go to hell could purge their sins and eventually be admitted into heaven.

IV. The process of redemption

Even though Adam had sinned and been severely punished, God did not abandon humanity entirely. He planned to offer human beings a way back to his favour, though it would take centuries to work it out. God had a plan to reveal himself again to fallen humanity and to save at least some humans from their inherited sin. In the generations after Adam's Fall, his descendants had gone from bad to worse. In Genesis 6:9–9:17, God sent a flood to destroy all but Noah, a just man, and his family. After the flood, God made a covenant, that is, an agreement, that he would never again destroy the natural world by flood. The symbol of God's covenant with Noah was the rainbow. That covenant included all mankind, but the subsequent stages of God's plan narrowed in on a specific people, the Israelites or Hebrews (known to later generations as the Jews), who were God's 'chosen people'.[2]

God subsequently made a covenant with Abraham, the father of the Israelites, in which he promised that he would be their God and they would be his special people, who would worship only him. He would give Abraham's descendants a promised land, where they could be a nation (Gen. 15–17). The sign of that covenant was the circumcision of every male child. After the covenant with Abraham, the Israelites – descended from Abraham's grandson Jacob, whom an angel renamed Israel – migrated during a famine into Egypt. There they lived as slaves until God gave them a deliverer named Moses, who led them out of Egypt and into the land of the Canaanites (roughly modern Palestine), which God had promised to them so long ago. Moses received God's third covenant on Mount Sinai, where he was given the Ten Commandments inscribed on stone tablets by the finger of God himself. The 'Law of Moses', which was far more complex, specific and demanding than just the Ten Commandments, filled most of the biblical books of Leviticus and Deuteronomy.

Even after their escape from Egypt, the Jews continued to be persecuted by occupying forces, for example, by the successors of Alexander the Great, and later by the Romans. One of the chief promises of God was that he would raise up a messiah, an 'anointed one', to save the Jews. Most Jews today believe that this messiah has not yet come. In the Christian tradition, however, the messiah was born in an eastern province of the Roman Empire, during the reign of Augustus Caesar. This was Jesus.

The life and teachings of Jesus were recorded four times, in the **gospels** of Matthew, Mark, Luke and John. The gospels of Luke (2:1-7) and Matthew (2:1) both claim that Jesus was conceived without a human father, but by supernatural means in the womb of a virgin named Mary, and was born as a human being at Bethlehem. In looking back, Christians have seen many 'messianic' texts in the Old Testament, that is, texts that seemed to them to predict the coming of Jesus. In Christian understanding, the coming of Jesus created a new and final covenant between God and all mankind, which replaced the Mosaic covenant with the Jews.

V. The Incarnation

That God's son became a human being is the doctrine of the Incarnation, which derives from a Latin word meaning 'to be put into flesh'. The Incarnation occurred through Jesus's miraculous birth from the Virgin Mary, whom God had specially chosen to become Christ's mother.

During his life on earth, Jesus taught, performed miracles and gathered disciples in and around Jerusalem. He was betrayed by one of his own followers and arrested by the Jews, who turned him over to their Roman overlords. The Romans executed Jesus by crucifixion. Christians believe that Jesus's willing suffering and death made up for the sin of his and every human's ancestor, Adam, and satisfied his heavenly father's just anger. Jesus's satisfaction of the penalty for human sin is comprehended in various doctrines of Atonement. For example, Augustine taught that Christ suffered in humanity's place, and thus freed humanity from death and the devil. This is called the 'substitution' or 'ransom' theory of atonement: Jesus acted as a substitute for humankind, paying the ranson for our sins. Contrast this with the 'satisfaction' theory of atonement, developed by the theologian Anselm of Canterbury. According to Anselm (c. 1033-1109), Adam's original sin was such a great insult to God that only Jesus, who was both God and man, could be a perfect sacrifice to satisfy it.

Christianity was built on the conviction that Jesus's death was not the end. On the third day after the crucifixion, God the Father undid the effects of death and brought Jesus back to life, which was his Resurrection, a word meaning 'to rise up again'. Jesus remained on earth for 40 days in his resurrected state, teaching his followers, especially the 12 apostles. He created his church by commissioning the apostles to make disciples of all nations. They were to baptise their converts in the name of the Father and of the Son and of the Holy Spirit, and were to teach them to obey Jesus's commands (Matt. 28:19–20). Jesus then rose to heaven, an act called his Ascension, where he was seated at the right hand of his Father.

VI. The nature of the Trinity

God came to be understood as a Trinity of three persons sharing one divine nature, or one God in three persons: Father, Son and Spirit. The most common ritual gesture of Christianity, the sign of the cross, reminds believers constantly of 'the name of the Father and of the Son and of the Holy Spirit'. But this doctrine did not come into being uncontested. The passage in 1 John 5:7 gives biblical authority to the idea of the Trinity: 'And there are Three who give testimony in heaven, the Father, the Word [Jesus], and the Holy Ghost. And these three are one.' Yet some early Christians questioned the nature of the Trinity based on the nature of Jesus. For example, Paul of Samosata (200–75), **Bishop** of Antioch, believed that Jesus was born an ordinary man, but became the son of God after his **baptism**, an idea that was condemned at the **Synod** of Antioch in 269. Arius (*c.*250–336), a **priest** in Alexandria, offered the most prominent counter to the doctrine of the Trinity. He taught that God the Father had come before God the Son, and that the Son was therefore created, and hence of lesser divinity than the Father. This may seem like so much theological nitpicking, but for Jesus to be central to the story of salvation, he would have to be fully God and fully man in one and the same person. In 325, the Council of Nicaea settled the matter, declaring that Jesus was 'of the same being' as the Father, and that the complete Godhead was comprised of 'three persons in one being'. Despite this decree, **Arianism** continued into the seventh century, and was especially popular among the Germanic kingdoms of the early medieval period, as we will see in the following chapters.

VII. Eve and Mary

Christianity gave the world two iconic images of women: Eve and Mary. (See Figure 1.) According to a long-developed tradition, Eve was essentially flawed, perhaps even wicked. In spite of the fact that both Adam and Eve ate from the forbidden fruit, in what became the normative reading of the Genesis story,

Figure 1 Eve and Mary
This image from a book of hours shows Eve and the Virgin Mary on opposite sides of the
'tree of knowledge'. Eve receives the forbidden fruit from the serpent, while Mary holds the
infant Jesus. Eve is shamefully naked, covered only by a leaf, while Mary is heavily clothed.
The differences between the two women are highlighted by the banderole held by the angel
above their heads, which reads: 'Eve, Authoress of Sin. Mary, Authoress of Merit.'

it was Eve who was cast as the temptress, Eve who instigated the 'Fall' of humans, and Eve who was responsible for humans being tainted with original sin. Augustine was one of the greatest promoters of this idea, which would have a profound effect on medieval views of women for centuries. For example, in one of his letters, he wrote:

> What is the difference whether it is in a wife or a mother, it is still Eve the temptress that we must beware of in any woman. I fail to see what use woman can be to man, if one excludes the function of bearing children.[3]

Mary, on the other hand, was the pinnacle of goodness and virtue. By the seventh century, Christians celebrated her conception with a feast day, and as this feast spread it eventually found the word immaculate (from the Latin *immacula*: without stain) attached to it. The idea of **immaculate conception** was that Mary had been born free from Eve's original sin, thus making her worthy to be the virgin mother of Jesus. Readers should not confuse Mary's immaculate conception – in her mother's womb, the product of sexual intercourse, yet free from sin – and the **virginal conception** of Jesus in Mary's womb through the Holy Spirit. The idea of Mary's immaculate conception was not without its critics, including Bernard of Clairvaux (1090–1153) and Thomas Aquinas. If Mary was conceived without sin, it made it look as if she did not need Jesus for redemption. The Franciscan theologian John Duns Scotus (1265–1308) argued that Mary could be immaculately conceived and still be redeemed by Christ, but that redemption would be special because of Mary's special role as Christ's mother. The church did not formally proclaim the doctrine of Immaculate Conception until 1854.

VIII. The Last Judgement

Jesus promised, or threatened, to return unexpectedly to judge the living and the dead. In every generation (of the Middle Ages and even today) people have believed that the return of Jesus, called his 'Second Coming', would be soon. At that moment, dead bodies would rise and be reunited with their souls. The final chapter of history would then be written, with the just and the unjust receiving what they deserved in a cosmic judgement.

In spite of how frightening this may sound, it reveals one of the lasting attractions of Christianity: that it seeks to explain the universe, that its story is cosmic in scope, embracing the full sweep of prehistory, history and post-history. It began before time and will end, according to tradition, after time comes to a violent halt. Therefore the future is also a part of the Christian account of history. Christian tradition posited not only where the universe had come from but also where it was headed. The age of grace, which began with Jesus, was not permanent, since it too was a stage in God's cosmic plan. Time would end, material creation would pass away, and only the spiritual worlds of heaven and hell would remain. Every human being who had ever lived would be judged when Jesus returned to earth on the clouds in majesty. The New Testament had vivid descriptions of the troubled last days that would precede the end of temporal things and the general judgement of all humans.

As this chapter has shown, even those teachings of Christianity that believers might consider basic (unchanging, eternal) did not come into existence all at once. Many of them grew out of interpretations that developed over time, as a direct result of historical contingencies. Let us turn now to those earliest contingencies, to begin to see how the medieval church and its doctrines developed.

Suggested reading

Primary sources

The Jerusalem Bible (Garden City, New York, 1985)

The Other Gospels: Non-canonical Gospel Texts, edited by Ron Cameron (Philadelphia, 1982, reprinted 2006)

Modern scholarship

Bamberger, Bernard Jacob, *Fallen Angels: Soldiers of Satan's Realm* (Philadelphia, 2006)

Bauckham, Richard, *The Theology of the Book of Revelation* (Cambridge, 1993)

Collins, Adela Yarbro, *Cosmology and Eschatology in Jewish and Christian Apocalypticism* (Leiden, 2000)

McDannell, Colleen and Bernhard Lang, *Heaven: A History*, 2nd edition (New Haven, 2001)

Pagels, Elaine, *Adam, Eve, and the Serpent: Sex and Politics in Early Christianity* (New York, 1989)

Rubin, Miri, *Mother of God: A History of the Virgin Mary* (New Haven, 2009)

Russell, Jeffrey Burton, *Lucifer, The Devil in the Middle Ages* (Ithaca, New York, 1984)

Torrance, Thomas F., *Incarnation: The Person and Life of Christ* (Downers Grove, Illinois, 2008)

Notes

1 Throughout this book, we will use masculine pronouns to refer to God. Aware of present day discussions regarding inclusive language, I have decided to retain Lynch's use of 'he', 'his', and 'him', as divine referents, not the least because this was likely the practice of most medieval people.

2 The Old Testament refers to God's chosen people as 'Israelites' or 'Hebrews'. In the New Testament, they are called 'Judeans' – after their geographical locale and after the Hebrew/Aramic word *Yehudim*. This was likely the term favoured by non-Jews in the first century. 'Jew' is a Middle English rendition of the French version of 'Judean'.

3 Augustine, Epistle 243.10, in Peter Brown, *Augustine of Hippo, A Biography, Revised Edition with a New Epilogue* (Berkeley and Los Angeles, 2000), p. 52.

2

Ancient Christianity

Notions such as 'ancient Christianity' or 'medieval Christianity', like so many attempts to chop history into manageable pieces, are modern constructs created by historians. People living between the fifth and fifteenth centuries might have been aware of some change, but saw no significant break between their religion and that of the earliest Christians. In one sense they were correct: Christianity had developed organically, step by step from a small community in Palestine in the late first century. However, the modern perception that Christianity during the years 900 or 1200 was different in significant ways from Christianity in 200 or 300 is also correct. Christianity's history had shaped it (and continues to shape it) in ways that no one in first-century Palestine could have predicted.

In the history of Christianity, the period of origins has had an immense impact on later forms of the religion. For generations of believers, the early years were a perfect time, when the voices of Jesus and his apostles still echoed in the ears of the faithful. Luke's idyllic description in Acts 4:32–5 set a standard that later ages yearned for but could rarely achieve:

> The whole group of believers was united, heart and soul; no one claimed for his own use anything that he had, as everything they owned was held in common. The apostles continued to testify to the resurrection of the Lord Jesus with great power, and they were all given great respect. None of their members was ever in want, as all those who owned land or houses would sell them, and bring the money from them, to present it to the apostles; it was then distributed to any members who might be in need.

Modern historical research has not confirmed this idealised early church, which was so peaceful, simple and united in belief and practice. In fact, the early years of Christianity were turbulent, as different Christian groups struggled to assert that their understanding of Jesus was the correct one. But the image of that perfect church of the apostles has been a recurring force in Christian belief and life.

Christianity began as a movement within Judaism, which was in a tumultuous period of its history, a period that ended in armed rebellion against Rome in 66, a smashing defeat and the destruction of the Jewish Temple at Jerusalem in 70. The root of the unrest in Palestine was foreign domination. With memories of the glorious kingdom of David and Solomon, which had ended a thousand years earlier, and with a conviction that only God should rule his people, many Jews resented both Roman rule and the cultural pressure to conform to Greco-Roman civilisation. However, first-century Jews did not present a united front against the threat of political and cultural domination. Some parties of Jews recommended accommodation with the Romans; others kept Roman culture at arm's length by a careful observance of the Mosaic law and passively awaited God's intervention to sweep away the hated gentiles; still other Jews recommended assassinations and armed resistance to provoke the Romans to violence and force God to intervene for his chosen people. There was a widespread, though not universally accepted expectation that God would send a messiah ('anointed one') to save the Jews. There was great diversity of opinion about what the messiah would be like, but most Jews probably expected a victorious war leader who would drive out the Romans. In the fevered atmosphere of first-century Judaism, sullen hostility alternated with high hopes and desperate action. Periodically, local rebellions broke out, such as the one led by Judas of Galilee in 6. Jerusalem was occasionally the scene of riots and assassinations when the religious or political sensibilities of important groups were offended. The situation came to a head in a desperate and unsuccessful rebellion in 66–73, which was crushed by Roman legions.

It is not surprising that in such an atmosphere there were charismatic preachers who attracted followers. John the Baptist was one of them, a prophet dressed in camel skins who ate locusts and wild honey. He preached that the Kingdom of God was very near and that Jews should repent and change their behaviour so as to be ready for the end. Those who accepted his message washed away their former life and sins in water, that is, they were baptised. There were other preachers far less well known than John and one far better known, who inspired a movement that survived in the Christian church. That man, Jesus, had accepted the baptism of John (Matt. 3:13–15) and became a wandering preacher in Palestine after John was executed. He was active for no more than two or three years. Like John, Jesus taught that the end was near and preached a message for how to act in the end-time. Ever since the Hebrew prophets of the eighth to sixth centuries BC, there had been a tension in Judaism between an emphasis on scrupulous observance of the Mosaic law and one on ethical behaviour and social justice. Jesus did not directly attack the Mosaic law, but he stressed the primacy of love of God and of generous altruistic behaviour to fellow humans. When he was asked which was the greatest of the commandments, Jesus responded 'You must love the Lord your God with all your heart, with all your soul, and with all your mind. This is the greatest and the first commandment. The second resembles it: You must love your neighbour as yourself. On these two commandments hang the whole law, and the prophets also' (Matt. 22: 34–40). Thus, even the Mosaic law must take second place to the demands of love.

So far as we know, Jesus wrote nothing and no one wrote about him in his lifetime. We are primarily dependent for our knowledge of him on four works written between 35 and 70 years after his death. These works are called gospels (from the Old English *go:d spel*, meaning 'good message', which is a translation of the Greek word, *eu-angel*, meaning 'good news', whence came the word 'evangelist'). The four evangelists – Matthew, Mark, Luke and John – composed the gospels after Jesus's followers had come to believe that he was the long-awaited messiah of Israel, and also the son of God. They described him as an itinerant preacher and miracle worker, proclaiming the approaching Kingdom of God through stories, pithy sayings and dramatic actions. He travelled with an inner circle of 12 companions, called apostles, and had a wider following of disciples as well. His criticism of contemporary Judaism and of the religious establishment at Jerusalem gained him many enemies. He was arrested about the year 30 and through a collaboration of the Jewish religious authorities and the Roman procurator, Pontius Pilate, he was condemned to die by crucifixion.

Jesus's followers were initially disheartened by his execution. The Jewish messiah was not supposed to die painfully and shamefully at the hands of the hated gentiles. Soon, however, they came to believe that three days after the crucifixion he had come to life again; he had been raised from the dead by his heavenly Father. The belief in the resurrection of Jesus was the pivotal event in the history of early Christianity: Jesus was believed to be alive again and would come again soon to judge humanity. As Christians pondered Jesus's death in the light of their belief in his resurrection, they interpreted it as a willing offering – a sacrifice – to God the Father that reconciled to him all who believed in Jesus.

The Jewishness of early Christianity must be stressed. All of the main figures were Jewish, who thought and lived in ways that contemporaries recognised as Jewish, including the practice of circumcision, the observance of dietary laws and worship in the Temple. The first missionary activity was among Jews. Jesus's followers, led by Peter and James, Jesus's brother, tried to convince their fellow Jews at Jerusalem that Jesus had been the messiah, whom they had not recognised. They urged them to accept him since there was still time to rectify that mistake before the end. Although preaching among Jews had some success, Jesus's movement failed to attract the majority of his fellow Jews. It remained just one small sect in the broad spectrum of first-century Judaism. After the military defeat and the destruction of the Temple in 70, Judaism regrouped under the leadership of the religious party of the Pharisees. Jewish Christians, that is, Jews who lived in the traditional ways but also believed that Jesus was the messiah, were increasingly out of step with their fellow Jews and gradually separated or were expelled from the synagogues. They survived in small groups in the Near East for centuries.

The future of Christianity lay with missionaries who took the bold move of offering the good news to gentiles. There must have been many such missionaries, but the best known is Paul, the author of influential letters to churches and individuals, which were later included in the New Testament. The pious Jew Paul (*c*.10–64), earlier named Saul, had never met the man Jesus and had been a persecutor of Jewish Christians. He had an experience that made him believe that the risen Jesus had come to him on the road to Damascus, had struck him temporarily blind, and had spoken to him. Once Paul was convinced of the correctness of Christianity, he became its most dynamic missionary and most profound theologian of the first generation. Paul's view of Jesus's message as universal, directed to all human beings, offended many Jewish Christians. He argued that it had been offered first to the Jews, God's chosen people, but they had rejected it. He then felt justified in taking the message to the Greeks, Romans and other gentiles, that is, non-Jews. For 30 years, he travelled in the eastern and central Mediterranean preaching and creating communities of converts, some of whom were Jews but most of whom were probably gentiles. Paul's theology lies at the very root of historic Christianity. For example, he argued against the need for Christian converts to first become Jews. Paul transformed the physical act of circumcision – which he said was no longer required for conversion – into a spiritual mindset, a 'circumcision of the heart' (Romans 2:25–9). Without this painful ritual to endure, more men adopted Christianity, helping it to spread. Paul's writings on women have remained influential and controversial. In a letter to Timothy, Paul wrote that he 'suffer[ed] not a woman to teach, nor to usurp authority over the man, but to be in silence. For Adam was first formed, then Eve' (1 Timothy 2: 12–13). Subsequent generations have seen this as Paul subjugating women to men. Yet in Paul's famous phrase from Galatians 3:28, 'There is neither Jew nor Greek, slave nor free, *male nor female*', the Apostle seemed to envision a Christian world in which nationality and social class and even gender would not matter.

I. Proto-orthodox Christianity

In the first and second centuries, the Roman Empire bubbled with old and new religions. The peace and prosperity of the empire had encouraged the migration of peoples, who brought their gods and rituals with them. The Roman authorities were tolerant in religious matters, so long as neither immorality nor the threat of rebellion was involved. In the cities, the variety of religious beliefs and choices was very wide. The Christians must originally have appeared to be one more of the groups jostling for recognition and members. They were organised as private associations, called churches, from the Greek *kuriakos*, meaning '(house) of the lord'. They had no way beyond moral persuasion to force anyone to do or to believe anything. Almost from the beginning, there were differences among Christians themselves about how to understand Jesus and his teaching. Those differences became more pronounced in the second century as leaders who had known Jesus or his early followers died and as the expectation of Jesus's quick return faded with the passing of years. In the second century, Christianity experienced a severe crisis of authority. With no living eyewitnesses, which of the competing views of Jesus was one to believe?

One of these competing views was Gnosticism, from a Greek word meaning 'knowledge'. In simplest terms, Gnostics believed that knowledge would bring them to God. Much of what we know about early Christian Gnosticism comes to us through a collection of papyrus manuscripts discovered at Nag Hamadi, Egypt, in 1945. These manuscripts include the Gospels of Philip, Thomas, Judas and the Egyptians. There is a Gospel of Truth, and a book called the 'Sophia' (Wisdom) of Jesus. There is even a translation of Plato's *Republic*, though this is highly modified toward Gnostic thinking. In fact, though they considered themselves Christians, Gnostic writers borrowed heavily from Platonic thought, and even pagan myth. For example, concerning the creation of the universe, the Gnostics adopted Plato's view of the creator as demiurge, rather than God, and posited Sophia (Wisdom) as the mother of that demiurge. Gnosticism offers one example of the forms of Christianity that were in opposition to what would become orthodox. In fact, the move to orthodoxy should be seen as a move away from these opposing views, which the church would eventually declare heretical. The crisis of authority in Christianity was a battle for which teachings would win. This was crucial for the direction that the future development of Christianity would take, and it was not a foregone conclusion.

Scholars have found it difficult to give unambiguous names to the winners of this second- and third-century struggle over authority in Christianity. We shall call them 'proto-orthodox', since they were the clear predecessors of the orthodox ('right-believing') or catholic ('universal') Christians of later times. The proto-orthodox Christians developed institutions that generally satisfied themselves as to where they might find reliable teachings about Jesus. The development of these institutions was slow and fitful because the proto-orthodox Christians were not centrally organised, but lived in independent communities scattered around the Mediterranean. By about the year 200, they had nonetheless succeeded in creating a consensus among themselves on how to organise, what to regard as scripture and what to believe.

Proto-orthodox Christians organised under a single leader in each community, called a bishop, from the Greek word *episcopos*, which means 'overseer'.

He was assisted by a group of **presbyters** ('elders') and **deacons** ('servants'). The position of the bishop and his **clergy** was strengthened by the doctrine of '**apostolic succession**', which taught that they derived their authority from Jesus through the apostles. The Holy Spirit had been transferred by a ceremony of laying on hands in an unbroken succession from Christ to apostles to living bishops, who were regarded as the only legitimate successors of the apostles. In about 115, Bishop Ignatius of Antioch, who was being led to execution by Roman soldiers, was already encouraging the Christians at Smyrna in Asia Minor to rally around their bishop:

> Flee from division as the source of mischief. You should all follow the bishop as Jesus Christ did the Father. Follow, too, the presbytery as you would the apostles; and respect the deacons as you would God's law. Nobody must do anything that has to do with the Church without the bishop's approval. You should regard that **Eucharist** as valid that is celebrated either by the bishop or by someone he authorizes. Where the bishop is present, there let the congregation gather, just as where Jesus Christ is, there is the Catholic Church.[1]

This is the earliest known text to use the term '**Catholic Church**'. Ignatius is an early witness to the gradual development within Catholic Christian communities of clear lines of authority, recognised teachers, and a firm structure that enabled them to withstand persecution from outside and the internal dissent that rarely disappeared.

Proto-orthodox Christians also developed brief statements of the essentials of their beliefs. The modern name for such a statement is '**creed**' because the most important Latin statement of belief began with the word *credo* ('I believe'). In the ancient church they were called the 'rule of faith', since they laid out the essentials of belief against which to judge other statements. Converts memorised a creed as part of their preparation for baptism into the community. It is likely that almost everyone in a church knew the local creed by heart. The creed could serve as a touchstone of belief for the ordinary members of the Christian community, to enable them to sort out the many competing forms of Christian belief. If they encountered a Christian teacher who disagreed with any element of it, then he was not their kind of Christian. Creeds varied in wording and details from church to church. The oldest surviving creed comes from Rome about the year 180 and runs as follows:

> I believe in God almighty. And in Christ Jesus, his only son, our Lord, Who was born of the Holy Spirit and the Virgin Mary, Who was crucified under Pontius Pilate and was buried and the third day rose from the dead, Who ascended into heaven and sits at the right hand of the Father, whence he comes to judge the living and the dead. And in the Holy Spirit, the holy church, the remission of sins, the resurrection of the flesh, the life everlasting.[2]

The creeds represented the proto-orthodox Christian communities' consensus on the core of belief, which could serve as a barrier between them and their many Christian rivals.

The third fundamental institution of proto-orthodox Christianity was the authoritative list of the books ('**canon**') making up the New Testament, which is an anthology of 28 documents, including four gospels, letters of varying length and an apocalypse. The New Testament documents were written between *c*.40 and 125 by different authors, some of them anonymous or difficult to identify. But the early Christian movement did not produce just 28 documents. In the first 200 years there was a flood of written works, including the Gnostic texts mentioned above, but also many others. These took the form of gospels, letters, apocalypses, sermons and treatises. Almost all were written under the name of a prestigious apostle or apostles and claimed to carry the authentic teaching of Jesus. The internal divisions of Christianity were mirrored in written works that presented diametrically opposed views of who Jesus was and what he had said. By the late second century, proto-orthodox churches were making lists of acceptable books. They quickly agreed on the acceptability of the four traditional gospels, the letters of Paul and Luke's *Acts of the Apostles*. Disagreement persisted for more than a century about some of the lesser letters and the *Apocalypse* of John. The first time that a list of New Testament books contained precisely the same items as the modern canon was in a letter written in 367 by Bishop Athanasius of Alexandria (*c*.295–373). Even though hesitation over peripheral books continued for a long time, the proto-orthodox Christians had settled the core of the New Testament scriptures by about 200.

The combination of bishop, creed and scriptural canon defined what we can properly call Catholic Christianity after the third century. They gave it a firmness of structure and clarity of belief that served it well in theological struggles with other kinds of Christianity, and in the struggle for survival against the Roman authorities.

II. Persecution

The persecutions of early Christianity had a great impact, but their nature has often been misunderstood by later generations. Christians were unpopular with their pagan neighbours because they seemed antisocial in all sorts of ways. They were regarded as atheists because they denied the existence of the Greco-Roman gods. They were suspected of horrible crimes such as incest and cannibalism because they met in secret, talked about loving one's brothers and sisters, and said that they ate the flesh and drank the blood of someone. They criticised the morals of their neighbours and spoke with too much eagerness about the time when their god would come from the sky and punish everybody but them. The widespread unpopularity of Christians broke out occasionally in mob attacks or efforts by local magistrates to punish or drive out the Christians. Arguably the most famous persecutor of Christians was the Emperor Nero (37–68), who tortured and killed Christians, according to the Roman historian Tacitus, in retaliation for the great Roman fire of 64 – which some historians argue was set by Nero himself to clear land for a new building project. Yet even Nero's persecution was just one of many sporadic and widely scattered attacks over the course of two centuries, from about 29–248. The Christians in one place might be viciously attacked, but even a few miles away their coreligionists lived peacefully. Such local episodes of persecution posed no serious threat to a religion scattered across the Roman Empire, though some Christian communities were damaged or even obliterated. From Jesus's death until about 248, Christians lived in relative peace, marked by general dislike, with intermittent local attacks from their neighbours.

The Christians were an unauthorised group and technically illegal, but the Roman central government had little interest in them for the first 200 years of their existence. In the third and early fourth centuries, that official attitude changed. On several occasions, over a period of about sixty years (249–313), the imperial government tried unsuccessfully to break down the infrastructure of Christian society, in effect, to exterminate it. That change in attitude was brought about by several developments. The Christians had grown more numerous and prominent. The empire had suffered military rebellions and economic problems for which some leaders sought people to blame. But the central issue was the Christians' refusal to honour the emperor, who was regarded as a god by his pagan subjects. Emperor worship was a form of patriotism and refusal to participate seemed to endanger the wellbeing of society, particularly when that society was severely threatened, as it was in the third century. Two systematic attempts to force the Christians to conform to emperor worship were launched between 249 and 260, but the deaths of the emperors involved, Decius (249–51) and Valerian (253–60), cut them short. Succeeding emperors were distracted by a breakdown of military and economic order, which gave the Christians 40 years of freedom from attack.

The last and most determined persecution occurred under the Emperor Diocletian (284–305), who had restored order in the empire after his accession in 284. Diocletian distrusted the loyalty of the Christians and favoured the old gods over newcomers such as Christ. He launched a series of measures to put an end to Christianity. On 23 February 303, Diocletian's soldiers demolished the main Christian church in his capital at Nicomedia. At first, they seized and burned scriptures, and confiscated and destroyed churches. They soon ordered all bishops and clergy to be arrested. If the Christians would offer sacrificial worship to the emperor, they would be freed. Many gave in under threats and torture, but those who flatly refused were executed. Finally, in 304 every citizen of the empire was ordered to sacrifice to the gods and obtain a certificate from official witnesses. Christians, whether clergy or **laity**, who refused to sacrifice were executed or had an eye put out and a hamstring muscle in one leg cut before they were sent to work in the imperial mines until they died.

Though it was the longest and most systematic effort, the persecution of Diocletian failed. By the early fourth century there were too many Christians and they had entered the mainstream of society. Their neighbours thought them odd, but many felt they did not deserve this cruelty. Some Roman officials, particularly in the west where Christians were less numerous, were willing to seize property and burn scriptures, but they would not enforce orders for widespread slaughter. In Egypt and Asia Minor, much of the rural population was Christian and some of them resisted by holding back taxes and grain and even by violence. Finally, the Christians found a champion in Constantine (312–37), who believed that he had defeated his rivals and become emperor with the help of the Christian God. Constantine tolerated Christianity and eventually became a Christian, though at first he probably did not understand clearly what that meant. He did not join 'Christianity' in the general sense of that term; he chose a particular kind of Christianity. There are no reliable religious statistics from the fourth century, but it seems clear that the largest and best organised Christian group was that of the Catholics, successors of the proto-orthodox, with their bishops, canon and creeds. It was that group which Constantine embraced and favoured at the expense of rival groups of Christians – though, as we shall see, other groups persisted.

III. Normative Christianity

The conversion of the Emperor Constantine was a major turning point in the history of Christianity. In one lifetime, the Christian church moved from a position of illegality and ferocious persecution to one of favour. The church historian Eusebius of Caesarea (*c.*260–339) had been imprisoned during the persecution of Diocletian and had seen friends, including his beloved teacher, killed. Yet in his later years he was a personal acquaintance and occasional guest of the Emperor Constantine. During the fourth century, the church moved from being an association of outsiders to a central position in Roman society.

Constantine did not make Christianity the official religion of the Roman Empire. His conversion was a personal matter and the majority of his subjects was still pagan. But in a military dictatorship, for that is what the late Roman Empire was, his example and patronage set in motion the conversion of large numbers of people. Imperial favour was crucial to the success of Christianity. As the privileged status of Christianity became evident to all, a great surge of converts occurred in the fourth and fifth centuries. By 380, the situation had shifted so much that the Emperor Theodosius (379–95) declared orthodox Catholic Christianity the official religion of the Roman state. The practices of paganism and of heretical forms of Christianity were forbidden; Judaism was permitted under tight restrictions.

Between the fourth and the sixth centuries, Christianity adapted to being a state church. The transition was not always smooth and there were tensions between the claims of the church and of the state that were never fully resolved. In spite of that, the church entered into a close and lasting alliance with the Roman state. We call the consequences of that alliance 'normative Christianity', because later generations often looked back with admiration to that time when so many of the traditional structures and practices of Christianity were clarified or even created. For centuries, the church of the late Roman Empire was the standard against which to judge subsequent developments. This coincided with the age of the great church fathers. Augustine, Jerome, Ambrose and Gregory in the Latin west and Gregory of Nazianzus, Gregory of Nyssa, Basil of Caesarea and others in the Greek east. For example, it was Augustine who framed the concepts of original sin, divine grace and just war that still impact Christian teaching today. And it was Jerome (*c.*347–420) who translated the entire Bible into Latin, known as the Vulgate. This was a sign that Christianity was becoming 'romanised'. The original books of the Bible were in Hebrew and Greek and Aramaic. To translate the Bible into Latin was a sign of the enduring importance of the city of Rome and its language. Many other aspects of Roman culture would come to influence Christian institutions.

The most obvious feature of normative Christianity was the privileged position that it held in Roman society, a position buttressed by laws in its favour and by laws against its external rivals and internal dissenters. When Constantine became a Christian, he expected that his new religion would be a unifying force in the weakened empire. However, spontaneous unity has always been elusive in the history of Christianity. There have been two long periods when Christianity did not enjoy the support of the state: the three centuries before Constantine and the two centuries since the eighteenth century when some European states and the United States of America abandoned Christianity as the state religion. Even some European countries, such as England, which kept a state church, relaxed their efforts to compel unity. The experience of both periods suggests that when it is left to its own resources, Christianity is very prone to split over disputes concerning belief, organisation and discipline. Constantine and his successors discovered that religious unity was difficult to achieve. They were repeatedly drawn by personal conviction and by political necessity to try to preserve the unity of Catholic Christianity, especially when serious internal disputes broke out in the fourth and fifth centuries concerning the nature of the Trinity and the nature of the God/man Christ.

For the sake of peace and unity, emperors often favoured theological compromises worked out at numerous councils that issued painstaking and detailed creeds. One such council, which took place at Nicaea in 325, tried to resolve the so-called Arian heresy. (See Figure 2.) Arianism is named for the priest Arius (died c.336), who lived in Alexandria, Egypt. His belief that Christ was a created being, subordinate to God the Father, and hence 'God' only in some restricted sense of that word, found avid supporters and violent opponents in the Roman Empire of the fourth century. The council at Nicaea voted overwhelmingly against the Arians, and codified orthodox teaching in the Nicaean Creed. But such efforts to split the difference or to obscure with a flood of words a disagreement about something so important as the nature of Christ or of God generally failed, as they often do in matters of deeply held convictions. The modern notion of freedom of conscience was not acceptable to fourth- and fifth-century Christians, who were convinced that there were true beliefs about God and that it was necessary to get them right for the salvation of individuals and for the safety of the empire. In such circumstances, the Roman state discouraged the losers in these theological struggles, whom they called **heretics**, by legal and economic harassment. In the Christian Roman Empire the death penalty was not ordinarily inflicted on heretics. But bishops who dissented from a major conciliar decision or from imperial religious policy were often deposed and exiled far from their bases of support. The clergy of the heretics lost the economic and legal privileges that the orthodox clergy enjoyed. Congregations of heretics lost their church buildings and endowments.

Such measures had only limited success, especially where heresies found popular support. Arianism continued and spread in areas outside the Roman Empire, as did Donatism in North Africa (the belief that **sacraments** were only valid if administered by morally upright priests), and Monophysitism in Egypt (the belief that Christ had only one nature, his humanity subsumed by his divinity). But it is important to note that the habit of repressing religious dissent was built into normative Christianity. The laws to carry out that repression were embodied in the prestigious Roman law and in the church's **canon law**.

In the Christian Roman Empire, internal theological quarrels were the most serious problems for Catholic Christianity, but there were external rivals as well. There, too, the support of the state was important. For at least a generation after Constantine's conversion, the majority of the empire's population,

Figure 2 Constantine at Nicaea
This manuscript from *c.* 825 shows the Emperor Constantine – *Imp*[*erator*] *Constantinus* – at the council of Nicaea. Notice the burning of Arian books at the bottom of the folio, with the phrase *Heretici Arriani damnati*, 'Arian heretics condemned'.

including soldiers and bureaucrats, remained adherents of the unorganised, complex religious practices often lumped together as 'paganism'. In the course of a century (320–420), the Christian emperors chipped away at the underpinnings of paganism. They closed temples, confiscated temple endowments, disbanded the traditional pagan priesthoods, withdrew state subsidies for pagan worship and forbade the traditional sacrifices to the gods. This policy of gradually sapping the strength of paganism and 'beheading' it, using that word figuratively, was successful. People could still believe in the old gods, but increasingly they could not openly express those beliefs in the time-honoured ways of offering sacrifices and worshipping publicly at shrines or temples. Traditional Greco-Roman paganism gradually ceased to function as a complex religion with priests and temples. However, important elements of it, including astrology, fertility magic and family rituals, survived tenaciously in popular culture in spite of the Christian clergy's efforts to uproot them as outmoded superstitions or the worship of demons.

There was one exception in the midst of all this. From 361 to 363, an emperor named Flavius Claudius Julianus Augustus, better known as Julian the Apostate, attempted to weaken Christianity's hold on the empire and fully reinstate the old Roman religion. He reconfiscated Christian temples that had originally been pagan, rescinded stipends and other privileges that Constantine had awarded to Christian bishops, and instituted laws that promoted freedom of religion, but in essence favoured paganism over Christianity. It was the Church that gave Julian the title 'Apostate', from a Greek word meaning defection, revolt, or in the case of religion, renunciation. Julian's successor, Jovian (331–64), immediately restored Christianity to its prior place of prominence, revoking Julian's many edicts against it. The episode of Julian the Apostate shows the tenuous nature of Christianity's relationship to the state, when the religious whims of one emperor could so quickly threaten its demise, while its restoration and survival depended, in part, on the accident of history that all future emperors were Christian. Thanks to the Christian Emperor Theodosius I, after 380, Christian heretics and pagans had no legal right to exist, although the empire often compromised or pulled its punches when dealing with potentially rebellious groups.

The Jews were in a very different situation, since their religion was legally tolerated and protected. Roman armies had crushed two major Jewish rebellions in Palestine (66–73 and 135–38). The Temple at Jerusalem was destroyed in 70 and all Jewish inhabitants were expelled from Jerusalem in 138. After those defeats, the Jews ceased to be a military threat and the pagan Roman state permitted them to regroup and to carry on with their religion. There remained a legacy of suspicion on the part of the Romans and of resentment on the part of the Jews. When the empire became Christian, that pre-existing tension was reinforced by the long-standing religious rivalry between the

Christians and Jews, who both claimed to be the true Israel that God had chosen. There was recurrent friction that occasionally burst out into riots, particularly in the eastern Mediterranean where the Jews were numerous. However, the prestigious antiquity of Judaism, long-standing legal precedents and their considerable number gained for the Jews a grudging toleration in the Christian Roman Empire.

Individual Jews could not legally be forced to become Christians and Judaism as an institution had a right to exist, to hold property and to perform rituals, such as circumcision and kosher butchering that were necessary for their religious life. However, for fear of a nationalist resurgence, the Roman authorities would not permit the rebuilding of the Temple at Jerusalem or the repopulation of Jerusalem with Jews. In spite of their legal protection, neither individual Jews nor the religion of Judaism stood on an equal legal footing with Catholic Christians and their church. Emperors from Constantine to Justinian (527–65) issued laws that curtailed the economic and religious activities of Jews. For instance, they were forbidden to make converts, to marry Christians, to own Christian slaves, and to hold honourable public offices – though they could hold burdensome offices, of which there were many in the late Roman Empire. They could not easily get permission to build new synagogues, though they could repair existing ones. The Jews remained an important minority in the cities of the Roman Empire, but legally and socially they were merely tolerated as outsiders in a society committed to normative Christianity.

The support of the Roman Empire was a key factor in the victory of Catholic Christianity over internal dissenters and external rivals – though this victory was hardly inevitable. But Christianity was not merely a religion imposed from the top. Its beliefs, expressed in complicated scriptures and precise theological language for the educated minority and in story and ritual for the majority, provided an explanation of the human situation in a flawed universe that satisfied many people. It promised salvation from that situation. People with outstanding intellectual and administrative abilities were attracted to its service, particularly as bishops. Its holy men, who were usually **hermits** and monks, spoke effectively to the hopes and fears of the masses and of the elites.

Normative Christianity was also firmly rooted in the world of tangible things. It was well organised and energetic. Its numerous clergy, its considerable landed wealth, its prominent buildings, its public rituals, its symbols and pictorial art, and its gradual but visible triumph over its rivals made normative Christianity seem a natural feature of the late Roman landscape.

Normative Christianity was also characterised by an elaborate hierarchical and territorial structure. Even before Constantine's conversion, there was a rudimentary hierarchy in proto-orthodox Christianity. This hierarchy became more conspicuous in the new circumstances. By the late first century, the Christian church had developed a distinction between the laity, from the Greek word *laos* meaning 'the people', and the clergy, from the Greek word *kleros* meaning 'the lot or inheritance (of the Lord)'. Within the clergy there were also gradations. A letter of **Pope** Cornelius (251–3) described the personnel of the Roman church in about 250 as 1 bishop, 46 presbyters, 7 deacons, 7 subdeacons, 42 acolytes and 52 exorcists, readers and doorkeepers.[3]

In the pre-Constantinian church, there were also distinctions among bishops. Most Roman towns were small places and their bishops had nothing like the personnel and income available to Pope Cornelius. The bishops of the numerous little towns were comparable to a modern **parish** priest or minister, since they had neither the time, nor the resources, nor the education to play much of a role outside their local church. Already in the late second and third centuries, a few important bishoprics exercised leadership and even a degree of control over the lesser bishops in their region. The leading bishoprics usually had an early founding, preferably by an apostle, a large number of Christians, a sizable body of clergy and a tradition of well-educated, activist bishops. The leading bishoprics of the pre-Constantinian church were Rome, Alexandria and Antioch, with regionally significant bishoprics at such places as Jerusalem and Carthage.

The impulse to orderly hierarchy, already visible in the pre-Constantinian church, blossomed in the favourable conditions of the Christian Roman Empire. The empire's administrative structure became the model for a parallel church hierarchy. The lowest unit of civil government was the *civitas* (city) with its rural district. Virtually every city had its bishop whose area of authority (**diocese**) was the same as that of the Roman *civitas*. At the next level, the Roman cities were grouped together in provinces; the dioceses of the church were also grouped in provinces headed by the bishop of the chief city (the 'metropolis'), whose title was metropolitan. The administrative provinces of the empire were grouped into four large secular dioceses (a use of the word that should not be confused with the church's dioceses). By the fifth century, the church provinces were grouped into patriarchates, headed by the major bishops of the church who stood in the following order of dignity: Rome, Constantinople, Antioch, Alexandria and Jerusalem, which was a small, poor place but was included as a patriarchate because of its venerable association with the beginnings of the church. The close parallels between the organisation of the church and the state broke down at this point. The emperor was the absolute ruler of the empire, but the church had no single head, though the bishop of Rome was first in honour among the bishops. That honour was expressed mostly in symbolic ways, such as having the most dignified seat at councils. The bishop of Rome was the patriarch of the west, but had very limited practical authority outside his own patriarchate.

Another characteristic of normative Christianity was the widespread use of meetings of bishops to define church discipline and doctrine. Since the second century, bishops had settled (or at least tried to settle) disputes in meetings, called councils in Latin and synods in Greek. The legalisation of Christianity allowed the flowering of councils as a regular part of church government. The ideal was that the bishops of each province meet once or twice a year under the presidency of the metropolitan bishop. In 325, the Emperor Constantine summoned the bishops of the entire church to meet at Nicaea in modern Turkey to settle the problems posed by the teachings of the aforementioned Arius concerning the nature of Jesus. The emperor's action set a series of important precedents. He made it possible for the first time that the entire church meet in a council to settle a serious issue. He personally took an active role by summoning the council and by subsidising the expenses of the bishops. He was present and participated in the deliberations. He took an interest in doctrine and used imperial power to gain adherence to the decisions. The consequence of Constantine's initiative, repeated by his successors, was to identify the **ecumenical** ('universal') council with imperial power: all seven of the ecumenical councils up to II Nicaea (787) were summoned by a Roman or Byzantine emperor.

Normative Christianity had considerable wealth and economic privileges. Pre-Constantinian Christian churches had owned modest amounts of property, mostly church buildings and cemeteries. However, since Roman law did not sanction them, their legal title was not secure and the property was liable to be confiscated during persecutions. During the Christian Roman Empire, the wealth possessed by churches grew considerably. The legalisation of Christianity meant that churches and later monasteries could hold wealth as corporate bodies, and could receive gifts of land and money as well as legacies in wills. Since churches were undying corporations, over the generations the favoured ones accumulated considerable wealth (there were, of course, many poor churches as well).

Constantine himself set the pattern of lavish generosity when he built impressive churches at the holy sites of Christianity, including churches dedicated to Christ's resurrection in Jerusalem, to Christ's birth in Bethlehem, to Christ's baptism at the River Jordan and to Peter's martyrdom at Rome. Successive emperors also gave churches and clergy valuable exemptions from taxation and forced labour. Other believers gave gifts of precious objects, money and land. Normative Christianity was comprised of numerous endowed and independent institutions that together held a significant portion of society's wealth.

The legalisation of and imperial favour toward Christianity led to one further characteristic of normative Christianity that later generations admired: an orderly church law, called canon law. Pre-Constantinian Christian churches had procedures and customs to regulate individual behaviour and community life. That development had already been initiated by New Testament writings, particularly the letters of Paul. In the second and third centuries, churches had developed rules for admitting members, for expelling sinners, for choosing clergy, for performing liturgical services and for administering property. There was considerable diversity from one end of the Mediterranean to the other, but the leading bishops and the decisions of councils gradually introduced some similarity of practice at the regional level.

In the Christian Roman Empire, the need and the opportunity for a more detailed church law arose. Regional and ecumenical councils treated not only matters of theology, but also the day-to-day problems of defining boundaries, settling disputes over rights, disciplining errant clergy and lay people, and protecting the growing church property from fraud, theft and mismanagement. Important bishops, but especially the bishops of Rome, issued letters, called **decretals**, which responded to requests for advice or forbade objectionable practices. The Christian emperors also issued laws for the church, touching occasionally on theology, but more commonly on the legal and economic privileges of churches and clergy, the protection of church property, and the repression of heretical forms of Christianity. In 438, the Emperor Theodosius II (408–50) ordered the codification of laws issued during the 120 years from Constantine's reign to his own, many of which concerned the church. A century later, the Emperor Justinian (527–65) also ordered the codification of the Roman law. The proportion of laws that touched directly or indirectly on the church was significant.

The move to bring order to the church's own internally created law was carried out by the learned monk Dionysius Exiguus (Dennis the Short), who was active from about 497 to 540 at Rome. Dionysius was a legal scholar who collected in one volume the canons issued by church councils. He also collected in a single volume the decretal letters of bishops of Rome from Pope Siricius (384) to Pope Anastasius II (498). To later generations, the imposing legal structure of the Christian church in the Roman Empire seemed admirable, orderly and proper, a normative standard to which they aspired.

Dionysius was also the man who calculated, apparently with an error of between four and seven years, the date of Christ's birth, which is used in the modern dating system of BC (before Christ) and AD (*anno Domini*: 'in the year of the Lord'). People throughout history have dated their own times according to whatever events they thought most important. For Roman historians this was the founding of Rome itself, so they dated events AUC (*ab urbe conditum*: 'since the foundation of the city'), which corresponds to 753 BC. For Dionysius, the most important date was the birth of Jesus. That the Dionysian dating system took hold shows how great the influence of Christianity was in the late Roman Empire and beyond. The convention of using BC and AD, now thought to be too 'Christo-centric', has fallen out of favour in many history books, especially in the United States. It has been replaced by BCE (*before the common era* of Judaism and Christianity) and CE (the *common era* of Judaism and Christianity), which are thought to be more inclusive and/or 'politically correct'. One of the questionable aspects of the BCE/CE method is that the dates are exactly the same as in BC/AD. Judaism itself continues to have its own calendar, based on its tradition of when the world was created. In 2012, as we write this paragraph, the Jewish calendar marks the year 5772. And while this newer dating system is slightly more inclusive, there are all sorts of religions and cultures that are not included. For example, **Islam** uses the year of Mohammed's pilgrimage (*Hijrah*) as the starting point of its calendar (which corresponds roughly to AD 622). And BCE/CE does not begin to account for the Chinese or the Mayans. The important thing to remember here is that all dating systems are human inventions, based on something that humans in a certain time and place deemed important.

IV. The beginnings of monasticism

There was another development that can be understood as a reaction against the growing formalism of normative Christianity. Since its beginnings, Christianity had placed a high value on voluntary asceticism, that is, self-denial for religious motives. Such self-denial usually involved sexual abstinence, fasting and avoidance of worldly entanglement. Many Christian communities in the second and third centuries had ascetic members, mostly widows and virgins, but some men as well. Such ascetics lived among their fellow Christians and, if they were able, they earned their own living, though the community supported some of them. In the fourth and fifth centuries, the ascetic impulse became stronger and took a new form. As Christian churches became larger and more structured, some fervent Christians saw them as tepid and too compromising with the world. Some of them, mostly men though there were certainly a fair number of women, abandoned urban life and ordinary careers and sought remote places, where they lived lives of systematic and severe self-denial, coupled with prayer and meditation on the scriptures. These were the first monks. Some, like Saint Antony (*c.*251–356), chose the eremitic or hermit life, and according to tradition found themselves tempted by boredom and apparitions of women. The eremitic life had its own challenges, but since its practitioners lived alone, it did not offer much opportunity to practise Christian charity – one needed other people around for that. Saint Pachomius (*c.*292–348) chose the cenobitic or communal form of monasticism. Living in community, with other flawed humans, there were ample opportunities to practise Christian charity.

Monks posed a challenge to normative Christianity, since they represented traditions of religious behaviour that directly or indirectly criticised the development of a structured church with many ties to society. However, normative Christianity found ways to accommodate them. By the fifth century, monasticism in its many forms had become a part of normative Christianity, a safety valve for the zealous minority who might otherwise have split from the main body of believers.

Normative Christianity was the direct outcome of the close alliance between the Catholic Christian church and the Roman Empire. The empire was the leading partner and the church was generally content with that, though it had values and beliefs that it defended even against the insistence of emperors. The alliance became unstable in the fifth century, particularly in the west, because the imperial partner was in serious political and economic decline. However, normative Christianity, embodied in sturdy structures such as the office of bishop, the written creed, the canon of scripture, the patriarchates and the conciliar tradition, and preserved in books such as the codes of Roman and canon law and in the writings of the church fathers, remained one of the ideals to which later generations of Christians looked back.

Suggested reading

Companion website
www.routledge.com/cw/lynch

2.1   Athanasius confirms the New Testament Canon
'Athanasius, Letter 39', in S. Athanasius, *Festal Epistles of S. Athanasius Bishop of Alexandria, Translated from the Syriac with Notes and Indices*, trans. Henry Griffin Williams, (Oxford: F. and J. Rivington, 1854), 137–139.

2.2   Constantine's Conversion
Excerpts from Eusebius, *The Life of the Blessed Emperor Constantine*, in *The Greek Ecclesiastical Historians of The First Six Centuries of The Christian Era* (London: Samuel Bagster And Sons, 1845), 25–30.

2.3   Early Christian Creeds
'The Nicene Creed of 325' and 'The Constantinopolitan Creed of 381', in Philip Schaff, *The Creeds of Christendom with a History and Critical Notes* (New York: Harper & Brothers, 1919), 28–29.

Primary sources

Eusebius of Caesarea, *The Ecclesiastical History*, translated by G. A. Williamson, as *The History of the Church* (London, 1965)

The Gospels and Acts of the Apostles

The Other Gospels: Non-canonical Gospel Texts, edited by Ron Cameron (Philadelphia, 1982, reprinted 2006)

The Theodosian Code and Novels, and the Sirmondian Constitutions, translated by Clyde Pharr (Princeton, 1952).

Western Asceticism, edited by Owen Chadwick (Philadelphia, 1958)

Modern scholarship

Blackburn, Bonnie and Leofranc Holford-Strevens, *The Oxford Companion to the Year: An Exploration of Calendar Customs and Time-Reckoning* (Oxford, 1999)

Chadwick, Henry, *The Church in Ancient Society. From Galilee to Gregory the Great* (Oxford, 2001)

Daniélou, Jean, *The Theology of Jewish Christianity*, translated by John A. Baker (London and Philadelphia, 1978)

Deane, Herbert A., *The Political and Social Ideas of St. Augustine* (New York, 1963)

Jones, A. H. M., *Constantine and the Conversion of Europe* (London, 1948; reprinted 1962)

Lynch, Joseph H., *Early Christianity: A Brief History* (Oxford, 2009)

Mitchell, Stephen, *A History of the Later Roman Empire, AD 284–641* (Malden, Massachusetts, 2007)

Pelikan, Jaroslav, *The Christian Tradition: A History of the Development of Doctrine*, especially vol. 3, *The Growth of Medieval Theology (600–1300)* (Chicago, 1978)

Schoeps, Hans J., *Jewish Christianity*, translated by D. R. A. Hare (Philadelphia, 1969)

Simon, Marcel, *Jewish Sects at the Time of Jesus*, translated by James H. Farley (Philadelphia, 1967)

Vauchez, Andre, *Sainthood in the Later Middle Ages*, translated by Jean Birrell (Cambridge, 1997)

Weinstein, Donald and Rudolph Bell, *Saints and Society: The Two Worlds of Western Christendom, 1000–1700* (Chicago, 1982)

Wills, Garry, *Saint Augustine* (New York, 1999)

Notes

1 Ignatius, *Letter to the Smyrnaeans*, ch. 8, in Cyril C. Richardson, *Early Christian Fathers*, The Library of the Christian Classics, vol. 1 (Philadelphia, 1953), p. 115.
2 *Documents of the Christian Church*, 2nd edition, edited by Henry Bettenson (London, 1963), p. 23 (translation adapted by the authors).
3 Eusebius of Caesarea, *The Ecclesiastical History*, book 6, ch. 43, translated by G. A., Williamson, *The History of the Church* (London, 1965), p. 282.

3

Beginnings of the medieval church

There is no precise date at which we can say with assurance that the ancient church ended and the medieval church began. The transition from one to the other was not an event but a long process of which contemporaries were unaware. The fate of the Roman Empire had immense implications for the future of Christianity. In the eastern parts of the empire, the alliance between Christianity and the Roman state remained unbroken and developed into the close intertwining of the Greek **Orthodox Church** and the **Byzantine Empire**. In the western territories of the Roman Empire, the course of development was very different. The alliance between normative Christianity and the imperial government was unstable because the empire was slowly collapsing in the west under the weight of economic, political and military problems. The decisive centuries of transition were the fifth and sixth. In the fifth century, the imperial government in the west collapsed in one region after another under the pressure of invaders who spoke Germanic languages. By the sixth century, the territories of the western empire had been divided among Germanic tribes, although a few small territories, including the city of Rome, remained as outposts under the control of the Roman emperors who resided at Constantinople, modern Istanbul in Turkey. For the purposes of this book, the medieval church began when Christianity outlived the Roman state in the west and had to come to terms with a different environment. The normative Christianity of the Roman Empire continued to offer models of behaviour and ideals after which to strive, but the key development was adaptation to a new situation.

I. The decline of the Roman Empire

It is one of the ironies of history that Christianity had allied itself with an empire in decline. In the third and fourth centuries, severe social, demographic, economic and military problems were already sapping the vitality of that empire. The Roman Empire was contracting by almost every measure that we can apply. If we had the statistics, which we do not, we could probably demonstrate that the socio-economic vigour of the empire peaked around the year 150. Thereafter, a long-term decline set in, more severe in some regions than others, sometimes slower and sometimes faster, sometimes marked by temporary recoveries, sometimes perceptible to contemporaries but usually not. A witch's brew of problems reinforced one another and contemporaries had neither the intellectual tools to understand them nor the means to halt them.

The fifth century was the turning point in the course of decline in the western part of the empire, which was attacked by numerous foes, the so-called barbarians, who disrupted economic and political life further. For centuries, the Romans had alternately traded peacefully and fought with Germanic peoples on the borders, but the balance of power had been with the Romans. When the Visigoths crossed the Danube and entered the empire in 375, something new emerged. The Visigoths were fleeing from the Huns and received permission to enter the empire. They came not as raiders, but as migrants with their families, their animals and their belongings. As a consequence of harsh treatment at the hands of Roman officials, they rebelled in 378, defeated a Roman army and killed the Emperor Valens in a battle at Adrianople, near Constantinople. They then began a migration within the empire that lasted more than twenty years, seeking a suitable place to settle down. Their military success revealed the fundamental weakness of the empire, which could not stop the wanderings of what must have been a modest-sized tribal group. Other Germanic peoples were emboldened to enter the empire in order to settle down. The migrations of these peoples eventually redrew the map of the western empire.

The Roman Empire gradually split into two parts, east and west, which had very different futures. The eastern part of the empire survived in a battered and shrunken form as what modern historians call the Byzantine Empire, whereas the western part sank under the weight of its problems and by 476 was divided up among the Germanic invaders – many of whom were Arian Christians – who ruled the much larger native Roman population. There were still Roman emperors, but they resided in Constantinople. These emperors kept their claim to be the rulers of the west. The Emperor Justinian (527–65) temporarily reconquered Italy, and parts of North Africa and Spain, though his successors could not hold more than a few fragments of territory in Italy and the Mediterranean islands. The rise of Islam in the seventh century amputated even more of the old Roman Empire, including the Near East, North Africa and Spain. The Byzantine Empire survived in Asia Minor and the Balkans. Hard pressed by its dangerous northern and eastern enemies, it was less and less able to intervene in western affairs.

By 750, a new balance of power had emerged. The former Roman Empire had been divided into three distinct and lasting entities: the Byzantine Empire, the Islamic world and the Latin west, each of which was based on a religion (Greek Orthodoxy, Islam and Catholicism) and on a sacred language (Greek, Arabic and Latin). For centuries, the Latin west was the poorest of the societies that were heir to the Roman past. In spite of modest regional recoveries, the decline and subsequent stagnation in the west continued for six or seven centuries after the Roman government had vanished, until a major revival began in the eleventh century. From the point of view of the Christian church in the west, the practical effects of its alliance with the Roman/ Byzantine Empire, which was far away and developing in different directions, had become mostly theoretical.

II. Byzantine Christianity

Although this book will concentrate on the Christian church in the west, the church in the Byzantine Empire remained an important heir to the normative Christianity of the fourth and fifth centuries. The Byzantines did not call themselves 'Byzantine' (that is a modern word derived from the city, called Byzantion, on whose site the city of Constantinople was built). They regarded themselves as Romans and indeed they were the heirs of the old empire, although such major changes had occurred that a second-century Roman emperor would have had difficulty recognising his seventh-century successors and their empire. By 476, the west had been lost to Germanic invaders. Between 632 and 650, Islamic armies had conquered Egypt, Palestine, Lebanon and Syria. Thereafter, the shrunken Byzantine Empire was Greek in language and Orthodox Christian in religion. In spite of its territorial losses, it remained a sophisticated society, with highly developed legal and bureaucratic systems. It was centred on the great commercial city and military stronghold of Constantinople, which was colossal by the standards of pre-modern times. There might have been 500,000 people in Constantinople in the tenth century, when Paris and Rome had fewer than 10,000. At its height, Constantinople was the largest Christian city on earth. For most of its long history, the Byzantine Empire was on the defensive against the **Muslims** to the south and east, the Slavic and Turkic peoples to the north, and the Latin Christians to the west. Until serious military defeats in the eleventh century, it remained a world power, rich, populous and highly sophisticated in its arts and crafts.

Orthodox Christianity was at the heart of the way the Byzantines understood themselves and their empire. God had preserved their empire because they were the guardians of true belief – which is what 'orthodoxy' means in Greek – amid the dangers of pagans, Muslims and heretics, among whom they sometimes put the Latin Christians. Until the ninth century, the Byzantine church carried on the ancient tradition of theological debate so passionately that it spilled over into rioting and rebellion. At times, religious conflict was also influenced by the ethnicity of the participants. For example, the seventh-century Islamic conquest of Byzantine Egypt happened to some extent because Coptic Christians in Egypt clashed with their Greek Orthodox overlords on the question of Monophysitism – the belief that Christ had one nature, rather than having two separate natures, human and divine – which the Orthodox considered heresy. Once the Muslims took control, they tolerated Coptic Christians, and did not much care if the Byzantines considered them heretics. The very ferocity of religious quarrels in the Byzantine Empire points to the seriousness of religious concerns. Although Islam blocked the empire's expansion in the south and east, and Latin Christianity blocked it in the west, in the ninth and tenth centuries Byzantine missionaries carved out a zone of influence among the Slavic peoples of Russia and eastern Europe, in areas never reached by its Roman predecessors. To an observer at most moments from the sixth to the eleventh centuries, the Byzantine Empire must have appeared to be the very heartland of Christianity, its economic, theological and political centre of gravity.

III. Islam

Islam was heir to a second major portion of the territory of the Roman Empire. Mohammed (*c.*570–632), an Arab merchant living in the city of Mecca, claimed that the angel Gabriel brought him revelations from the one God, Allah, whom Mohammed believed to be the God of the Old and New Testaments. These revelations were recorded in the Islamic holy book known as the Qur'an. God had revealed much to the prophets of earlier periods, among whom Muslims counted Jesus, but God's final revelation was to Mohammed, who was to be the last in the line of the prophets. Mohammed's prophetic message – that there was no God except for Allah – found great success among the warring clans of the Arabian Desert, who had traditionally worshipped many gods. Those who submitted to his call (the literal meaning of 'Islam' is 'submission') and became Muslim ('one who has submitted') were united in their zeal for the true faith and quickly turned their energies toward raiding and conquest of their neighbours, the Byzantines to the north and west and the Persians to the east. Within an astonishingly short period, no more than two human lifetimes, Arab armies under the unifying power of Islam had redrawn the religious and political map of the Greco-Roman world. They conquered the shores of the Mediterranean from Syria to Spain, and even Persia, which had never been held by the Romans. The armies and fleets of Islam pressed hard on both the Byzantine Empire and the Latin west in the eighth and ninth centuries. If circumstances had been different, the entire Mediterranean basin might have been reunited under Muslim domination, but Constantinople held out against a major siege in 717, while Christian Franks defeated Muslim raiding parties at Tours in 732, forcing the Muslims to withdraw south of the Pyrenees into Spain. A military stand-off in the Mediterranean between Islam and Byzantium allowed the Latin west to survive.

Large numbers of Christians lived under Muslim rule. They were not generally forced to convert to Islam, but they lived under conditions of second-class status similar to those their Christian predecessors had imposed on Jews in the Christian Roman Empire. The Christian communities in Muslim lands withered over the centuries as their members converted to Islam, sometimes for social and economic advantages, but also out of conviction. There are still Christian minorities in most of the Muslim Near East, descendants of the conquered peoples. The Muslim Arabs borrowed much from the Greco-Roman past and created a lively urban and commercial civilisation that extended from Toledo in Spain to Baghdad in Iraq, united by the religion of Islam, the Arabic language and vigorous economic ties.

IV. The Latin west

Byzantium and Islam were comparable to one another in their wealth, military power, urbanisation and sophistication. They were the possessors of territory that in Roman times had been the most prosperous and highly developed. In sharp contrast, the Latin west cut a poor figure. It developed in territories that were among the poorest and least developed parts of the Roman Empire. Its problems, which had begun in the late Roman Empire, continued between the fifth and the eighth centuries even after the political collapse of the empire in the west: cities withered, population stagnated or fell, violence disrupted life, trade shrank, economic production shifted to rural estates owned by great lords who dominated an impoverished peasantry, and standards of living and literacy declined. In modern terms the Latin west was an underdeveloped region until the twelfth century, inferior to Byzantium and Islam in most measures of economic and social life. Yet the west avoided both absorption by Islam and domination by Byzantium. It was the third heir to the Greco-Roman past. Like the other heirs, it also spread its religion and culture beyond the former Roman boundaries, into the Germanic and Slavic lands of northern and central Europe. It created new institutions or adapted old ones and created a religious structure that proved remarkably resilient.

V. Gregory the Great

The career of Pope Gregory I (590-604) illustrates in microcosm the period of transition of the western church from the Christian Roman Empire to the Middle Ages. He was an heir of the Greco-Roman past and a staunch defender of normative Christianity. (See Figure 3.) At the same time, his life and career pointed to future developments. A brief overview of the situation in Gregory's lifetime will serve as a starting point for the history of the medieval church.

When Gregory was elected bishop of Rome in 590, the Christian movement was more than 500 years old and normative Christianity was 250 years old. The alliance of the church in the west with the Roman state was in bad repair because of political circumstances, but not because either party wanted to abandon it. The weaker partner in the alliance was now the empire. No emperor had lived in the city of Rome for 120 years. The migration and settlement of Germanic peoples in the western empire had pushed effective imperial authority into the eastern Mediterranean. (See Map 1.) From 476 to 554, Italy had been ruled by Germanic kings, first Odovacar and then Theodoric, king of the Ostrogoths (493-526), and his successors. Theodoric was the most romanised of the barbarian kings and favourable to Roman ways. The native population of Italy lived in traditional ways under Roman magistrates answerable to the Ostrogothic king. In 535, the vigorous Roman Emperor Justinian began the reconquest of Italy from Theodoric's weak successors. The Ostrogoths resisted valiantly and Italy was devastated during 19 years of warfare (535-54) between Roman and Ostrogothic troops. It is symbolic of the period that the city of Rome itself, formerly the mistress of the entire Mediterranean, was empty for 40 days in 549, its inhabitants evacuated by the Ostrogothic king Totila. Gregory, who was born about 540, spent his childhood during those hard years.

By 554, the Ostrogoths had been defeated but the Byzantine Empire was financially exhausted by its effort to reconquer the west. Even though Italy was impoverished and depopulated by war and the outbreak of plague, the imperial government demanded heavy taxes to recoup its expenses, which only worsened the situation. Justinian's conquests in Italy remained intact for only 14 years. In 568, the Lombards, a fierce and unromanised Germanic tribe, crossed the Alps and began their conquest of Italy. The imperial government was able to save only coastal enclaves, including Ravenna, Naples and Rome. In 573, Gregory, who was about 33 years old and still a layman, was the prefect of Rome, the highest civil official in the city, and participated in the successful defence of the city against a Lombard attack. His entire life was spent against a backdrop of an impoverished and depopulated Italy and under the constant threat of Lombard attacks and epidemics.

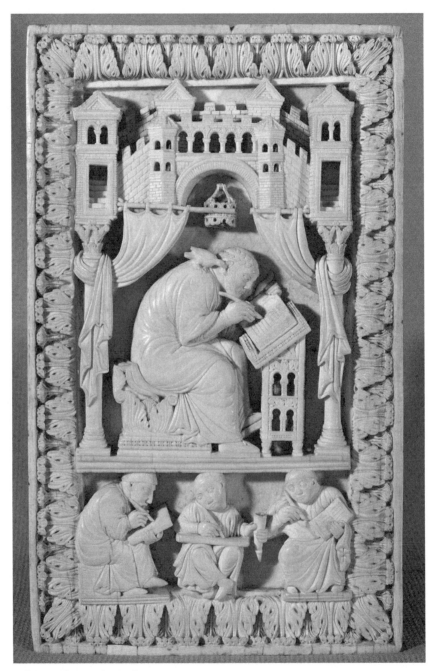

Figure 3 Pope Gregory I, the Great
This ebony book cover shows Pope Gregory I, the Great, who by tradition was considered the author of the Roman Mass. We see Gregory composing the Mass, as scribes in the register below copy his work. Notice the tiny dove on Gregory's shoulder, a symbol of the Holy Spirit, whispering into his ear to inspire him.

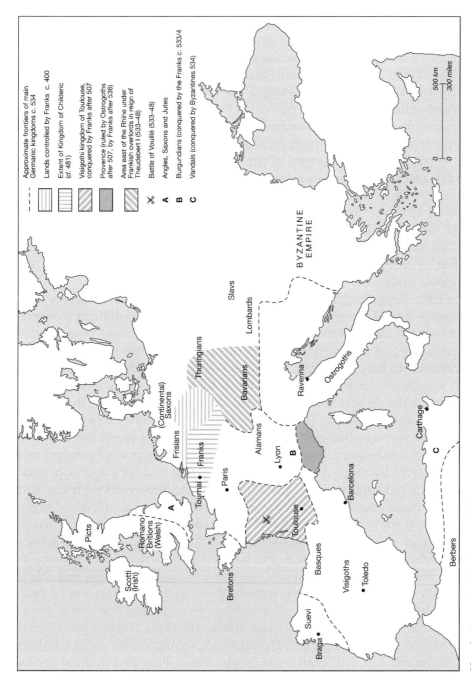

Map 1 Germanic kingdoms, c.534

Gregory came from a pious, wealthy family. One of his ancestors was Pope Felix III or IV, his parents were religious and he had three aunts who were lifelong ascetics. When he was about 34, he abandoned his secular career. He used his family estates to found six monasteries in Sicily and the monastery of St Andrew on the Caelian hill in Rome itself, which he entered as an ordinary monk. He spent four years in rigorous self-denial and, like many ascetics, he probably damaged his health. He was periodically ill for the rest of his life.

Talented men of good education and practical experience were in short supply in sixth-century Rome. In 578, Gregory was reluctantly drawn from the monastery into the service of the pope, first as a deacon of the Roman church and then as the pope's representative (*apocrisarius*) to the emperor at Constantinople, where Gregory lived from 579 to 585. It is symptomatic of how far apart east and west had drifted that Gregory never mastered Greek, even though he had a good education and lived in a Greek-speaking city for six years. When Gregory returned from Constantinople, he became **abbot** of St Andrew's monastery, where he continued his asceticism and scripture studies.

In 590, Pope Pelagius died in an outbreak of plague and Gregory was elected bishop of Rome. He was about 50 years old. In very difficult economic and political circumstances, Gregory showed the traditional Roman traits of efficiency and managerial skill. The Byzantine emperor was far away and occupied with his own problems. The empire could not defeat the Lombards and would not make peace with them. In those circumstances, Gregory undertook the defence and management of the city of Rome and the territory around it that was still in Roman control. He had no official civil title to do so, but he was the chief citizen of the city of Rome, its moral leader and its wealthiest inhabitant. Gregory provided for the thousands of refugees who had fled from Lombard territory, he organised and paid for a militia, he guaranteed the food and water supply of the city, and he negotiated truces with the Lombards, much to the annoyance of some imperial officials. Gregory was a loyal subject of the Roman Empire and took it for granted that he was part of that world, living on its western fringe. He shouldered secular responsibilities in an emergency, but had no desire to break with the empire. Quite the opposite, he wished that the emperor might be willing and able to fulfil his traditional role as protector of the church and guarantor of peace and order.

By birth, education, experience and managerial skills, Gregory had many of the traits of a Roman magistrate. He was similar to many of the greatest bishops of the fourth and fifth century, men who could have had brilliant secular careers if they had not chosen a different path. But his career also pointed to future developments in the history of western Christianity. He was the first monk to be elected pope and to continue to live in a monastic way even as pope. More significant for the future, he was a protector and promoter of monasticism, and laid the foundations for the important alliance between monasticism and the papacy.

He was also a pioneer in his interest in the Germanic peoples who lived to the north and west. Earlier bishops of Rome had made almost no effort to deal systematically with the frightening pagan or heretical conquerors who now held the western empire. Gregory reached out to the invaders. He cultivated good relations with the Lombard Queen Theodelinda, who was Christian, and corresponded warmly with the Spanish Visigothic King Reccared, who had abandoned Arianism for Catholic Christianity in 587. He maintained relations with the Frankish rulers, who were Catholic Christians but by no means models of Christian behaviour. He was the first pope to sponsor a missionary expedition to pagan Germanic peoples, the Anglo-Saxons.

He was also the first pope to exercise major social and military responsibility in central Italy, forced on him when the Byzantine emperors were unable to provide effective help against the invading Lombards. He foreshadowed not only the activist papacy of later times, but also the growing social role of the church in a society undergoing rapid change and probably cultural decline. He lived in a beleaguered outpost of the Byzantine Empire. Gregory's city was in real danger of falling to the Lombard invaders and he looked, often in vain, for protection from the emperor. Finally, he had to undertake the military defence of the city and the negotiations with the Lombards. Across the Alps, to the north and west of Italy, disorder reigned. Christian populations lived under the domination of Germanic rulers, some of whom were pagan (the small Anglo-Saxon kingdoms in lowland Britain and some Lombards in Italy) or Arian Christian (other Lombards in Italy, and until 589 the Visigoths in Spain), while others were Catholic Christian but highly independent (the Franks in Gaul).

As bishop of Rome, Gregory was the patriarch of the west and the first in dignity among the patriarchs of the entire church. He was very careful to safeguard that honour, especially against his chief rival, the patriarch of Constantinople. But his practical powers in churches other than his own were quite limited. The day-to-day workings of local churches had always been in the hands of bishops, who were traditionally quite independent. There had never been a centralised church and there was no assumption, even in the west, that the bishop of Rome could actively intervene in the routine business of other bishops.

Political and military circumstances strengthened the traditional independence of bishops. In some places, bishoprics that had existed in Roman times had lapsed due to the disorder and violence of the invasions. Even though the majority of western bishoprics survived the invasions, they were functioning in a hostile environment, under the rule of pagans, Arians or brutal Catholic kings. Gregory exercised considerable powers of supervision over the nearby bishops and abbots of central and southern Italy. But those powers were limited by canon law and tradition. Except in emergencies or great scandals, Gregory could not easily appoint or depose Italian bishops, could not supervise them or have anything to do with their finances. Further off, the bishops of Gaul, Spain and northern Italy generally acknowledged the bishop of Rome to be the most dignified of bishops, the first in honour, who should be consulted on important matters of **liturgy** or discipline or theology (which in fact did not arise very often), but they gave him no right to interfere with their ordinary business.

It is difficult to get a clear view of the Roman bishop's situation in the early sixth century. He had a unique position in the west that was quite independent of the personality or ability of any particular pope. In Gregory's day, there was no significant quarrel with the view that Christ had made Peter the rock on which the church was built and had entrusted to him the keys to the kingdom of heaven (Matt. 16:16–19). Nor was there dispute that the bishop of Rome was Peter's successor and heir to his responsibilities and privileges. Even the patriarch of Constantinople and other eastern bishops accepted the pope's primacy, but put strict limits on its practical applications. In the west, only the church at Rome could claim a founding by two apostles, Peter and Paul, a fact that enhanced Rome as the 'apostolic see' (from the Latin *sedes*, meaning 'seat'). The bishops of Rome were also the custodians of a great treasure of saints' bodies, in particular that of Peter, who was believed to be buried beneath the large church on the Vatican hill paid for by the Emperor Constantine in the fourth century, and that of Paul, who was believed to be buried in the Constantinian church of St Paul Outside-the-Walls. In Gregory's day, Rome was already the major **pilgrimage** site in the west and the popes shared in the glory of their saints and martyrs.

The bishop of Rome also had great financial assets in the 'Patrimony of St Peter', a collection of estates that had been gifted from emperors and others. Since the estates were widely scattered in southern Gaul, central and southern Italy, Sicily, Sardinia, North Africa and the Balkans, it was unlikely they would be devastated or confiscated at the same time. With such a firm economic base, the popes had considerable resources at their disposal for charity, for building projects and for defence. It was from the resources of the church that Pope Gregory supported the refugees who had fled from the Lombards and organised the defence of the city of Rome. There was no bishop in the west and few in the east who could be compared to him in religious prestige or material wealth.

That was one side of the picture: primacy of honour, guardianship of the most venerable sites of the Christian world and considerable wealth. But little of that translated into practical authority. The bishops of the west were quite independent within their own dioceses. The conciliar practices of normative Christianity continued, in spite of the invasions and arrivals of new rulers, though perhaps on a less grand scale than in the days of Constantine. Bishops met in provincial and kingdom-wide councils to decide matters of controversy. If they answered to anyone, it was to the Germanic kings in whose realms they lived and whose protection they desperately needed. In the Visigothic kingdom, which renounced Arianism and converted to Catholic Christianity in 587, the bishops met regularly with the king and his nobles in 'national' councils at Toledo, where they decided religious and secular business. Similarly, the bishops of Gaul were in close contact with the Frankish kings, who often appointed them. Catholic Christianity survived the end of the western Roman Empire and the creation of Germanic kingdoms on the continent, but it was organised around the Germanic kings, as it had been earlier (and still was in the Byzantine Empire) around the Christian Roman emperors. In such a situation, the bishops of Rome were distant figures with considerable religious prestige and plenty of problems to occupy them in Italy.

VI. Monasticism takes hold in the west

The bishops were the official leaders of the local Christian churches, but since the fourth century they had rivals in the holy men who were admired by many ordinary Christian clergy and lay people. Monasticism was a complex and independent movement within Christianity. By Gregory's lifetime, it had been a prominent feature of normative Christianity for more than 250 years. Gregory himself had been a monk for about fifteen years before his election as pope and he was deeply interested in monasticism's organisation and success.

From its beginnings Christianity had a world-denying strand within it, based on Jesus's uncompromising sayings about marriage ('And there are eunuchs who have made themselves that way for the sake of the kingdom of heaven' – Matt. 19:12); family life ('And everyone who has left houses, brothers, sisters, father, mother, children or land for my sake will be repaid a hundred times over, and also inherit eternal life' – Matt. 19:29); and property ('If you wish to be perfect, go and sell what you own and give the money to the poor, and you will have treasure in heaven; then come and follow me' – Matt. 19:21). Jesus called for a whole-hearted commitment ('Anyone who does not take his cross and follow in my footsteps is not worthy of me. Anyone who finds his life will lose it; anyone who loses his life for my sake will find it' – Matt. 10:38). In pre-Constantinian Christian communities, there was a minority of members who took those sayings literally and lived in a celibate, poor and generally self-denying way.

In the late third and fourth centuries, some ascetics, as these people are called, moved into desert regions in Egypt and Palestine to find a more demanding arena for their spiritual struggles. Since monasticism was eventually integrated into normative Christianity, in fact became one of its basic foundations, it is easy to forget that it began as a counterculture, a criticism of contemporary life. It was a spontaneous, disorderly, grassroots movement. The earliest monks were not clergy, were not ordinarily well educated, and were sometimes hostile to what they saw as the moderation or luke-warmness of urban Christian communities and their clergy, particularly when they were measured against Jesus's hard sayings. During the fourth and fifth centuries in the eastern Mediterranean, the virtually unregulated monastic experimentation produced a wide variety of types, from individual hermits and column-sitters ('stylites') to large, disciplined villages of monk-farmers and monk-craftsmen. As is often the case with experiments, there were failures, disorders and scandals. However, the popularity of the monks as holy men, wonder-workers, and intercessors with God was very great among ordinary Christians. Some urban bishops and clergy, who were literate, often married and possessed personal property, regarded the monastic movement with suspicion and even disapproval. Monasticism might have broken with the greater church, but in the fifth century the bishops successfully asserted their right to approve monastic foundations and to supervise monks as they did all other Christians. Although they tamed the monastic movement somewhat, they never had full control over it. For centuries, monasticism remained a source of controversy, reform and innovation within the church. It was no accident that most movements of renewal within the church grew out of monasticism.

Monasticism spread to the western parts of the Roman Empire about a century after it had arisen in the east. Hermits appeared occasionally in the west, but the more extreme and individualistic forms of eastern monasticism generally did not transplant well to that region. The normal setting of western monastic life was a small community under the leadership of an abbot, who was supervised by the local bishop. Gregory's own monasteries in Sicily and Rome, founded on his family property, fit that pattern.

After he had been elected bishop of Rome, Gregory wrote an immensely popular work called the *Dialogues*, which dealt in part with the monks and holy men of Italy. He intended to show that even in the midst of wars, invasions, plague and terrible suffering God continued to work miracles through his saints. He devoted book two of the *Dialogues* to Benedict of Nursia (*c.*480–545), who had died when Gregory was a young child. Although Gregory's book is not history and has almost no firm chronology, it is the only source for biographical details about Benedict, the key figure in western monasticism.

According to Pope Gregory, Benedict had been born to a good family in the central Italian town of Nursia and was sent to Rome for an education. He was repelled by the immorality at Rome and withdrew to a cave at Subiaco, where he lived for three years as a hermit. His reputation for holiness was such that he was invited to become abbot of a monastery in the region. His reforming zeal alienated the monks, who tried unsuccessfully to poison him. He left that monastery and eventually founded a dozen small houses, each with 12 monks, over which he presided. Conflict with a neighbouring priest, who led an immoral life, forced him to leave again. He went about 90 miles south-east of Rome to Monte Cassino, where his preaching converted the local pagans. He burned the groves where the pagans worshipped and took possession of a temple and ruined citadel on top of the mountain. In about 529 he founded a new monastery at Monte Cassino, where he lived for the rest of his life.

Gregory's *Dialogues* make clear that there were many holy men in sixth-century Italy, but he also tells us about holy women, who were just as adept at performing miracles. Benedict's sister and companion in religious life, Scholastica, headed a convent for nuns. According to Gregory, the siblings only visited each other once a year and when they did, they always met in a special place, a respectable distance from their own monasteries. This let them set an example for how male and female monastics were to act. At one particular meeting, night began to fall and Benedict rose to leave. His sister asked him to stay, but he insisted this would be inappropriate. Scholastica was so saddened by her brother's departure that her tears turned the entire sky into a thunder storm, which forced Benedict to stay the night. They talked until dawn about religious matters, then returned to their respective monasteries. Three days later Scholastica died, and Benedict 'beheld the soul of his sister, which was departed from her body, in the likeness of a dove to ascend into heaven'. He rejoiced and gave thanks to God, and asked his fellow monks to 'bring her corpse to his abbey, to have it buried in that grave which he provided for himself . . . as their souls were one with God whilst they lived, so their bodies continued together after their death'.[1]

Benedict might have been remembered as just one more abbot, except for the fact that he wrote directions for organising and living the monastic life, a document called the *Rule*. It is a relatively short work, only 73 brief chapters, some of which are only a paragraph in length. It is not entirely original, since Benedict had read widely in the works of earlier monastic writers, including Basil of Caesarea (*c*.330–79) and John Cassian of Marseilles (360–435). Modern scholarship has also demonstrated that he borrowed large sections of his rule from an anonymous Italian document called the *Rule of the Master*.[2] Benedict's *Rule* was intended to govern life in his own monastery and it did not spread quickly. There were many other monastic rules in circulation and for about two centuries Benedict's *Rule* was only one among them. In the eighth and ninth centuries, however, Benedict's *Rule* won out over its rivals with the support of the Carolingian kings and became the norm for western monasticism.

The *Rule* was a flexible and sensible document, the distillation of wide reading and personal experience. Benedict described his monastery as 'a school for beginners in the service of the Lord: which I hope to establish on laws not too difficult or grievous'.[3] In view of later developments that brought monasticism to the centre of cultural and religious life, it is useful to stress that Benedict himself intended no external or socially useful tasks for his monks: no manuscript copying, no teaching outsiders and no missionary work. At most, he encouraged the monks to provide food and lodging to travellers, who were to be received as if they were Christ himself. Men, predominately laymen, joined the small community to work out their own salvation through obedience, manual labour and, above all, the worship of God. Benedict wrote that nothing should take precedence over worship, which he called the 'work of God' (Latin: *opus Dei*).[4] The *Rule* gave detailed instructions for the **divine office**, that is, eight periods of public prayer, distributed through each day from before dawn to just after dusk. The prayers consisted mostly of the singing of psalms, hymns and readings from the Bible. There were also periods of the day given over to the reading of religious works, particularly the Bible and the church fathers. Finally, during the intervals between prayers and religious study, Benedict's monks did manual labour of the sort needed to support an agricultural community, though it was assumed they would have slaves or dependents to do field work that might interfere with the eight daily periods of group prayer.

Benedict's *Rule* also laid down an organisational framework within which the life of prayer should be organised. The idea of a 'Benedictine order' is a later development. Benedict's *Rule* was written for an independent and self-contained house, answerable only to the local bishop and then only in serious circumstances. The head of the monastery was an elected monarch, called the abbot. The monks chose him and advised him on important matters, but they could not overrule his decisions or remove him. The abbot was responsible for every aspect of the house, including its spiritual life, its finances and its recruitment.

The guiding image of Benedict's monastery was that of a family under the control of a strong father figure. Benedict advised that the abbot seek to be loved rather than feared. Adults wishing to become monks were not to be admitted too easily, since the candidate needed to ponder carefully a lifelong commitment. At first the candidate was to be put off, and if he persisted, he was to spend a year in a probationary status in the community as a novice, during which time the *Rule* was read to him three times. If at the end of his testing he still wished to join and if the abbot and community would have him, he made his solemn promises, called **vows**. In later Catholic religious **orders**, the traditional vows were poverty, chastity and obedience. For Benedict, chastity was taken for granted; his monks promised to remain in the monastery for life, to adapt to the life of the monastic community, and to obey the abbot.

Benedict also allowed for the reception of children who were offered by their parents. He demanded that the parents disinherit the child so that he would not be tempted to return to the world. The child was offered to the church along with the bread and wine during a mass, and his parents' decision bound him for life. These child-monks were carefully supervised until about age 15, when they became adult members of the community.

Good sense marks the *Rule* in such matters as the care of children and of the sick, diet, the treatment of the unruly and disobedient, and the choice of officials. Benedict discouraged the personal eccentricities and spectacular acts of self-denial that had been common in eastern monasticism. He encouraged a communal life with an adequate vegetarian diet, adequate sleep, and a daily pattern of work and prayer. In the disrupted times of the early Middle Ages, a self-contained and self-sufficient monastic house was a flexible institution, capable of adapting to widely differing circumstances and of recovering from many calamities. Benedict's *Rule* slowly gained ground because of its merits of workability, moderation and humaneness. As we shall see, historical developments thrust Benedictine monks into situations that Benedict could not have imagined, but the foundation of their successes was the *Rule* itself.

VII. Pilgrimage, relics and the cult of the saints

As monasticism developed in the early medieval church, so did another institution: the practice of pilgrimage. Reading or hearing the stories of Jesus, Christians wanted to journey to the places where the events of his life had taken place. Pilgrimage often contained a spiritual dimension, transforming these locales into magical spaces, which could in turn transform the pilgrims who visited them. Saint Jerome, one of the early church fathers, encouraged pilgrimage as a way of completing a Christian education:

> If a famous orator [Cicero] blames a man for having learned Greek at Lilybaeum instead of Athens, and Latin in Sicily instead of Rome . . . can we suppose a Christian's education to be complete who has not visited the Christian Athens? [i.e. Jerusalem].[5]

One of the earliest Christian pilgrims was a woman named Egeria, who around 381 left her native Galicia, in the north of modern-day Portugal, to travel to the Holy Land. She wrote about her pilgrimage in a long letter to her female friends back home. Egeria's journey was a difficult and remarkable demonstration of her faith and piety:

> Early Sunday morning, accompanied by that priest and the monks who lived there, we began climbing the mountains one by one. These mountains are climbed with very great difficulty, since you do not ascend them slowly going round and round, in a spiral path, as we say, but you go straight up the whole way as if scaling a wall. Then you have to go straight down each of these mountains until you reach the very foot of the central mountain, which is properly called Sinai. By the will of Christ our God, and with the help of the prayers of the holy men who were accompanying us, I made the ascent, though with great effort, because it had to be on foot, since it was absolutely impossible to make the climb in the saddle. Yet you did not feel the effort, and the reason it was not felt was because I saw the desire which I had being fulfilled through the will of God.[6]

Travel in the pre-industrial world was slow, expensive and often dangerous, hence the well-worn truism that most medieval people did not venture far beyond their own villages. Egeria undertook a journey from her homeland in western Europe to the other side of the Mediterranean. Others would follow in her footsteps.

In spite of the significance and religious allure of Jerusalem, most medieval pilgrims made more modest journeys to local shrines that contained the **relics** of saints whom they venerated. Christians believed that many people were saved and some of them could be identified because God chose to make them known. The identified holy dead, the saints, were important intermediaries between God and their fellow humans. It was only in the twelfth century that canonisation – the official declaration that some particular person is a saint – became formalised and organised. Before that there was a great deal of popular initiative and spontaneous canonisations at the local level. In the first three centuries of Christianity, the most obvious saints were the martyrs who, like Christ, had died for their beliefs at the hands of the Roman authorities. The cult of the saints grew out of the Christian community's admiration for those who died for their faith, imitating Jesus, the first martyr. After Christianity became the legal religion of the Roman Empire, martyrdoms became rarer and the ranks of known saints grew by the addition of ascetics, that is, people who lived notably self-denying and holy lives. Most saints of the early Middle Ages were monks and nuns, with a smattering of bishops, many of whom had been monks before their election to the episcopate. Their canonisation and veneration was usually local and popular.

The formalities of the cult of saints must not obscure the living reality of the Christian people's belief in the saints, who were thought to be alive, active and interested in the welfare of their fellow humans struggling with life on earth. At the theological level, the saints were intercessors for the living, that is, they stood near God's throne in heaven and asked him for mercy, favours or forgiveness for living humans. That static view of intercession was fleshed out in popular belief, where the saints were very prominent. Saints appeared in dreams to warn or cajole the errant. They punished those who injured their living devotees. They healed the sick or the mentally ill who came to their shrines. Like the human beings they were, saints could enter into bargains. It was common to promise to give something or to do something if the saint's intercession obtained a favour. The strongest point of contact with saints was to be found in their relics, which literally meant 'the things left behind'. A relic might be an object used by the saint – a walking stick, cloak or Bible. But the most precious relic was the saint's body or portions of it.

For medieval communities, saints and their relics were also a source of local pride and assurance. The saint's victories were miracles, especially healings for individuals and favours for the community. Towns honoured their saints with fine receptacles for their remains, called a **reliquary**, and perhaps a church or chapel dedicated to their name. A saint's annual festival could be a genuinely popular mixture of piety and revelry in honour of the local hero. The saint was the pride of the community, the intercessor with God for that comunity. Yet a saint's fame was in many cases very localised. For example, St Kentigern (died *c*.612) was honoured in Scotland, but not too far away his sphere of honour faded as those of other local saints rose.

To an observer in the year 590, when Gregory was elected bishop of Rome, the situation of western Christianity probably would not have appeared hopeful. The decay of economic life and the decline in population, which contemporaries probably could not comprehend because they had no statistics from earlier times, certainly limited options. The decline of urban institutions, including schools, led to increasing illiteracy and a general lowering of cultural standards. Contemporaries were certainly aware of the disorder brought by the Germanic invaders. Lowland Britain, which had been romanised for 350 years, had by 600 been divided for more than a century among pagan Germanic peoples and Christianity there had vanished. Christian Germanic kings – brutal, disorderly and quite independent in church matters – ruled Gaul and Spain. The Lombards, who were among the latest invaders (568) and quite terrifying in their ferocity, were less than a day's march from Rome. They had destroyed Benedict's monastery at Monte Cassino in about 589. The Byzantine Empire was on the defensive in the east against Persians, Slavs and Avars and unable to provide much practical aid in Italy (and of course no aid whatsoever further west). In his more sombre moods, Gregory was convinced that he lived at the end of time and that the Last Judgement was near.

A pessimistic observer might well have agreed with him. However, the pessimistic observer was to be proven wrong. In Gregory's lifetime, there were already in place the peoples and institutions that would eventually create a new civilisation in the west: the papacy itself, the sturdy late-Roman structure of bishops and councils, monasticism, pilgrimage, and the Germanic tribes, particularly the Franks, whose conversion to Christianity will be treated in Chapter 4.

Suggested reading

Companion website
www.routledge.com/cw/lynch

3.1   The Qur'an
Excerpt from The Qur'an, trans. E. H. Palmer, *The Sacred Books of the East Vol. VI*, ed. F. Max Müller (Oxford: Clarendon Press, 1880), 1, 19–26.

3.2   Pope Gregory the Great and the Lombards
Excerpts from Paul the Deacon, *History of the Langobards*, trans. William Dudley Foulke (Philadelphia: The Department of History University of Pensylvania, 1907), 153–158.

3.3   The Rule of Benedict on Property
The Rule of Our Most Holy Father St. Benedict, Patriarch of Monks, from the Old English edition of 1638, edited in Latin and English by one of the Benedictine Fathers of St. Michael's, near Hereford (London, 1875), pp. 148–151.

Primary sources

Athanasius, *The Life of Saint Antony*, translated by Robert T. Meyer, Ancient Christian Writers, vol. 10 (Westminster, Maryland, 1950)

Benedict of Nursia, *The Rule of St. Benedict in English and Latin with Notes*, edited by Timothy Frye (Collegeville, Minnesota, 1980)

Cassian, John, *Conferences* translated by Robert T. Meyer, Ancient Christian Writers, vol. 10 (Westminster, Maryland, 1950)

Egeria: Diary of a Pilgrimage, translated and annotated by George E. Gingras (New York, 1970)

Gregory I, *Dialogues*, translated by Odo J. Zimmerman, Fathers of the Church, vol. 39 (New York, 1959)

Gregory I, *Life and Miracles of St. Benedict*, edited by Edmund Luck (New York, 2007)

Gregory I, *The Letters of Gregory the Great*, translated with introduction and notes by John R. C. Martyn, 3 vols (Toronto, 2004)

Wilkinson, John, *Egeria's Travels: Newly Translated, with Supporting Documents and Notes*, 3rd edition (Warminster, England, 1999)

Modern scholarship

Brown Peter, *The Cult of the Saints: Its Rise and Function in Latin Christianity* (Chicago, 1981)

Butler, Cuthbert, *Benedictine Monachism. Studies in Benedictine Life and Rule*, 2nd edition, reprinted with an introduction by David Knowles (Cambridge, 1962)

Dudden, F. Holmes, *Gregory the Great. His Place in Thought and History*, 2 vols (London, 1905)

Grégoire, Henri, 'The Byzantine Church', in Norman H. Baynes and H. St L. B. Moss, *Byzantium. An Introduction to East Roman Civilization* (Oxford, 1948), pp. 86–135

Gregory, Timothy, *A History of Byzantium*, 2nd edition (Malden, Massachusetts, 2010)

Herrin, Judith, *The Formation of Christendom* (Oxford, 1987)

Kennedy, Hugh, *The Prophet and the Age of the Caliphates. The Islamic Near East from the Sixth to the Eleventh Centuries* (London and New York, 1986)

Mitchell, Stephen, *A History of the Later Empire, AD 284–641* (Malden, Massachusetts, 2007)

Moss, H. St L. B., *The Birth of the Middle Ages* (Oxford, 1935)

Richards, Jeffrey, *The Consul of God: the Life and Times of Gregory the Great* (London, 1980)

Straw, Carole, *Gregory the Great: Perfection in Imperfection* (Berkeley, 1988)

Watt, M. W., *Muhammad, Prophet and Statesman* (Oxford, 1961)

Notes

1 Gregory the Great, *Life and Miracles of St. Benedict*, ch. 43–4, pp. 82–5.
2 On the links of the *Rule of the Master* to Benedict's *Rule* see David Knowles, *Great Historical Enterprises* (London, 1963), pp. 135–95.
3 *Rule of Saint Benedict*, Prologue, in Owen Chadwick, *Western Asceticism* (London, 1958), p. 293.
4 Ibid., ch. 43, *Rule*, p. 319.
5 Jerome, Letter 46, *Nicene and Post-Nicene Fathers*, Second Series, vol. 6, edited by Philip Schaff and Henry Wace (Buffalo, New York, 1893 [reprint New York, 2007]), pp. 63–4.
6 *Egeria: Diary of a Pilgrimage*, translated and annotated by George E. Gingras (New York, 1970), pp. 51–2.

4

The conversion of the west (350–700)

It was not inevitable that Christianity would survive the disintegration of the western empire. Yet Christianity's long history is filled with adaptations to different economic, political and social situations. During the three centuries of the Christian Roman Empire, Catholic Christianity had created elaborate theologies, liturgies and traditions of learning, as well as detailed bodies of canon law to manage such practical necessities as the election of officers, the handling of wealth and the settling of disputes. Agreement in belief was regarded as essential, but centralisation and uniformity were not. The large regional groupings of churches shared much and were generally tolerant of one another's differences. Christianity had grown to depend on the order and security of Roman society, though the price for that security was a wide measure of control by the emperors, who were its protectors and masters. The collapse of Roman power in the west meant that Christianity in that region could no longer depend on the state for support. On the one hand, this meant liberation from the heavy hand of the Roman state, though it also meant struggling against the forces of diversity. Regional distinctions, which had always been present, flourished, and regional varieties of Christianity developed, though a Christian ideal remained enshrined in custom, in law and in church books. Because the Roman Empire survived in the eastern Mediterranean (the so-called Byzantine Empire) the church–state symbiosis of the fourth and fifth centuries continued there until the fifteenth century. So: the early Middle Ages exhibited diversity and regionalism in the western church, and a more or less unified church state in the east.

The situation in the west between about 350 and 700 is confusing both geographically and chronologically. The surviving sources are sparse and difficult to interpret. We shall try to impose some order on the swirl of events by looking at the conversion of three large groups: the rural inhabitants of the Roman Empire; the Germanic invaders who settled inside the empire; and the peoples who lived outside the empire.

I. Conversion of the internal 'pagans'

There is a long-standing myth, promoted by the Christians as an argument for God's favour to them, that Christianity swept quickly over the empire.

Already in the early third century, the North African Tertullian (*c*.155–after 220) was taunting his pagan opponents:

> Day by day you groan over the growing number of Christians. You cry aloud that your city is under siege, that there are Christians in the countryside, in the military camps, in apartment buildings. You grieve over it as a calamity that every sex, every age, and every rank is passing from you [to us].[1]

That theme was repeated with even more vigour in the fourth century, when Christian apologists pointed triumphantly to the rapid growth of their religion and especially the conversion of the emperors as proof that God favoured them. When examined critically, however, the growth of Christian numbers inside the Roman Empire takes on a more restrained look. Modern estimates show that when Constantine was converted in about 312, approximately 8 to 10 per cent of the Roman population was Catholic Christian, with the majority of members in the east.[2] Thus, after 250 years, Christianity could at most claim only one person in ten – hardly spreading like wildfire. The pace of growth sped up when the empire actively favoured Christianity, but fervent bishops were under no illusions about the lukewarmness of many of those who converted for social or economic reasons. The flow of converts became a flood in the later fourth and fifth centuries. Christianity had its earliest successes in Greco-Roman cities and towns. The church in the Roman Empire was a relatively loose federation of bishoprics, which were almost always located in cities. Individual Christians proselytised their neighbours and relatives, but the responsibility for receiving and testing converts rested with the local bishops. In the cities of the empire, the bishops had developed an orderly process called the catechumenate to instruct, test and exorcise those who asked to be baptised. The adult converts in each diocese were initiated into the Christian church through elaborate ceremonies lasting about forty days, which culminated in baptism at dawn on **Easter** Sunday. In the cities, where there were plenty of clergy to instruct, where imperial encouragement and threats worked best, and where there was social pressure, Christianity had by the late fifth century probably become the religion of the urban majority, although a substantial minority of Jews, some hard-pressed pagans and some Christian heretics were present as well.

The Greco-Roman countryside had a different course of development. Great obstacles stood in the way of the Christianisation of the countryside, where the vast majority of the empire's people lived. There were no missionary orders or societies to devote personnel and resources to the conversion of unbelievers. In areas of the east, notably in the Nile valley and in Anatolia (modern Turkey), Christianity had become the dominant religion of some rural districts by the late third century. By the fifth century, wealthy landowners and their immediate entourage were generally Christians. But those were exceptions. For many centuries, large areas of the countryside, without resident clergy or permanent churches, were superficially Christianised or not at all. The beliefs, rituals, values and worldviews lumped together under the word 'paganism' were deep-rooted and very much alive. The word pagan comes from the Latin *'paganus'*, meaning 'country dweller', which is where most non-Christians could be found. Traditional ways in religion hung on tenaciously in rural areas, where violent resistance to Christianity was unusual, but passive resistance was common.

One sign of Christianity's penetration of the countryside was the growth of the number of churches and clergy. In 300, there were about twenty-six bishoprics in Gaul, whereas within a century there were about seventy. In northern Italy, the growth was even more impressive: from five or six bishoprics in 300 to about fifty in 400.[3] As bishoprics multiplied, the network of churches became tighter and the local, small-scale efforts at missionary activity more effective. Within dioceses, the creation of rural churches with resident priests was also an effective technique for the conversion of the countryside. For much of the early Middle Ages, the number of such churches was limited by cultural and economic conditions. They required more trained clergy than were available to staff them and they required more capital and annual income to support their operation than was readily available in the impoverished countryside. But since bishops were unable (or unwilling) to put a church in every hamlet, they left the field open to others – a form of private enterprise in religion. Some landlords built churches for their tenants, often humble buildings of wood with dirt floors; some monasteries built them for their peasants; some hermits, holy men and wandering priests created chapels that served rural people; and some free villagers took the initiative to found churches for themselves. Privately built and privately owned churches eventually outnumbered in many places the official churches of the bishops. Bishops did not control those **private churches**. They remained the property of their founders, who often appointed the priest from among their own peasants and dependents, and shared in the revenues from fees for religious services, gifts and sometimes **tithes**. A bishop was needed to ordain the priest for the church, but for all practical purposes many village churches of early medieval Europe were the property of the founders and their successors, who might be lay aristocrats or monastic houses. Such private enterprise did, however, bring the Christian sacraments and a priest, however poorly trained, to the masses of western European peasants. It was not until after the year 1000 that western Europe was fully divided into parishes with resident priests and defined territories. When the imperial government in the west gave way to Germanic rule during the fifth century, Christianity was still primarily an urban religion in a society where cities had entered a serious decline. Yet Christianity did penetrate the rural world between the fifth and the eleventh centuries. Its movement into every nook and cranny of the west is a remarkable proof of its vitality and adaptability in difficult circumstances.

Christianity has often been described as a missionary religion, but the missionary impulse was stronger in some times than in others. One must not imagine that the urban bishops of the late Roman Empire were ceaselessly attacking the paganism of the rural masses. A bishop's efforts could often be reduced to mere sermons, or less, on account of inertia, lack of personnel and resources, passive resistance by the rustics, and the protection of powerful Christians who did not want their dues-paying peasants upset. However, there are reports of some late Roman bishops who vigorously promoted the conversion of the rural population. Sometimes they used sermons and peaceful persuasion, but at other times they could be forceful. In the Roman law of the Christian Empire, paganism had no legal protection. Furthermore, Christian intellectuals had long regarded paganism either as a worn-out creed whose time had passed or as a trick of demons with whom compromise was impossible. Finally, in a highly stratified society where bishops were men of social dignity and rural farm workers were close to the bottom of the heap, the wretched social, educational and economic conditions of the rustics only intensified the scorn that educated people, including bishops, heaped on traditional religious practices and their believers. Despite some exceptions, bishops were not vigorous in their efforts to convert the 'internal' pagans.

One exception was a bishop who lived in Roman Gaul. Martin of Tours (*c*.330–97) had been born in the area of modern Hungary to pagan parents. Although he became a **catechumen** at an early age, like many contemporaries he put off baptism for a number of years. After service in the Roman military, he became a Christian monk and founded the first monastery in Gaul in about 360. Because of his reputation for holiness, he was elected bishop of Tours in 372, when it was still unusual in the west for monks to be chosen bishops. He continued to live in a monastic way even after his election as bishop, withdrawing to his monastery at Marmoutier whenever the burdens of being a bishop allowed it. Although the Roman Empire was officially Christian, there were many pagans in the countryside around Tours in western Gaul. They held a variety of beliefs beyond the Greco-Roman gods, including remnants of Celtic customs, worship of Mithra and Isis, who had been popular among Roman soldiers, and other eastern cults. Martin toured the countryside preaching, and backed up his preaching with bold (one might say high-handed) actions that demonstrated the weakness of the pagan gods. He smashed statues, cut down sacred trees, burned temples, and founded churches and monasteries on their sites. He was thought to have the power to drive out demons, cure the sick, and bend the forces of nature with his prayers. Perhaps wowed or cowed by these powers, rural people seem to have converted in groups, implying a superficial Christianisation, at least in the early stages.

The reliance on bishops and their clergy to evangelise the inhabitants of their dioceses was relatively effective in some settled areas within the former boundaries of the empire, especially near the Mediterranean Sea. However, the migrations/invasions of Germanic peoples into the Roman world between the fourth and sixth centuries posed problems that overwhelmed the isolated efforts of local bishops.

II. Conversion of the invaders

If many bishops were not zealous about converting peasants in the regions around their cities, they made even fewer efforts to convert the so-called barbarians who lived north of the empire's borders. There is no report of a late Roman bishop sent as a missionary to purely pagan peoples outside the empire. Now and then a bishop went to minister to Christian merchants and captives who had been carried off by raiders, but these were often special requests.

The Germanic invasions that began in 378 introduced more religious complexity into the empire. Many rural Roman 'citizens' remained un-Christianised or superficially Christianised as entirely new religious groups invaded. Not all invaders who entered the empire between the fourth and sixth centuries were Germanic pagans. Of course, some were adherents of native Germanic religions. By a fluke of history other invaders were Christians, although of the Arian variety that was regarded as heretical inside the empire.

Arianism held brief sway because the Emperor Constantius II (337–61) supported it. During Constantius' reign, Ulfilas, a descendant of Christian captives who had lived among the Goths beyond the River Danube for several generations, was ordained a bishop and sent to minister to Gothic Christians outside the north-eastern borders of the empire. When a Gothic king began to persecute Christians, Ulfilas and his followers fled into the Roman Empire. Bishop Ulfilas continued to defend Arianism until he died about 383. He translated the Bible into the Gothic language, which may have helped Arian Christianity to spread among the western Germanic peoples (including the Visigoths, Ostrogoths, Burgundians and Vandals). When these peoples settled in the empire, they brought with them their Arian Christianity with its own clergy and churches. Some Germanic invaders adopted Arian Christianity after they were inside the empire, perhaps to put a barrier between themselves and their Roman subjects, who were generally Catholic Christians.

By the year 500, Arian Germanic minorities ruled Catholic Roman major-
ities throughout the former empire. The way the different tribes ruled could
vary. The Arian Vandals in North Africa actively persecuted Catholics, and in
488 forced them to convert. In Spain, the Arian Visigoths practised a more
passive resistance, for example, by leaving bishoprics empty, causing a decline
in the Catholic priesthood. In the Rhone valley of France, Avitus, Archbishop
of Vienne (c.494–523), preached Catholicism to the Arian, Burgundian king
Gundobad (473–516), who accepted Catholic doctrine privately, but not in
public. The ruling minority could often be quite tolerant of the Catholic
majority, as was the case in northern and central Italy under the Ostrogothic
king Theodoric (454–526), who largely let the Catholic bishops manage their
own affairs. In fact, in spite of other behaviours we might justifiably call
'barbaric', Theodoric showed remarkable religious tolerance, even toward the
Jews. According to a letter collected by the historian Cassiodorus, Theodoric
said, 'We cannot order a religion, because no one can be forced to believe
against his will.'[4]

Within a few generations of their creation, the Arian/Germanic kingdoms
found themselves in a political crisis that was rooted in demography. The
invading groups, which were not large, settled in a sea of Roman Christians.
As with many minority groups that migrate into dominant societies, they
found assimilation attractive or at least unavoidable: their servants spoke the
local dialect of Latin; they began to use the local language in their dealings
with the majority; they adopted many features of the comfortable way of
life of urban Romans; some even intermarried with Romans. The growing
cultural assimilation, coupled with the hostility of the Catholic Christian
majority to the Arian heresy, created instability in the Arian kingdoms. By
about 600, none of them remained Arian. The Byzantine Emperor Justinian
reconquered the Arian Vandals in North Africa (534) and the Arian Ostrogoths
in Italy (554). In 534, the Catholic Franks conquered the Burgundians, who
had abandoned their Arianism in 517, too late to save themselves from the
Franks. The Arian Visigoths adopted Catholic Christianity in 589. The heir to
the Lombard kingdom was baptised a Catholic in 603. These conversions
were generally not the result of missionary work in the modern sense, or of
the individual conversions typical of the Roman Empire before the fifth
century. They were political decisions, taken by rulers faced with grave problems, who needed the support of the Catholic bishops and their native
Roman subjects.

To complicate matters more, not all invaders were Arian Christians. Some
were pagan Germans (Franks, Angles, Saxons and Jutes) who settled in the far
north-western parts of the empire. They were the most difficult and threatening of the invaders with whom the church had to deal. They come the closest

to the stereotypes of 'barbarians' that the cinema has given us: fierce warrior/ farmers with their own distinctive forms of art, social organisation and religion. Most, though not all, were illiterate – the earliest Germanic runes can be dated to around 200. They had come from remote areas in the Rhineland and Denmark, where Roman culture had influenced them very little. In northern Gaul, the Frankish advance in the 300s and 400s had serious consequences for Christianity. Pagan Germanic religion put the church on the defensive, and some bishoprics were actually abandoned. In eastern, lowland Britain, the invasions were catastrophic for Roman civilisation, including Christianity, which seems to have vanished from there after 450. The surviving British Christians regrouped in the rugged western parts of the island, where the Germanic invaders did not succeed in making conquests.

III. Conversion of the Franks

As far as contributing the most lasting changes to medieval Europe, the most important Germanic invaders were the Franks, who lived along the Rhine in the 350s and advanced slowly into modern Belgium, western Germany and northern France, where they settled in considerable numbers. They pushed south of the River Loire and conquered the remnants of Roman territories in Gaul (486), the Visigothic lands north of the Pyrenees (507), and Burgundian lands (534), although they did not settle in their southern conquered territories in large numbers. Both Catholic and Arian Christians wooed the Franks, who worshipped the Germanic gods, but the Arians, at least, may have had some success: when King Clovis was baptised between 496 and 506, one of his sisters was said to be an Arian.

Clovis (481–511) was a key figure in the religious evolution of the Franks. The story of his conversion, related by Bishop Gregory of Tours (579–94) 75 years after the event, is a model of how the church won over pagan invaders. Clovis was a teenage boy when he inherited royal power from his father. He retained that power by shrewdness, military valour and brutality. For instance, he killed all his male relatives so as to concentrate power in his nuclear family, the Merovingian dynasty, which ruled the Franks until 751. In tribal societies such as the Franks, religious individualism, which had existed in the Roman Empire and exists in modern western societies, was unusual and perhaps unthinkable. Religion was part of the social glue binding a Germanic king to his warriors and religious diversity often led to political instability, as the Arian rulers learned. There was no practical hope for conversion of the Franks one at a time. A change of religion had to be a group decision: the ruler's role was crucial, but he needed the assent of his people, which in practice meant his warriors.

Clovis wanted to conquer central and southern Gaul, where the population was overwhelmingly Catholic with Arian Visigothic rulers. It was useful to Clovis to be on good terms with the bishops, who had taken a leading role in society when Roman government ended. Even when he was a pagan, he tried to keep his unruly warriors from alienating the bishops by looting their churches.

Clovis's wife was a Catholic Burgundian princess named Clotild. Bishop Gregory of Tours tells us how she tried to convert her husband:

> 'The gods whom you worship are no good,' she would say. 'They haven't even been able to help themselves, let alone others. They are carved out of stone or wood or some old piece of metal . . . You ought instead to worship him who created at a word and out of nothing heaven, and earth, the sea and all that therein is, who made the sun to shine, who lit the sky with stars, who peopled the water with fish, the earth with beasts . . . by whose hand the race of man was made.'[5]

Such theological arguments would not be sufficient. The native Germanic religion was 'instrumentalist' in nature: the gods were expected to be powerful enough to give good things to their worshippers, such as fertility, or wealth, or victory in war. Germanic kings like Clovis loved the example of Constantine, the Roman emperor who centuries earlier had converted to Christianity after victory in battle. When Clotild had their first son baptised, and the child immediately died, Clovis took this as a sign that the Christian god was weak:

> 'If he had been dedicated in the name of my gods,' he said, 'he would have lived without question; but now that he has been baptized in the name of your God he has not been able to live a single day.'[6]

Clotild kept her faith, even after a close call following the baptism of a second son. But it took Clovis being hard-pressed in a war with the Alemanni, a tribe located in the area of the north Rhine River, to see the instrumental superiority of the Christian God:

> 'Jesus Christ,' he said, 'you who Clotild maintains to be the Son of the living God, you who deign to give help to those who are in travail and victory to those who trust in you, in faith I beg the glory of your help. If you will give me victory over my enemies, and if I may have evidence of that miraculous power which the people dedicated to your name say that they have experienced, then I will believe in you and I will be baptized in your name. I have called upon my own gods, but, as I see only too clearly, they have no intention of helping me. I therefore cannot believe that they possess any power, for they do not come to the assistance of those who trust in them. I now call upon you. I want to believe in you, but I must first be saved from my enemies.'[7]

Figure 4 Baptism of Clovis
This ivory plaque shows legendary scenes from the life of Saint Remigius. In the top register, Remigius revives a young girl. In the middle, the hand of God fills two vials with chrism (consecrated oil) for the baptism of the dying pagan on the right. On the bottom, Remigius baptizes Clovis, King of the Franks. Notice the Holy Spirit, in the form of a dove, delivering an ampoule of chrism just above Clovis's head.

Clovis's victory over the Alemanni convinced him of the power of Christ, and he kept his promise to convert. Bishop Remigius of Reims (died 533) instructed him in secret because his warriors had not yet agreed to abandon their traditional gods. At a meeting with his warriors, Clovis won them over and 'more than three thousand of them' were baptised with the king some time between 496 and 506. (See Figure 4.) Catholic Christianity was henceforth the religion of the Franks, although as a practical matter it took generations for the new religion to oust the old one. But the implications of the conversion of the Franks must not be underestimated. The only long-lasting kingdom founded on the continent by the Germanic invaders, occupying a large landmass that became the economic and military heart of western Europe, had thrown in its lot with Catholic Christianity. This was not an inevitable development, and its consequences shaped the west religiously and politically.

IV. Conversion of the outsiders

The Franks, who settled on territory that had been inside the empire, were the most significant early medieval converts to Christianity, but developments in the British Isles deserve notice because, as we shall see, conversion was successful there even though most of the converted peoples had never lived inside the functioning empire. In an area of approximately 120,000 square miles inhabited by what was probably a modest-sized population, in the year 600, there were several antagonistic ethnic groups, each with its own internal divisions: Picts in northern Britain; Germanic Angles, Saxons and Jutes in the south and east of Britain; and romanised Celts in the west of Britain and non-romanised Celts in Ireland. There were three families of languages, Celtic, Pictish and Germanic, each with distinct dialects. In addition, there was a good knowledge of grammatical Latin among the monastic elite in the Celtic lands. There were probably two-dozen men in the British Isles who could have been described as 'kings', who alternately allied with and waged war on one another. The religious situation was also complex. There were large numbers of Celtic Christians. Those on the island of Britain were descended from the people who inhabited Roman Britain before the Anglo-Saxon invasions. Those in Ireland had been converted during the fifth and sixth centuries by the missionary Patrick and his successors. On the island of Britain, there were also Germanic and Pictish pagans, as well as remnants of Celtic paganism. By 700, all these peoples were officially Christians. The way in which their conversion happened is a complicated tale.

V. Christianity in Ireland

Since the Romans had never conquered Ireland, there had developed on the island a Celtic society divided into many small tribal units that were constantly at war with one another, as well as raiding or trading in Roman territory to the east. Commerce and the slave trade had brought small numbers of Christians into Ireland by the early fifth century, but they were neither organised nor a significant element in the population. In 431, Pope Celestine I (422–32) may have sent those Christians a bishop named Palladius, but we know nothing about his work. We know more, though not enough, about Patrick (active in the 400s), a Christian of Celtic ancestry who was born in the western part of Roman Britain. Pirates captured the 16-year-old Patrick and sold him into slavery in Ireland, where he remained for six years. He tells us in his *Confessions* that after he had escaped from slavery, he had a vision in which a man handed him letters, one of which was titled 'The Voice of the Irish'. At the same time, voices called out to him to return to Ireland. Patrick may be the first clear case of a missionary who felt called to direct his efforts specifically to the conversion of pagans. He probably received his clerical training and ordination in Britain, where his grandfather had been a priest, and his father a deacon. He was ordained a bishop and returned to Ireland about 430, where he set in motion the conversion of the Irish in tribal groups. The Irish were the first people in the west to become Christian without having been in the Roman Empire.

Patrick probably tried to plant in Ireland the organisational pattern with which he was familiar in Christian Britain and Gaul: territorial dioceses headed by bishops who resided in cities and who consciously or unconsciously acted within the leadership models given by Roman culture. That is not how things turned out. In the century after Patrick (about 450–550), Ireland was isolated while the churches in Britain and on the continent were reeling under the blows of invasions and subsequent rule by Arian or pagan kings. As a consequence of difficult communications, the regional differences among the churches grew more intense everywhere. For instance, the churches in Spain and those in Italy, which had never been precisely the same, diverged from one another in such things as liturgical practices and religious art. Ireland is the most extreme example in the west of the consequences of isolation. Conditions in Ireland were so different from those on the continent that the traditional bishop-centred organisation did not dominate. When sources are available after about 550, they reveal a church in Ireland that differed in significant ways from the churches on the continent.

The important differences were in church organisation rather than in theology, in which the Irish were generally conservative and quite orthodox. In the decades after Patrick's death, Christianity adapted to life in a society where there were no cities, no coined money, no central government and no Latin language. In Ireland, monasteries often replaced dioceses as the chief Christian institution. Each monastery was closely allied with a clan. The abbot and some monks were kinsmen of the tribal chief, and organised the religious life of their clan. Abbots were the leading religious figures in society, and often important economic and political forces as well. Bishops were needed because Christianity could not function without them. Only they could perform certain essential religious rites, especially the ordination of other clergy. Some Irish bishops lived in monasteries and were available when the abbot needed their services. But they had little of the power and social importance associated with bishops on the continent. In addition to this distinctive way of organising church life, there were other matters in which the Irish differed from their continental counterparts: they continued to calculate the date of Easter in a way that had been abandoned by fellow Christians on the continent; their clergy cut their hair (**tonsure**) in a distinctive way; and they baptised in a different way, though we do not know precisely what that difference looked like.

Monasteries were also the places where the intellectual and theological side of Christianity was preserved in Irish society. Adoption of Christianity posed a hard linguistic problem for the Irish, who spoke a Celtic language. The church's books of scripture, canon law, theology, saints' lives and liturgy were written in Latin, a language quite distinct from their own. The Irish could have translated the essential books into Old Irish, but they did not. They retained Latin as the language of sacred things and hence had to learn it from scratch (just as we do). It required a long training for an Irish boy to gain facility in Latin. Only monasteries had the wealth to support the teachers and the copying of books that permitted bright boys to master the holy texts. Hence the monasteries took over the functions of schools, at least for their own members. In a strange twist, the Irish mastered grammatically correct Latin since they learned it out of books, whereas many Christians on the continent learned a living Latin that was diverging significantly from the norms of classical Latin; indeed, it was dividing into the Romance languages. Until the Carolingian Renaissance that took place in the Frankish Kingdom in the ninth century, classically correct Latin survived best in the monasteries of the Irish and of their Christian Anglo-Saxon disciples.

Another feature of Irish monasticism was important for the future of Christianity. Self-denial (asceticism) was highly valued and actively pursued in Irish monasteries, which had very severe discipline, similar to the monasticism that had arisen in Egypt in the fourth century. The biographies of Irish monastic saints and the written rules that organised their lives are full of accounts of severe fasting, long periods of sleeplessness called vigils, physical discomfort eagerly sought out, and whippings administered for serious lapses as well as for what may seem to us minor infractions. By the sixth century, the Irish monks began collecting these punishments for lapses and infractions into books called penitentials, which were basically guidebooks for assigning specific **penance** for specific sins. Many entries in the penitentials offer great insight into the culture and mentality of this period, including family obligations, witchcraft and pagan practices, and even rather folksy interpretations on complex matters like the Eucharist. For example, if a person took communion and accidentally vomited up the eucharistic host (the bread that had been transformed into the body of Christ), and a dog ate the vomit (essentially eating Christ), dogs not being allowed to participate in communion, this was a sin, and the person who vomited would need to do penance for this sin. Penitentials became popular on the continent, but by the ninth century they had fallen out of favour, and were condemned at the Council of Paris in 829.

In a society based on strong bonds of kinship, separation from family and region was a particularly demanding form of self-denial. Beginning in the sixth century, some Irish monks imitated the Jewish patriarch Abraham (Gen. 12:1–3) and abandoned all earthly ties of kinship and country to go 'on a pilgrimage for the sake of Christ'. They went to remote islands in the Irish Sea and the North Atlantic, to England, to Gaul, even to Italy and Palestine. The monk-pilgrims did not set out to be missionaries, but when they met pagans or Christians whose behaviour seemed lax, they often began to preach among them. The revival of continental Christianity after the invaders had been nominally converted owed much to the Irish monks. Between the sixth and the ninth centuries, wandering Irish monks were a familiar feature of western Christianity, sometimes admired for their zeal, self-denial, learning and missionary work, and sometimes criticised for their independence, their peculiar ways and their disruption of local practices.

VI. Conversion of the Anglo-Saxons

The other island on which important religious changes took place between the fifth and seventh centuries was Britain, which had a long period of Roman occupation. Julius Caesar had landed in Britain in 55 BC and the Emperor Claudius began the conquest of the eastern and central portions of the island in AD 43. Roman control, which lasted until 410, was effective only in the lowlands, since in the north and west rugged terrain, fierce natives and general poverty discouraged the Romans from further conquest. Roman Britain attracted few settlers from the Mediterranean regions, but some soldiers and administrators stayed on. As a consequence of three and a half centuries of imperial control, the elite of the Celtic population was somewhat romanised in language and lifestyle.

Christianity probably reached Roman Britain in the third century, brought by traders and soldiers. When the empire embraced Christianity in the fourth century, the religion spread in the romanised portions of the island, but there is archaeological evidence for the vigour of paganism in the fourth century and there is no way to know with precision the extent of Christianisation. Three bishops from Roman Britain attended the Council of Nicaea (325). In spite of this, Germanic invaders of the later fifth and sixth centuries uprooted this first planting of Christianity. The conquerors were outsiders, just as the Irish were.

The problems of the western empire in the fifth century had a disastrous impact on Roman Britain, which was a relatively unimportant place in the eyes of far-off and hard-pressed emperors. In 410, Rome withdrew its troops from the island to fight in a civil war in Gaul. They never returned. The Romano-British population was left to defend itself against the Picts, who lived beyond the northern borders, as well as against Irish and Germanic pirates. Centuries of Roman rule had apparently left the native population unwarlike. Following Roman precedent, they hired Germanic mercenaries to help defend their lands. The mercenaries, members of the Saxon tribe living on the coasts of Denmark and Holland, soon took the opportunity to seize land for themselves, led by the brothers and chiefs Hengest and Horsa, in about 450. For more than two centuries thereafter, the migrating Saxons, Angles and Jutes pushed up the river valleys, driving the Romano-British before them. We know very little about the details of the struggles. When the situation stabilised in the eighth century, the descendants of the Romano-British population, who had remained Christians, lived in the western and north-western parts of the island. There were bishops, but as in Ireland monks and monasteries were important. Because the Anglo-Saxons had come from areas virtually untouched by Roman influence, they were among the most purely Germanic and primitive invaders of the empire. Roman culture and institutions, including Christianity and the Latin language, disappeared from lowland Britain. Illiterate, pagan and warlike, the invaders divided lowland Britain into numerous small kingdoms constantly warring with one another and with the Christian Celts to the west.

In theory, the Romano-British abbots and bishops in Wales, Devonshire, Cornwall and Strathclyde – or even Ireland – might have undertaken the conversion of the invaders, but the bitterness created by conquest and continuing warfare made that impossible. There were Frankish bishops across the English Channel, only 30 miles from Kent, but they took no initiative in the matter. In a remarkable development, missionaries arrived in the south of England from Rome in 597 and in the north from Ireland in 635.

VII. The Roman missionaries to the Anglo-Saxons

Pope Gregory I (590–604) was the moving force behind the Roman mission to the Anglo-Saxons. In a story told a hundred years later by an Anglo-Saxon biographer of Gregory, the future pope saw captives for sale in the slave markets of Rome. When he asked who the blond, blue-eyed folk were, he was told they were 'Angles' (*Angli* in Latin); he responded that they were 'angels (*angeli*) of God'. The anonymous biographer says that Gregory received permission from Pope Benedict (575–79) to go as a missionary to the Angles, but the Roman populace forced the pope to call him back. In a less legendary source, Gregory himself reported in a letter to the patriarch of Alexandria, written in July 598, that he had sent monks from his monastery to the Angles 'who dwell in a corner of the world and remain in the wicked worship of wood and rocks'. He asked the patriarch to rejoice with him that 10,000 Angles had been baptised at Christmas 597.[8] Gregory's effort was an unusual one. The popes (and most bishops inside the Roman Empire) had not previously been active in missionary work of any kind. Gregory could not have known the long-term impact of his decision to send missionaries to the pagans in Britain.

Gregory took another important initiative when he entrusted the mission to monks. Traditionally, monks withdrew from the world for the salvation of their own souls. They were not expected or encouraged to do missionary work or any sort of pastoral work among the laity because such work was the responsibility of the bishops, priests and deacons. Gregory himself had been a monk and may have realised the potential of organised, disciplined and self-sufficient communities of monks to provide a sturdy infrastructure for missionary work in such a primitive place as Anglo-Saxon England.

In 596, Gregory sent a band of 40 Italian monks under the leadership of a monk named Augustine (597–*c*.607), named for the great fifth-century bishop of Hippo in North Africa. The monks were terrified of what they might encounter and even tried to come home when they were in Frankish territory. Gregory would not permit it and in 597 they landed in Kent, the kingdom closest to the Frankish realm and most influenced by Frankish ways. The favour of the local king was crucial, as it was so often in the conversion of the early medieval Germanic tribes. King Ethelbert of Kent (560–616) had married Bertha, a great-granddaughter of the Frankish king Clovis, and had permitted her to have in her household a Frankish bishop to minister to her spiritual needs. King Ethelbert allowed the Roman missionaries to settle in Canterbury, where the monks founded the monastery of Saints Peter and Paul (later St Augustine's). Augustine, the first archbishop of Canterbury, restored a surviving Roman church, which he dedicated to the Saviour. (This was known as Christchurch in later times; we know it today as Canterbury

Cathedral.) Within a few years, King Ethelbert was baptised and the Roman mission had a small but secure base of operations in Kent.

The situation that developed in the south of England in the seventh century was new. For the first time, missionaries sent directly from Rome had converted a pagan people. The fledgling Anglo-Saxon church was proud of its ties to St Peter and the papacy. It was the first regional church outside Italy to acknowledge in continuing, concrete ways the religious pre-eminence of the bishop of Rome. In the seventh and eighth centuries, a modest traffic in letters and pilgrims moved from England to Rome and back. Anglo-Saxon bishops and kings asked the popes for guidance on difficult questions of liturgy, morality and organisation. They appealed occasionally to the pope for the decision of disputed religious matters. They sent newly chosen archbishops of Canterbury to Rome to obtain the *pallium*, a woollen liturgical garment that served to confirm them in office. In short, Pope Gregory's mission had created a church loyal to the papacy at the western fringe of the Christian world.

VIII. The Irish missionaries to the Anglo-Saxons

About a generation after the arrival of Roman missionaries, Irish monks began a mission to the northern Anglo-Saxon kingdom of Northumbria. Anglo-Saxons of royal blood, living as exiles among the Irish, had accepted Christianity. When one of them, King Oswald (634–42), was restored to power, he invited Irish missionaries from the important monastery on the island of Iona into the Kingdom of Northumbria. The Irish brought their ways with them, including their tonsure, their method for determining the date of Easter, their love of monasticism, and their ascetic lifestyle. The island of Lindisfarne off the north-eastern coast of England became the centre of their mission, with Bishops Aidan (634–51), Finan (651–61), and Colman (661–64) winning over the Northumbrian court to Irish Christianity. The Irish and their northern Anglo-Saxon disciples were not anti-papal, but they were not attached to the papacy in the way that the converts of the Roman missionaries were.

The Roman and Irish missions functioned in their separate spheres for about thirty years with some friction, but no serious breach. Each church had its supporters among the royal families of the Anglo-Saxons. For example, the Northumbrian king Oswiu favoured the Celtic rite, but his contracted bride, the Kentish queen Eanfled practised the Roman rite. Women in such marriage alliances often kept the right to practise their own religion, but although Eanfled had no such marriage agreement, she kept to her own religious practices anyway. She did not want it to look like her family, from Kent, was submitting to the king of Northumbria. This was an alliance, after all, not one group accepting the other as overlord. For his part, if the king accepted his wife's religion, especially if her family was the stronger of the two in the marriage alliance, then it could look like the king was submitting to the side of the new queen. So on the matter of Easter each followed his or her own practice. As Bede tells us:

> In those days it sometimes happened that Easter was celebrated twice in the same year, so that the king had finished the fast and was keeping Holy Sunday, while the queen and her attendants were still in Lent and observing Palm Sunday.[9]

One can imagine that this might create discord in a marriage, but historian Stephanie Hollis called this a 'micro-cosmic resonance of a wider conflict'.[10] In 664, King Oswiu called for a synod at the monastery of Whitby, at which the Roman and Irish parties might debate their case. Whitby was a centre of learning, especially under its founding **abbess**, Hilda (c.614–80). One can speculate whether Oswiu was trying to stack the deck, since Hilda herself was an influential woman, who practised the traditions of Irish monasticism. No one in the debate pulled any punches. Wilfrid of York, a staunch Romanist, told the Irish contingent from Iona that their great monastic founder Columba, may have been holy, but where the dating of Easter was concerned he was 'obstinate', 'foolish' and showed a 'rude simplicity'.[11] According to historian Peter Brown, the necessity for the Irish contingent to change their dating of Easter was not something they heard for the first time at Whitby. As early as 630, an Irish monk named Cummian had brought this same issue to the monks of Iona, admonishing them to get in line with the rest of the church, for they were nothing more than 'a pimple on the chin of the earth'.[12] And this from their own countryman! In the end, Wilfrid argued the primacy of the Roman pope – 'Christ gave Peter the keys to the kingdom of heaven' – and the Irish bishop Colman gave in. In the face of such heavenly power, King Oswiu opted for the Roman ways: he did not want heaven's doorkeeper to turn him away. Hilda of Whitby also accepted the Roman practice, as did many of the Irish clergy, though some did not and returned to Iona.

By the 690s, all the Anglo-Saxon kingdoms had formally accepted Roman Christianity, although native pagan ways were tenacious and hung on for centuries. The Anglo-Saxon church presented a new church type: proud of its conversion to Roman Christianity; loyal to St Peter and his representative, the bishop of Rome; possessing a disciplined clergy, of whom some were literate in Latin; and marked with impulses to strict asceticism and missionary work imparted by their Irish teachers.

When Pope Gregory died in 604, the situation in the west had appeared bleak for his form of Christianity. Arianism was receding but still a threat; Germanic paganism was a tenacious force in important parts of the north-west; the vigorous Celtic Christianity of Ireland and western England was quite independent; and even the Catholic Franks were ruled by brutal, immoral kings who dominated their bishops and had little regard for the wider church or the papacy. By 700, the situation had changed significantly. The descendants of the native Roman population were still largely Christian and most of the invaders were in the process of being assimilated in language, culture and religion, though the word conversion must not be used too simplistically. The official acceptance of Catholic Christianity by Germanic royal families and aristocrats was just a first step in the much more complicated process of replacing traditional behaviours, values and beliefs with Christian ones. By 700, all of the Arian kingdoms had disappeared, either by conversion or by conquest. The Christianised Anglo-Saxons had recently begun missionary work on the continent among pagan Germans, where they promoted loyalty to St Peter and the pope. The Roman Empire in the west was gone, but Christianity survived in the new circumstances and showed glimmers of revival and expansion.

Suggested reading

Companion website

www.routledge.com/cw/lynch

4.1   St. Patrick's Confession
Excerpts from 'St. Patrick's Confession', in Daniel De Vinné, ed., *History of the Irish Primitive Church together with The Life of St. Patrick and his Confession in Latin, with a parallel translation* (New York: 1870), 207–214.

4.2   St. Augustine of Canterbury converts the pagans
Excerpts from *Bede's Ecclesiastical History of England: A Revised Translation*, translated by A. M. Sellar (London: George Bell and Sons, 1907), 42–73.

4.3   The Synod of Whitby
Excerpts from *Bede's Ecclesiastical History of England: A Revised Translation*, translated by A. M. Sellar (London: George Bell and Sons, 1907), 192–201.

Primary sources

Bede, *A History of the English Church and People*, edited by Bertram Colgrave and R. A. B. Mynors (Oxford, 1969)

Gregory of Tours, *History of the Franks*, translated by Lewis Thorpe (Harmondsworth, Middlesex, 1974)

Medieval Handbooks of Penance: A Translation of the Principal Libri Poenitentiales and Selections from Related Documents, edited by John T. McNeill and Helena Gamer (New York, 1965)

Patrick, *Confession* and *Letter to Coroticus*, in R. P. C. Hanson, *The Life and Writings of the Historical Saint Patrick* (New York, 1983)

Soldiers of Christ: Saints and Saints' Lives from Late Antiquity and the Early Middle Ages, edited by Thomas F. X. Noble and Thomas Head (University Park, Pennsylvania, 1995)

The Earliest Life of Gregory the Great by an Anonymous Monk of Whitby, edited by Bertram Colgrave (Cambridge, 1985)

Modern scholarship

Bieler, Ludwig, *Ireland, Harbinger of the Middle Ages* (London, 1963)

Bowes, Kimberly, *Private Worship, Public Values, and Religious Change in Late Antiquity* (Cambridge, 2008)

Charles-Edwards, T. M., *Early Christian Ireland* (Cambridge, 2000)

Crawford, Samuel John, *Anglo-Saxon Influence on Western Christendom, 600–800* (Cambridge, 1933)

Dunn, Marilyn, *The Christianization of the Anglo-Saxons, c.597–700: Discourses of Life, Death and Afterlife* (London, 2009)

Hughes, Kathleen, *The Church in Early Irish Society* (London, 1966)

Mayr-Harting, Henry, *The Coming of Christianity to Anglo-Saxon England*, 3rd edition (University Park, Pennsylvania, 1991)

McNeill, John T., *The Celtic Churches; a History A.D. 200 to 1200* (Chicago, 1974)

Riché, Pierre, *Education and Culture in the Barbarian West*, translated by John J. Contreni (Columbia, South Carolina, 1978)

Russell, James C., *The Germanization of Early Medieval Christianity: A Sociohistorical Approach to Religious Transformation* (Oxford, 1996)

Stenton, Frank M., *Anglo-Saxon England*, 3rd edition (Oxford, 1970)

Stutz, Ulrich, 'The Proprietary Church as an Element of Medieval Germanic Ecclesiastical Law', in Geoffrey Barraclough, *Medieval Germany*, vol. 2 (Oxford, 1938), pp. 35–70

Thom, Catherine, *Early Irish Monasticism: An Understanding of its Cultural Roots* (London, 2006)

Van der Meer, Frederik, *Augustine the Bishop. Church and Society at the Dawn of the Middle Ages*, translated by Brian Battershaw and G. R. Lamb (London, 1961)

Wallace-Hadrill, J. M., *The Frankish Church* (Oxford, 1983)

Wolff, Philippe, *Western Languages, AD 100–1500*, translated by Frances Partridge (London, 1971)

Wood, Ian, *The Missionary Life: Saints and Evangelization of Europe 400–1050* (Harlow, 2001)

Wood, Susan, *The Proprietary Church in the Medieval West* (Oxford, 2009)

Yorke, Barbara, *The Conversion of Britain: Religion, Politics and Society in Britain, 600–800* (London, 2006)

Notes

1 Tertullian, *Ad nationes*, I.1.2, edited by Janus Borleffs, *Ad nationes libri duo* (Leiden, 1929), p. 1.

2 Ralph Martin Novak, *Christianity and the Roman Empire: Background Texts* (Harrisburg, Pennsylvania, 2001), p. 103. The footnote on that same page cites Robin Lane Fox, *Pagans and Christians* (New York, 1989) p. 592, which 'favors a somewhat lower number, estimating that Christians may have formed only 4 or 5 percent of the population by 312 C.E.'.

3 Calculation based on data in *Atlas zur Kirchengeschichte*, edited by Hubert Jedin, Kenneth Scott Latourette and Jochen Martin (Freiburg im Breisgau, 1970).

4 'King Theodoric to all the Jews living in Genoa', Cassiodorus, *Variae Epistolae*, Book II, Letter 27, in *The Letters of Cassiodorus, Being a condensed translation of the Variae Epistolae of Magnus Aurelius Cassiodorus Senator*, with an introduction by Thomas Hodgkin (London, 1886), p. 186.

5 Gregory of Tours, *History of the Franks*, translated by Lewis Thorpe (Harmondsworth, Middlesex, 1974), book 2, ch. 29, pp. 141–2.

6 Gregory of Tours, *History of the Franks*, book 2, ch. 29, p. 142.

7 Gregory of Tours, *History of the Franks*, book 2, ch. 30, p. 143.

8 Gregory I, *Registrum epistularum*, book 8, letter 29, edited by Dag Norberg, Corpus christianorum, Series latina 140A (Turnhout, Belgium, 1983), p. 551.

9 Bede, *A History of the English Church and People*, book 3, ch. 25, p. 297.

10 See Stephanie Hollis, *Anglo Saxon Women and the Church* (Woodbridge, Suffolk, 1992), pp. 234–40.

11 Bede, *A History of the English Church and People*, book 3, ch. 25, pp. 301 and 307.

12 Cummian, *On the Paschal Controversy* 107–110, translated by M. Walsh and D. O'Cróinín (Toronto, 1988), p. 72, cited in Peter Brown, *The Rise of Western Christendom: Triumph and Diversity, AD 200–1000*, 2nd edition (Malden, Massachusetts, 2003), p. 362.

5

The Papal-Frankish Alliance

In the middle of the eighth century, Anglo-Saxon monks working as missionaries on the continent brought the popes and the Franks into an alliance that did much to shape the medieval church. The 'Papal-Frankish Alliance' of 751 was the outcome of a process that began in the 680s with three independent developments: the beginning of missionary work by the Anglo-Saxons on the continent; the rise to political domination of a Frankish aristocratic family called the Carolingians; and the growing alienation of the popes from their political protectors and masters, the Byzantine emperors at Constantinople.

I. The Anglo-Saxon missions

In the winter of 677–8, an Anglo-Saxon bishop, Wilfrid of York (634–709), was on his way to Rome to appeal to the pope over a decision that had gone against him. Because he had offended the Frankish ruler and could not cross his territory, he had to spend the winter in Frisia (modern Holland), where the native Frisians were Germanic pagans. He used his time to attempt to convert them, though without lasting success. However, his efforts were the first of what became a wave of missionary enthusiasm in the church of his homeland. Within three decades there were perhaps hundreds of Anglo-Saxon monks and nuns working as missionaries among the pagan or partly Christianised Frisians, Saxons, Alemanians, Thuringians and Bavarians who lived beyond the northern and eastern borders of the Frankish kingdom.

Roman and Irish missionaries had introduced the Anglo-Saxons to Christianity only 90 years earlier. Their full adoption of Christianity had been secure for only about forty years. Yet with the zeal characteristic of recent converts, the Anglo-Saxons had created the most orderly, learned and dynamic church in the west. They knew Christianity almost entirely from books and they endeavoured with much success to carry out what the books told them. Monks living under the *Rule* of St Benedict set the tone of the Anglo-Saxon church. Monasteries trained native clergy both to read Latin and to use the native language in religious instruction. In an unexpected twist, the most learned westerner in the eighth century, the monk Bede (672–735), lived at the northern fringe of the civilised world in what is now Northumberland.

An exodus of missionaries came out of Anglo-Saxon England, Christian monks who were loyal to Rome.

In modern times, the Rhine delta and valley are among the most highly developed regions in the world. It is necessary to imagine them in a very different state to understand the problems faced by the Anglo-Saxon missionaries. In 700, the Rhine region was part of a primitive, illiterate, violent world, sparsely populated, where people lived in disorderly villages of wooden huts and earned their keep from primitive agriculture and herding. Human effort had not yet remade the region, where vast forests, marshes and moors marked the landscape. In such an environment, missionary activity had to pay its own way and meet most of its own needs – though the missionaries did receive some support from England and from the generosity of Frankish kings and aristocrats. Monks, nuns and kings in Anglo-Saxon England sent gifts to their compatriots in the mission lands: books, liturgical vestments, clothing and some money, but certainly not enough to support for decades the day-to-day activities of the missionaries.

The Anglo-Saxons were quite familiar with an institution that adapted well to sparsely inhabited regions without cities, markets or a plentiful supply of money: monasteries had flourished in the primitive material conditions of Ireland and Anglo-Saxon England itself. St Benedict had intended that his monastery be economically self-sufficient, although his motive was a religious one, that of minimising the contact of his monks with secular life. The Anglo-Saxon missionaries built on that monastic self-sufficiency to support their work economically. Since unoccupied or sparsely settled land was plentiful beyond the Rhine and north of the Alps, there was little difficulty in finding suitable sites. The ideal monastery was built in a well-watered place, with buildings for monastic life (a church, a dormitory, a dining hall and an infirmary), as well as for economic life (workshops, stables, granaries and a mill). Wealthy patrons sometimes gave huge grants of land where agriculture could be carried on by the monks' peasants and slaves. The sturdy, workable monastery, often though not always Benedictine, was the backbone of missionary work on the continent.

The missionaries were immigrants from England, but they willingly accepted native boys to be trained as the next generation of monks and rural clergy. Each monastery evangelised and organised the surrounding region, supplying priests and building churches. The Anglo-Saxons were well-suited for the task of converting Germanic peoples, whom they consciously regarded as their kinsmen. They themselves spoke a Germanic language and must have learned the local Germanic dialects with relative ease. They could soon preach and teach in the language of their converts, but many were also educated in Latin and capable of creating orderly churches built on the theology and organisational patterns derived from scripture, canon law and liturgy.

The Anglo-Saxon missionaries were skilful organisers, who maintained their work for about a century. (See Map 2.) They produced two long-lived and outstanding leaders, Willibrord/Clement and Winfrith/Boniface. Willibrord (658–739) was a Northumbrian monk and a disciple of Wilfrid of York. He had spent 12 years in an Irish monastery, where his desire to do missionary work among Germanic pagans and lax Christians had grown. In 690 his abbot dispatched him with 11 companions to continue the work of Wilfrid among the Frisians. The Frisian ruler, Radbod, was not favourable to Christianity, probably because he rightly feared that conversion would be a prelude to conquest by the neighbouring Franks. To counter Radbod's hostility, Willibrord realised that he needed the support of the paramount Christian power in the region, the Franks. The Frankish king was by then a figurehead. The real power lay with Pippin of Herstal (died 714), who held the position of the king's chief minister, called the mayor of the palace. Since the aggressive Franks saw in the conversion of their neighbours a promotion of their own plans for conquest, they were willing to help, endow and protect the missionaries. When Willibrord founded a monastery in about 698 at Echternach in modern Luxembourg, the endowment in land came from Pippin of Herstal, Pippin's wife, and his mother-in-law. Pippin's protection enabled Willibrord to work in western Frisia, which was under Frankish control, but more importantly it drew the Frankish mayors of the palace into continuing support for the Anglo-Saxon missionaries.

Willibrord needed not only military protection but also legitimate authority to undertake the ecclesiastical organisation of new territories, where there had never been bishoprics before. He did what Anglo-Saxons had done since their conversion to Christianity: he turned to the pope. Here was the fruition of the seed Pope Gregory I had planted a century earlier, when he sent missionaries to the Anglo-Saxons. Now the Anglo-Saxon missionaries turned to the papacy. In 695, Pope Sergius I made Willibrord archbishop of the Frisians, with headquarters at Utrecht in the modern Netherlands. Pope Sergius also gave Willibrord a good Roman name, Clement, to replace what must have seemed to Romans a barbaric one. It is important to note that it was Willibrord's initiative to involve the pope. The popes had not sponsored any missionary work since that of Pope Gregory about a century earlier, though they had kept sporadic contact with the Anglo-Saxons and the Franks. Sergius and his successors welcomed the missionaries' spontaneous acknowledgement of their authority, but it was the Anglo-Saxons who sought them out. Thus, Willibrord drew both the Frankish rulers and the popes into support of his missionary work, although they were not yet cooperating much with one another.

The other Anglo-Saxon organiser of missions, who worked on a much larger geographical scale than his mentor Willibrord, was the monk Winfrith (c.675–754), renamed Boniface by Pope Gregory II. (See Figure 5.) From the

Map 2 Christianity and paganism in western Europe, *c*.350–750

Figure 5 Martyrdom of Boniface
Saint Boniface on his mission to the Frisians. In the left frame, Boniface baptizes a pagan. In the right frame, he is martyred by the Frisians.

North Sea coast of Frisia to Thuringia and Bavaria, Boniface worked for 40 years both to convert Germanic pagans and to reorganise church life in areas where there were nominal Christians and much religious disorder. His chief monastic foundation was at Fulda in western Germany. His papally granted title was archbishop of the Germans, with the site of his archbishopric fixed late in his life (745) at Mainz.

While the standard narrative of the Anglo-Saxon missions centres on Willibrord and Boniface, we should not ignore the contributions of women missionaries, such as Boniface's relative, the nun Leoba. In addition to the bishops and priests who travelled in order to take the Christian message to the pagans, stationary communities of monks and nuns also attracted and inspired followers in the missionary territories. Leoba (c.710–82) was a relative of Boniface, perhaps his niece. She was abbess of the monastery of Tauberbischofsheim (German for 'the bishop's home on the river Tauber'), founded by Boniface, but she also was involved in the foundation of other monasteries. Leoba was famed for her learning, and – counter to the ideal for cloistered nuns – actively participated in theological discussions with bishops and members of the nobility. According to her biographer, Rudolph of Fulda, she was the only female allowed to enter the all-male monastery of Fulda to pray and consult with the abbots there on matters of monastic discipline. Leoba was so important to the missionary effort that in 754, when Boniface left on his mission to Frisia, he gave Leoba his monastic cowl, partly as a symbol of their close relationship, but perhaps as a sign that she carried his authority in his absence.

To secure the success of his mission, Boniface followed Willibrord's pattern of seeking both Frankish and papal support for his work. Pippin of Herstal's son and successor as mayor of the palace, Charles Martel (714–41), took the missionaries under his protection, but Boniface was never at ease in the court of that tough warlord, where the Frankish bishops seemed too worldly for his strict views. Boniface's ties to the papacy were particularly close, indeed no other bishop in the north had enjoyed anything like them. The pope authorised his missionary work in 719, consecrated him bishop in 722, and appointed him archbishop from the pope in 732. Boniface swore an oath of loyalty to St Peter and to the pope, which he renewed when successive popes died. He also carried on a steady correspondence with four popes, seeking their advice and approval in many matters. Where he was successful in converting pagans and revitalising pre-existing Christian communities, he spread an orderly, Rome-oriented Christianity.

The story of Boniface's missionary work can make him seem like a lone hero, single-handedly transforming the pagan landscape to Roman Christianity through the power of his preaching. In fact, there were many other missionaries at work. Some of these were the Irish missionaries mentioned in Chapter 4. Others were people Boniface had dispatched to certain territories, monks like Lullus, Willibald, Burchard. In addition to Leoba, mentioned above, there were other women as well, like Walburg and Thecla. And persuasive preaching was not the only tool these missionaries used. They often resorted to violence against the pagans, in the form of destroying their shrines or cutting down their sacred trees and groves, in an attempt to demonstrate the powerlessness of the pagan gods. Carolingian leaders and their armies, in addition to protecting missionaries, also participated in the destruction of shrines, as Charles Martel did in his campaign against the Frisians in 734. Two generations later, Charlemagne would continue this practice of using force as a tool of conversion, when he conquered the Saxons in 776, forcing them to be baptised as part of their acceptance of his lordship. Missionaries supported this violence, often urging Carolingian rulers, as one modern historian put it, 'to root out paganism with the sword, destroying every sign and symbol of the pagan gods'.[1]

By the 740s, the Franks had been Christians for about two hundred and fifty years. They had developed a church organisation centred on bishops and on the kings and, when royal power declined, on the mayors of the palace. For 50 years, Pippin of Herstal and Charles Martel supported missionary work beyond their northern and eastern borders, but they did not allow Willibrord, Boniface or the pope to interfere in the running of the Frankish church itself. The Frankish rulers regarded the popes as dignified, respected figures. They corresponded with them and even accorded them a vague authority in theological, liturgical and moral matters, but they did not permit them to intervene in the financial or personnel decisions of the Frankish church.

When Charles Martel died in 741, he was succeeded by two sons, Pippin the Short (741-68) and Carloman (741-54), who divided the office of mayor of the palace. They had spent part of their youth in the monastery of St Denis, just north of Paris, and were more pious than their brutal father. In 747, Carloman abandoned his position as mayor of the palace to become a monk at Monte Cassino in Italy, leaving full control of the Frankish kingdom to his brother. Both Pippin and Carloman wished to retain control of the Frankish church, but they also favoured a moral and intellectual reform of the clergy. They sought the advice of the veteran missionary Boniface, who encouraged them to undertake the reforms with papal participation. A strict religious person might have disapproved of many common practices in the Frankish church, including bishops of noble birth who lived like their secular kinsmen, the survival of paganism, the religious mixing in the countryside, and a decline of church discipline from earlier ideals. It was a symptom of the decline of the church in the Frankish kingdom that in 742 there had been no council of bishops there for 50 years. Boniface and the mayors of the palace revived the use of councils (they held four of them between 742 and 747) and consulted the pope on what to do. Boniface himself presided over three of these councils, at the mayor's invitation and as the **legate** (representative) of the pope. In cooperation with Frankish rulers and popes, Boniface ignited a reform movement that transformed the Frankish church, promoted its 'romanisation' and ultimately led to the cultural revival of the ninth century called the 'Carolingian Renaissance'.

In his middle seventies, Boniface returned to his work as a missionary where he had begun, in Frisia. According to his biographer, Willibald, Boniface was martyred in 754 and buried at his monastery of Fulda.[2] Before his death, he asked that his kinswoman and fellow missionary Leoba be buried with him in the same grave, 'so that they who had served God during their lifetime with equal sincerity and zeal should await together the day of resurrection'.[3] Interestingly, this last request of the martyred saint does not appear in Willibald's *Life of Boniface*, but in Rudolph's *Life of Leoba*. (In fact, Willibald makes no mention of Leoba at all!) Boniface's request to be buried with his kinswoman echoes that of Saint Benedict and his sister Scholastica, who was also a kind of partner in spreading religious life. Although they were both buried at Fulda, Boniface and Leoba were put in separate graves.

Seventy years of Anglo-Saxon and Irish missionary work – sometimes by preaching, sometimes by the sword – had transformed the north-eastern borders of Latin Europe. A string of bishoprics and monasteries had advanced the conversion of the pagan Germans and the re-Christianisation of neighbouring regions. A vigorous reform movement, loyal to the papacy, was spreading within the Frankish church as well. The popes and the Frankish mayors of the palace (soon to be kings of the Franks) had been brought into ever more intense contact by their mutual interests, first in supporting the missionaries and more recently in promoting the reform of the Frankish church.

II. The Frankish mayors of the palace

The Merovingian dynasty produced its last effective king with Dagobert I (died 639). There continued to be Merovingian kings, but real power lay with the king's chief steward, the mayor of the palace. After 687, that office was monopolised by an aristocratic family whose base of power was in vast estates and in allied aristocratic families in northern Gaul, a region that includes modern Belgium and northern France. These people had no last names, so we need to identify them in other ways. A personal name used for generations was Pippin, so they are sometimes called Pippinids, but historians more commonly call them Carolingians, from the Latin 'Carolus', Charles in English, which was another characteristic name. The Carolingian mayors of the palace controlled the Frankish church in the traditional ways, in particular by choosing bishops and abbots from their circle of kinsmen and other allied aristocrats. The control of the national church by the ruler was so normal that there was no serious resistance even when a ruler pushed that power very far. For instance, Charles Martel seized vast amounts of land from the church, with the grudging approval of the bishops, to support his warriors.

As a consequence of long-term trends quite beyond the control of contemporaries, the economic and cultural regression in Gaul, which had begun in Roman times, probably reached its low point in Charles Martel's lifetime, during the first half of the eighth century. In a landlocked agricultural society, trade had become rare, cities vestigial, violence common and brutal poverty the norm for all but the elite. After generations of decline, literacy had finally become restricted almost entirely to the clergy, and even many of them were only marginally literate – which would remain the case for 500 years. This economic, cultural and political decline affected the church at every level. Reformers, such as Boniface, admired the church of the late Roman Empire and of his native England, and by those standards the contemporary Frankish church fell far short. Boniface complained that the behaviour of some Frankish bishops was so scandalous that he wanted to avoid contact with them. For instance, he informed the pope that some Frankish bishops had purchased their positions (which was considered a sin called **simony**), others were married or fornicators, and still others enriched their relatives from church property, carried weapons, shed blood, and generally acted like lay members of the aristocratic class to which they belonged. But he could not avoid them because he needed to go to the royal court for support for his missionary work. Boniface's observations on the rural priests he encountered were also negative: they knew little or no Latin, were incapable of preaching, and some even worshipped the Germanic gods as well as Christ. Not only were many of the Frankish clergy ignorant and immoral, but there were also structural problems larger than any individual. The traditional mechanisms for supervision had broken down: the organisation of the bishops into provinces under archbishops had disappeared, as had the practice of holding councils to define and enforce discipline.

In response to such a sorry state of affairs, the Carolingian mayors of the palace, Pippin and Carloman, asked Boniface to lend his prestige and advice to the reform of the church. The canons of the reform councils over which he presided restated 'the ancient canon law', that is, the canon law of the late Roman Empire, and called for basic reform in the behaviour of the clergy. A letter from Boniface to Archbishop Cuthbert of Canterbury reported on the decisions of the Frankish synods. Among other things, they forbade 'pagan rites, divination, fortune-telling, soothsaying, charms, incantations, and all Gentile vileness'. They also forbade the clergy from wearing 'showy or martial dress or to carry arms'.[4] Monks were to live by the *Rule* of St Benedict. The councils also called for the reinstitution of an orderly church organisation, including annual councils of bishops, annual meetings of bishops with their priests, obedience of priests to bishops, and restoration of church finances, which had been disrupted by Charles Martel's confiscations a decade earlier to support his soldiers.

The councils issued brave words ('we command that . . .'), but change was glacially slow on some issues and non-existent on others. The abuses that the reformers attacked in the Frankish church were deeply rooted and had the authority of long tradition behind them. Many important people had an interest in their continuance. Significant reform in some areas would have cost some people power or money or jobs. Furthermore, Frankish society had few means to propagandise for the reforms. One notes that even in modern societies with sophisticated mass communication, activists of various sorts are frustrated by how hard it is to persuade people to abandon racial hatred, to practise safe sex or to stop smoking. In the primitive conditions of the eighth century, it was very difficult to change minds and behaviour. But the Anglo-Saxons, cooperating with their Frankish sympathisers and the mayors of the palace, succeeded in disseminating three notions that were in the long run subversive of the status quo. They held that the present state of affairs in the church was wrong; that the proper guidelines for Christianity were to be found in the 'ancient canons'; and that the pope (and through him, St Peter) was the appropriate person to consult when uncertainties arose about liturgy, law and belief. In short, the Franks began to behave more like Anglo-Saxons when it came to religious and ecclesiastical life.

The first stages of the reform of the Frankish church put Boniface in close contact with the mayors of the palace. His advice was not only religious but also political. Carloman's decision in 747 to become a monk reunited the Frankish kingdom in the hands of his brother and mayor of the palace,

Pippin. The Merovingian royal family, weak as it was in reality, had a halo of antiquity (they had ruled for eight or nine generations) and a quasi-pagan divinity, a kind of sacred bloodline, which Pippin's upstart family could not match. Pippin wanted to become king in place of the nominal ruler, Childerich III (743–51). He certainly had the military power to seize the throne, but in order to be recognised as a legitimate ruler, Pippin needed to counter that sacred bloodline and the traditional authority of the Merovingians. Boniface may have suggested to him that he seek legitimation from the pope. Even if the idea came from Pippin himself, the Anglo-Saxon missionaries had prepared the way and supported the decision.

III. The papacy

In the late 740s, the popes were hard-pressed by their neighbours, the Lombards, and increasingly alienated from the distant, relatively weak and heretical Byzantine emperors. Around 750, circumstances were right for a major reorientation of papal political alliances. The roots of the change lay a century earlier in the Middle East. After 632, the entire face of the Mediterranean world was changed by the spread of a new religion, Islam. As Islamic armies swept rapidly around the Mediterranean, reaching Damascus in 637, Jerusalem in 638, Egypt in 641, Carthage in 698 and crossing into Spain in 711, the Byzantine Empire shrank back to its core in Turkey and Greece with outlying territories in Italy and the Balkans. Most of the ordinary Christian population in the conquered areas had no choice but to remain under Muslim rule. However, many monks, nuns, clergy and wealthy lay people fled into Christian territory, including Italy. Rome, which was still politically Byzantine territory, had its character as an eastern outpost reinforced by the influx of refugees. Between 687 and 751, 11 of the 13 popes were Greek-speakers from Sicily or the east. They were loyal subjects of the Byzantine emperor until they felt pushed to seek other protectors because of two developments, one theological and the other military.

First the religious split. In 726, the Byzantine Emperor Leo III (717–41) attacked the use of religious images, called **icons**, and inaugurated 50 years of **iconoclasm** (literally 'image smashing') as the official policy of the Byzantine Empire. The popes, and westerners in general, were not troubled by the use of religious images and regarded iconoclasm as a serious heresy that seemed to deny that Christ was a real human being and, as such, could be depicted in such material substances as paint or ivory. In efforts to force successive popes to accept iconoclasm, Leo threatened to arrest them, as his predecessors had actually done in earlier theological/political disputes.

He was unable to make good that threat, but he did seize papal estates and rights in the Balkans. In reaction, the popes were increasingly alienated on religious and economic grounds from their centuries-long imperial protector.

Now the military split. The popes could not easily break away from the emperor because of the military threat from the Lombards, who held territory both north and south of the city of Rome. The Lombards had been Catholics for almost one hundred and fifty years, but they were fierce warriors and under their vigorous king Liutprand (712-44) they attempted to conquer all Byzantine territories in central Italy, including Rome. Pope Gregory III (731-41) had appealed in 739 to the Frankish mayor of the palace, Charles Martel, but he refused to intervene because he was allied to the Lombards. That crisis passed when the Lombard King Liutprand died. Under King Aistulf (749-56), the Lombards renewed their military pressure and Popes Zachary (741-52) and Stephen II (752-57) were again looking for help from the only place they could hope to get it: the Franks.

IV. The Papal-Frankish Alliance of 751

Pippin's need to gain approval for his overthrow of the Merovingian king accorded well with Pope Zachary's need for protection against the Lombards and the iconoclastic Byzantines. In the preceding two generations, the Anglo-Saxon missionaries had reinforced the Frankish reverence for St Peter and his representative and had accustomed the Franks to look to the pope for religious authority. In 749, Pippin sent a delegation to Pope Zachary:

> To inquire whether it was good or not that the kings of the Franks [i.e. the Merovingian king Childerich], should wield no royal power, as was the case at that time. Pope Zacharias instructed Pippin that it was better to call him king who had the royal power than the one who did not. To avoid turning the country upside down, he commanded by virtue of his apostolic authority that Pippin should be made king.[5]

One might reasonably question the trustworthiness of this story, recorded in the Royal Frankish Annals, since it related the events from the winner's point of view. Whether or not it really happened as described above, and for the reasons given, the pope legitimated Pippin's revolution by making him king. The ousted King Childeric was sent to a monastery. Pippin was elected king by the Franks and anointed by the clergy (maybe by Boniface), just as the kings of the Old Testament had been anointed. Holy oil consecrated by the church replaced venerable tradition and the sacred blood of family lineage as the legitimiser of Frankish kingship.

Pippin owed the pope a favour and some sort of agreement was struck during the negotiations with Pope Zachary. In 754, Pope Stephen II came in person to Gaul, where he reanointed Pippin and his dynasty in the persons of his sons Charles (768–814) and Carloman (768–71). Stephen asked Pippin to defend St Peter and the Roman church against the Lombards. After some diplomatic manoeuvring and military preparations, Pippin invaded Italy, defeated the Lombard King Aistulf, and gave to St Peter the territory that he had taken from the Lombards in central Italy, territory which the Byzantine emperor believed was his. This 'Donation of Pippin' was the origin of the Papal States. The Papal States persisted until the unification of Italy in 1870 and survive today in the 109 acres of Vatican City.

The Papal-Frankish Alliance, for which the Anglo-Saxon missionaries were intermediaries, set in motion developments that changed the face of western Christianity. Instead of being a western outpost of Byzantium, the papacy moved permanently into the western world, which was dominated by the Franks. The Frankish church became more consciously Roman in its liturgy, its canon law, its learning and its monasticism. The Carolingians, who became the anointed kings of the Franks, took seriously their role as protectors of the church of St Peter and of western Christianity in general. But the Carolingian kings were no more willing to give up control of the church than their predecessors had been. As the popes soon discovered, under a forceful king, protection could become domination.

Suggested reading

Companion website
www.routledge.com/cw/lynch

5.1   The Missionary Work of St. Boniface
Excerpts from Willibald, *The Life of Saint Boniface*, trans. George W. Robinson (Cambridge: Harvard University Press, 1916), 40–45.

5.2   The Frankish Kingdom and the Roman Church
Excerpts from Willibald, *The Life of Saint Boniface*, trans. George W. Robinson (Cambridge: Harvard University Press, 1916), 69–76.

5.3   Pippin's Donation
Excerpts from the *Liber Pontificalis I*, in Oliver Thatcher and Edgar McNeal, eds., *A Source Book for Medieval History: Selected Documents Illustrating the History of Europe in The Middle Age* (New York: Charles Scribner's Sons, 1907), 101–105.

Primary sources

Emerton, Ephraim, editor and translator, *The Letters of Saint Boniface* (New York, 1940), new edition by Thomas F. X. Noble (New York, 2000)

Noble, Thomas F. X. and Thomas Head, editors, *Soldiers of Christ: Saints and Saints' Lives in Late Antiquity and the Early Middle Ages* (University Park, Pennsylvania, 1995)

Scholz, Bernhard, editor, *Carolingian Chronicles* (Ann Arbor, Michigan, 1970)

Talbot, C. H., editor, *The Anglo-Saxon Missionaries in Germany* (New York, 1954)

Modern scholarship

Easton, Stewart and Helene Wieruszowski, *The Era of Charlemagne: Frankish State and Society* (New York, 1961)

Hollis, Stephanie, *Anglo Saxon Women and the Church* (Woodbridge, Suffolk, 1992), pp. 283–8

Levison, Wilhelm, *England and the Continent in the Eighth Century* (Oxford, 1946)

McKitterick, Rosamond, *The Frankish Kingdoms under the Carolingians, 751–987* (London and New York, 1983)

Noble, Thomas F. X., *The Republic of St. Peter. The Birth of the Papal State, 680–825* (Philadelphia, 1984)

Richards, Jeffrey, *The Popes and the Papacy in the Early Middle Ages, 476–752* (London, 1979)

Sullivan, Richard E., 'Early Medieval Missionary Activity: A Comparative Study of Eastern and Western Methods (600–900 A.D.)', *Church History* 23 (1954), pp. 17–35

Sullivan, Richard E., 'The Carolingian Missionary and the Pagan', *Speculum* 28 (1953), pp. 705–40

Notes

1 Richard E. Sullivan, 'The Carolingian Missionary and the Pagan', *Speculum*, vol. 28, no. 4 (Oct., 1953), pp. 720–1.
2 Willibald's *Life of Saint Boniface*, translated by C. H. Talbot, in Noble, *Soldiers of Christ*, pp. 107–40.
3 Rudolph's *Life of Saint Leoba*, translated by C. H. Talbot, in Noble, *Soldiers of Christ*, p. 272.
4 Boniface, Letter 78, to Archbishop Cuthbert of Canterbury (747), Emerton, *The Letters of Saint Boniface*, pp. 114–19.
5 *Royal Frankish Annals* for the year 749, in Bernhard Scholz, editor, *Carolingian Chronicles* (Ann Arbor, Michigan, 1970), p. 39.

6

The church in the Carolingian Empire

I. The new Europe

The Latin west stabilised politically for about a century (750–850) under the rule of the Carolingian dynasty. During that crucial period a civilisation emerged in western Europe that differed enough from its Roman predecessor as well as from contemporary Byzantium and Islam as to be something recognisably new, what many historians call 'the First Europe'. The characteristic features of the new civilisation were discernible by 800 and persisted for a long time. Europe had a new geographical focus. It was not centred on the Mediterranean, as Roman civilisation had been, but on the fertile plains that extended from southern England across northern France into Germany. It also had a new economic base. Whereas Rome, Byzantium and Islam were built on varying degrees of commercial activity, Europe was until the twelfth century an agricultural society in which cities, trade and manufacturing played a minor part. Its religious and intellectual core was Catholic Christianity, with the pope holding an important, though not precisely defined, position of religious pre-eminence. As heir to the Roman and Christian past, Europe had a sacred language, Latin, which was used by the educated elite in matters of religion, high culture and some governing activities.

Even though most of the new Europe was temporarily united in the Carolingian Empire, it remained deeply divided by languages and cultures, and especially by a fundamental split between the Germanic north and the Roman south. Those regional divisions and rivalries reasserted themselves as the Carolingian Empire disintegrated in the later ninth century, making European history often violent but also endowing it with the creative force and cultural diversity that grew out of those conflicting elements. The new Europe also had a complicated cultural heritage, because in many places Germanic values and institutions dominated in government, military behaviour and social structures, while the heritage of the Roman and Christian pasts dominated in intellectual and religious life. The new Europe of the ninth century was no match for the contemporary urban and commercial civilisations of Byzantium and Islam, but it was independent, aggressive and strong enough to survive.

The kingdom of the Franks was the heart of the new Europe. By force of arms and organisational ability, the Carolingian kings Pippin (died 768) and his son Charlemagne (742–814) roughly doubled the size of their kingdom in about forty years, conquering Saxony, Bavaria, the Lombard kingdom in Italy,

Aquitaine, Brittany and a buffer zone in northern Spain. Such military conquests sometimes showed the darker side of Christianisation, where newly subjected pagans were forced to convert under the sword. This was not a moral problem for the Carolingians, whose expanded realm was the largest political entity in the region since the fifth century, when the western Roman Empire had collapsed. Most of western Christianity was within the Frankish Empire, though the small kingdoms of the Anglo-Saxons, the Irish, and the Visigothic refugees from Islam in north-western Spain remained independent.

The Franks achieved remarkable successes in politics and probably increased the economic resources of their society by imposing a greater degree of internal peace. They certainly increased those resources by the plunder, slaves and land seized in successful wars against their neighbours. However, the fundamental economic and demographic facts that had marked the west for centuries had not changed substantially. Frankish society supported itself from primitive, precarious and low-yielding agriculture; consequently it was poor and had only a modest-sized population to bear the economic and military burdens of an empire. The profound poverty of the masses and the modest prosperity of the small elite formed the backdrop against which Christianity developed in the eighth and ninth centuries.

II. The restoration of order

The new political conditions created by the rise of the Carolingian dynasty had a profound influence on the church. Since the 740s, Pippin and his successors had favoured 'reform' in the church and had supported the champions of reform, including Anglo-Saxon Benedictine monks and the papacy. As the power of the Carolingian family grew, they were increasingly in a position to do concrete things to promote change. To put it simply, the Carolingian programme of reform was intended to restore proper 'order' to society, including the church. 'Order' is a simple word covering a complicated idea, which needs to be unpacked.

Until the American and French Revolutions of the late eighteenth century, the western world was committed to a hierarchical view of society. People and institutions were imagined to stand on the steps of a ladder; the higher positions were reserved for kings, nobles and important churchmen, while their subordinates held the lower positions. The hierarchy was ordinarily thought to be given by God or rooted in nature and hence fundamentally right and unchangeable. Carolingian intellectuals, who were almost all churchmen, also thought in hierarchical terms, though the components of their hierarchies changed over time. For example, in 802, in Charlemagne's capitol at Aachen, churchmen developed a hierarchy in which God had divided human society into three distinct orders (from the Latin *ordo*, plural *ordines*). These *ordines* were the **secular clergy** (bishops, priests and deacons); the **regular clergy** (monks, nuns and canons, all of whom were living under a rule, called in Latin a *regula*); and finally, the laity (everyone who was not a member of the clergy). Half a century later, a monk and scholar named Heiric of Auxerre developed another theory containing three orders of medieval society: those who work, those who pray and those who fight. Heiric's theory would not become the dominant view of medieval societal structure until post-Carolingian times, so we will leave it for now to focus on the earlier theory – with secular clergy, regular clergy and laity – and how it affected Carolingian church reforms.

The Carolingian reformers believed their society's problems were due to the fact that the *ordines* were intermingled and confused with one another. They were convinced that if each *ordo* was granted its rights and performed its duties, society would function as it was supposed to. Carolingian reform can be condensed to the attempt to define for each *ordo* its rights and to enforce on each its duties. Canon law was the complicated set of rules and recommendations that laid out for each *ordo* its religious rights and duties. The earliest inklings of a Christian canon law are found in the New Testament, where, for instance, Paul regulated difficult questions of marriage (1 Cor. 7) and laid down requirements for men to be officers of the church (1 Tim. 3:1–13), and where the apostles regulated the admission of gentile converts to their essentially Jewish group (Acts 15). As the Christian movement grew, it encountered new problems, new situations and new cultures, which in turn called for new decisions, some of which were eventually incorporated into canon law.

Canon law developed out of a variety of sources. Councils of bishops meeting at the local, regional and ecumenical levels settled disputes over belief and behaviour. The decisions of such councils were later gathered in collections and became basic parts of the church's procedures. Sometimes leading bishops issued their views on controversial topics in the form of letters, of which some were eventually accepted into the canon law. In the fourth century, the bishops of Rome had begun issuing such letters, called decretal letters. In the late Roman and Byzantine Empires, secular laws concerning church property and personnel sometimes became part of the canon law. Finally, excerpts from the works of prestigious theologians such as Augustine, from monastic rules such as Benedict's, and from the Old and New Testaments became part of the canon law. Already in the sixth century, the accumulation of diverse texts made the canon law complex and even contradictory. Here and there, scholars attempted to bring order to the canon law by selecting texts and arranging them systematically under topic headings. A bishop could use such a canonical collection, which might be a single thick volume, to manage his church.

Because the church had never been centralised and the invasions of the fifth and sixth centuries had increased its regionalised character, it was only natural that canon law collections would differ, sometimes quite significantly, from place to place. When the ninth-century Carolingian reformers sought to strengthen links between their church and that of the late Roman Empire, they stimulated a revival of canon law. As the Carolingian reformers did in so many religious matters, they looked to the papacy for authoritative legal texts. Charlemagne accepted for the Frankish church the canonical collection sent to him by Pope Hadrian I in 774, called the *Dionysio-Hadriana*, because it had been created about 500 by the monk Dionysius and was transmitted in an updated form by Pope Hadrian. The canon law grew significantly in the ninth century, and later copyists even expanded the *Dionysio-Hadriana*, adapting it to new situations. New collections were made as well. Sometimes those collections gathered new texts or arranged well-known texts in new ways. Sometimes forgers created canonical collections to bolster their reform efforts and to defend views, for which they had few or no authentic authoritative texts.

In the mid-ninth century, many Frankish bishops sought to safeguard their independence from aggressive archbishops, and their property and freedom of election from lay rulers. They did so by asserting their historical right to decide matters as a body and by stressing the pope's right to intervene and to receive appeals from them. Those ideas were embodied in the most influential Carolingian canonical forgery, the Pseudo-Isidorean Decretals, created about 850 and attributed to Isidore the Merchant. The collection contained authentic material mixed skilfully with letters purporting to be from popes who had lived before the fourth century. Whoever composed it was both educated and clever. Within a century, the Pseudo-Isidorean Decretals were being cited in arguments over church government and relations among lay and ecclesiastical powers. The Carolingian age, with its insistence on proper order in the church, made the gathering of canonical collections and the study of canon law a creative activity with great implications for the future.

The greatest of the Carolingian kings was Charles, often called by the French version of his name, Charlemagne, 'Charles the Great'. He was a big man, over 6 feet tall, and a successful general, an important attribute in a warrior culture. He lived a long time (about seventy-two years) in a society where life expectancies were low. His dynasty was new and until he was in his late thirties, he had to struggle to maintain his power against rebels. (See Map 3.) When he had assured his political control, he turned to the search for order in his kingdom and was particularly interested in the reform of the church. Charlemagne had a dominating personality and exercised vigorously the tradition of royal control over the personnel and finances of the Frankish church. He appointed bishops and some abbots. He summoned church councils, and even in more secular meetings he consulted with bishops and abbots. After such consultations, he issued commands to churchmen that touched on their finances, their behaviour, their religious duties and even on their beliefs.

Charlemagne's biographer, Einhard (*c*.770–840), who knew him, recorded many details of his great piety. Carolingian society has been called a liturgical

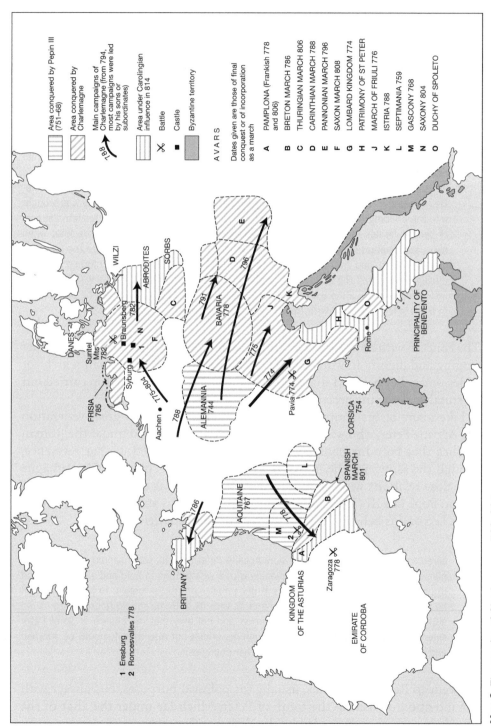

Map 3 The empire of Charlemagne, 768–814

Area conquered by Pepin III (751–68)

Area conquered by Charlemagne

Main campaigns of Charlemagne (from 794, most campaigns were led by his sons or subordinates)

Area under Carolingian influence in 814

Battle

Castle

Byzantine territory

A V A R S

Dates given are those of final conquest or of incorporation as a march

A PAMPLONA (Frankish 778 and 806)
B BRETON MARCH 786
C THURINGIAN MARCH 806
D CARINTHIAN MARCH 788
E PANNONIAN MARCH 796
F SAXON MARCH 808
G LOMBARD KINGDOM 774
H PATRIMONY OF ST PETER
J MARCH OF FRIULI 776
K ISTRIA 788
L SEPTIMANIA 759
M GASCONY 768
N SAXONY 804
O DUCHY OF SPOLETO

1 Eresburg
2 Roncesvalles 778

DANES

WILZI

ABRODITES

SORBS

Suntel Mts 782

Braunsberg 782

Frisia 785

Syburg

Aachen

788

ALEMANNIA 744

BAVARIA 778

791

796

D

E

C

F

N

1

775

774

J

K

G

H

Pavia 774

Rome

CORSICA 754

PRINCIPALITY OF BENEVENTO

O

BRITTANY

786

AQUITAINE 767

M

A

2

B

L

SPANISH MARCH 801

Zaragoza 778

KINGDOM OF THE ASTURIAS

EMIRATE OF CORDOBA

society because the liturgy – the church's formal ritual of public prayer – absorbed so much energy and surplus wealth. Frankish Christians believed that God both wanted and was pleased by liturgical services sung in beautiful surroundings by attentive, dignified and morally upright clergy. Charlemagne valued the liturgy highly, though as a layman he was mostly a spectator and a financial patron. If Einhard is correct, a great portion of the king's day was given to the liturgy:

> As long as his health permitted, he used to go to church morning and evening with great regularity, and also for mass and the night hours of prayer. He used to take great care to ensure that all ceremonies in church were performed with the greatest dignity possible. He warned the sacristans frequently to see that nothing inappropriate or dirty was brought into the building or permitted to remain there. He provided in the church such a supply of sacred vessels made of gold and silver, and so many priestly vestments, that when mass was celebrated even those who opened and closed the doors, who are the lowest in church orders, had no need to perform their duties in their ordinary clothes. He very diligently corrected the practice of singing and reading in church. For he was rather well instructed in both, although he did not personally read in public nor did he sing except in a low voice and along with the rest of the congregation.[1]

The concern with appropriate clothing, sacred vessels, clean buildings, proper singing and dignity in worship is characteristic of the Carolingian search for order, since they believed that God would be pleased with worship carried out by suitable clergy in special, pure surroundings.

Like many of his contemporaries, Charlemagne held in great veneration the Apostle Peter, who was universally believed to be buried under the Roman basilica that bore his name. The bishop of Rome shared in that reverence, though the saint, not the individual pope, was the focus of it. Charlemagne had close relations with Pope Hadrian I (772-95), but did not trust his successor, Pope Leo III (795-816). He once instructed his ambassadors to lecture Pope Leo on his behaviour. Einhard tells us that Charlemagne:

> cared more for the church of the holy Apostle Peter than for other sacred and venerable places in Rome. He enriched its treasury with a vast fortune in gold and silver coins and in precious stones. He sent many and uncounted gifts to the popes. In his whole reign he thought nothing more important than that the city of Rome should flourish with its old authority as a result of his work and effort and not only that the church of Saint Peter should remain safe and protected through his efforts but also that it should be adorned and enriched by his wealth beyond all other churches.[2]

He went to Rome four times, usually for political purposes, but always with the intention of visiting the tomb of Peter, which lay under the altar of the fourth-century church funded by the Emperor Constantine.

Charlemagne's political position and political self-interest reinforced his piety. Since his childhood, he had been told that he was the protector of the church and the promoter of missions to the pagan peoples living to the north and east of his borders, duties that he took seriously. He believed that he held an exalted, almost priestly role in society. In 754, Pope Stephen II had anointed him, his father and brother, like an Old Testament king. On Christmas Day 800, Pope Leo III crowned him emperor at Rome, an event that consolidated the Papal-Frankish Alliance, and, in theory, revived the Roman Empire in the west. In a letter to Leo III, Charlemagne expressed his view of the proper distribution of power in Christian society:

> For it is our task, with the aid of divine goodness, to defend the holy church of Christ everywhere from the attacks of pagans outside and to strengthen it within through the knowledge of the Catholic faith. And it is your duty, O Holy Father, with your hands raised high to God, after the manner of Moses, to aid our armies so that by your intercession with God, who is our leader and benefactor, the Christian people may always and everywhere be victorious over the enemies of His Holy Name, and the name of Our Lord Jesus Christ be proclaimed throughout the world.[3]

Charlemagne saw himself as the military leader and religious reformer of the Christian people, with whom the pope should cooperate and for whom he should pray. The popes had a higher view of their role, but could do little to resist their powerful protector.

Charlemagne's interest in church reform was not just religious. The church's wealth and personnel were crucial to the military, governmental and cultural successes of all Carolingian kings. The bishops and abbots, who were often chosen by the king, were his collaborators in the work of government, providing advice, staffing rudimentary bureaucracies and disseminating royal orders through society. They contributed money and soldiers to the kings' wars from the income of their churches. In newly conquered areas east of the River Rhine and north of the River Danube, they were used to Christianise, control and stabilise the regions. In some areas they provided the kings with a counterweight to the power of lay aristocrats. The lower clergy were instrumental in the organisation of society at the local level. The monks made indispensable contributions to education, book copying and other cultural reforms. It was in such an atmosphere of the king's piety, his practical control of the church, and papal dependence on his protection that the reform of society's *ordines* was undertaken.

III. The reform of the *ordo* of the secular clergy

There were approximately 250 dioceses in the Carolingian Empire in 800, and tens of thousands of priests, deacons and lesser clergy. These were the 'secular' clergy, a term which designates them as working among the laity in the world, from the Latin *saeculum*. They were distinct from the regular clergy, that is, the monks, **canons** and nuns, who had withdrawn from the world to live under a rule. The reform of both sorts of clergy was a key goal of the Carolingian programme.

Christianity was a religion that the clergy had to learn at least in part from books written in a foreign language, Latin. The Bible was not a simple book, and neither were the books of canon law, the collections of sermons, the liturgical books, nor the writings of church fathers. The cultural decline of the sixth, seventh and early eighth centuries had affected all of western society, including the clergy. The decline of literacy in Latin among the clergy and the loosening of traditional discipline exercised by bishops over the clergy had transformed the church in Frankish lands, and not for the better. By the eighth century, many Frankish bishops behaved like the aristocrats they were, and much of the lower clergy behaved like the peasants they were. One could argue that the Frankish church had merely adapted to changed conditions in society, but when judged from the perspective of late Roman Christianity, as the Anglo-Saxon missionaries did, the situation appeared very objectionable indeed. The letters of the Anglo-Saxon missionary Boniface provide information about the reactions of a man well-versed in book-oriented Christianity to what he found in the Frankish kingdom before about 750. He was appalled at the drunkenness, the violence, the sexual sins and the ignorance of basic matters among the secular clergy. In 742, Carloman, Pippin's brother and a mayor of the palace, asked Boniface to take the lead in the reform of the Frankish church. Boniface wrote a long letter to Pope Zachary asking for advice on how to proceed. At one point he asked the pope:

> [What should I do] if I find among these men certain so-called deacons who have spent their lives since boyhood in debauchery, adultery, and in every kind of filthiness, who entered the diaconate with this reputation, and who now, while they have four or five concubines in their beds, still read the Gospel [in the Mass] and are not ashamed or afraid to call themselves deacons—nay rather, entering upon the priesthood, they continue in the same vices, add sin to sin, declare that they have a right to make intercession for the people in the priestly office and to celebrate Mass, and, still worse, with such reputations advancing from step to step to nomination as bishops—may I have a formal written prescription of your authority [i.e. Pope Zachary] as to your procedure in such cases so that they may be convicted by an apostolic judgment and dealt with as sinners? And certain bishops are to be found among [the Franks] who, although they deny that they are fornicators or adulterers, are drunkards and shiftless men, given to hunting and fighting in the army like soldiers, and by their own hands shedding blood, whether of heathens or Christian.[4]

Historians should be careful reading a source like this, with such inflammatory language, and question whether it reflected reality or the reform agenda of its author. What disorder there was among the secular clergy had probably been increased by the confiscations of church property that Frankish rulers occasionally ordered. Charles Martel, the mayor of the palace, justified such measures in the 730s by appealing to the need to support his army. The confiscated ecclesiastical estates were supposed to be held by soldiers only until the military emergency passed. In fact, the Frankish kingdom was constantly at war and the soldiers came to depend for their livelihood on the former church estates: it became politically impossible to return them to the churches from which they were taken. Martel's son, Pippin, compensated the churches by forcing the holders of their estates to pay rent to the religious institutions from which the property had been taken. In addition, he ordered all persons to pay a tithe (10 per cent) of their income to the local church from which they received the sacrament of baptism. The Old Testament had ordered tithing for the Jews and later some Christians had tithed voluntarily. Pippin's mandatory tithe was the first universal tax in European history and it put the secular church on a sound economic footing. The later successes of the Carolingian church were due in part to the fact that a tenth of society's income (in fact, it was usually less) was designated for its support, and that sum was in addition to the income from each church's own estates.

Not only did the reformers restore the secular church's income but they also tried to reform the behaviour of the secular clergy. In societies that value tradition, as the Franks did, a 'reform' usually means that what exists is reshaped to conform to some ideal based in the past. It is important to understand what the ideal was to which the reformers wanted the Carolingian church to return. Since the twelfth century, many Christians have been fascinated by the 'primitive church', that is, the church described in the New Testament. That idealised primitive church has been and continues to be the model for all sorts of successful and failed reforms. When Carolingian intellectuals looked backward, what they found most understandable and appealing was the church of the later Roman Empire, that of Augustine, Ambrose, Jerome and Gregory, which seemed to them a stable, orderly, sophisticated and admirable structure, in comparison with which the church in the contemporary Frankish kingdom was quite deficient.

The Carolingian reformers knew about the fourth-, fifth- and sixth-century church only through written documents, including collections of canon law, which gave an idealised picture of how things should be. At an important meeting of bishops, abbots and lay aristocrats in 789, Charlemagne issued a set of commands, called the *General Admonition* (*Admonitio generalis*), which borrowed heavily from the *Dionysio-Hadriana*, the canonical collection sent to Charlemagne in 774 by Pope Hadrian I. Those commands, called canons, that were directed specifically to the secular clergy are a good indication of what the reformers wanted and, by implication, what they thought was wrong with the contemporary church.

One of the striking concerns of the *General Admonition* was for the restoration of hierarchical control, which had been loosened by generations of disorder. The bishops themselves, who were often independent and aggressive, needed reminding that they functioned in a larger church. The reformers tried to restore the grouping of bishops into provinces under the general supervision of archbishops. The *General Admonition* commanded that archbishops and bishops cooperate with one another; that they meet twice a year in councils; that bishops not be appointed in rural places, since the proliferation of bishops reduced the dignity of the office; that bishops not meddle in the affairs of other dioceses; that bishops not receive into their service without permission the clergy of other bishops; and that bishops reside near their cathedral churches.

In the canon law of the idealised past, the clergy were carefully set apart for God's service by their ordination, their knowledge, their behaviour and their legal status. The Carolingian reformers thought that the boundary between the secular clergy and the laity in their own day was not sharp enough. Some clergy acted like and were treated like laymen. The *General Admonition* reasserted the need for the clerical *ordo* to separate from the 'world'. The reformers wanted the clergy to be a self-regulating organisation, as they believed it had been in the past. The legal privileges of the clergy were spelt out. Several canons ordered that if a cleric committed a crime, he was to be judged by the bishop or the semi-annual council, but not by laymen. In order to protect the dignity of the clergy, the reformers made it more difficult to accuse clergy of misconduct by specifying that only persons worthy of trust could bring charges against them. Quarrels among clergy were to be settled by the church, not by secular judges. No cleric could appeal his case to the king without permission of a church council or his archbishop.

According to the *General Admonition*, the moral behaviour of the clerical *ordo* must also separate it from the laity. Bishops, priests and deacons were forbidden to live with women, except for close blood relatives such as mothers or sisters, who were above suspicion. Bishops must not ordain slaves or unfree persons without their master's permission. Since clergy lived from the tithe, they were not to have ordinary jobs, and in particular not to lend money at interest, which was the sin of usury. They were never to frequent taverns or do anything else to lessen their claim to a superior moral status.

Since many clergy were not financially dependent on their bishop, they were often quite independent and beyond the reach of effective discipline. The reformers tried to reassert control by insisting on the subordination of priests, deacons and the lower clergy to their bishops. Bishops were ordered to guard more carefully entry to the clergy. No one was to be ordained a priest before the age of 30. Bishops had to examine candidates for the priesthood on their knowledge and morals before they ordained them. Bishops were not to take gifts or bribes from candidates for ordination. Even the ordained clergy were placed more firmly under the bishops. A clergyman who was deposed but refused to cease ministering was to be excommunicated. Priests were to know and obey the canon law. They should not rebel or conspire against their bishop. They should not seek a position outside their diocese without their bishop's permission.

Since the *Dionysio-Hadriana* had been composed in the late Roman Empire, its canons took for granted such things as widespread literacy and urban life. Because the Frankish kingdom was quite different from the Roman Empire in its economic, cultural and social structures, it had problems that the ancient canon law had not anticipated. Charlemagne and his advisers therefore added some things to the *General Admonition* of 789 that were not in the *Dionysio-Hadriana*. Those additions throw more light on the conditions of the Carolingian secular clergy and on the ideal to which the reformers looked. The level of learning among the clergy was low and the minimum knowledge expected from priests was very basic. Bishops were instructed to inquire whether their priests knew the essentials of belief as expressed in the *Apostles' Creed*, and whether they could explain the *Our Father* to the people. In a society that valued liturgy, the bishops were to find out if priests knew how to carry out a proper baptism, a proper mass and the proper singing of the psalms, all of which had to be done in the foreign language of Latin. Bishops were to make sure that church buildings, altars and sacred vessels were kept from any unworthy or secular use.

By 789, the growing influence of the papacy in the Frankish church was leading to a 'romanisation' of its practices. The *Dionysio-Hadriana*, a Roman collection of canons, came in 774. In 786/7, Pope Hadrian sent Charlemagne a copy of a Roman liturgical book, the Gregorian sacramentary (a book on how to carry out a mass, a baptism and perhaps other liturgical acts), which was reworked and supplemented to fit Frankish needs and tastes. The *General Admonition* instructed bishops to see to it that liturgical services were carried out as closely as possible to the way they were done in Rome. (See Figure 6.)

Charlemagne and his advisers were very concerned about preaching, which was the chief means to give religious instruction in a basically illiterate society. In the ancient church, only bishops preached on a regular basis. In the Carolingian world, with its growing network of rural churches, ordinary priests needed to preach, but had little training and few resources to help them. The *General Admonition* of 789 included a brief explanation of the creed and a model sermon, which avoided complex theology and treated simple moral and social themes that priests should stress to their people, including love of God and neighbour, social peace, treating one another justly, prohibiting such things as perjury, superstitious practices, envy, private vengeance, theft, illicit sexual unions. During the ninth century, a rise in educational standards and the provision of collections of sermons that the clergy could read or

Figure 6 Charlemagne with Popes Gelasius and Gregory
Charlemagne (center, 742–814), wearing a halo and being crowned from above by
the hand of God, with Popes Gelasius I (left, died 496), and Pope Gregory I (right, 540–604).
Notice from their dates that the three figures were not contemporaries. Their depiction
together may be a kind of propaganda, possibly to link the Frankish king to two important
figures of the early church. By tradition, both Gelasius and Gregory had prominent roles
in developing the liturgy. This folio is from a sacramentary, a book of instructions for
conducting the liturgy. The words tell the celebrant to chant '*excelsa voce*', i.e.
'in a loud voice'.

paraphrase into the vernacular languages probably provided more preaching, although the ordinary rural priest was rarely equipped to do the job well.

For the secular clergy, the reformers put forward an ideal of rights and duties drawn from the ancient canon law and updated to meet the needs of the contemporary church. The ideal was disseminated in collections of canons, councils and bishops' letters, and especially in bishops' statutes for their dioceses, of which more than thirty survive from the ninth century. The reformers sought to set the secular clergy above and apart from the laity by legal privileges, behaviour, knowledge, economics and even social class. The Carolingian period solidified a trend that was already old. The highest positions in the secular clergy were reserved for men who were noble by birth. Noble families saw it as their right to monopolise the highest offices for their relatives. That introduced a significant social rift between bishops and priests that persisted for a thousand years.

Secular clerics were expected to function within an orderly hierarchical structure in which each level was obedient to those above and responsible for those below it. The reality fell short, but this ideal had an immediate impact on the Carolingian church and an enduring influence in the medieval church.

IV. The reform of the *ordo* of the regular clergy

Carolingian leaders tried to draw a sharper line between the *ordo* of the secular clergy and the *ordo* of the regular clergy. In spite of some overlap, the rights, duties and way of life of the one were not supposed to be the same as those of the other. The first monastic communities in Gaul and Italy had been founded in the fourth century, based on the monasticism of Egypt. Monastic life responded to deeply felt religious and social needs. By the year 800 there were more than 650 monasteries in the Frankish Empire, excluding Italy, where there were several hundred more. Each monastery was theoretically independent and self-governing, though kings, bishops and powerful aristocrats controlled many houses.

Like modern institutions of higher education, the diversity of Carolingian religious houses was striking: some were large but most were medium sized or small; some were rich but most were middling and some were quite poor; some stood out for their religious fervour but most were orderly and some were scandalously mismanaged; some had a widely known reputation but most had only regional or local fame. Religious houses had widely different origins and traditions. Some houses had been founded in the late Roman Empire, others were founded by Irish missionaries in the seventh century, others by Anglo-Saxon missionaries in the eighth century, and still others by Franks between the sixth and ninth centuries. By 800, monasteries were governed in a bewildering range of ways: some used the *Rule* of Saint Benedict; others used Gallo-Roman monastic rules such as that of Caesarius of Arles (*c.*470–542); still others used Irish monastic rules, such as that of Columbanus (543–615). In addition to monks and nuns there was another form of quasi-monastic life practised by religious men and women called canons. These were most often communities of secular priests, who lived according to a rule and served non-monastic churches. One example of a rule for canons in the Frankish church is that of Chrodegang (died 766), Bishop of Metz, whose rule of 34 chapters borrowed from the *Rule* of Benedict and the so-called rule of Saint Augustine. The rule of Saint Augustine began as a letter written in 423 to a community of nuns. Over time, its guidelines for religious life in community gained the status of a rule for canons. The sheer numbers of canons, monks and nuns, including their wealth and visibility, made the regular clergy a major force in Carolingian society and its church.

In simplest terms, regular clergy had abandoned life in the world to save their individual souls. Both the ancient canon law and the monastic rules discouraged monks from providing direct service to lay congregations. In particular, the regular clergy were not supposed to preach and administer sacraments to the laity because that was the right and duty of the secular clergy. Monks were not supposed to receive from the laity tithes, which were intended to support the secular clergy's pastoral work.

But historical developments had led to significant modifications in the monastic ideal of separation from the world. Irish, Anglo-Saxon and other monks had been the backbone of early medieval missionary work. As a legacy of the days when the Anglo-Saxon monks were missionaries to the Germans across the Rhine, they frequently continued to minister to the laity in villages dependent on their religious houses. Many monasteries had founded churches on their estates for their dependants and, like all owners of private churches, they controlled them, chose the priest, and might even staff them with monks. Some Carolingian reformers saw the pastoral activity of the regular clergy as a disorder and wanted to return to the ancient ideal of the late Roman Empire, which they found in the *Dionysio-Hadriana* and the *Rule* of Benedict. They had little success, and many monks continued to minister to their dependent peasants.

The Carolingian reformers' most far-reaching innovation in monastic life was their decision that all monks and nuns should adopt Benedict's *Rule*. The *Rule* had been composed in sixth-century Italy, but it was thanks to the Carolingians that it became *the* monastic rule of the medieval west. That was not an inevitable development. In the two centuries between the *Rule*'s composition and its adoption by the Carolingian reformers, monastic life in the west was extremely diverse. In sixth- and seventh-century Gaul, abbots were free to choose any rule they liked, to mix several rules or to use no written rule but to govern their monasteries by traditional, unwritten norms. In

Merovingian monasticism, the *Rule* of Benedict was respected and played a part, but not a dominant one.

Three factors were decisive in the decision of the Carolingian rulers to promote Benedict's *Rule*. One factor was historical: the Anglo-Saxons used the *Rule* at home and had brought it with them to the continent, where it was observed in their many houses. A second factor was theological: in the atmosphere of admiration for things Roman, Benedict's *Rule* was a 'Roman' rule, which had been praised by Pope Gregory I in his *Dialogues*. The third factor was suitability: Benedict's *Rule* embodied the virtues of orderliness, hierarchy and stability that the reformers sought as an antidote to the social, religious and political reality they confronted. Beginning with Pippin, the Carolingian kings ordered all monks to adopt the *Rule* of Saint Benedict. Older traditions of monastic diversity were tenacious and the transition to Benedictine monasticism was slow, but it did occur during the ninth century.

The most ambitious and successful effort at 'Benedictinisation' took place under the Emperor Louis the Pious (814–40). A Visigothic abbot named Witiza (751–821), who changed his name to Benedict, was a close adviser to Louis and a champion of Benedict's *Rule*. Benedict of Aniane, as he is called to distinguish him from Benedict of Nursia, tried to introduce uniformity in monasteries, something quite new in monastic history. Benedict of Aniane supplemented Benedict's *Rule*, which consists of a prologue and 73 relatively brief chapters, with legislation intended to adapt it to contemporary conditions and to promote uniformity. With the emperor's help, Benedict of Aniane created a model Benedictine monastery at Inde, later called Cornelimünster, where two monks from every Carolingian monastery were sent to learn Benedictine ways, so that they could introduce them to their home monasteries.

Ultimately, Benedict of Aniane's ambitious plans to supervise all monasteries and to apply the Benedictine *Rule* to hundreds of them in a uniform way failed: the Carolingian Empire was not capable of enforcing unity over so great an area. Furthermore, the empire itself began to crumble politically and militarily within a generation of his efforts. However, monks accepted the notion that they were 'sons of Saint Benedict'. The Benedictine *Rule*, with additions and interpretations to accommodate local traditions, ousted rival rules and became the norm for monastic life between the ninth and twelfth centuries, a period called the 'Benedictine Centuries' because of the prominence of Benedictine monasteries in religious, cultural and economic life.

The *General Admonition* of 789 prescribed for regular clergy an ideal that drew heavily on Benedict's *Rule*. There was the same concern for order and hierarchy that was so prominent in the reform of the secular clergy. The authority of the abbot over the monks was reasserted. The stability of life in the community was to be strengthened. The *General Admonition* argued that wandering monks – some of whom might be charlatans or mentally unstable – were a problem in Frankish society, and ordered wanderers who said they were monks to settle down in a monastery or be forced to do so. There were legitimate reasons why monks needed to leave their monasteries, for example, to manage monastic estates. In those cases, abbots were instructed to permit only mature, virtuous monks to do so. Hasty acceptance of candidates for monastic life could lead to years of unhappiness and problems. Those who wished to join a monastery should be tested for a year before being admitted, as Benedict's *Rule* commanded. To enhance the dignity of monastic life, more youngsters of free birth were to be recruited and fewer youngsters of servile birth. Instead of undertaking pastoral work among the laity, monks were to support the educational and cultural revival of the church. They should learn and teach Latin grammar, reading, proper singing of the liturgical chant, and the complicated computations of the ecclesiastical calendar. Mature, well-trained monks should copy the scriptures and liturgical books so as to keep them free from the errors that poorly educated scribes introduced into the copies. Communities of regular clergy were to practise hospitality, providing food and lodging to travellers. The ideal for members of the regular *ordo*, both monks and nuns, was that of detachment from worldly occupations, so as to live a life within a community devoted to personal sanctification, liturgical prayer, the copying of manuscripts, and the education of boys (in the case of nuns, girls) intended for the monastic life or the secular clergy.

V. The reform of the *ordo* of the laity

The *ordo* of the laity was numerically the largest. It was divided into a small aristocratic, military elite and the mass of peasant farmers. The reformers were most concerned about the secular and regular clergy, though members of the Carolingian family and some important lay people received personal pastoral advice. Most of it must have been oral, but some survives in letters and treatises, which are sometimes called 'mirrors for princes', composed by abbots and bishops. At times, lay people themselves tried to reform their *ordo*. Between 841 and 843, a time of civil war among Charlemagne's descendents, a Frankish noblewoman named Dhuoda wrote a 'handbook' (Latin: *liber manualis*) of moral advice for her son William. Here, Dhuoda tells her son not only to love Christ but to become better educated about him:

> I also admonish you, O my handsome and lovable son William, that amid the mundane cares of this world you not neglect the acquisition of many books, in which you may understand and learn something greater and better than is written here concerning God, your Creator, through the teaching of the most blessed doctors. Beseech Him, cherish Him, love Him; if you do so, He will be a Keeper, a Leader, a Companion, and a Fatherland for you, the Way, the Truth, and the Light, granting you generous prosperity in the world, and He will turn your enemies to peace.[5]

When we have writings of women, it is safe to assume those women were privileged, particularly in terms of education. For example, Dhuoda recommended to her son that he read 'the teaching of the most blessed doctors': Augustine, Jerome and others. Either Dhuoda read these herself or had them read to her.

In spite of the privileges of nobility, the reformers did not entirely neglect the religious needs of the great mass of lay people, although in such primitive material and educational conditions success was minimal. Illiteracy was the greatest impediment to every plan for lifting the religious and moral level of the laity. Even most of the aristocratic elite were illiterate, although there were some noble men and women who could read and a few had modest-sized libraries. But the crushing majority of the laity, including the soldiers, the peasant farmers and the serfs, was entirely illiterate. Direct contact with the scriptures, the church fathers, the canon law and the liturgical texts was not possible for them. Consequently, there was much more stress on their religious duties than on their religious knowledge. The reformers had a notion of the minimum that every lay Christian should know. Although the official religious texts remained in Latin, teaching in the languages of ordinary people, called the vernacular languages, was not unusual. Essential prayers, such as the Our Father and the Creed, were translated into local dialects, as were the promises made at baptism. In 813 an important Frankish council ordered preaching in the Germanic and Romance vernaculars.

The laity stood at the bottom of the religious hierarchy and was expected to accept the supervision provided by the secular clergy above them. In fact, the political power and wealth of the lay elite disrupted the neat hierarchical arrangement of *ordines*. The kings, counts and important aristocrats had considerable authority over churches and monasteries. Virtually all of them controlled private churches on their estates where they appointed and dismissed priests. The more powerful of them chose bishops and abbots. In dealing with upper-class people, the clergy was limited mostly to exhorting them to use their power justly and to avoid the grossest personal sins and political abuses. In reality, such people were usually beyond the church's ability to enforce more than minimal obedience.

In the face of great difficulties, the Carolingian church did find ways to structure the religious behaviour of ordinary lay people, particularly by creating small, defined religious communities, the parishes. By 900, many more people were living inside the religious, social, legal and economic framework of the parish than had been in 750. Perhaps the single most important point to realise about the parish is that it was not a voluntary organisation but a compulsory one, a reflection of the fact that society was legally Christian. It took a long time to work out the details, but already in the ninth century Christians were being pushed to follow a way of life centred in the parish, where they baptised their children, attended the mass and sought blessings for all sorts of occasions.

Life in the parish had its economic side: the tithe was a compulsory payment to the parish, and there were often additional customary fees for religious services. Time was structured by the rhythms of the liturgical calendar, which required lay people to attend church on Sundays and feast days, as well as to avoid manual labour on those days. For more than 100 days a year, the church required fasting and sexual abstinence to honour holy days and holy seasons. We do not know much about preaching to ordinary people, but it seems to have focused on simple moral teaching, such as charity to the poor and fairness in social dealings. There was a modest intellectual expectation in the ideal for the lay *ordo*: men, women and children were instructed to know by heart in Latin or in their native language the Lord's Prayer and the Apostles' Creed. The difficulty in getting everyone to learn the 212 Latin words of the Lord's Prayer is a sobering reminder of the conditions to which Christianity adapted.

In the hierarchical ordering of Christian society, there was some tension between the regular and secular clergy. The life of the ideal monk or nun – chaste, poor, obedient, otherworldly and self-denying – was usually the most admired. But the secular clergy, particularly the bishops, were the ordained pastors and legal leaders of the church, responsible both for the laity and the regular clergy. From a legal, organisational perspective, the secular clergy were the first *ordo*. But in the reputation for holiness and popular esteem, the regular clergy were often first. The laity stood near the bottom of the ladder, though Jews, Muslims and pagans were regarded as below them. Lay people were to some degree pitied by the clergy for their situation. Because lay people lived a life that was involved in varying degrees with violence, pride, greed and sexuality, it was thought to be inevitable that they would be sinners. The Carolingian church expanded the practice of private confession – as opposed to public confession, which involved public shaming that discouraged many sinners from coming forward – and made penance a major feature of the religious life of the laity. Marriage, which concerned the laity so directly, was still a private contract not yet under church supervision. A priest might be asked to bless a marriage, but his participation was not required, as it would be later. However, the reformers wanted the laity to observe the marriage laws of the church, particularly the ban on remarrying while a spouse was alive and the increasingly elaborate rules forbidding marriage with relatives. It was necessary to remind the laity repeatedly that they must avoid the old religious ways and that they should not worship both Christ and the pagan gods. Like the secular and regular clergy, the laity were encouraged to adopt a way of living to fit their *ordo*, including charity to the needy, confession of sins, payment of tithes and fees, knowledge of the Lord's Prayer and the Creed, regular attendance at mass on Sundays and religious feast days, and sexual activity only within marriage and even then observing the frequent times of sexual abstinence imposed for religious reasons.

The results of the Carolingian reform of the church must not be exaggerated. In a very poor society, where illiteracy and poor communications were normal, the reform measures touched primarily the elites of the laity, of the secular clergy and of the regular clergy. But the results of the reform must not be minimised either. In such a society, the views of the elite filtered down to the mass of clergy and laity, though slowly and imperfectly. The Carolingian rulers, bishops, abbots and learned monks set the religious life of western Europe on a new course. It included a desire for order and hierarchy, a growing respect for the prestige and authority of the papacy, a sharper separation of the clergy from the laity, a 'Benedictinisation' of monasticism, and an incorporation of the laity into a sturdy parish framework in which they received the sacraments, paid their tithes, and shaped their moral behaviour and social lives.

Suggested reading

Companion website
www.routledge.com/cw/lynch

6.1   Charlemagne crowned Emperor
Excerpts from Einhard, *Life of Charlemagne*, trans. Samuel Epes Turner (New York: American Book Company, 1880), 65–66.

6.2   The Apostles' Creed
'The Apostles' Creed', in Philip Schaff, *The Creeds of Christendom with a History and Critical Notes*, vol. II (New York: Harper & Brothers, 1919), 45.

6.3   The Monastic Rule of St. Columbanus
Excerpts from the Rule of St. Columbanus, in George Metlake, *The Life and Writings of Saint Columban* (Philadelphia: The Dolphin Press, 1914), 71–76.

6.4   Introitus: 'Gaudeamus omnes', Anonymous, plainchant, mode I
Musical recording: The Rose Ensemble, *Seasons of Angels, Harmony of the Spheres* (Saint Paul, MN, 2001)

6.5   Communio: 'Angeli, Archangeli', Anonymous, plainchant, mode II
Musical recording: The Rose Ensemble, *Seasons of Angels, Harmony of the Spheres* (Saint Paul, MN, 2001)

Primary sources

Dhuoda, *Handbook for William: A Carolingian Woman's Counsel for Her Son*, translated by Carol Neel (Lincoln, Nebraska, 1991)

Einhard, *Life of Charlemagne*, translated by Lewis Thorpe, *Two Lives of Charlemagne* (Harmondsworth, Middlesex, 1969)

King, P. D., editor, *Charlemagne: Translated Sources* (Kendall, 1987)

The Reign of Charlemagne: Documents on Carolingian Government and Administration, translated by H. R. Loyn and John Percival, Documents of Medieval History, 2 (New York, 1976)

Modern scholarship

Barbero, Alessandro, *Charlemagne: Father of a Continent*, translated by Allan Cameron (Berkeley, 2004)

Burns, Cecil Delisle, *The First Europe: A Study in the Establishment of Medieval Christendom* (New York, 1948)

Duby, Georges, *The Three Orders: Feudal Society Imagined* (Chicago, 1982)

Hamilton, Sarah, *The Practice of Penance, 900–1050* (Woodbridge, Suffolk, and Rochester, New York, 2001)

Innes, Matthew, Marios Costambeys and Simon Maclean, *The Carolingian World* (Cambridge, 2005)

Jasper, Detlev and Horst Fuhrmann, *Papal Letters in the Early Middle Ages* (Washington, DC, 2001)

McKitterick, Rosamond, *The Frankish Church and the Carolingian Reforms, 789–895* (London, 1977)

McKitterick, Rosamond, *The Frankish Kingdoms under the Carolingians, 751–987* (New York, 1983)

McKitterick, Rosamond, *Charlemagne: the Formation of a European Identity* (Cambridge, 2008)

Van Engen, John, 'Decretals, False', *The Dictionary of the Middle Ages* 4 (New York, 1984), pp. 124–7

Notes

1 Einhard, *The Life of Charlemagne*, in *Einhard and Notker the Stammerer: Two Lives of Charlemagne*, translated by Lewis Thorpe (Harmondsworth, Middlesex, 1969), ch. 26.

2 Einhard, *The Life of Charlemagne*, ch. 27.

3 *Letter of Charles to Pope Leo*, in Monumenta Germaniae historica, *Epistolae* IV: *Epistolae Aevi Karolini* 2 (Berlin, 1895), pp. 137–8, partly translated in Marshall W. Baldwin, *Christianity Through the Thirteenth Century* (New York, 1970), pp. 119–20.

4 Boniface to Pope Zachary, Letter 50 (742), in Ephraim Emerton, editor and translator, *The Letters of Saint Boniface* (New York, 1940), new edition by Thomas F. X. Noble (New York, 2000), pp. 56–61.

5 'Dhuoda, Manual (841)' in Amy Oden, editor, *In Her Words: Women's Writings in the History of Christian Thought* (Nashville, Tennessee, 1994), p. 95.

7

The Carolingian Renaissance

'Reform' in the Carolingian church was based on texts composed centuries earlier and available only in a dead, non-spoken language, Latin. They included the scriptures, the church fathers, the canon law, the liturgical books and Benedict's *Rule*. The reformers were convinced that much of the disorder in the contemporary church was due to ignorance. They gave a high priority to the instruction of the clergy and the monks. Serious instruction of the laity was beyond their resources, although they did try. The Carolingian reformers created schools and libraries to further their ends, and in so doing they shaped intellectual life around the study of Latin grammar. That remained the focus of education until Aristotle's writings on logic were made the basis of advanced education in the twelfth century. They also launched the first major cultural revival of the new Europe, often called the Carolingian Renaissance.

I. Cultural decline

The slow economic and demographic decline of Roman civilisation that had begun in the third century extended to education as well. As Greco-Roman civilisation aged, the sheer weight of its intellectual past grew unmanageable. Already at the height of the Roman Empire, teachers were producing textbooks, summaries and anthologies to enable students to master the immense heritage of Greek and Roman literature. In subsequent generations, those books were in their turn condensed and simplified. By the late empire, formal education was increasingly dried out, lifeless and uncritical, based more on summaries and textbooks than on the great literature of the past. Education, already in decline, fell on very hard times after the western empire collapsed. Between the late fifth and early eighth centuries, the Roman schools, which taught grammar and rhetoric based on the pagan classics and were run by masters who worked for fees, disappeared in one region after another as urban life withered.

Even though the formal schools ceased to function, ancient textbooks, summaries and reference books survived to provide a starting point for later generations. Martianus Capella (early fifth century) created a basic textbook on the seven liberal arts in the literary form of an allegory called *The Marriage of Mercury and Philology*. Mercury (Eloquence) is about to marry Philology (Learning) and Jupiter arranges a great celebration. The attendants of Mercury are the seven liberal arts who are defined and described elaborately in both verse and prose. Likewise Cassiodorus (*c*.490–585), the cultured statesman who founded a monastery devoted to Christian learning, wrote the *Institutes of Divine and Human Learning* in the 550s. In it, he synthesised precious information for later generations of monks. In book I, he included the names of the books of the Old and New Testament, the names and works of the chief biblical commentators, the major church historians and the chief fathers of the church. His *Institutes* has detailed information on the duties of a good scribe, including the rules of manuscript copying, spelling and bookbinding. In book II of the *Institutes*, Cassiodorus gave a brief survey of the seven liberal arts, basing his work on ancient authorities. Another contributor in this vein was Isidore of Seville (*c*.560–636), a Visigothic scholar and bishop, and a prolific author. Isidore summarised a vast amount of ancient learning in his encyclopaedia called the *Etymologies*, which treated objects and institutions by analysing the meanings of their names. In 20 sections, he took up such topics as the seven liberal arts, medicine, law, history, theology, zoology, cosmology, psychology, architecture and agriculture. Modern readers might find some of Isidore's 'scholarship' to be questionable. His attempts were often more 'folk etymologies' rather than anything resembling the modern study of linguistics. Some of his medical assertions also seem to be based more on contemporary attitudes rather than scientific method. For example, on women's menstrual cycle, Isidore wrote:

> Woman is the only menstruating animal. If they are touched of the blood of the menses, crops cease to sprout, unfermented wine turns sour, plants wither, trees lose their fruit, iron is corrupted by rust, bronze turns black. If dogs eat any of it, they are made wild with rabies.[1]

Yet in his own day, Isidore's work was immensely popular, a fixture in most medieval libraries, and it survives in almost one thousand medieval manuscripts. It was on the basis of the works of Martianus, Cassiodorus, Isidore and others that the intellectual heritage of the Ancient World survived into the Middle Ages.

The fate of the Latin language itself had a great impact on learning and on the church. Latin was not immune to the forces that make all languages change. In Italy, Spain and southern Gaul, where Latin had been the language of ordinary life for centuries, the spoken versions of the language drifted away from the written version. The Romance languages (versions of Italian, Spanish and French) were emerging, but that meant the eclipse of classical

Latin as a living tongue – nobody spoke as Cicero or Augustine had. By the eighth century, even clergy born in Romance-speaking regions had to study in order to distinguish their spoken language from the Latin used in the books of their religion. The language of religion and the languages of ordinary life were losing touch with one another.

The settlement of Germanic invaders on Roman soil during the fifth and sixth centuries and the subsequent conversion of Germanic peoples living beyond the former Roman borders during the eighth and ninth centuries created in those regions a massive gulf between the language of religion and that of everyday life. The clergy of Germanic origin had to learn Latin as a foreign tongue, sometimes with little success. The Anglo-Saxon missionary Boniface was so troubled by a priest in Bavaria who could not say the 11-word baptismal formula in Latin that he ordered a person rebaptised. Pope Zachary gently criticised Boniface's zeal:

> If the ministrant [priest performing the baptism] introduced no error or heresy but simply through ignorance made a slip in the Latin language, we cannot agree that the baptism should be repeated [i.e. the original baptism was good enough].[2]

The difficulty of learning Latin placed a barrier against the success of Christianity in the Germanic parts of the new Europe. In the early Middle Ages, no one could approach the crucial books of Christianity without formal instruction in Latin. But that instruction grew less available in the hard conditions of the seventh and eighth centuries.

The secular and regular clergy could not function without some sort of school, however rudimentary. As the traditional Roman schools vanished, bishops, who wanted at least a minimal literacy for their clergy, created schools. Abbots, who accepted young children as monks, also sought to educate at least some of them for the needs of the liturgy. But such early medieval church schools were makeshift, dependent on the energy and education of the local churchmen, and quite variable in their results. The growing regionalisation of the church meant that the level of education could vary enormously. Between the sixth and the eighth centuries, local conditions were sometimes favourable to cultural revivals. These always involved a turning back to the Roman past and are sometimes called with exaggeration 'renaissances', with reference to the later, arguably more famous Renaissance of Italy. Learning and education blossomed briefly in Spain around Isidore of Seville, among Irish monks in the late sixth and seventh centuries, in Anglo-Saxon Northumbria, whose greatest teacher was the monk Bede (*c.*672–735), and in northern Italy at the Lombard royal court in Pavia in the decades around 700. Excluding Pavia, these regional revivals were on the periphery of the Latin Christian world.

II. The court school

In the Frankish heartland, learning reached its low point in the first half of the eighth century. Serious church leaders knew that there was no way to reform the Frankish church without an extension of the availability and an improvement in the quality of education. By the mid-eighth century, some abbots and bishops were taking independent measures to educate their subordinates. After 780, Charlemagne and his advisers supported such efforts and generalised them to the whole empire, as a part of their reform of the secular and regular clergy. The Carolingians drew heavily on the experience and personnel of the areas where regional educational revivals had taken place in the recent past (the British Isles, Spain and Italy).

The educational revival of the Frankish kingdom started in several independent centres but received a major boost when the royal court became involved. For generations, it had been customary for Frankish aristocrats to spend part of their youth at the king's court. Their presence served several functions: they grew to know the king, his heirs and one another; they learned by observation the behaviour appropriate for an aristocrat – fighting, giving and taking advice, rendering judgement and leading their social inferiors; and they were hostages for the good behaviour of their powerful fathers. Although some of the boys learned to read, intellectual pursuits were not the main purpose of this court 'school'.

Charlemagne kept the traditional practice, but added to it an educational dimension. The leader of Charlemagne's court school for about fifteen years was Alcuin (c.730–804), an Anglo-Saxon educated at York by a pupil of Bede. (See Figure 7.) By the time Alcuin came to the Frankish court in 781, he was already a middle-aged man. Alcuin was not an original thinker, but he was an educated man and a good schoolmaster. His Irish and Anglo-Saxon predecessors had developed techniques to teach Latin to their pupils. Alcuin transferred those techniques to the court school where some young Franks of high birth learned to read, compose and perhaps even speak grammatically correct Latin. Initially it was very elementary instruction, but it set in motion the Carolingian revival of learning.

Alcuin did not instruct only young boys. Charlemagne himself had a poor education but possessed a good native intelligence and curiosity. As a mature man he tried to make up for his deficiencies. His biographer Einhard says that:

> he was eloquent and lively in speech and could express very clearly whatever he had to say. He was not content with just his native language [Frankish], but gave attention to learning foreign ones. Among which he learned Latin so well that he was accustomed to speak both in it and in his native language, but he was better able to understand Greek than to speak it. He was so skilled with words that he might appear to be glib. He most zealously cultivated the liberal arts and he respected very much those who taught them and gave them great honours. In learning [Latin] grammar he studied with the aged deacon

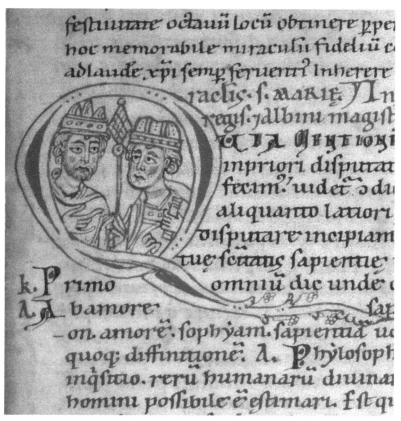

Figure 7 Charlemagne and Alcuin
This detail of the initial Q from Alcuin's *De Dialectica* ('Concerning Dialectic') shows
Charlemagne and the great scholar Alcuin of York. Notice how Alcuin, right, points to the book
in his hand, perhaps a sign of his authorship, or at least of his education.

Peter of Pisa; in other subjects he had as teacher Albinus of Britain, surnamed Alcuin,
also a deacon, a man of the Saxon race, who was the most learned man of the time. With
him he gave much time and effort to the study of rhetoric, dialectic, and especially of
astronomy. He learned the art of computation and talked with wise attention and care
about the course of the stars. He also tried to write and kept tablets and little books in
bed under his pillows so that when he had free time he might accustom his hand to form-
ing letters. However, the labour was begun late in life and did not achieve much success.[3]

Charlemagne encouraged other adults in his court to pursue intellectual
interests. The better educated members of the court, many of whom were
from Ireland, England, Spain and Italy, met to discuss theology, to compose
and engage in criticism of poetry, and even to discuss scientific questions of
an elementary sort. The members of this seminar, if that is the right word for
it, drank plenty of beer or wine and enjoyed calling one another by the names
of heroes of the classical and biblical past – Charlemagne was 'David', his son

Louis was 'Solomon', Alcuin was 'Flaccus' (i.e. the Roman poet Ovid), and Einhard, who had skill as a craftsman, was 'Bezaleel', the inspired workman on the Lord's sanctuary in the Old Testament (Exod. 31:2 and 35:30–5).

The numbers involved in the court school and the seminar were small, but because their ranks produced some of the leading counts, abbots and bishops of the next generation their impact was great, if short lived. At first, the Franks were the pupils and the teachers were foreigners imported and supported by Charlemagne. In addition to Alcuin, the most prominent immigrants were the Visigoth Theodulph (c.750–821) and the Italians Peter of Pisa (died before 799) and Paul the Deacon (c.720–99). But by the 820s, native Franks had taken their place among the intellectual leaders of the empire, although the international character of Frankish intellectual life remained.

The court alone could not have carried the burden of educating the Frankish clergy. But there were two institutions that had a long tradition of education and the resources to support schools: the cathedral churches of the bishops and the monasteries. Beginning with Charlemagne, Frankish kings ordered bishops and abbots to create schools. Some did, particularly abbots and bishops who had lived at court or who admired the court school. None of these schools was large by modern standards, but their cumulative effect was important. The writing, book copying, artistic and architectural work, and thinking of the men trained in the cathedral and monastic schools stimulated a change in the quality and quantity of intellectual life.

III. Cathedral schools

The schools at bishops' main churches (cathedrals) were intended to train secular clergy. But there were not enough resources for them to train all of the thousands of priests and deacons who served rural and private churches. Most of those clergy learned their occupation by a form of apprenticeship with a local priest, who taught them the rudiments of reading Latin and performing the liturgy. Such clergy were much like their peasant neighbours in values and outlook. They were the objects of endless scorn, criticism, advice and exhortations from their ecclesiastical superiors, but in an impoverished rural world there were limits to what could be done to change them. The Carolingian period witnessed a growing split between the well-educated elite of the clergy and the poorly educated clergy of the masses – a split that would always mark the medieval church to some degree and limited its effectiveness.

A minority of clergy, generally sons of noble families, were educated in the cathedral schools and later received the leading positions in the church. Such boys entered the clergy early and lived, worked and studied within the extended household of the bishop. Since Carolingian bishops had many religious and political duties, they ordinarily delegated the teaching of boys to a learned cleric who ran the school. Normally, there was only one teacher who somehow taught every level from prepubescent boys learning to read to young adults studying the intricacies of the scriptures. One might compare them to teachers in a one-room schoolhouse. The greatest weaknesses of the cathedral schools were that so much depended on the attitude of the bishop and on the efforts of a single teacher. Since the royal appointment of bishops had a heavy element of politics in it, a bishop who was a patron of the school might be succeeded by a man who thought his resources could be better used elsewhere. The death or departure of a schoolmaster could also interrupt the existence of a school. Nevertheless, some cathedral schools sustained a tradition of teaching for several generations in the ninth century, including those at Laon, Mainz, Reims and Orleans.

IV. Monastic schools

The ninth century witnessed the beginning of the 'Benedictine Centuries' (approximately 800–1150), when monks were prominent in every aspect of religious, intellectual, economic and political life. The monastic schools were an important underpinning of that prominence. Monasteries had suffered from the general decline of secular education in the early Middle Ages. Many adults who sought to be monks needed instruction to enable them to carry out the liturgy that was based on Latin texts. Monasteries also had a special need for schools, caused by a practice called 'oblation' (literally 'the giving') of children. Benedict's *Rule* (ch. 59) permitted parents to offer their young children to be monks. By the ninth century, monasteries received many members in that way. It was unquestioned that they needed some education if they were to be good monks. In small religious houses, the training of the young was probably informal, entrusted to senior monks who taught them enough reading and singing to carry out the liturgy. But in the larger monasteries of the Frankish Empire, there were formal schools presided over by learned monks. The pupils were mostly **oblate** boys, but pupils might also be older monks, youngsters intending to be secular priests and some boys whose families wanted them to remain in secular life but also to become literate. In at least one rich, large monastery, St Gall in Switzerland, there were two schools, one for the monks and one for the non-monks. That arrangement was ideal since it sheltered the boy-monks from worldly ideas and conversation, but it was expensive, and in most monasteries the lay boys were trained alongside the monks. Monastic schools had advantages over cathedral schools: they were built into the stable routine of monastic life and were less dependent on the good will of the abbot or the presence of a single teacher. Between the ninth and eleventh centuries, monastic schools generally outshone cathedral schools, though they did not replace them.

V. The seven liberal arts

Both cathedral and monastic schools had primarily professional or voca-
tional purposes: to train their students to meet the obligations of their *ordo*.
The *General Admonition* of 789, canon 72, specified the chief subjects of the
curriculum: 'And let there be schools to teach boys to read. In every monastery
and bishop's house, teach the psalms, notation, chant, computation and
[Latin] grammar.'[4] These were the skills needed to read the religious texts and
to perform the liturgy properly.

As the educational reform gained momentum, a more ambitious plan took
shape. Since the Germanic peoples had no tradition of formal education
based on books, the Carolingians looked quite naturally to the Roman past
for a model. Roman intellectuals, including Varro (116–27 BC), Cicero (106–
43 BC), and Quintilian (AD 35–95) had drawn on the experience of the Greeks
to formulate a curriculum to train wealthy Roman boys for political and
administrative careers. Since such boys were free men (the word for 'free' in
Latin was *liber*), the subjects in the curriculum were the *artes liberales*, the liberal
arts, which were thought to be appropriate for a wealthy free man's education.

Since Roman culture idealised the orator, the focus of education in the
liberal arts was on words. Three of the liberal arts (grammar, rhetoric and
dialectic) taught the young man to read, write, speak, think and argue in
proper Latin. He polished his linguistic facility by intense study and imitation
of speeches, letters, poems and essays written by the great writers of the past.
In the course of his studies, he learned a great deal about the subjects needed
to make literature comprehensible, especially mythology, history and geography. The Roman intellectuals recommended that the educated man also
be conversant with certain mathematical subjects: geometry, astronomy (which
was close to astrology), arithmetic and music, which made up the other liberal
arts. The ideal of an eloquent learned orator monopolised the education of
the upper classes until the end of the Roman Empire.

The early Christians, mostly uneducated or educated in a lower-class way,
were indifferent or hostile to the liberal arts education, especially because they
thought it referred too often to sexual immorality and the pagan gods, who
were prominent in the literature that provided models of good writing and
speaking. In the fourth century, men educated in the liberal arts tradition
began to convert in numbers to Christianity and their skills and social standing often made them very prominent in the church. Sometimes congregations
eager to have a well-educated leader elected such men as bishops. Ambrose of
Milan (374–97), Augustine of Hippo (395–430), and Jerome (340–420), who
was not a bishop but a monk, were the most important of these educated
Latin speakers, who had a great impact on the way Christianity regarded education in the liberal arts.

Augustine wrestled with the problem of the relationship between Christianity and the liberal arts in his influential book *On Christian Doctrine*. He recommended a cautious acceptance of the traditional educational subjects and techniques. The objectionable parts of ancient education (especially the paganism and sexual immorality) should be avoided, but the aspects of liberal education that could be adapted to train students to be effective preachers and interpreters of scripture should be retained. In Augustine's judgement, the seven liberal arts were an ideal way to prepare students to understand and explain the scriptures, which were bulky, difficult texts that required just the sort of careful analysis that the rhetoricians and grammarians were so good at.

The reconciliation between Christianity and the education built on the liberal arts occurred when the Roman Empire was already in decline. The vigour of the ancient educational tradition was drying up, dependent on summaries, handbooks and encyclopaedias, and its clientele was shrinking. But whenever conditions were favourable, educational revivals in the Latin west always tried with varying success to return to the liberal arts, especially the literary subjects of grammar, rhetoric and logic.

The Carolingian reformers also looked to the seven liberal arts as an ideal framework within which to educate the elite of secular and regular clergy. Already in antiquity, the mathematical subjects had been reduced to summaries and textbooks that were studied less intensely than the literary subjects. That continued to be true in Carolingian practice. The four mathematical arts, called the *quadrivium*, usually received only superficial treatment in the Carolingian schools. Because the acquisition of the ability to read and write well in Latin was a great task in itself, emphasis was placed on the literary subjects of grammar, rhetoric and dialectic, which the Carolingians named the *trivium*.

The traditional narrative of the Carolingian Renaissance claims that creativity was not the dominating characteristic of intellectual life: that educated Carolingians usually sought to recreate an earlier golden age, and in particular to write and think as their great predecessors had. Carolingian intellectuals approached the past with an inferiority complex, judging themselves lesser in literary abilities than a Cicero or an Augustine. They adopted a reverential attitude toward the biblical and classical writers, who seemed to have said everything so well that there was no possibility of surpassing them. Even the pagan writers of the past were admired for their language and wisdom, provided they did not contradict Christian theology or morality. For centuries, medieval education in every field was based upon written texts, called authorities, which were thought to contain the essential features of a particular subject. For most students, the goal of education was to learn what the authorities thought, and not necessarily to construct one's own thoughts. This was true to some extent, but newer scholarship is showing that Carolingians were much more creative than previously thought, especially in the area of exegesis, the scholarly practice of interpreting the Bible.

Not only the curriculum but also the atmosphere of the Carolingian schools had important implications for the future. From the ninth to the thirteenth century, formal education outside Italy was oriented to the clergy in every way: the teachers were clergy; the students were overwhelmingly clergy; and the interests that dominated the schools centred on the scriptures, the canon law and the liturgy. Carolingian thinkers achieved originality most often in matters where the revered past did not offer a decisive answer or model. For instance, the effort to understand the presence of Christ in the Eucharist provoked a lively debate in the ninth century, with the monk Paschasius Radbertus defending a very literal view of Christ's presence and the monk Ratramnus of Corbie defending a more symbolic understanding. Likewise, the Saxon monk Gottschalk raised the thorny theological issue of predestination and, after a lively debate, was condemned in 848 for his belief that some humans were predestined to salvation and others to damnation. In matters relating to liturgical worship, which was a central concern of Frankish society, Carolingian intellectual and artistic creativity was at its best. In the ninth century, the liturgy was embellished in many ways. It was performed in impressive stone churches with the use of precious liturgical objects such as gold chalices and silver crosses. Poets and musicians also created new forms of chanting, new religious texts to be sung aloud, and new techniques to preserve music through written notation.

The Carolingian Renaissance is sometimes described in modern books as if it primarily involved the recovery of ancient pagan authors such as Cicero and Virgil. That is neither an accurate statement of what the Carolingian reformers set out to do nor of what they accomplished. The overwhelming proportion of intellectual energy was directed to religious ends and particularly to copying and composing religious texts. The scriptures, church fathers, sermons, saints' lives, liturgy and canon law dominate in the surviving manuscripts. However, there was a small niche reserved for the pagan Latin classics, which were regarded as models of fine literary style that could be used to add dignity to God's service, though they were also regarded as potentially dangerous because of their paganism, immorality and pre-Christian worldview. For example, when Einhard set out to write the life of Charlemagne, he studied intensely what may have been the only surviving copy of the *Lives of the Caesars*, by the second-century writer Suetonius, and used it as his model of how to write the life of an emperor.

VI. Books and handwriting

During the ninth century, a minority of scholars within the educated elite – a minority within a minority – found some pagan writings aesthetically and intellectually satisfying. Their interest was crucial for the very survival of the ancient pagan authors, whose works had generally ceased to be copied in the fifth or sixth century, as the ancient schools and libraries vanished. Very few of the pagan Latin classics survive today in ancient copies, no more than a few stray pages from the fifth century and some papyrus fragments from Egypt. The oldest surviving copies of the vast majority of both the well-known and the obscure ancient Latin authors were made in the ninth century by Carolingian scribes who saved them from oblivion. But that fact, important as it is in the cultural history of the west, is only a by-product of the religious aims of the reformers. About 8,000 books copied during the eighth and ninth centuries in the Frankish kingdom survive and they are overwhelmingly religious in content. For every copy of works by Cicero, there were dozens of copies of works by church fathers, such as Augustine, Jerome and Gregory, and probably hundreds of copies of biblical and liturgical books.

In a culture based on books, libraries of some sort are indispensable. Every Carolingian church, however poor, needed a book or two, if only to say mass or carry out a baptism. The leading monasteries and bishoprics, the same institutions that created schools, also created collections of books. Although tiny by our standards, these collections are impressive in the context of the ninth century. A major university library can have as many as 5 million books, or more, whereas the greatest collections that we know of in the ninth century were at the monastery of Lorsch, with about 600 volumes, and at the monastery of Fulda, with almost 1,000. The acquisition of a manuscript was both expensive and time-consuming, since each was handmade. Much energy and surplus wealth in Carolingian society was devoted to copying books, to enable the recovery of the learning of the past.

Not only did the Carolingians seek out earlier manuscripts to copy but they also developed a new form of handwriting, called Carolingian minuscule, in which to copy them. One of the symptoms of the regionalisation of the west between the fifth and eighth centuries was the development of styles of writing so different from one another that someone trained in one style could not easily read another. (If you have ever seen the flowery German script called *Fraktur*, similar to 'Gothic' computer fonts, then you have some idea of the difficulty the form of writing can place in the way of reading.) Even before Charlemagne supported reform, scribes at several monasteries, especially Corbie in modern northern France, had begun to develop a clear, neat and legible style of writing that gradually replaced earlier styles within the empire and made it possible to read a manuscript produced anywhere. When the Italian humanists of the fifteenth century encountered this Carolingian minuscule, they admired it greatly. Since they thought everything admirable was of Greek or Roman origin, they mistook it for 'Roman' writing. As a consequence, Carolingian minuscule handwriting was revived in the Italian Renaissance and became the basis for the printed letters on this very page.

It is possible both to overestimate and to underestimate the consequences of Carolingian educational reform. Few people were directly affected. The educated elite may not have included more than a thousand persons at any one time. The vast majority of laymen were totally illiterate; many of the rural secular clergy were barely literate; and many of the ordinary monks were sufficiently literate to perform the liturgy, but little else. But the admittedly small beginnings had a great future ahead of them. The Latin west re-established contact with the Roman past, which stimulated and challenged it until modern times. Formal education was for centuries based on the seven liberal arts, particularly the literary subjects. Mastery and analysis of authoritative texts was the mark of the educated person. The revival of the use of grammatically correct Latin meant that western society would be bilingual, with Latin for high culture and many aspects of religion and the vernacular languages for ordinary life. The Carolingian reform also reinforced the church's monopoly on learning. Until the revival of towns in the eleventh and twelfth centuries, literacy was a preserve of clergy and monks. Finally, the reform solidified a three-fold division within the body of the church, based in part on education and social class. An elite, usually well born, economically secure and well educated in the liberal arts tradition, was heavily entrenched in the higher positions in the church. The vast majority of clergy, monks and nuns were drawn from the lesser groups in society, literate but often poorly educated. And the illiterate laity, whatever their wealth and social status, were unfamiliar with the learned, normative aspects of Christianity. As a consequence of the Carolingian reforms, Christianity, a religion based on written texts, was never again without considerable numbers of clergy and monks capable of using those texts intelligently.

Suggested reading

Companion website

www.routledge.com/cw/lynch

7.1   St. Augustine of Hippo, On Christian Doctrine
Excerpts from Aurelius Augustine, *The Works of Aurelius Augustine, Bishop of Hippo*, vol. 9, ed. Marcus Dods (Edinburgh: T & T Clark, 1892), 55–56.

7.2   Concerning the Body and Blood of the Lord
Ratramnus of Corbie, 'Concerning the Body and Blood of the Lord', in Monk of Corbie, *The Book of Bertram*, trans. W.F. Taylor (London: Simpkin Marshall & Co., 1880), 6–13.

Primary sources

Augustine of Hippo, *On Christian Doctrine*, translated by D. W. Robertson, Jr (Indianapolis, Indiana, 1958)

Barney, Stephen A., W. J. Lewis, J. A. Beach and Oliver Berghoff, editors, *The Etymologies of Isidore of Seville* (Cambridge, 2006)

Cassiodorus Senator, *Introduction to Divine and Human Readings*, translated by Leslie Webber Jones, Columbia Records of Civilization, 40 (New York, 1946, reprint 1966)

Stahl, William H. and Richard Johnson, editors and translators, *Martianus Capella and the Seven Liberal Arts*, 2 vols (1971-7)

Modern scholarship

Chazelle, Celia and Burton Van Name Edwards, editors, *The Study of the Bible in the Carolingian Era* (Turnhout, 2003)

Dales, Richard C., *The Intellectual Life of Western Europe in the Middle Ages* (Leiden, 1992)

Duckett, Eleanor Shipley, *Carolingian Portraits* (Ann Arbor, Michigan, 1962)

Laistner, M. L. W., *Thought and Letters in Western Europe, A.D. 500 to 900*, 2nd edition (Ithaca, New York, 1957)

Marrou, Henri I., *A History of Education in Antiquity*, translated by George Lamb (New York, 1956)

McKitterick, Rosamund, *The Carolingians and the Written Word* (Cambridge, 1989)

Reynolds, Leighton D. and Nigel G. Wilson, *Scribes and Scholars: A Guide to the Transmission of Greek and Latin Literature*, 2nd edition (Oxford, 1974)

Riché, Pierre, *Education and Culture in the Barbarian West from the Sixth Through the Eighth Century*, translated by John J. Contreni (Columbia, South Carolina, 1976)

Too, Yun Lee, editor, *Education in Greek and Roman Antiquity* (Leiden, 2001)

Wolff, Philippe, *The Awakening of Europe* (also published as *The Cultural Awakening*), translated by Anne Carter (Baltimore, 1968)

Wolff, Philippe, *Western Languages, AD 100–1500*, translated by Frances Partridge (London, 1971)

Notes

1 *The Etymologies of Isidore of Seville*, translated by Stephen A. Barney, W. J. Lewis, J. A. Beach and Oliver Berghof (Cambridge, 2006), book XI, ch. 140, p. 240.
2 Pope Zachary to Boniface, Letter 68 (July, 746), in Ephraim Emerton, editor and translator, *The Letters of Saint Boniface* (New York, 1940), new edition by Thomas F. X. Noble (New York, 2000), pp. 100-1.
3 Einhard, *The Life of Charlemagne*, ch. 25, in *Einhard and Notker the Stammerer. Two Lives of Charlemagne* (Harmondsworth, Middlesex, 1969).
4 *Admonitio generalis*, canon 72, in Monumenta Germaniae historica, Legum sectio II, *Capitularia regum Francorum*, vol. 1 (Hanover, 1883), p. 60.

8

The collapse of the Carolingian world

The Carolingian Empire was built on a fragile economic and political base, a fact that became evident in the 840s. Civil war among Charlemagne's heirs and invasions from the south, north and east destroyed political unity and impoverished society. For the next two centuries, the west was battered by increased violence, political disintegration and economic decline. The bishops supported the ideal of strong, anointed rulers like Charlemagne who would protect the church and expand the boundaries of the Christian world, but the reality was quite different. Local and regional strongmen seized political power, and filled church offices as they saw fit. Vast amounts of church land and tithes passed to the direct control of these strongmen. Church councils and kings criticised the confiscation of church property, but with little success.

I. Civil wars

In part, the political troubles of the Carolingian Empire were caused by friction within the royal family and in part by the ambitions of the important aristocrats who wished to gather power into their own hands. Although the intellectual life of the Carolingian world owed much of its form and content to the Roman and Christian past, its political life was conducted according to Germanic customs. Frankish inheritance practices within the royal family followed a formula guaranteed to produce conflict. Among the Franks, every able-bodied son inherited an equal portion from his father and that view was so deeply rooted that even kings had to obey it. The idea of favouring the king's first-born son, a practice called primogeniture, had not yet emerged in political life. The Merovingian kings had regularly divided their kingdom among sons, who often fought one another over the fairness of the division, thus contributing to the progressive weakening of that dynasty in the sixth and seventh centuries. The Carolingian kings were bound by the same rules of succession, but between 741 and 840, by a series of lucky developments, power passed quickly to only one son and the kingdom kept its unity. In 806, Charlemagne, who was about 64 years old, drew up a document dividing his empire among three adult sons. He also had some young illegitimate sons who were not included in the division. But when he died in 814, Louis

(814–40) was his only surviving adult son and the empire once again passed on undivided.

With Louis the Pious, the dynasty's luck changed for the worse. Louis had three sons from his first marriage, Lothair, Louis the German and Pippin of Aquitaine, who died before his father, and another son from his second marriage, Charles the Bald (843–77). The multiplicity of heirs revived the family feuding that had weakened the Merovingian kings. The older sons did not want to share power with their young half-brother, Charles, and resisted their father's plans for redividing the empire. When Louis the Pious decided to give the imperial title and the bulk of his estates to Lothair in order to preserve the unity of the empire, the two half-brothers, Louis and Charles, allied against their father and Lothair. After Louis the Pious died in 840, civil war broke out with Charles the Bald and Louis the German united uneasily against Lothair. After the bloody but indecisive battle of Fontenoy (842), the brothers agreed to divide the empire three ways. Charles received west Francia (roughly the kingdom of France), Louis the German received east Francia (roughly the kingdom of Germany) and Lothair received the title of emperor and a central strip of land running from the North Sea to Italy. Lothair's share, which had no linguistic, economic or political unity, was very unstable. Its inevitable disintegration led to struggles over its control that recurred periodically until the Second World War.

A pattern of violence in royal politics persisted for almost sixty years, as shifting alliances pitted brothers, uncles and cousins against one another. The major gainers in the civil wars were the important aristocrats, particularly the counts and dukes. Under a strong king like Charlemagne, they were forced to curb their ambitions for power and independence. The civil wars of the later ninth century weakened the monarchy and strengthened the great aristocrats, who traded their support to one claimant or another in return for concessions of royal lands and rights. By the late ninth century, the kings had impoverished themselves by giving away their estates and rights to gain support that often proved unreliable. The disunity of the royal family helped power to pass into the hands of the kings' most powerful subjects, who eagerly consolidated their position in society, often by impoverishing bishoprics and monasteries under their control.

II. Invasions

Around the time of these civil wars, invaders crossed the borders of the empire. The Franks were traditionally a formidable military power on land when they were the aggressors who could choose the time and place of attack. But when they were unexpectedly attacked, their army was slow to assemble.

They had neither experience nor success at naval warfare. When the heirs of Charlemagne were fighting one another, they delighted to see invaders ravage the lands of their opponents. Because of such short-sightedness, they did not cooperate against the invaders and were unable to cope with the seaborne attackers who appeared in the north and the south.

The biggest threat to the future of Christianity in the west came from Scandinavian invaders, whom contemporaries called *Nordmanni*, 'Northmen', which eventually became the modern word 'Norse'. We lump them together as Vikings. The Vikings were Germanic peoples, similar in culture to the Franks and other tribes who had migrated into the Roman Empire during the fifth and sixth centuries. While the Carolingian Franks and other successors to the invaders of the Roman Empire had been culturally assimilated and converted to Catholic Christianity, the Scandinavian Vikings retained traditional features of Germanic society, including paganism. (See Figure 8.) One could argue that both the Carolingian Franks and the Vikings shared a common set of Germanic warrior values, though each group applied those values to different purposes.

In the 790s, the Northmen began to raid the northern outposts of Latin **Christendom**. We do not know the reasons that propelled them outward. They may have been stirred by a growing population in a land of few resources or by the restrictions placed on local warfare by emerging monarchies in Scandinavia. The first targets were Christian monasteries with their poor defences and valuable property. In 793, Vikings looted and destroyed the monastery on the island of Lindisfarne, off the coast of northern England. Alcuin wrote to the bishop of Lindisfarne that 'the misfortune of your suffering saddens me every day, even though I am far away. The pagans defiled the sanctuaries of God and shed the blood of the saints in the vicinity of the altar, they ravaged the home of our hope, they trampled the bodies of the saints in the temple of God as if they were dung in the street.'[1] In 794, Vikings looted and burned the monasteries of Wearmouth and Jarrow in Northumbria, where Bede had lived. In 795, they attacked the Irish monastic and missionary centre on the island of Iona, and its monks had to flee to Ireland. The raids continued off and on for almost 300 years (793–1066), and the Northmen extended their range of activity from Ireland in the west to Russia and the Byzantine Empire in the east.

Any discussion of the Northmen must be careful not to perpetuate the old stereotypes of Vikings as marauders whose sole activity was rape and pillage. Whatever the experience of contemporary monastic chroniclers, modern archaeology has shown Viking society to be much more nuanced and complex. The Northmen were farmers and herders. They wove woollen textiles with intricate designs, and crafted objects in wood and leather, bone and antler, iron and precious metals. They held markets and eventually participated in money economies, even minting their own coins, some with combinations of Christian and pagan symbolism. They were great traders and

Figure 8 Viking animal-head post
Important Vikings were buried with their ships and other grave goods. Archeologists found five animal-head posts, like the one shown here, with the famous Oseberg ship burial. The heads are carved from maple, in various styles, and measure between 19 and 21 inches long (50 to 54 cm), with handles of roughly the same length. The fact that they have handles suggests that the animal heads were not attached to something else, but were designed for people to carry them, perhaps in processions. No one knows the purpose of the animal heads, but their placement in the ship's burial chamber, and their richly detailed carving, may be signs that they were some kind of magical or religious talisman.

travellers. Indeed, while the origins of the contemporary word *víkingr* is contested, most scholars argue that it came from an Old Norse word for 'sea warrior', though it might also mean 'a man travelling with others on a long voyage', perhaps for the purposes of trading. The Vikings were also settlers, for example, founding the city of Dublin in Ireland. In Iceland, where they found Irish monks, they converted peacefully to Christianity. The Swedish Vikings turned their attentions east and south, moving down the river systems through modern Russia and into the Black Sea, toward Byzantium – where they were known as Varangians – founding trading posts for furs, slaves, amber and other products of the east.

Some Vikings did attack Christians, especially churches and monasteries. The Vikings themselves, living in a predominantly oral culture, left no written record of these attacks. The reason the written record has been so biased against the Vikings is that their Christian victims constructed that record. It would be interesting to know how the Vikings might have portrayed this activity. One-sided as it is, here is just a portion of the record. In 860, Swedish Vikings in dug-out canoes attacked the greatest city of the Christian world, Constantinople. They were beaten back, but periodic attacks continued. The Byzantine emperors made economic treaties with them and recruited some Vikings into their bodyguard. In the west, Vikings from Norway attacked and eventually settled in Scotland (ninth century), the Orkney and Shetland Islands (ninth century), Iceland (874), Greenland (980s) and Ireland, where the monasteries were plundered, causing their intellectual life to be snuffed out. The Danes turned south and west to the kingdoms of the Franks and of the Anglo-Saxons. Between 876 and 890, Danes conquered Anglo-Saxon England north of the River Thames, leaving only the southern kingdom of Wessex independent under the rule of the Christian king Alfred (871–99) and his descendants. In the Frankish kingdom, raids began in 814 when Viking ships moved up the many river valleys. Between 840 and 860, raiding activity devastated the western Frankish kingdom, where the cities of Rouen, Nantes, Bordeaux, Tours, Blois, Poitiers, Orleans and Paris were sacked at least once, as well as the surrounding countryside with its churches and monasteries.

The Northmen's military tactics were successful against the Franks and the Anglo-Saxons. They were skilled, fearless sailors who crossed the North Sea in open boats and attacked with the advantage of surprise. They were ferocious fighters, whose battlefield behaviour encouraged their opponents to flee rather than to fight. Since neither the Franks nor the Anglo-Saxons had standing armies, only local people resisted the raiders initially, if at all. By the time an army had been assembled, the Vikings had departed with their loot. Although they took whatever they could, the Vikings were drawn particularly to monasteries and big churches, where a century of Carolingian peace and prosperity had often built up a considerable amount of gold, silver, jewels, books and precious cloth for the liturgy. The same was true in England and Ireland. Parish life, which rested on a simple economic basis, probably recovered quickly. Monastic, canonical and cathedral communities were more complex organisms that did not recover so easily. In some places, they were obliterated along with their schools and libraries. In the regions worst hit by the Northmen, including Ireland, Anglo-Saxon England and the western parts of the Frankish Empire, Christianity became deprived of its intellectual centres.

The usual pattern of the early ninth-century attacks was for the raiders to operate in the summer and to return to their Scandinavian homes before the onset of the fierce North Sea winter. In the 840s and 850s, Viking raiding parties began to winter over on islands just off the coasts of England and France. The bases soon turned into permanent settlements from which the raiders could more easily attack. After 871, only the kingdom of Wessex in Britain hung on as an independent Christian power. Scandinavian chiefs ruled two-thirds of the Anglo-Saxon lands. Dublin and York were the centres of Norse kingdoms. The lively monastic culture of the earlier period had died out. It seems that no Benedictine monastery was still functioning in Anglo-Saxon England. By 911, a Carolingian king had been forced to grant territory at the mouth of the River Seine to the Viking chief Rollo (c.846–c.931), who created Normandy, the land of the Northmen. Interestingly, Rollo accepted baptism as part of this negotiation, and seems to have done his best to integrate and unify Viking and Frankish culture. According to an eleventh-century chronicler, 'Rollo was not long in bringing together men of various extractions and crafts, shaping all races into one single people.'[2]

A somewhat lesser threat came from Muslim pirates, who in the 820s began raiding along the Mediterranean coast from northern Spain to Italy, for slaves, plunder and ransom. During the ninth century, they conquered the islands of Sicily, Corsica and Sardinia and seized some ports in southern Italy and along the French Riviera. They did not create large settlements on the mainland, but their attacks had devastating effects. Travel by sea as well as by land through the Alpine passes from France to Italy became dangerous. In 846 they looted the Church of St Peter at Rome, the holiest shrine of the west. The Muslim pirates inflicted serious economic and psychological damage in the southern parts of the Frankish Empire. Economic life was disrupted, terrorised populations withdrew into fortified towns on hilltops, monasteries and churches were destroyed, and the south of France, which had earlier been an important economic and intellectual centre, regressed. However, Islam's explosive energy, which had carried it around three-quarters of the Mediterranean shore between 632 and 732, had spent itself in the west. The Muslim raiders made no successful attempt to conquer large areas on the mainland. In spite of serious damage to some areas, there was little danger that they would obliterate the native Christian culture.

Largely because of geography, the eastern Frankish kingdom (modern western Germany, Switzerland and Northern Italy) was spared any raiding by Muslim pirates and any sustained attacks by Vikings, who did occasionally raid in the Mediterranean. However, the eastern Frankish kingdom did not escape invaders entirely. Between 895 and 955, horsemen raided deep into east Frankish territory from their base in the plain of Hungary. The Magyars, ancestors of the modern Hungarians, were an Asiatic people who had migrated into the gap created when Charlemagne destroyed the kingdom of the Avars between 791 and 796. Using horses instead of ships, the Magyars sought loot and slaves in the territories of the east Frankish kingdom. Their mounted expeditions often covered long distances, reaching such places as the Po valley in Italy (899), Saxony (906) and Reims (937). Individual districts suffered seriously, but the cumulative effect was not so great as that of Muslim and Viking attacks to the south and west. The east Frankish kingdom survived intact and many churches and monasteries escaped harm. As the Magyars settled down to agricultural life, their nomadic raiding declined. In 955, the German king Otto I (936-73) inflicted a severe defeat on them at the River Lech and the raiding ceased, though warfare did not. Under King Stephen (997-1038), the Hungarians converted to Latin Christianity and became participants in the political and religious system of Christendom.

III. The east Frankish kingdom (Germany)

In the face of these civil wars and invasions, which reached their climax in the generation after 850, Carolingian political unity, which was barely a century old, collapsed. The empire split into several large regions, including the west Frankish kingdom, the east Frankish kingdom and the middle kingdom, each of which developed in its own way. The greatest continuity with the Carolingian past survived in the eastern part of the empire, which was less severely disrupted by invasions. The last Carolingian of the eastern line, Louis the Child (899-911), died without heirs. In 919, the important aristocrats and churchmen of the east Frankish kingdom reacted to the need for a leader against the Magyar invaders by electing the duke of Saxony, Henry the Fowler (919-36), to be king. Three of his descendants, all named Otto, ruled the east Frankish kingdom until 1002.

Otto I (936-73) took measures that had a great impact on the church in his kingdom. Otto's major internal political problem was that he did not have sufficient personal, military and economic resources to control the great lords of his kingdom, particularly the dukes of Bavaria, Swabia, Lotharingia and Franconia, who did not want him to be strong enough to dominate them. Traditionally, medieval kings depended to some degree on their control of the church for political allies, bureaucratic personnel, 'gifts' and patronage. In order to obtain resources to give him the power to control the dukes, Otto also turned to the church, which retained vast amounts of land in his kingdom. Control of bishops and abbots had great advantages. Churchmen were expected to be celibate and even if there were illegitimate children, they had no right to succeed to their fathers' church offices. Whenever a bishop or abbot died, a successor had to be chosen, without the limitations to the exercise of royal power that were posed by the hereditary rights of noble families. Otto I emphasised his role as the anointed king and the successor of Charlemagne. He vigorously asserted his right to fill high church offices, even in the territories of the other dukes. He succeeded often, though not always, in appointing bishops and abbots loyal to him. Their considerable resources in wealth and soldiers were a major source of support for Otto's plans. In addition, he appointed some churchmen to secular posts, giving them counties that might otherwise have been held by lay aristocrats, who would try to make them hereditary in their families. These count-bishops combined secular and religious power that a strong king could use to his advantage. Yet the Ottonian programme may not have been as clear-cut as all that. According to historian Timothy Reuter, modern scholars have oversystematised Ottonian practices in controlling the church: they were neither so well thought out nor so unique as was once held.[3]

The Ottonian imperial church system, with its close alliance between king/ emperor and church, meant that the ruler's power depended on his ability to continue to control the high offices of the church. Even though the system was advantageous for the king, it did not work badly for the church either. The Ottonian kings generally chose competent, reliable men to serve them and the church. Barefoot saints were rare among the German hierarchy, but many bishops and abbots were builders, patrons of the arts, serious administrators, and efficient organisers of missions that spread Christianity eastward into Poland, Hungary and Bohemia. Large, orderly monasteries carried on the Carolingian tradition of schools and libraries.

IV. The west Frankish kingdom (France)

The situation in the west Frankish kingdom (roughly modern France) was quite different. That region bore the full force of three generations of Viking and Muslim raids. There continued to be Carolingian kings of the western line until 987, but in wealth and political power they were pale shadows of their great ancestors and were weaker than some of their contemporary dukes and counts. Their landed estates were few and their rights were sharply curtailed by the rise of local and regional strongmen. Constant warfare undermined the traditional social and political hierarchy. Strong kings, like Charlemagne, had appointed and dismissed their officials as they wished, but in the struggles of the later ninth and tenth centuries, the kings failed to retain that right. Power moved down the social scale to men who could exercise it effectively: the man who could protect a region became its actual ruler. Powerful men made counties and duchies hereditary in their families and struggled to control all who lived in their territory, including churchmen. In some places, effective power was even more fragmented: a local strongman with a few dozen soldiers and a fortified house exploited the local peasants and parish church in return for defending them against Vikings and other strongmen. Such men paid little attention to the figurehead king, who was sometimes militarily weaker than they were.

The breakdown of royal control in the western kingdom was a disaster for the church. Local and regional strongmen seized the traditional royal right to fill church offices, but exercised that right more crudely than Frankish kings had usually done. The local rulers gave bishoprics, abbacies and parish churches to their kinsmen and supporters or to the highest bidder, with little regard for their qualifications. Massive portions of church wealth, including land and tithes, were seized by lay rulers as their own or were given to them with the connivance of the prelates who were their subordinates and often relatives. Monasteries that had escaped the Viking raids were exploited by local strongmen, who appointed abbots and milked the resources of the houses for their own benefit. Life in accordance with the Benedictine *Rule* became rare as local custom, economic problems, and the ignorance and brutality of the times took root. At every level, the written norms for the clerical *ordo*, so laboriously restored by the earlier Carolingian rulers, were ineffective, either because they were ignored or simply forgotten. Custom, which had the force of law in the period, allowed many things that a Carolingian bishop a hundred years earlier would not have tolerated: laymen taking fees to appoint clergy, bishops taking fees to ordain clergy and priests taking fees to give sacraments – all examples of the sin of simony – as well as married priests, hereditary positions in the church and violent seizure of church property. In general, religious interests in the west Frankish kingdom were subordinated to the power of laymen, ranging from kings, whose religious anointing at least gave them some appearance of legitimacy, to local thugs who held power by their strong right arm, with no pretence of legitimacy.

The church made one significant attempt to protect clergy against local warlords in the absence of effective royal power. This was the *Pax Dei*, or Peace of God, a proclamation that the church would excommunicate any person who attacked or robbed a church or member of the clergy. This protection was later extended to other non-combatants, such as women, children, unarmed peasants and merchants.

V. The papacy and Italy

In the tenth century, the situation of the papacy was like that of many contemporary bishops. A fundamental problem for the papacy throughout the Middle Ages was that the popes wanted freedom of action and independence, but usually lacked the territorial base, the soldiers and the wealth to achieve those ends on their own. Hence the popes needed a protector, yet one who would not control them too closely. For centuries, the protector had been the Byzantine emperor. In the 750s, the popes allied themselves with the Frankish kings, who protected them until the late ninth century when Frankish power in Italy vanished. Without a strong royal power, the papacy was subjected to the same struggles among local aristocratic families that marked the development of so many bishoprics elsewhere. From 850 to 1050, the average length of a pope's reign was about four years: hence the struggle to choose a pope was barely over before it began again. The main players were central Italian aristocratic families and the kings of Germany. Intrigue, bribes, street violence, assassinations, and rumours of sexual misconduct and poisoning hung over many of the popes. From about 900 to 963, the house of Theophylact, a Roman aristocratic family, controlled the papacy and appointed kinsmen and favourites, including a 16-year-old boy, John XII (955–64).

The title of emperor, given to Charlemagne by Pope Leo III on Christmas Day 800, had fallen on hard times as the Carolingian realm disintegrated. By the early tenth century, it was held by relatively minor Italian rulers and was finally left vacant after 924. In 962 the German king Otto I came to Rome, where Pope John XII crowned him emperor in recognition of his defeat of the Magyars at the River Lech (955), and of his commanding position among Christian rulers. John XII hoped Otto would be a protector but when the pope realised that the new emperor intended to control Rome, he went against him, but failed. In a synod of bishops, Otto had John XII deposed and appointed a successor. For the next century, the popes were integrated into the imperial church system. The kings of Germany claimed the right to approve the election of popes or even to appoint them. When the kings were able to exercise their right, they generally appointed respectable men. But they had preoccupations in Germany and did not always succeed in making their choices stick. Rome was far from Germany and Roman aristocratic families continued to want the position. Depending on circumstances, local candidates alternated with imperial choices.

It might seem surprising, but the prestige of the papacy did not decline noticeably in this period, perhaps because in an age without news media its problems were not widely known. Even when contemporary popes were negligible figures or worse, the papacy continued to benefit from the prestige of its saints and its great past. Pilgrims came, as they had come for 800 years, to visit St Peter's tomb and the other holy sites of Rome, where they saw magnificent buildings, solemn liturgy and dignified bishops. The weight of holiness in the holy city left its visitors in awe, and sent them home edified.

But if papal prestige remained, papal power was much reduced. Pope Nicholas I (858–67) had been powerful enough to force the Carolingian Emperor Lothair to take back a wife he had repudiated. Nicholas faced down important Frankish archbishops in disputes over their relative power. But for about the next two hundred years, there were no popes to compare to Nicholas. After the political collapse of the Carolingian realm, the papacy became an object of competition among Italian aristocratic families, with occasional interventions from Germany. During the tenth and early eleventh centuries, short papal reigns, local problems, the disorder throughout western

Christendom, and the power of the king of Germany reduced the popes to almost purely religious figures without significant moral or political leadership. They took few initiatives and had little influence in the wider church. The Christian church continued to function, even to expand by converting the Scandinavian and Slavic peoples. But laymen held the leadership at every level in Christian society. Some exercised their power well, particularly the powerful kings and emperors in the east Frankish kingdom, but others exploited the church ruthlessly. In such conditions, church life wandered far from the orderly church that the Carolingians had tried to create.

VI. Signs of revival

The tenth century was an age of the sword, but it was not a 'dark age' comparable to the sixth and seventh centuries when the heritage of antiquity was radically transformed or, as some would argue, died. In spite of invasions, the Carolingian ideals lived on, particularly in monasteries with their schools and libraries, some of which had an unbroken survival through the time of troubles.

With the benefit of hindsight, we can detect late in the tenth century the first glimmerings of important social and economic changes, although contemporaries probably could not see them. The most fundamental change concerned population: for the first time since the Carolingian period and perhaps since the third century, population began to grow in some favoured regions of the west. The causes for this were varied. Some had to do with the end of the invasions. As Northmen and Magyars settled down and were converted to Christianity, their raiding and warfare tapered off. The Mediterranean coasts became safer as Italian merchants gained experience at sea and resisted the Muslim pirates. Other causes of population growth were political: the consolidation of power in compact principalities began to reduce violence, though there was still plenty of it. Agriculture, the economic basis of life, became more stable. In north-western Europe, the climate seems to have grown warmer and drier and consequently more favourable to agriculture. The diet of peasants was improved by the wider use of legumes such as peas and beans. The more settled conditions encouraged the opening of new lands to agriculture, which in turn provided a livelihood for a growing population. Whatever the exact mix of causes in any region, a long-term demographic rise had begun in the Latin west, which continued until the climate change and epidemic diseases of the fourteenth century.

The second fundamental change was economic. In 950, the west was economically anaemic, far inferior to the commercial and manufacturing societies of Byzantium and Islam. But in some places, especially in northern Italy and Flanders, the first faint stirrings of new economic forces based on commerce and manufacturing appeared. Traders, many of them mere peddlers, began to carry goods for sale, promoting both production and consumption. The success of the traders stimulated the revival of urban life, as they repopulated the almost empty shells of ancient Roman towns and founded entirely new ones. The tenth century was still a miserably poor and disordered time in western Christendom, but the momentum of population growth and economic life had begun to shift, even though local strongmen and worldly prelates still dominated the scene.

VII. Monastic reform: Cluny

Even as the church in the western Frankish kingdom and in Italy – the most disrupted areas in the later ninth and tenth centuries – sank into sometimes unbelievable squalor, there were scattered signs of its revival as well. The secular church of dioceses and parishes was so enmeshed in the control of laymen that it was unlikely that serious reform would be successful there. To be sure, there were conscientious bishops who sought to enforce minimal standards on the clerical *ordo*, especially literacy, sexual continence, and avoidance of buying and selling holy things, called the sin of simony. They kept alive the memory of earlier standards, but their task was comparable to bailing out the sea, and their successes were generally local and short-lived.

Monasteries were the surest incubators of religious revival. Since the emergence of monasticism in the fourth century, that broad and messy movement had often been the place where religious ferment and dissent found a home. In modern times, if arguments about matters of religious discipline become bitter enough, they can result in a new denomination. In the Middle Ages, such arguments often resulted in a new monastic movement. Monasticism was a flexible institution. Individual houses or groups of houses were quite independent and could adapt to a wide variety of circumstances. Until the thirteenth century, there was an abundance of unoccupied land in western Europe for new monastic foundations, where the zealous or the malcontent could work out their vision of the Christian life. It may seem paradoxical, but the exploiters of some churches were also the generous patrons of other churches. Even in the disorders of the period from 850 to 1050, local thugs, who accepted the Christian view of the world even if they did not live by it, generally valued the prayers of good (i.e. chaste and personally strict) monks. They wanted good monks to pray for them and their families, and they were willing to give them gifts and protection.

Monastic reform movements began independently in several places in the tenth century, including Brogne near Namur in the 920s, Gorze near Metz in the 930s, and Anglo-Saxon England under Archbishop Dunstan of Canterbury

(909–88) in the 940s. The most famous and largest of the monastic reforms was centred at **Cluny** in Burgundy. It followed a classic pattern: a reforming abbot attracted patronage from a lay lord, who might well exploit other churches but wanted the prayers of reformed monks for himself and his family. In 909, Duke William I of Aquitaine, who had no direct heirs and felt guilty about a murder, gave an abbot named Berno his property at Cluny to be the site of a new monastery. William stated his reasons in the document drawn up to record the gift:

> To all who think sanely, it is clear that God's providence counsels those who are rich to use well those goods that they possess temporarily, so that they may be able to gain rewards which last forever. God's word shows and encourages this when it says 'A man's riches are the redemption of his soul' [Proverbs 13]. I, William, by the gift of God, Count and Duke, thinking carefully about this and wishing to provide for my own salvation while it is possible, have judged it to be proper, indeed very necessary, that for the benefit of my soul I share a small portion from the goods which have been entrusted to me for a time . . . that this deed may last not for a time, but forever, I shall provide from my own wealth for men living together under a monastic vow. [I act] with this faith and hope that although I myself cannot despise all things, at least by sustaining those who despise the world, men whom I believe to be just, I myself may receive the reward of the just. Therefore . . . let it be known that for God's love and that of our Saviour Jesus Christ I hand over my property to the holy apostles Peter and Paul . . . I give on this condition, that a monastery living under a rule be established at Cluny in honour of the holy apostles Peter and Paul; that the monks there form a congregation living according to the *Rule* of St. Benedict; that they shall for all time possess, hold, have and manage these properties, so that this honourable house of prayer shall be unceasingly full of vows and petitions, that in that place a heavenly life may be sought with all desire and deeply felt ardour, and that prayers, petitions and supplications may be faithfully addressed to the Lord, both for me and for those persons commemorated above [i.e. the king, William's parents, his wife, his sister Avana, his other sisters, brothers and nephews, all his male and female kinsmen, his servants, and the Catholic faith].[4]

Abbot Berno's reform looked back to the monasticism of the Carolingian golden years. He wanted his monks to observe completely the *Rule* of Benedict, as Benedict of Aniane interpreted it. A key to the success of the reform was freedom from lay interference, which the monks regained with the restoration of their right to elect their own abbot – Duke William agreed to abandon for himself and his heirs any claim to the traditional practice of making that appointment. In an era of disorder and widespread lay control of monasteries, Abbot Berno and Duke William placed their monastery under the protection of the pope or, more accurately, of the Roman apostles, Peter and Paul. Duke William's language reflects the fear that his monastery might fall under the control of some less pious ruler or churchman:

It is pleasing to be inserted in this testament that from this day forward the monks gathered in Cluny should not be subjected to us, or to our kinsmen, or to the splendour of royal greatness, or to the yoke of any earthly power. I beg and pray through God and in God and all his saints and in the day of the fearful judgement that none of the secular princes, nor any count, nor any bishop, nor the bishop of the Roman church ever invade the possessions of these servants of God. Let no one take, diminish, or exchange their goods, or give them as a **benefice** to anyone. Let no one impose an abbot over them against their will . . . I beg you, O holy apostles and glorious princes of the earth, Peter and Paul, and you, bishop of bishops of the Apostolic See, that you cut off from the communion of the Holy Catholic Church and from life eternal, by the canonical and apostolic authority that you received from God, thieves, usurpers and alienators of these things which I give to you with a cheerful mind and an eager will. Be guardians and defenders of Cluny and of God's servants who dwell there.[5]

The symbol of the protection requested from Saints Peter and Paul and from the pope was a payment of 10 gold pieces every fifth year for the upkeep of the lights in the Roman church. Because the popes were far away and in no position to exercise effective control over Cluny, Berno had the prestige of papal protection for his house, but also independence.

In the tenth and early eleventh centuries, many monasteries underwent reform, which meant in practice that they attempted to observe Benedict's *Rule* and to reduce interference by outsiders in monastic affairs. In its beginnings, Cluny did not differ significantly from many reformed houses, but its energetic abbots, particularly Odo (926–42), the long-lived Odilo (994–1049) and Hugh (1049–1109), shaped Cluny into a distinctive force in the western church. Internally, the monks of Cluny lived under Benedict's *Rule* in an expanded and interpreted form that emphasised the monks' devotion to liturgical prayer, particularly intercession for living and dead patrons. During the eleventh century, Cluny represented the high point of what historians call liturgical monasticism, in which the monks cultivated the celebration of elaborate liturgy in splendid surroundings. The church at Cluny, whose main altar was dedicated in 1095 by Pope Urban II, a former monk of Cluny, was the largest church built until the new St Peter's at Rome in the early sixteenth century. (Most of the monastery at Cluny was demolished in the early nineteenth century and many of its stones are now in the breakwater in the harbour of Marseilles.) In an impressive physical setting, more than 300 monks sang the monastic hours prescribed by Benedict, and added to them processions and prayers for the monastery's benefactors and for the dead who had donated gifts in order to be remembered. The Cluniac monks were not severely ascetic or overly intellectual. But in a disorderly world, life at Cluny was orderly, dignified and centred on the liturgy. The Cluniac ideal did not replace other forms of Benedictine monasticism, but it had many lay and clerical supporters in the eleventh century.

Cluniac monks opposed such uncanonical activities as simony and clerical marriage, but their weapons of opposition were example and exhortation. They did not fundamentally oppose lay control of the church, but they encouraged lay rulers to exercise that control responsibly. Cluniac abbots were welcome at the courts of princes and kings, where they promoted with some success the reform of lay power in the church rather than its abolition.

Abbots Odilo and Hugh were also active in the reform of other monasteries, many of which were owned by laymen as a consequence of the scramble for church property that occurred in the ninth and tenth centuries. Some laymen asked the abbot of Cluny to reform their monasteries. If the abbot agreed, he sent Cluniac monks to train the local monks and to make the local house more Benedictine, orderly, dignified and liturgical – in short, to make it more like Cluny. Although some lay rulers retained control of their reformed monasteries, others gave them permanently to the abbot of Cluny. Without following any sort of blueprint, a religious order centred on Cluny began to take shape in the eleventh century. The Cluniac system was monarchical, with full authority in the hands of the abbot of Cluny. Aside from a few special cases, the abbot of Cluny was the abbot of each and every reformed house, whose monks professed their vows to him. A **prior** appointed by the abbot of Cluny exercised day-to-day control of the local house. The maintenance of discipline in distant houses depended on the energy and good sense of the abbot of Cluny and his appointees.

There is no precise way to count the number of Cluniac houses, in part because bonds to Cluny were loose and shifting. It is clear that in the eleventh century the admiration for Cluniac monasticism, particularly in Spain, southern France and Italy, led to a rapid expansion of the order. From fewer than 30 monasteries in the year 1000, the Cluniac network had grown to an estimated 600 houses with about 10,000 monks by 1100. By the abbacy of Peter the Venerable (1132–56), there were more than 1,000 Cluniac monasteries and hundreds of others influenced by Cluny, though not all of them were actually governed by the abbot of Cluny.

Without planning for it, Cluny had created the first international religious order. During his 60-year abbacy, Hugh of Cluny stood second to the pope in religious prestige, and first in the human and material resources at his command. The ramshackle structure of far-flung houses answerable to the abbot of Cluny was a great force in the eleventh century, although its simple organisation carried the seeds of decay when conditions changed, fervour declined and weaker abbots took charge. In particular, Cluny had no general meeting of priors with the abbot to discuss problems, coordinate policies and maintain discipline. As the order grew, there was less likelihood that the abbot of Cluny could really supervise all of the houses. Since the order expanded by reforming existing houses, many exceptions to the rules survived from the days when houses were independent. Such localism reasserted itself when central control weakened in the later twelfth and thirteenth centuries.

Cluny's impact in eleventh-century Europe was enhanced by the fact that Cluniac monks were often chosen by pious or reform-minded rulers to be abbots of non-Cluniac monasteries. They were also chosen to be bishops, even popes. The Cluniac ideals of living according to a detailed written rule, of independence from but cooperation with lay rulers, and of commitment to the moral regeneration of the church and its clergy were a powerful force for reform, especially since they were backed up by vigorous abbots and impressive resources in wealth and personnel.

VIII. Missionary successes

In addition to monastic reform, the further conversion of pagan peoples settled within Latin Christendom and beyond its borders was also a sign of religious recovery. The tenth-century Latin west suffered in comparison to contemporary Islam or Byzantium, but to the more primitive peoples to the north and east it must have seemed very advanced indeed. Its elaborate religion, its literacy, its metal work, its stone buildings and its kings, particularly the powerful rulers in Germany, were just some of the expressions of its cultural superiority. When pagan invaders settled among Christian populations, as did the Vikings in Normandy and in the Danelaw in England, the price of peaceful coexistence generally included conversion to Christianity. King Alfred sponsored the Danish chief Guthrumin's baptism in 878. The Viking ruler of Normandy, Rollo, accepted baptism about 911 as part of his settlement with the west Frankish king Charles the Simple (893–923). In the beginning, these were political arrangements that led to a superficial Christianisation. During the tenth and eleventh centuries, the process of assimilation continued. Settlers adopted the language and religion of the natives. Although one might say that Christianity 'absorbed its attackers', the process was probably more complicated than that.

In the lands beyond the northern and eastern boundaries of Latin Christendom, conversions were still group decisions with strong political overtones. Almost everywhere, a pagan king was associated with the conversion of his people. There were political reasons why a pagan Germanic or Slavic ruler might want to become Christian. Christianity helped in the building of more centralised states since it favoured strong monarchy over the violence and disorder associated with an independent nobility. As a practical matter, the founding of dioceses, parishes and monasteries created an infrastructure that supported rulers in their efforts to unify their loosely organised territories. Since conversion to Christianity had implications that favoured strong kings, the native nobility often resisted conversion violently. In Scandinavia, the decisive period was 950-1050. Christianity found promoters in Harold Bluetooth (*c.*960) in Denmark, Olaf Trygvesson (969-1000) and Saint Olaf Haraldsson (1015-30) in Norway, and King Olaf (*c.*1000) in Sweden. In Iceland, which had no king, the assembly of leading men (the *Althing*) accepted Christianity in 1000, with permission for worship of the old gods to continue for a while, just in case the new religion disrupted the order of nature.

In eastern Europe, the Ottonian rulers of the east Frankish kingdom were vigorous in promoting Christianity beyond the River Elbe from their missionary base in the bishopric of Magdeburg, established by Otto I in 968. German missionaries brought Christianity, but local Slavic rulers resisted German ecclesiastical control since it might lead to German political control. To escape such political domination, some Slavic rulers successfully sought independent native bishoprics from the pope, including King Stephen (997-1038) in Hungary and Prince Mieszko (966-92) in Poland. By the first half of the eleventh century, Latin Christianity was well on its way to becoming the religion of the peoples on its northern and eastern borders, smoothing their entry into the political, economic and cultural sphere of the west.

IX. The revival of canon law

The third important development in the late tenth and early eleventh centuries was more intellectual, but highly significant for the future: the revival of the study of canon law, particularly in monasteries. The Carolingian period had seen significant interest in canon law: more collections, more manuscript copies, more councils of bishops and more regular application of the law.

When the Carolingian Empire crumbled in the later ninth century, one of the casualties was the observance of canon law. Its provisions were often unknown, ignored or unenforceable in the darkest decades of the later ninth and tenth centuries. However, the manuscripts survived, as did the fundamental idea that each *ordo* in the church ought to live by the canon law. When relative peace returned in the later tenth and early eleventh centuries, some scholars, mostly monks, rediscovered the canonical collections and learned from them how different the church of their day was from what the canonical ideal said it ought to be. In particular, they became aware that the canon law said bishops and abbots should be elected rather than appointed by lay rulers; that the buying and selling of church offices was forbidden as the serious crime of simony; and that clergy guilty of sexual immorality deserved deposition from office. The rediscovery of the canon law unleashed ideas that helped eventually to overturn the dominance of lay rulers in church matters.

The collapse of Carolingian order had great consequences for the church, which may be summed up in the phrase 'lay domination'. However, monks, missionaries and students of the canon law laid the foundations for the recovery of the church that occurred in the second half of the eleventh century when Europe entered on a new phase of relative peace, population growth and economic revival.

Suggested reading

Companion website

www.routledge.com/cw/lynch

8.1   Division of the Carolingian Empire
Nithard, 'The Strassburg Oaths' (842), and Annales Bertiniani, 'The Treaty of Verdun' (843), in Oliver J. Thatcher and Edgar H. McNeal eds., *A Source Book for Medieval History: Selected Documents Illustrating The History of Europe in The Middle Age* (New York: Charles Scribner's Sons, 1907), 60–64.

8.2   The Foundation Charter of Cluny
'Foundation Charter of Cluny', in Ernest F. Henderson, trans., *Select Historical Documents of the Middle Ages* (London: George Bell and Sons, 1905), 329–333.

8.3   Olaf Trygvesson is baptized
Excerpts from Snorri Sturlason, *The Heimskringla: A History of The Norse Kings*, trans. Samuel Laing (London: Norrcena Society, 1906), 151–152.

8.4   Odin and Christ
Excerpt from 'Rúnatal', in *The Elder or Poetic Edda, commonly known as Sæmund's Edda, part I: The Mythological Poems*, edited and translated by Olive Bray (London, 1908), pp. 99–100; and a rendering by Phillip C. Adamo of Harald's Stone, based on the tenth-century runestone in Jelling, Denmark.

Primary sources

John of Salerno, 'The Life of Abbot Odo' in Gerard Sitwell, *St. Odo of Cluny* (London, 1958), pp. 1–87

Njal's Saga, translated by Magnus Magnusson and Hermann Palson (Harmondsworth, Middlesex, 1960)

Snorri Sturluson, *Heimskringla*, translated by Lee Hollander (Austin, Texas, 1991)

The Sagas of the Icelanders, introduction by Robert Kellogg, various editors (New York, 2001)

Modern scholarship

Barraclough, Geoffrey, *The Origins of Modern Germany*, 2nd edition (Oxford, 1947), pp. 24–71

Bernhardt, John W., *Itinerant Kingship and Royal Monasteries in Early Medieval Germany, ca. 936–1075* (Cambridge, 1993)

Brink, Stefan and Neil Price, editors, *The Viking World* (London and New York, 2008)

Constable, Giles, *Cluny from the Tenth to the Twelfth Centuries: Further Studies* (Brookfield, Vermont, 2000)

Evans, Joan, *Monastic Life at Cluny, 910–1157* (Oxford, 1931)

Foote, Peter and David M. Wilson, *The Viking Achievement: The Society and Culture of Early Medieval Scandinavia* (London, 1980)

Hadley, Dawn, and Julian Richards, editors, *Cultures in Contact: Scandinavian Settlement in England in the Ninth and Tenth Centuries* (Turnhout, 2000)

Hunt, Noreen, *Cluniac Monasticism in the Central Middle Ages* (Hamden, Connecticut, 1971)

Johnson, Edgar N., *The Secular Activities of the German Episcopate, 919–1024* (Chicago, 1932)

Lawrence, C. H., *Medieval Monasticism: Forms of Religious Life in Western Europe in the Middle Ages*, 3rd edition (2001)

Logan, F. Donald, *The Vikings in History*, 3rd edition (New York, 2005)

Lopez, Robert S., 'Still Another Renaissance', *American Historical Review* 57 (1951), pp. 1–21

Lopez, Robert S., *The Commercial Revolution of the Middle Ages, 950–1350* (Englewood Cliffs, New Jersey, 1971)

McKitterick, Rosamond, *The Frankish Kingdom under the Carolingians, 751–987* (London and New York, 1983)

Nicholas, David, *The Growth of the Medieval City: From Late Antiquity to the Early Fourteenth Century* (London, 1997)

Reuter, Timothy, 'The "Imperial Church System" of the Ottonian and Salian Rulers: A Reappraisal', *Journal of Ecclesiastical History* 33 (1982), pp. 347–74

Rosenwein, Barbara, *Rhinoceros Bound. Cluny in the Tenth Century* (Philadelphia, 1982)

Notes

1 Alcuin, *Letter 24*, Monumenta Germaniae historica, *Epistolae*, 4 (Berlin, 1895), pp. 32–3.
2 From the *Miracles of Saint Vulfran*, quoted in Stefan Brink, editor, *The Viking World* (London and New York, 2008), p. 456.
3 Timothy Reuter, 'The "Imperial Church System" of the Ottonian and Salian Rulers: A Reappraisal', *Journal of Ecclesiastical History* 33 (1982), pp. 347–74.
4 *Recueil des chartes de l'abbaye de Cluny*, edited by A. Bernard and A. Bruel, Collection de documents inédits sur l'histoire de France, vol. 72, part 1 (Paris, 1876), pp. 124–5.
5 Ibid., pp. 126–7.

9

The church in the year 1000

After the middle of the eleventh century, reform movements that had begun in several different regions gained control of the papacy and introduced great changes into the western church. To understand the revolutionary nature of those changes, it will be useful to look at the structures of the church about the year 1000, before the reformers set to work.

I. Diversity and unity

By the year 1000, Christian Europe had survived the Viking, Muslim and Magyar invasions; we are able to discern the outlines of a new stability, though contemporaries could not. In the new order that was emerging from the debris of the Carolingian Empire, several enduring traits of European history had already appeared. In 1000, Christian Europe was multi-ethnic and multilingual. Since prehistoric times, waves of migrants had entered the European peninsula, usually from the east and north, carrying with them their languages and cultures. After the tenth century, the ethnic make-up of medieval Europe was never again significantly altered by invasions. In fact, some western Europeans became the migrants during the central Middle Ages, moving permanently into eastern Europe and Spain, and temporarily into the crusader states on the shores of the eastern Mediterranean. The main linguistic groups (Celtic, Germanic, Romance and Slavic) were settled more or less where their descendants still live. The boundary that divided speakers of Romance languages from speakers of Germanic languages was more or less where it is now (roughly the Rhine River). The ancestors of the Poles, Hungarians, Czechs and Slovaks were already in the general regions their descendants still inhabit. In 1000, some of those border peoples were in the process of Christianisation, and the rest soon would be.

European political life was also multi-centred. The large, loosely organised Carolingian Empire had only survived as a political unit for about a century. From the tenth to the twentieth centuries, Europe was never again united politically. Napoleon and Hitler failed in their attempts to unite it by force and the verdict is still out whether the European Union can survive the nationalism of its member states. In 1000, European politics were centred in medium-sized and small units: the German Empire, six or seven monarchies, and a multitude of more or less independent duchies, counties, city-states and ecclesiastical principalities, including the Papal States.

Even though Europe in 1000 was diverse, there were unifying forces. Economic bonds remained weak until the twelfth and thirteenth centuries, but cultural and religious bonds preserved strands of unity within the complex make-up of the Latin west. In 1000, the church was the only institution that spanned the diversity of languages and political structures in a region that ran approximately 1,350 miles from York in Northern England to Brindisi in southern Italy and approximately 1,500 miles from Poland to Spain. The highly centralised church of the thirteenth and fourteenth centuries did not yet exist. In 1000 the church was not tightly organised: such matters as finances, the choice of bishops, the details of the liturgy and relations with lay powers were very localised. Even without a centralised power structure, the church was present everywhere in its liturgy, its sacraments, its customs and rules, its clergy and its monasticism. The popes were the symbols of unity in belief but their power to command was modest. Although the church's structures were loose and varied, it enjoyed a special status in society because almost everyone believed that it mediated God's grace and taught His truth to its members. That conviction was made concrete in the great wealth, numerous personnel and legal privileges that many, but not all, churches possessed. There were frequent disputes about church property and offices, but apparently few doubts about the truth of the church's religious beliefs.

The other force for unity was a shared culture, which was literary for the educated elite and religious for the majority. The Latin language was used in liturgy, theology and other matters of high culture, as well as in diplomacy, and in almost everything that was written down. The knowledge of Latin gave a few people access to the rich literary culture of the Roman Empire, which repeatedly stimulated the creativity of the Latin west. Even when they were not deeply versed in ancient learning, the educated clergy everywhere shared the ideas and imagery of the Latin Bible, a knowledge of the Latin liturgy, and an adherence to formal creeds written in Latin. The overwhelming majority of ordinary Christians were illiterate, but they too participated in a shared religious culture. In spite of practices that varied by region, every Christian lived within a sacramental framework that was fundamentally the same and adhered to basic beliefs that were recognisably part of the same religion. This interplay of diversity and unity, already visible in 1000, gave later European history much of its tension and openness to change.

The Christian church in 1000 was the product of historical developments almost ten centuries old, though the Carolingian period and the upheavals that followed had contributed heavily to the shape of the contemporary situation. The basic structures of the church included the secular rulers, the papacy, the bishops, the parishes and the Benedictine monasteries. Since they were linked in ways that the eleventh-century reformers attempted to change, our study will benefit by looking at them before the changes occurred.

II. Church structures: the king

It may seem strange to make kings a part of the church structure, but that is how it was. Since the fourth-century Roman Empire, the church had been in alliance with rulers, a situation that was reinforced by the important role that some early medieval rulers had played in the conversions of their people. Everywhere, rulers were important in the functioning of the church, though the precise situation varied considerably from place to place. Some rulers shared power with the bishops but others dominated the church quite openly. Nowhere was the church independent of lay rulers.

Kings were quite distinct from other lay rulers, such as dukes or counts, whose practical power was often very great. Bishops and other church leaders regarded the king's authority in the church as legitimate and more desirable than that of multitudes of lay lords. That view was based partly in the practical experience of church leaders: it was better to deal with one king than with many potentially ignorant and irresponsible lords. However, it was also based in religious ideas. Only kings had biblical approval: kings anointed by God had ruled Israel, and the New Testament told Christians to honour the king (1 Pet. 2:17). No mere duke or count could look to the clear authority of scripture to justify his independent power.

During the Carolingian period, kings had taken on sacred characteristics that symbolised and justified their leading role in the church. Both the Christian Visigoths in Spain and the Christian Anglo-Saxons had probably anointed their kings on the model of Old Testament Hebrew kings. When the Franks adopted royal anointing for King Pippin's consecration in 751, it became customary for many western kings to be inducted into office in ceremonies that closely resembled those used to consecrate bishops. No duke or count took political power in the context of such a religious ceremony. Since the Greek word *christos* means 'one who has been anointed', an anointed king was the only layman who could be called another 'Christ'. Even some theologians thought that the royal anointing was a sacrament given to those few human beings whom God called to be kings. There was also a theology of Christian kingship, which argued that Jesus had combined in himself the offices of priest and king. After his death and resurrection, those offices had been separated within a unified Christian society. Bishops represented Jesus's priestly powers and Christian kings embodied his royal power. Just as the bishops were called to exercise an essential role, so the kings were called by God to protect, defend and expand the church. In the ideal situation, bishops and kings would cooperate to govern the *populus Christianus*, the Christian people. Since kings were not clergy but laymen, some ecclesiastical matters were beyond their powers. For instance, they could not say mass. But their involvement in other church matters was a duty, not an intrusion. Their powerful role in Christian society was regarded as a God-given right, provided that they acted justly and respected the rights of the bishops.

In such a situation, the modern distinction between church and state was unknown. There was one Christian society within which bishops and kings functioned in distinct but complementary ways. There were quarrels among them, but they were not about church–state relations in the modern sense. They were about how to divide God-given power within a unified Christian society. In practice, kings with sufficient political power, as in Germany, were the senior partners in the cooperative arrangement. That was the way things had been for as long as anyone living in 1000 could remember, and all parties, including the bishops and popes, accepted it as legitimate.

In many places political reality in the tenth and eleventh centuries ran counter to the view that kings were the chief laymen in the church. In the confusion of the Carolingian decline, political power had fragmented and fallen into the hands of nobles and warriors, particularly in France and Italy. Lay rulers with titles such as duke or count exercised some degree of control over the bishops and abbots in their territory. Even minor lords, some of them mere soldiers, appointed and dismissed the priests of the private churches located on their estates. The power of such laymen was not legitimated by anointing or scripture. It was rooted in custom and in their willingness to use force to keep what they had seized. Where there was no strong king to control them, they often fought among themselves without regard for the sufferings of peasants or churchmen. Around 1000, peace movements emerged, particularly in south-western France. Under the leadership of bishops and abbots, these popular movements tried to limit violence by forcing nobles to swear on relics that they would not fight on certain holy days and seasons (the '**Truce of God**') and that they would not harm churches, peasants, women, clergy and other non-combatants (the '**Peace of God**'). But such efforts had only limited success in the political free-for-all that followed the Carolingian collapse. Since many clergymen were related to or appointed by the lay nobles, they took the system for granted, though they might regret its violence. But in 1000, a few intellectuals, generally bishops and abbots, criticised the power of these petty tyrants, though they had to live with it.

When a lay ruler in 1000 gave someone a position or property, he 'invested' him with it in a public ceremony. Because there was no sharp distinction between secular and church offices, churchmen also received their positions and lands by **investiture**. For instance, when a man had been chosen bishop, he would come before the king, kneel down and swear loyalty to him. The king then invested him with the office of bishop by handing him its symbols, which were the pastoral staff and ring. To onlookers it seemed that the king gave the man the bishopric, even though he then needed to be consecrated by other bishops in a religious ceremony. Other church positions were given in an analogous way, right down to the priest of a private church, who received the door keys or some other symbolic object from the local lord. Such public, visible investitures were a powerful expression of the dominance of lay rulers, particularly kings, in the life of the church. Such lay investiture was part of the normal state of affairs and provoked little controversy in 1000, though two generations later it was the object of bitter and successful attacks by reformers.

In spite of the theology of kingship, not all kings were equally effective. The French king, Robert II (996–1031), was politically, militarily and economically weak. Most of his kingdom was really ruled by dukes, counts and even lesser lords who had seized power for themselves. His authority was effective in a modest territory around Paris though even there he had to struggle to prevent local strongmen from ignoring him. But he had something no duke or count could claim: he was anointed with oil believed to be brought to Reims by an angel each time a new king was installed. Even at the French king's weakest, the church supported him because he was God's anointed ruler. In Anglo-Saxon England, King Aethelred II (978–1016) was also weak, distrusted by his great lords, and hard pressed by Danish invaders who finally triumphed under King Canute in 1016. Yet the Anglo-Saxon church supported Aethelred, perhaps because they had no place else to turn.

The most fully developed anointed or sacred kingship was in Germany, in the eastern portion of the old Frankish Empire, where the kings remained politically and economically strong. As noted earlier, Otto I (936–73) used the higher offices of the church as a major support for his regime. He also took seriously his responsibilities as protector and promoter of Christian society. He founded the archbishopric of Magdeburg (968) to spearhead the missionary effort among the peoples in eastern Europe. German missionaries, supported by the German Empire's diplomacy and armies, had considerable success in Poland, Bohemia and Hungary. When Otto went to Rome in 962 to be crowned emperor, he acted as a sacred king should by reforming the papacy, which had been mired in local politics. He presided over a synod of bishops that deposed Pope John XII, the man who had crowned him, and elected a successor. He confirmed papal possessions in Italy, but required all future popes to be elected with his consent and to swear loyalty to him and his successors. For 75 years, Otto's successors were the models of anointed kings, occasionally called vicars ('representatives') of Christ, dressed in royal robes that resembled bishops' vestments, depicted in art with symbols of religious majesty (see Figure 9), and in effective control of the church in their realm, including the papacy.

Figure 9 Coronation of Otto III
As with the image of Charlemagne (Figure 6), this manuscript illumination shows the
Emperor Otto III being crowned by the hand of God. But Otto III pushes his divine
connections further. We see the emperor seated in a mandorla, the almond-shape that
frames his throne. This is a convention usually reserved for Christ, as is the presence of the
Evangelists' symbols: the angel, lion, ox, and eagle, for Matthew, Mark, Luke, and John,
respectively. Notice, also, how the image depicts both secular and sacred powers (knights
and clergy) beneath the emperor.

Of course, some churchmen disapproved of crude abuses of ecclesiastical property and offices by laymen, such as the selling of offices, known as the sin of simony. Occasionally, there was tension when churchmen chastised individual kings who were notorious sinners in their personal lives. But fundamentally, the leaders of the church in the year 1000 accepted that it was God's will that kings defend and to some degree control the church, especially in the choice of its office-holders and the use of its possessions.

III. Church structures: the pope

In 1000, the western church also had a spiritual head, the bishop of Rome, who was honoured as the successor of the apostle Peter. The dignity of his office, the 'apostolic' bishopric, was unchallenged in the west. The popes of the tenth and early eleventh centuries were not activists who dealt frequently with the affairs of distant churches, but they had a functioning bureaucracy, archives, libraries, and an institutional memory that made them potentially more efficient than any other ruler in the west. Disputes about theology, liturgy and morality were referred to them in letters written in very respectful language. Churchmen who thought they had been treated unfairly at the local level appealed to the pope for a judgement. Pilgrims came to Rome for the sake of the relics and the liturgy. But in the year 1000, the pope's power was also limited. Pope Sylvester II (999–1003), a learned man who had briefly been tutor to the young emperor Otto III (983–1002), owed his position to the emperor's favour. His effective authority in no way matched his prestige and dignity. In particular, his power over church money and personnel outside central Italy was severely limited. Occasionally, he received appeals in disputes about elections, but he could not intervene at will. He was a figure of religious dignity, called on to bless and approve the initiatives of others but with little practical power. The popes of the early eleventh century did not oppose the dominance of kings within the church and they were not 'reformers' in any strong sense of that word. They accepted the world as it was.

IV. Church structures: the bishop

The bishops were the most important persons involved in the day-to-day running of churches. In 1000, there were approximately two hundred and fifty dioceses in the western church. They were especially thick on the ground in the areas near the Mediterranean that had been Christianised early. Virtually every town in the former Roman Empire, including very small ones, had its own bishop. In the fifth century, there had been a reaction against the indiscriminate creation of bishoprics, since the office seemed to be cheapened by the existence of impoverished, relatively ignorant bishops from little backwater villages. Tradition was powerful, however, and the little bishoprics survived (there were more than one hundred and eighty bishoprics in Italy, Sardinia and Corsica in the year 1000), but after the fifth century newly founded bishoprics were considerably larger and therefore fewer in number. In 1000 there were 17 dioceses in Anglo-Saxon England and only about 30 in Germany and eastern Europe between the Rivers Rhine and Elbe.

The basic procedures for choosing bishops had developed in the ancient church between the fourth and sixth centuries. Pope Leo I (440–61) described a proper election as one that took place in peace and calm. He thought that the clergy should take the lead in the choice, the local important people should give testimony to the candidate's fitness and the rest of the people should consent. No candidate should be imposed against the will of the local faithful. The metropolitan bishop of the province and his senior colleagues should ratify the local election and approve the fitness of the candidate before they ordained him. The radical change in circumstances brought about by the collapse of the western empire and the creation of Germanic kingdoms had undermined the workability of the old formal procedures, but their presence in the conservative canon law preserved an ideal that pleased eleventh-century reformers and had considerable influence on medieval practice.

The Roman imperial government had only a modest role in the choice of most bishops, who were the only elected persons in the late empire, which was otherwise a dictatorship in which appointment to office flowed down from the sacred emperor. The usual candidates were local clergy with seniority and the electors often chose a competent, experienced middle-aged priest or deacon who had worked his way up through the clerical offices of that diocese. It was very unusual to choose a cleric from outside the diocese or to choose a layman. Men who were already bishops were never supposed to move to another diocese. Sometimes, however, the people wanted a man outstanding for holiness and championed the candidacy of a monk. This was the case with Martin of Tours (371–97). Or they wanted a rich, powerful protector and supported the candidacy of a highborn man, who might even be a layman, as was the case of Ambrose of Milan (374–97). Neighbouring bishops, preferably three, supervised the election, attempted to mediate disputes, judged the bishop-elect on his suitability and laid hands on him to confer the Holy Spirit in the sacrament of ordination, also called consecration. Ambition to be a bishop was frowned on, but existed nonetheless. Conflicting interests and personal ambition could make the election a real contest, with violence a possibility. For example, serious rioting marked the election of Pope Damasus (366–84), and required the intervention of the civil authorities at Rome.

In the Germanic kingdoms of the early Middle Ages, the older procedures for electing bishops changed considerably. By Charlemagne's day, bishops owed their positions directly to the king, even when the formalities of election were carried out. By 1000, laymen chose and invested most bishops with their offices. In more or less orderly places such as the German kingdom, kings performed this investiture. In more politically fragmented regions, powerful local aristocrats did it. Where no single authority predominated, elections could be hotly, even violently, contested by candidates of opposing factions.

Canon law required that a bishop be at least 30 years old and sexually continent. A married man could be elected bishop, but he and his wife were expected to give up sexual intercourse. This was to avoid the bishop fathering children, who might threaten church property if their fathers used it to provide them with dowries or an inheritance. A married bishop's wife remained his wife, and he provided for her financial support, though preferably under someone else's roof. The requirement of **celibacy** on the part of the higher clergy (bishops, priests, deacons and eventually subdeacons) had been part of western canon law since the fourth century, though its enforcement varied. The disruptions of invasion, civil war and lay dominance during the late ninth and tenth centuries had not created favourable conditions for the observance of celibacy. In 1000, a bishop or priest with a wife or a concubine was not unusual.

A conscientious bishop (there were many) was a busy man. He had a whole range of religious duties, such as ordaining clergy; carrying out heavy liturgical obligations; consecrating altars, churches and liturgical objects; confirming new converts; and supervising the regular and secular clergy in his diocese. The property and rights of the bishop's church were a constant drain on his time and energy; he had to manage them and defend them at law against all claimants. One of the bishop's fundamental duties was to ensure the numbers and quality of the clergy who assisted him. That was a burdensome task in a society where schools were scarce. The clergy, who were quite numerous in a large diocese, were organised in a ladder-like hierarchy, with a succession of **holy orders** given at specified minimum ages. A boy could enter the clergy quite young through a simple ceremony of cutting his hair, called tonsure, which symbolised his commitment to God's service. Through successive ceremonies, he received the 'minor orders' of acolyte, exorcist, lector and doorkeeper, though it was possible to omit any or all of them, especially for older candidates. The minor orders placed no permanent commitment on the child, who decided at puberty whether to seek the major orders of subdeacon, deacon and priest, which committed him to lifelong celibacy. The bishop controlled admission to the senior ranks of the clergy, because only he could ordain men to the major orders.

Because of their wealth, education and aristocratic ties, bishops were also leading men in secular society. In many places, bishops had secular duties, either usurped by their predecessors in unsettled times or given to them by rulers who had few educated men at their disposal. For instance, the Ottonian rulers in Germany made some bishops into secular officials called counts, with fiscal, judicial and military duties. Bishops met regularly with their king or prince to advise him and to protect their interests. A bishop who offended his ruler and lost his favour was in a difficult position, since he might not receive the ruler's cooperation, which he needed to carry out his duties and to protect his church. Bishops were pillars of the established order of things and rarely questioned its legitimacy.

V. Church structures: the parish

There were many local churches in 1000 and their legal and economic relationships with one another and with the bishops were complex. Some churches had been founded by a bishop in the past and had been granted full rights to minister to the people of a defined area. They came closest to being parish churches in the modern sense: they had a theoretical monopoly on the religious services that the laity needed, including burial, the myriad traditional blessings, the mass, penance (though historians debate how common this was) and especially baptism. Such churches were sometimes called 'baptismal churches' because only they had a baptismal font in which new Christians were born. Christianity was not voluntary, as it is in the twenty-first century, and the baptismal churches collected legally enforceable tithes and fees from those dwelling within their boundaries.

Such was the ideal arrangement, but it had been overrun by historical developments. In 1000, the laity in fact received religious ministration in a bewildering variety of churches, which did not all stand on the same legal footing. The founding of churches by the rich and the pious was a respected activity that had gone on for centuries. The landscape was dotted with holy places, ranging from freestanding stone crosses to rough rural chapels, from little shrines to great stone monastic churches. They had not been founded according to any plan and gave rise to overlapping and conflicting claims. Virtually every movement and impulse in Christianity left a residue of churches. Hermits founded churches in remote places to serve their needs; churches were sometimes built to mark the burial place of a saint; wealthy persons founded churches in gratitude for cures, miracles or military victories; wealthy public sinners founded churches as part of their penance; villagers founded still others because there was no church in their remote or recently settled areas; lords had chapels in their castles; monasteries and nunneries had churches for their own services where their servants and dependants attended mass.

The most common origin of rural churches was foundation by a lord. Beginning in the ninth century, a growing population led to the clearing of land

and the creation of new rural settlements. In an age before easy transportation, many small villages or hamlets were too distant for their inhabitants to go every Sunday to the 'baptismal' church in whose territory they resided. For their convenience and his profit, the lord of the village might build a church, though the villagers still theoretically owed tithes to the baptismal church where they were required to take their infants for baptism. The lord's church, of which there were thousands in rural Europe, was a private church, owned by its founder. The Carolingian bishops resisted the development of private churches but could not stop it. The best they could arrange was a compromise between the lord's ownership and the needs of religion. They insisted that the private church have a permanent endowment of land that could not be taken away; that the priest of the private church be a free man or, if a serf, that he be freed before the bishop would ordain him; and that the lord and priest acknowledge the bishop's right to 'visit', that is, to inspect and supervise, the church. But within those requirements the lord could do almost anything he wished, including sell the church, subdivide its income into shares or give it as a dowry to his daughter. The lord appointed the priest and could remove him. Since the private church received no tithes, which were reserved for baptismal churches, the lord and his priest instituted fees for religious services. The lord gave the priest a share of the income, but in a good-sized village the church might be quite profitable to the lord, especially if he required his serfs to seek services and pay fees there. Private churches of every sort, particularly the lords' churches, encroached on the rights of the baptismal churches, since the lords wanted tithes and fees from their dependants. In the disrupted conditions of invasion and local warfare, many private churches simply usurped baptismal rights and tithes. The proliferation of churches meant that more people could easily receive religious services, but the overlapping jurisdiction of the churches also meant that there was much litigation over baptismal rights, tithes, fees for services and burial dues. It also meant that in 1000 the majority of churches were not under the direct control of the bishop but of a lay lord. The lay domination of the church was very evident in the villages of Europe.

The sources do not tell us as clearly as we would like what went on in the year 1000 in the thousands of rural churches. We do know some of the basic conditions in which ministry took place. The congregation was utterly illiterate and the priest was probably of peasant origin and poorly educated. The formal services were in Latin, though preaching (it is very unclear how much there was) might be in the vernacular. So far as we can tell, religious life centred on ceremony and liturgical prayer, of which there was a great deal. The model to be imitated was that of the bishop's cathedral church, where a group of clergy, called canons, carried out elaborate daily prayers. For instance, the morning mass in a cathedral was sung, and lasted perhaps two hours. In addition, the clergy of the bishop's church also performed the prayers of the canonical hours at intervals during the day. In parish churches, where there were fewer clergy and fewer resources, daily mass was probably normal in 1000. The local church also had prayer several times a day and celebrated saints' days, in imitation of the greater monastic and secular churches.

Communal and individual life at the parish level was structured around religious services, especially mass on Sunday, which was obligatory though attendance was difficult to enforce. The passage of time was measured by the annual round of saints' days and liturgical festivals, which were supposed to be observed as days without work and without sexual activity. The individual's life was built around the sacraments. Children born to a Christian family were baptised soon after birth, in a ceremony that admitted them both to the church and to society. Canon law said that a bishop should confirm each person, but that sacrament was less commonly received, in good part because bishops were distant figures. In 1000, the church did not have control of marriage, which was still in the hands of the couple's relatives, who celebrated the union with gifts, feasts, drinking and sexually oriented songs. Marrying couples had a choice whether to go to church for the priest's blessing. The church regarded marriage as an ordinance of God and tried to enforce complex rules about who could marry whom. Rituals and prayers surrounded serious illness, death and burial. There were also numerous liturgical ceremonies that were not performed at defined times but were used when they were needed, usually in connection with life's happy and sad times. God, angels, saints and demons were regarded as close by, constantly intervening in human life. Prayer and fasting were powerful tools to ward off evil and invite good. Consequently, there was a tendency to ask in liturgical prayers for God's blessing on every occasion and to seek his mercy for every calamity.

In a religious culture that placed a high value on liturgy and ceremony, what was the role of preaching? There was a great deal of preaching in monasteries and cathedral churches, but it was aimed at a very specialised audience: the monks and clergy of that community. Such preaching was in Latin, long winded, complicated, full of allegory and subtle biblical references. It suited an educated audience, but did not seem appropriate for a rural congregation or for an illiterate lord, his relatives or his knights. Some priests did occasionally paraphrase a Latin sermon in the vernacular for their parishioners, but such humble efforts were generally not thought worthy to be written down and so only scraps survive. A rare exception was in Anglo-Saxon England, where several translators, particularly the Benedictine abbot Aelfric (c.955–1010), created a large body of sermons in the native language for use by priests preaching to lay audiences. However, in continental Christianity, preaching in the language of the people was probably rare: at the parish level religion was more practised than understood.

VI. Church structures: religious houses

In 1000, the Benedictine form of monasticism was without rival in the west. The social and cultural importance of Benedictine monasticism was rooted in the high value that society placed upon liturgical prayer. Liturgy is worship that takes place in public, usually before a group, with a considerable degree of structure and fixity to it. The Episcopalian, Lutheran and Catholic eucharistic services are examples of liturgy in modern times, but there was a profusion of liturgical ceremonies in the Middle Ages, including such things as the sacraments, the monastic hours and even the anointing of kings. In the year 1000, no one questioned the notion that God was especially pleased by elaborate, devout and frequent liturgical prayer carried out with singing. As a consequence of that belief, the liturgy was the centre of formal religious practice from the humblest rural oratory to the large basilica of St Peter's in Rome. The desire to make the liturgy a beautiful, worthy offering to God absorbed much of the artistic and literary energy of society, as well as a good deal of its surplus wealth.

To perform the liturgy correctly required practice and learning. Centuries of development gave it a complexity that puzzles modern readers. Medieval clergy also needed at least one or two stout books to do it right. The liturgical services were in Latin, generally sung or chanted, and were basically a mosaic made up of words, phrases and passages from the Bible. There was a daily liturgy in most churches, consisting of mass and public prayer at fixed hours of the day. Since it would have been boring to repeat the same thing every day, parts of the daily liturgy, particularly scripture readings, prayers and hymns, changed according to a yearly cycle built around the religious feasts of Christmas, Easter and Pentecost. In addition, festivals in honour of saints were celebrated on particular dates throughout the year and a special service for the saint's day might be composed to honour the saint and tell his or her story. The complexity of the liturgy was increased by the fact that local areas honoured their special saints in addition to universal ones such as the Virgin Mary or Peter, and different kinds of churches carried out the liturgy in different ways.

Liturgical prayer was an activity of all churches, but monasteries and nunneries were specialists in liturgy, which Saint Benedict's *Rule* called 'the work of God' (*opus Dei*). Regular public prayer, especially prayers interceding with God for sinners, was a main reason why monasteries existed and why lay people and secular clerics gave them a considerable portion of society's wealth. The other occupations in which monasteries engaged, such as hospitality to travellers, management of their estates, copying of manuscripts and occasional preaching to lay people, were incidental to their main purpose, the continuous worship of God through liturgical prayer. In the monasteries, the entire day was marked out by periods of prayer, called the 'hours', whose time of day varied according to the seasons and the amount of daylight. There was much variety, but the daily pattern of prayer in one place can be reconstructed from the *Regularis Concordia*, a Benedictine document from tenth-century England. In the winter the monks rose at about 2:30 a.m. for nocturns and then celebrated matins at 6 a.m., prime at 6:45 a.m., terce at 8 a.m., sext at noon, none at 1.30 p.m., vespers at about 4:15 p.m. and compline at 6:15 p.m. Then they went to bed. The monks also offered masses on behalf of the community and its benefactors. Their intercession with God was highly valued.

We cannot overstress the importance of monasteries in religious life in the year 1000. The life of monks, particularly their chastity, fasting, self-denial and praying, was thought to make them more acceptable to God. Good monks and nuns received high praise from contemporaries, who often thought they lived the most holy form of life accessible to human beings on earth. For centuries, the canon law and popular pressure had slowly monasticised the lifestyle of the secular clergy: they too were expected to be celibate, to wear distinctive clothes, to say the daily hours, all of which were originally monastic practices. Even so, the secular clergy were often compared unfavourably to the regular clergy. The involvement of bishops and parish priests with the world meant that people did not think of them, as a group, as being equal to monks in holiness.

A key to monasticism's social importance and, indeed, to an understanding of medieval Christianity in general, is a firm appreciation of the central conviction that the prayers of one person could benefit another person, that the good deeds of one person could be shared with another. The individualism so strong in some forms of modern Christianity would have been out of place in the year 1000. Instead, the emphasis was on a sense of belonging to a group, conceived as the people of God or the church. The efforts of the group could compensate for the failings and sins of its individual members. In simplest terms, Christians could pray for one another, whether living or dead, and God would listen.

Because lay people's lives contrasted with everything the monks valued, many of them felt inferior: they were not celibate and even within marriage sex was thought to have a taint of uncleanness about it; many of society's leaders were men of violence in a violent world; all laymen were enmeshed in the need to earn a living, which smacked of greed, envy and pride. Living such a life, they feared that they could not please God, whose biblical description as the Just Judge who would make men answer for every idle word (Matt. 12:36) was terrifying to contemporaries. They were not without hope, however, for they believed fervently that holy humans, living and dead, could intercede for them with God. The fervour for saints and their relics was rooted in the belief that the holy men and women of the past, who were now before God's throne, could obtain mercy for sinners. Priests and bishops also interceded with God in liturgical prayer for their people. But the simony, ignorance and sexual behaviour of some of the secular clergy were always in the background, detracting from people's full confidence in their holiness.

In 1000, the best living intercessors were usually thought to be monks and nuns. Lay people looked to monks and nuns to compensate by their prayers and personal sacrifices for the inadequacies of ordinary Christians. The wealthy founded monasteries in which the monks commemorated their names, often daily, in their liturgical prayers. These prayers acted as a penance for the sins of the world, especially for those benefactors who could not possibly do enough penance themselves for the sins they had committed. This was particularly true for members of the military aristocracy who found themselves guilty of killing. Other lay people (and many secular clergy too) gave to monastic houses so that monks and nuns would pray for them, or, as the documents reporting the gifts expressed it, so that they could 'share' in the prayers, fasting, sexual abstinence and other good works of the religious. They particularly wanted to be remembered each year on the anniversary of their death. The great flowering of monasticism cannot be understood without a realisation that monks provided a valued social service: intercessory prayer for their patrons and for society itself.

VII. Church structures: the dissenters

In 1000, the Christian church in the west was firmly in place and expanding along its eastern and northern borders. In a violent and disorderly society, the dominant values in religion, as represented in a good monastery or in the sacred monarchy in Germany, were order and stability. However, there were dissenters from those views in 1000, unimportant in their own day but with an important future as society grew richer and more sophisticated.

The first group of dissenters were those monks who sought a stricter life, which usually meant greater physical hardship and more isolation from the world. Benedictine monasticism was no holiday on a tropical island, but it did favour a moderate form of asceticism: a plain but adequate vegetarian diet, sufficient but not excessive sleep, and simple but adequate clothes. In Benedictine monasteries, the individual was part of a group and personal oddities were discouraged; the monk was expected to conform to the routine of the house in such matters as prayer, diet and clothing. Despite a desire for separation from the world, the Benedictine monastery as a corporate body had many social roles: its abbot was a leader in society; the monastery often provided a destination for pilgrims, hospitality to travellers, charity to the poor, prayer for benefactors and education for the young. Because monasteries owned agricultural property, some monks devoted much energy to the management of estates and economic interests. Although the monks were individually poor, many monasteries were rich by the standards of their society.

The memory of a fiercer, more individualistic monasticism had survived in literary texts that originated in Egypt and the Near East as long ago as the fourth century. Here and there in the eleventh century, some individuals adopted the hermit's life in imitation of the Egyptian desert fathers of the fourth and fifth centuries or in imitation of John the Baptist, who had lived in the desert clothed in camel skins and eating a diet of locusts and wild honey (Matt. 3:4). They were consciously or unconsciously rejecting the Benedictine tradition of orderly, moderate, group life and choosing the rigours of a life in solitude, severe physical deprivation, real personal poverty and a more individualistic religious style. Their challenge to the Benedictine monastic establishment was just a tiny voice in the eleventh century, but it grew louder in the twelfth, thirteenth and fourteenth centuries as more people, both lay-men and clergy, sought in a bewildering variety of ways to find a more intense personal religious life.

The second group of dissenters, also few in number and quite powerless in 1000, were those who consciously rejected some important Christian belief or beliefs. These were called heretics. Ancient Christianity had been split many times by fierce quarrels engaging all levels of society over such matters as the nature of Christ or of the Trinity. Byzantine Christianity had continued that tradition of religious argument in the struggles during the eighth and ninth centuries over the use of religious pictures called icons. However, even in antiquity, the western Latin-speaking churches had been less prone than the Greek-speaking eastern churches to argue the finer points of theology. As political and economic conditions deteriorated in the west, conservatism in theology became ever more pronounced, perhaps as a defence mechanism or simply as a reflection of declining standards of education. In any case, between the sixth and the eleventh centuries, religious dissent was rare in the west, involving few people and almost never with a significant popular following.

Some dissent grew out of tendencies latent in Christianity itself. The Christian church had always harboured ambivalent attitudes toward the created world: it was good because God had created it, but it was saturated with sin because of Adam's Fall. The church had valued the spiritual aspects of life more than the material, but it had not condemned the latter outright. Some religious dissenters rejected such ambiguity and declared the material world evil, the product of, or at least under the control of, an evil being such as Satan. They recommended that their followers escape from the world by rigorous practices, including celibacy, vegetarianism and poverty, practices which in the larger church were thought appropriate for monks and nuns, but not for everyone else. The first hints of the re-emergence of heresy that attracted significant numbers of followers appeared in the eleventh century, although they were scattered and not easy to categorise. For example, the chronicler Ademar of Chabannes (*c.*988–1034) claimed that a dualist group known as Manichees were active in Aquitaine in the early eleventh century. Dualists emphasised more than the church the dichotomy between good and evil, spirit and matter, soul and body. Some historians have accepted Ademar's report as fact. Others have questioned whether the word Manichee was nothing more than a generic term for heretic, that is, they may have been heretics, but not necessarily dualists.

Other dissenters thought that every Christian should imitate the life of the apostles as it is described in the New Testament: wandering without a fixed residence, preaching, barefoot and self-denying. They too recommended to their followers a monk-like lifestyle, but carried out in the world rather than in a monastery. Such people were not necessarily heretics, but their views did implicitly or explicitly criticise simoniacal priests, princely bishops and wealthy houses of Benedictine monks. They, like the heretics, were unimportant in 1000, but their views grew in popularity in subsequent centuries.

A third group of dissenters, orthodox in their beliefs but intensely dissatisfied with the prevailing situation, had more immediate success – indeed they captured the leadership of the church by the mid-eleventh century. They were the reformers who attacked and eventually overturned the traditional pattern of a loose, decentralised church dominated by laymen. They were particularly opposed to the buying and selling of church offices, the marriage of the clergy and the abusive dominance of powerful laymen in the church. They favoured the application of the canon law on such matters as church elections and the moral purification of the clergy. They saw in the growth of papal power a means to those ends. Unlike the hermits and the heretics, the reformers had an immediate influence on the eleventh-century church and it is to them that we turn in Chapter 10.

Suggested reading

Companion website
www.routledge.com/cw/lynch

9.1   The Peace and Truce of God
'Peace of God, proclaimed in the Synod Of Charroux' (989), 'Peace Of God, proclaimed by Guy of Anjou, Bishop of Puy' (990), 'Truce of God, made for the Archbishopric of Arles' (1035–41), 'Truce Of God For The Archbishoprics of Besancox And Vienne' (ca, 1041), 'Truce for the Bishopric of Terouanne' (1063), in Oliver J. Thatcher and Edgar H. McNeal, eds., *A Source Book for Medieval History: Selected Documents Illustrating the History of Europe in the Middle Age* (New York: Charles Scribner's Sons, 1907), 412–418.

9.2   Pope Leo the Great on the election of bishops

'Leo the Great, excerpts from Letter XIV', in Philip Schaff and Henry Wace, eds., *A Select Library of Nicene and Post Nicene Fathers of the Christian Church*, 2nd series, volume 12 (New York: The Christian Literature Company, 1895), 18.

Primary sources

Aelfric, *The Homilies of the Anglo-Saxon Church; the first part, containing the Sermones catholici, or Homilies of Aelfric, in the original Anglo-Saxon, with an English version*, edited by Benjamin Thorpe, 2 vols (London, 1844–6)

The Lives of the Ninth-Century Popes (Liber Pontificalis): The Ancient Biographies of Ten Popes from A.D. 817–891, translated with an introduction and commentary by Raymond Davis (Liverpool, 1995)

Peters, Edward, editor and translator, *Heresy and Authority in Medieval Europe* (Philadelphia, 1980)

Regularis concordia, edited and translated by Thomas Symons, *The Monastic Agreement of the Monks and Nuns of the English Nation* (London, 1953)

Silvester II, *The Letters of Gerbert, with his Papal Privileges as Sylvester II*, translated by Harriet Lattin, Columbia Records of Civilization, 60 (New York, 1961)

Modern scholarship

Bak, János M., editor, *Coronations: Medieval and Early Modern Monarchic Ritual* (Los Angeles, 1990)

Barraclough, Geoffrey, *The Crucible of Europe: The Ninth and Tenth Centuries in European History* (Berkeley, 1976)

Bloch, Marc, *The Royal Touch: Sacred Monarchy and Scrofula in England and France*, translated by J. E. Anderson (London, 1973)

Canning, Joseph, *A History of Medieval Political Thought, 300–1450* (Abingdon, 1996)

Coleman, Janet, *A History of Political Thought from the Middle Ages to the Renaissance* (Malden, Massachusetts, 2000)

Cowdrey, H. E., 'The Peace and Truce of God in the Eleventh Century', *Past and Present* 46 (1970), pp. 42-67

Duckett, Eleanor Shipley, *Death and Life in the Tenth Century* (Ann Arbor, Michigan, 1967)

Fichtenau, Heinrich, *Living in the Tenth Century. Mentalities and Social Order*, translated by Patrick Geary (Chicago, 1991)

Focillon, Henri, *The Year 1000*, translated by Fred D. Wieck (New York, 1969)

Frassetto, Michael, editor, *Heresy and the Persecuting Society in the Middle Ages: Essays on the Work of R.I. Moore* (Leiden and Boston, 2006)

Head, Thomas, *The Peace of God: Social Violence and Religious Response in France around the Year 1000* (Ithaca, New York, 1992)

Johnson, Penelope D., *Prayer, Patronage and Power. The Abbey of La Trinité, Vendôme, 1032–1187* (New York, 1981)

Kern, Fritz, *Kingship and Law in the Middle Ages*, translated by S. B. Chrimes (Oxford, 1948)

Klauser, Theodor, *A Short History of the Western Liturgy*, 2nd edition, translated by John Halliburton (Oxford, 1979), pp. 45–93

Lambert, Malcolm, *Medieval Heresy. Popular Movements from Bogomil to Hus* (London, 1977)

Leclercq, Jean, *The Love of Learning and the Desire for God*, translated by Catharine Misrahi (New York, 1961)

Leyser, Henrietta, *Hermits and the New Monasticism. A Study of Religious Communities in Western Europe, 1000–1150* (New York, 1984), pp. 1–37

Lynch, John E., 'Marriage and Celibacy of the Clergy: The Discipline of the Western Church: an Historico-canonical Synopsis', *Jurist* 32 (1971), 14–38 and 189–212

Moore, Robert I., *The Origins of European Dissent* (New York, 1977)

Russell, Jeffrey Burton, *Dissent and Reform in the Early Middle Ages* (Berkeley, 1965)

Stutz, Ulrich, 'The Proprietary Church as an Element of Medieval Germanic Ecclesiastical Law', *Mediaeval Germany*, edited by Geoffrey Barraclough (Oxford, 1938), II, pp. 35–70

Ullmann, Walter, *Medieval Political Thought* (Harmondsworth, Middlesex, 1970)

Van Engen, John, 'The "Crisis of Cenobitism" Reconsidered: Benedictine Monasticism in the Years 1050–1150', *Speculum* 61 (1980), pp. 269–304

10

The eleventh-century reforms

Sacred kingship functioned well in the German Empire during the reign of the serious young king Henry III (1039–56). He was 22 years old when he succeeded his illiterate and brutal father, Conrad II (1024–39). Like his predecessors, Henry depended on the resources of the church to rule his kingdom and he exercised his right to appoint bishops and abbots. However, he was personally pious and conscientious in choosing suitable men for church offices. He favoured monastic reform in his realm and he encouraged the moral reform of the secular clergy. After surviving an illness, he refused to commit simony by taking payments from bishops and abbots, but he did not abandon the traditional right to invest churchmen with the symbols of their offices.

I. The Synod of Sutri

Henry III demonstrated his power during a disputed election to the bishopric of Rome. Pope Benedict IX (1032–44) was the son of a central Italian count who had thrust him into the papacy. He may have been as young as 18 when he assumed the papal throne. Benedict was harsh and immoral – his critics accused him of adultery and even murder. In 1044 a revolt in Rome led to the election of a rival pope, Sylvester III (1045). But Benedict's kinsmen drove out the new pope and restored him to power. After a short time returned in office, Benedict decided he wanted to marry and sold the office of pope to the archpriest John Gratian, who became Pope Gregory VI (1045–6). Gregory was a reformer who was willing, ironically, to commit simony to remove the scandalous Benedict. Then in 1046, Benedict IX reneged on his sale of the office to Gregory VI and attempted to become pope again, even though the rest of the church continued to recognise Gregory as the true pope. Then Sylvester III showed up again, reclaiming the papacy, so that in 1046 there were three men with claims to be bishop of Rome.

Quarrels about elections to bishoprics were not unusual, but this one was troubling because of the particular church involved and because there seemed to be no end in sight. Following the precedent of his great predecessor Otto I, Henry III came to Italy to restore order in Rome, the chief bishopric of his empire and of the entire church. In 1046 at Sutri, just outside Rome, he met in council with local bishops and the German bishops whom he had brought with him. The Council of Sutri was the high-water mark of sacred kingship, where the German emperor sat in judgement on the pope. The three men who had some claim to be pope (Benedict, Sylvester and Gregory) were deposed. Over the next three years, Henry appointed three respectable, moderate reformers to the papacy. The first was a Saxon noble, Bishop Suidger of Bamberg, who reigned briefly as Clement II (1046-7). Clement was succeeded by Henry's nominee Bishop Poppo of Brixen, who reigned as Damasus II (1047-8), who had to struggle against Benedict IX's third attempt to retake the papacy. In 1048, Henry III appointed a third candidate, his relative Bishop Bruno of Toul, who reigned as Leo IX (1049-56). In view of later struggles between the reformed papacy and Henry III's son, Henry IV (1056-1106), it is ironic to note that the papacy was put into the hands of reformers by Henry III, who had acted as a Christian king was supposed to act, protecting the church even against itself.

II. Moderate reform

Leo IX's pontificate marked a decisive moment in the history of the western church, since it allied the papacy firmly with the reformers, who had earlier worked in scattered centres with only occasional support from the popes. Leo also began the transformation of the papacy into an active force in church affairs. Since he was a relative of Henry III and owed his position to him, Leo was no radical demanding a massive transformation of society. He accepted the basic validity of sacred kingship, and he did not challenge the king's right to appoint high churchmen. What he and reformers like him wanted was primarily a moral reform of the clergy. They thought that if lay rulers could be convinced to use their authority to appoint good men it would hasten the reform.

Moderate reformers like Leo held the papacy from 1049 until 1073. They sought to cooperate with lay rulers in a moral reform of the clergy, no easy task since it challenged traditional ways and vested interests. In general the reformers wanted the clergy to live by the canon law. They stressed particularly that the clergy be celibate and that they avoid demanding or paying a price for holy orders or church offices (simony). They suggested rather timidly that lay rulers should not give churchmen the symbols of their offices, but they did not dare to forbid lay investiture or the existence of private churches.

Once the reformers had gained control of the papacy, they used its prestige and authority to promote their cause. No reigning pope had been north of the Alps in 250 years, but Leo IX travelled energetically in the interests of reform. At councils in southern Italy, France and Germany, to which he summoned the leading clergy of the region, Leo issued reforming decrees and exercised power to investigate and correct the wayward. For instance, in a dramatic confrontation at Reims in 1049, he had the body of Saint Remigius, the sixth-century bishop who had baptised the Frankish King Clovis, placed on the high altar of the cathedral. Each bishop and abbot present had to declare with his hand on the saint's relics that he had not committed simony to obtain his office. Two bishops, who confessed that their families had purchased their positions for them, were deposed and then reinstated by Pope Leo. The archbishop of Reims was summoned to Rome to explain his situation. A bishop who fled at night was excommunicated and one bishop was actually deposed. All over Latin Europe, two quite new things were happening. Upper clergy and highborn laymen were being compelled in large numbers to question the contemporary state of affairs in the church, and the formerly sleepy institution of the papacy was now leading a vigorous reform movement.

Leo IX also transformed the personnel of the papal court. His greatest impact was on the cardinals. Rome was a city filled with churches and, as the bishop of the city, the pope had a crushing burden of processions, masses, blessings and other liturgical services. Since the sixth century, popes had shared that burden with the underemployed bishops of seven little towns around Rome (Ostia, Porto, Silva Candida, Albano, Sabina, Tusculum and Palestrina). These men, called cardinal-bishops, substituted for the pope at liturgical functions and by a natural process became his advisers and helpers in other matters. The popes also drew on the administrative and liturgical services of other leading churchmen in the city of Rome itself, some of whom were priests and some deacons. The cardinal-bishops, cardinal-priests and cardinal-deacons (there were about forty of them in the second half of the eleventh century) were also important in the election of popes; in fact it was from their ranks that popes were often chosen. Traditionally the cardinals had been Romans and central Italians. Leo IX internationalised the cardinalate by appointing eminent foreigners who shared his reforming views. They in turn travelled around Christian Europe, summoning councils in the pope's name and promoting reform at the regional and local level. As a result of the activism of reforming popes and cardinals, the authority of the papacy was felt in places where it had never been exercised before.

The moderate reformers began with high hopes, but were soon frustrated by the difficulties of gaining lasting moral reform. The practices that they opposed had a long history behind them: in some places married clergy, simony and lay investiture had been the normal ways of doing things for at least two centuries. Many lay rulers depended on the money they received for appointing clergy. Other lay rulers, including the German kings/emperors, depended on the support of loyal church appointees for their power to control the lay nobility. Simony went on, but most disapproved of it. Simoniacal deals were often struck in private. It was generally accepted that monks living in a community should be celibate, but some contemporaries saw the imposition of celibacy on secular clergy as a more complicated matter. A distinction needs to be made between a priest who visited prostitutes and one who was married. No one defended the former priest, but some people did defend the respectably married rural priest. Married priests, their wives and their wives' relatives certainly did not see the woman as the whore that the reformers said she was. When in 1072 the archbishop of Rouen attempted to punish married canons in his cathedral, he was stoned and barely escaped alive. In many places the clergy resisted (actively and passively) the attempts to force them to put away their wives. Successful moral reform, which included both simony-free choices of clergy and a celibate clergy, was slow in coming. It depended on the good will of local lay rulers, and if an unfavourable ruler succeeded a favourable one, the old ways could well return.

III. Radical reform

Among the reformers, a more radical wing took shape, which argued that moral reform would not happen as long as powerful lay people dominated the clergy. Cardinal Humbert of Silva Candida (1049-61), a northerner from Lorraine well educated in canon law, was the chief spokesman for the radical reformers. Humbert wrote a work called *Three Books Against Simoniacs* (1058), which attacked not only abuses but also the system of lay control, which was symbolised by laymen investing bishops with their pastoral staff and ring. He argued that lay domination made moral and financial abuses among the clergy inevitable and he called for its abolition. For a generation, the more radical reformers were unable to put their views into practice, though they held a firm minority position within the circles of the reformed papacy. The situation shifted in their favour in 1056, when the German emperor Henry III died unexpectedly at the age of 39, leaving a 6-year-old son, Henry IV (1056-1106), as his heir. The rule of a young child weakened the German monarchy and reduced its influence in far-off Rome.

In the new circumstances, the radical reformers grew bolder. Their key desire was that high clergy be chosen by election according to the canons. In 1059, Pope Nicholas II (1059-61) issued a procedure for elections that changed the way popes were chosen. He gave the choice to the seven cardinal-bishops in consultation with the cardinal-priests. When the cardinal-deacons were later included, the election was in the hands of the College of Cardinals, as it still is today. Nicholas consciously eliminated the influence of the German king, who was notified only *after* the election that a pope had been chosen. The boy-king was in no position to stop them. While Henry IV was a minor, two popes were elected in the new way, thus setting a precedent that seriously reduced the king's power.

Henry IV assumed personal rule in 1071, when he was 21 years old. During the years of his long minority, the nobility in Germany had weakened the strong monarchy of his father and grandfather. The young king resolved to recover what he thought were his traditional rights. But he needed firm control of the church if he were to have the money and soldiers to carry out his plans. His political needs ran directly counter to the aspirations of the papal reform party. The clash with the reforming papacy came over the archbishopric of Milan, which was among the largest and richest cities in the German Empire. At Milan in 1072 there was a disputed election between a reform candidate and a more traditional candidate. Henry exercised his right to appoint. Pope Alexander II (1061–73) intervened in favour of a different candidate. Each side saw the struggle as crucial to its future and refused to back down. Alexander II excommunicated Henry's advisers for simony, but not the king himself, since he hoped that the young man, who was only 23, could be brought around. In the midst of the quarrel, Alexander died and an adherent of more radical reforming views was elected pope.

IV. Pope Gregory VII

Upon his election, Hildebrand, the cardinal-archdeacon of the Roman church, chose the name Gregory VII (1073–85). He had served the Roman church for 25 years in many ways: as a cardinal, as a travelling legate and as the archdeacon, who was the chief financial officer of the Roman church. He was an intense man, devoted to Saint Peter's rights as prince of the apostles and head of the church. He was fiercely committed to the view that, in the right order of things, the spiritual would dominate the material, and the Roman church, St Peter's church, would provide leadership as the head of all other churches and of Christian society itself. Even to contemporaries he was a controversial figure. In the heat of the struggle, 26 bishops of the German Empire agreed with their king that Gregory VII was 'not pope but a false monk' and called on him to resign. Cardinal Peter Damian, a long-time collaborator of Gregory but an advocate of moderate reform, once called him a 'holy Satan'.

Gregory intensified the campaign for moral reform of the clergy. For instance, he called upon lay people to refuse to accept ministrations from priests whom they knew to be simoniacs or sexual sinners. In an eleventh-century context this was a very radical idea: that the ordinary laity should judge the worthiness of their clergy. He added to the call for moral reform a direct challenge to sacred kingship. Like Cardinal Humbert, he was convinced that lay power over the clergy lay at the root of the many problems of the church. He insisted that all clergy be chosen according to the canons, which in practice meant that clergy should be chosen by other clergy, not by laymen. In 1075, Gregory struck at the most visible act of lay control by being the first pope to forbid the clergy from accepting investiture into office from a layman. He also put forward a theological argument that the clergy, headed by the pope, were superior to kings and other lay powers, whose role was to carry out the clergy's directions. In a long letter to his supporter, Bishop Hermann of Metz, Gregory attacked sacred kingship directly:

> Shouldn't an office [i.e. kingship] instituted by secular men, who did not even know God, be subject to that office [i.e. the pope] which the providence of Almighty God has instituted for his own honour and has compassionately given to the world? God's Son, even as he is without doubt believed to be God and man, is also considered the highest priest, sitting at the right hand of the Father and always interceding for us. He despised a secular kingdom, over which the men of this world swell with pride, and came of his own will to the priesthood of the cross. Who does not know that kings and dukes have their origin from men who were ignorant of God, and who, by pride, robberies, treacheries, murders – in short by almost every crime – at the prompting of the devil, who is the prince of this world, struggled with blind greed and intolerable presumption to dominate their equals, that is, their fellow men? To whom, indeed, can we better compare those who struggle to make the priests of God bow at their feet, than to him who is chief of all the sons of pride [i.e. Satan] and who tempted [Christ] the highest Pontiff himself, the chief of priests, the Son of the Most High, and promised him all the kingdoms of the world, saying, 'All these I will give to you, if you will fall down and worship me'? Who doubts that the priests of Christ should be regarded as the fathers and teachers of kings and princes, and of all the faithful? Isn't it seen to be wretched insanity if the son tries to subdue the father or if the pupil tries to subdue the teacher and tries to subject him to his power by wicked bonds?[1]

Such views were quite radical on a theoretical level. On a practical level Henry IV could not accept them since his power over the nobility of his empire depended on control of the resources of the church. The two camps waged a furious battle of words, expressed in councils, letters and pamphlets. Opponents ransacked the scriptures, the fathers and the canon law for authoritative texts and arguments to use against one another. This was the first complicated intellectual battle in medieval history in which the issues roused widespread passions. Words were not the only weapons. Military force was always a possibility, since Henry IV had a powerful army at his command and Gregory had almost no soldiers. But Henry also had many opponents, including German nobles, Italian princes and cities, and the Normans of south Italy, who supported Pope Gregory VII to thwart their enemy, King Henry.

There were other kings in Europe, particularly William the Conqueror (1066-87) in England and Philip I (1060-1108) in France, who controlled the church in their kingdoms in so far as they could. Gregory decided that he could not afford to attack them while he was embroiled with Henry IV.

King William and his adviser, Archbishop Lanfranc of Canterbury, tightly controlled the church in England. But since they appointed suitable men to be bishops and abbots and were in favour of the moral reform of the clergy as long as it did not decrease the king's power, Gregory avoided a direct challenge to William's power. Philip I was a different case. He was a simoniac who sold church offices, but his effective control of the church was weak since the aristocracy held most of the power in the kingdom of France. Gregory apparently saw no pressing need to confront him vigorously.

At first glance, the military advantage lay with Henry IV, whose resources dwarfed those of Gregory. In Italy, Gregory had the support of Matilda, the countess of Tuscany, and of the Norman adventurers, descendants of Vikings, who were carving out principalities for themselves in southern Italy at the expense of the Muslims and the Byzantines. However, the real key to Gregory's strength lay in Germany itself. While Henry IV was a minor, the German nobility had grown used to a weak king, and they did not wish for the return of a strong one. When the quarrel between Henry and Gregory grew heated, most of the German bishops stood with the king, but many lay nobles sided with the pope in order to prevent the king from regaining power over them.

In 1076, Gregory did what no pope had ever done. In response to Henry's attempt to depose him at a synod of imperial bishops, Gregory excommunicated Henry IV and deposed him from his office as king. In a Christian society, where social bonds were imbued with religious meaning, an excommunicated king could not function. In theory, and to some degree in practice, no Christian was to have contact with him. Henry's political enemies seized the opportunity and a rebellion centred in Saxony broke out against him. When his situation grew desperate, he took a bold move. In January 1077, Henry went to Italy dressed as a pilgrim and appeared before the castle of Canossa in northern Tuscany, where Gregory was residing. (See Figure 10.)

Canossa was the ancestral home of Matilda, Countess of Tuscany. Matilda had been married to the Duke of Lorraine, a man named Godfrey the Hunchback, who supported the emperor's cause, even as Matilda threw her support behind the papacy. In 1076, Godfrey's death left Matilda in control of considerable lands in Lorraine, as well as northern Italy. Matilda's relationship with Gregory VII was complicated. A recent biography of the countess has even suggested that she and the pope were lovers. In our own time, we have seen clergy of various denominations preaching high moral standards, yet acting quite differently in their private lives. A sexual affair involving a pope who advocated for clerical celibacy would make for a juicy scandal, yet even Matilda's biographer admits there is only circumstantial evidence for this claim. Whatever the details of their relationship, Matilda was a tireless supporter of Gregory and the reform cause. In 1077, she willed all of her lands to the pope, which would give him considerable resources, and a buffer zone

Figure 10 Encounter at Canossa
This image from the *Vita Mathildis* ('Life of Matilda') shows the Holy Roman Emperor, Henry
IV, kneeling before the Countess Matilda of Tuscany, seated under the arch. Behind Henry IV,
Hugh, the abbot of Cluny, holding a crozier, appears to be discussing matters with Matilda.
The Latin text, 'Rex rogat abbatem, Mathildim supplicat atq[ue]' ('The king entreats the
abbot, and also asks humbly of Mathilda') describes Henry's request of Matilda to intervene
on his behalf in his conflict with Pope Gregory VII.

between Rome and Henry's empire north of the Alps. Matilda often commanded her own armies in the pope's defence against the emperor in the
many battles that followed Henry's coming to Canossa.

Barefoot and in a nightshirt, Henry IV came on three successive days to
ask for reconciliation with the pope. In spite of Gregory's suspicions about
the sincerity of Henry's repentance, he finally consented to a conditional

reconciliation: Gregory would lift the **excommunication** but reserved the right to judge Henry at a future date. It looked as if the pope had won, but when news of the reconciliation reached Germany, the rebellion collapsed and within two years Henry was again firmly in charge. The issue of control of the church had not changed just because Henry had been temporarily reconciled with Gregory. The men continued to confront each other with sincerely, indeed desperately, held views of what was right. In 1080, conflict broke out again. Gregory VII excommunicated Henry IV again, but this failed to topple the king a second time. Henry invaded Italy and besieged Rome for three years. In 1084, he installed the cleric Guibert of Ravenna (*c.*1029–1100) as Pope Clement III – an 'anti-pope' to Gregory VII – who crowned Henry as Holy Roman Emperor. Gregory, still the legitimate pope, took refuge in Castel Sant'Angelo, the mausoleum of the Roman Emperor Hadrian, located in the centre of the city. Gregory's south Italian, Norman vassal, Robert Guiscard, rescued him, and caused Henry IV and his anti-pope to flee Rome. As the emperor headed north with his troops, engaging Matilda's forces, he took revenge on the countess for her support of Gregory by laying waste to her Tuscan holdings. Meanwhile, back in Rome, Robert Guiscard's Norman soldiers sacked the holy city, forcing Pope Gregory himself to flee to Salerno, where he died in 1085.

Even though Henry appointed a pope (Clement III), as Otto I and Henry III had done before him, the papacy had broken free from lay control. The reformers elected their own popes (Victor III, Urban II and Paschal II), who were accepted by the rest of the church. Henry IV struggled until his death in 1106 to win back secular and religious power in Germany, but he failed. In 1122, Pope Calixtus II (1119–24) arranged a treaty with Henry V (1106–25), called the Concordat of Worms. After 50 years of struggle, the matter of lay investiture ended in a compromise. The king agreed not to invest churchmen with the symbols of their offices and he permitted canonical election. In the German kingdom, where the king had to have some say in the appointment of important churchmen if he was to remain in power, he was permitted to be present at the election of bishops and abbots (where he could exercise influence), but the electors were technically free. After the person was elected, the king could invest him with his secular offices and properties, called the *regalia*, by touching him with his sceptre, but it was clear from the symbolism that he was not investing him with his spiritual office, which was conferred by the bishops who consecrated him. The German emperor was also the ruler of the kingdom of Burgundy and of much of northern and central Italy. In those regions, Henry V agreed that the bishops were to be elected canonically and within six months were to be invested with their temporal rights and properties by the king. In England, France and elsewhere, similar compromises had been reached in the first decades of the twelfth century. The lay ruler's power in the church was not abolished, but the right of canonical election limited that power, as did the right of appeal to the pope, who had the last word in disputed elections.

V. The consequences of reform

The outcome of the papal reform movement of the eleventh century is complex. There were two distinct issues at stake: who was to control Christian society? And who was to control the church? The answers to the questions were not the same.

In society as a whole, there was a shift, though by no means an avalanche, of power in favour of the spiritual over the temporal. The distinction between the sacred and the secular was sharpened to the advantage of the church, since spiritual things were acknowledged to be superior to secular ones. The attack on sacred kingship was successful: kings were recognised to be laymen and as such were in theory answerable to the clergy in religious matters, as all laymen were. The prestige of the papacy increased steadily in the century and a half after the pontificate of Leo IX. The popes benefited from the growing sense among laity and clergy that they belonged to a corporate body of Christians, increasingly called Christendom, which transcended politics and language. The pope was acknowledged to be the head of Christendom. For example, since the **crusades** were the armies of Christendom rather than of any particular kingdom, the popes took the lead in summoning and organising them – Pope Urban II called the First Crusade – though popes left actual military command to lay rulers.

However, on issues affecting the political and economic interests of lay rulers, compromise was the rule. Kings were forced to relax their iron grip on high church appointments but not to give up a major role in such appointments. The attack on lay control of parish churches and tithes at the local level failed almost completely because the lower nobility would not give up such control – they needed the income. The reformers had to settle for cleaning up the grossest abuses of buying and selling church offices. They encouraged lay lords to give churches as gifts to monasteries. Well into early modern times, however, lay nobles and other 'patrons' of churches appointed much of the lower clergy in Catholic Europe. As a consequence of the eleventh-century reforms, the papacy was a far more important actor in the politics of Europe in 1200 than it had been in the heyday of sacred kingship in 1000, but it was only one actor in a complicated drama. The papacy at that time certainly did not control society.

Within the church itself, the papal victory was more complete. The independence of regional churches and individual bishops was greatly curtailed by the growth of effective papal power. In the letter collection of Pope Gregory VII there is a series of short declarations, called the *Dictatus papae*, 'the thing dictated by the pope'. They might have been the chapter headings for a canon law collection that was never actually made. They certainly represent Gregory's expansive view of the power of the pope. There were 27 declarations, of which 23 concern the internal workings of the church. Virtually all of them were untrue in the year 1000, were still mostly wishful thinking in Gregory's day, but had become quite true by the year 1200. They outline in a dramatic way the reformers' ambition to increase papal power over the internal workings of the church:

1. That the Roman Church was founded by the Lord alone.
2. That only the Roman bishop is rightly called 'universal'.
3. That he [the pope] alone can depose or reinstate bishops.
4. That his legate, even if of lower grade, takes precedence in a council over all bishops and can give a sentence of deposition against them.
5. That the pope can depose those who are absent.
6. That, among other things, we should not stay in the same house with those excommunicated by him.
7. That for him alone is it lawful to enact new laws for the need of the time, to assemble together new congregations, to make an abbey of a canonry and vice versa; and to divide a rich bishopric and unite poor ones.
8. That he alone may use the imperial insignia.
9. That all princes shall kiss the feet of the pope alone.
10. That his name alone is to be recited in churches.
11. That his title is unique in the world.
12. That he may depose emperors.
13. That he may transfer bishops from one see to another, if necessity requires it.
14. That he has power to ordain a cleric of any church he wishes.
15. That anyone ordained by the pope may preside over another church but may not be a subordinate in it; and that [one ordained by the pope] should not accept a higher order from another bishop.
16. That no synod should be called 'general' without his order.
17. That no law and no book may be regarded as canonical without his authority.
18. That his decision ought to be reconsidered by no one and he alone can reconsider the decisions of everyone.
19. That he himself should be judged by no one.
20. That no one should dare to condemn a person who appeals to the Apostolic See.
21. That the more important cases of every church should be submitted to it [i.e. the Roman church].

22. That the Roman Church has never erred, nor will it ever err, as the scripture testifies.
23. That if he has been ordained according to the canons, the Roman bishop is undoubtedly made holy by the merits of the blessed Peter . . . .
24. That by his order and permission, subjects may accuse [their leaders].
25. That without a synod he can depose and reinstate bishops.
26. That he should not be considered as Catholic who does not agree with the Roman Church.
27. That he may absolve subjects from their fealty to wicked men.[2]

Notice number 12: that the pope had the authority to depose emperors. Issued in 1075 or 1076, the *Dictatus papae* seem to authorise Gregory VII's power to depose emperors just in time for his conflict with Henry IV, or at least to justify it after the fact. The *Dictatus papae* was probably not a description of actual practice when it was composed, but it did point to the main direction of church development over the next two centuries. The reformers created a new vision of order in the church. The clergy were to be separated from the laity and placed above them in the hierarchical chain of reality that stretched from God to humanity. The clergy in their turn were to be organised in a strict hierarchy under the pope, who would control that hierarchy so firmly that he could override custom, tradition, bishops and councils. No detail of church life was too large or too small to escape his supervision. Reality did not always match the reformers' vision, but that vision remained an ideal to be pursued. Successive popes put the ideal into practice by small and large steps, accumulating precedents that by the early fourteenth century had given the pope an effective control over the personnel, finances and law of the church that Gregory VII probably could not have imagined.

The reforms of the eleventh century touched many more people than kings and popes. Over the long run, they stimulated a religious ferment that could not be bottled up just because the kings and popes had compromised and signed treaties. The long struggle between the popes and the German rulers had forced many people to make choices in religious matters. Practices were no longer justified just because they were traditional, the way things had been for as long as anyone could remember. In particular, the clerical and lay elites were forced to choose among competing views of correct behaviour. In monasteries and cathedral chapters, in rural parishes and urban churches, in royal courts and meetings of knights, the clergy and nobility were sometimes reluctantly forced to take sides. Many people were unsure who was right. The king had tradition on his side: for as long as anyone could remember anointed kings had ruled the church. An argument based on tradition was a powerful one in medieval society. Yet the pope had the more convincing theological arguments on his side and his supporters appealed to even more ancient traditions, embodied in the scriptures, the canon law and the church fathers. Self-interest and economics played their part in swaying people one way or the other. Lay nobles sometimes supported reform to weaken their king. Lay recipients of tithes and owners of private churches resisted reform because they had considerable income to protect. Married priests, many of whom were respectable men, obviously did not like the idea of giving up their wives. Whatever individuals decided, the fact that they had to decide was new. Not since late antiquity, more than 700 years earlier, had so many Christians debated publicly about such significant religious issues. The lively debates of the reform period unleashed ideas that influenced religious life for centuries.

Even people of the lower classes, who could not follow the learned arguments based on scriptural, canonical or patristic texts, were stirred by the new ideas. A new lay activism in religion emerged that was to express itself in many ways, some acceptable to the clergy and others unacceptable. As a result of public conflicts about how the clergy should live, some lay people refused the ministrations of priests whom they regarded as unworthy. This was not a new problem. In the fifth century Bishop Augustine of Hippo had argued against the Donatist Christians in North Africa, who denied the validity of baptisms performed by sinful priests and bishops. Augustine had worked out the official theology, which said that Christ was the true giver of grace in the sacraments, though he used the priests and bishops as his human agents. Their failings, ignorance and sins could not hurt the transmission of grace from Christ to the individual believer. Augustine argued that a validly ordained priest, even if personally unworthy, performed valid sacraments for the faithful.

In spite of the assurance that a sinful priest could not contaminate Christ's sacraments, the real-life problem of how to react to a priest who was a fornicator or a simoniac remained for ordinary people. In fact, it became more acute in the twelfth century as the standards of behaviour applied to the clergy grew stricter. Even though the faithful were told that it did no harm to take the Lord's Body and Blood from the hands of such a priest, that was not the instinctive reaction of many people. In some places and among some people, there was a reluctance to honour and take ministrations from unworthy priests, a general attitude called donatism with a small 'd', named for those fifth-century North African dissidents with whom Augustine had argued. Gregory VII seemed to ratify such views when he ordered the laity to boycott unchaste and simoniacal priests. The spread of donatist attitudes among the laity created long-lasting problems for the church, since even after the Concordat of Worms (1122) there were priests who fell short – sometimes far short – of a priestly ideal that was more demanding than in earlier times.

In the towns, which were growing under the stimulus of trade, unregulated and unauthorised popular preachers roused people in their own language to religious fervour. The preachers criticised the local clergy because they fell short of the reformers' ideal of a chaste, high-minded and separate group. Such criticism was not in itself heretical, but could become so if the critics refused the ministrations of clergy whom they thought unworthy. The spread of popular heresy was one unanticipated consequence of the changes set in motion by the eleventh-century reformers.

A second consequence of decades of agitation about reform was also visible in other contexts. When Pope Urban II summoned the First Crusade in 1095, knights responded in considerable numbers, as the pope intended. But so did peasants and lower-class townspeople, whose zeal was uncontrollable. While the knights were organising for the expedition to the Holy Land, a man named Peter the Hermit led disorderly bands of the poor down the Rhine valley toward Jerusalem, slaughtering Jews whom they identified as God's enemies along the way. The church struggled, often but not always successfully, to channel and contain the religious energy that the reform movements had unleashed in society.

In a society energised by the growth of population, of economic activity and of urban life, the reforms of the eleventh century added a dimension of religious ferment and dissent that had repercussions for centuries.

Suggested reading

Companion website
www.routledge.com/cw/lynch

10.1 The Synod of Sutri
'An account of the Synod pf Sutri', in Oliver J. Thatcher and Edgar H. McNeal, eds., *A Source Book for Medieval History: Selected Documents Illustrating the History of Europe in the Middle Age* (New York: Charles Scribner's Sons, 1907), 121–124.

10.2 Lay Investiture: The Letters Of Henry IV and Gregory VII
'Letter of Gregory VII to Henry IV' (December 1075), 'Henry IV's Answer to Gregory VII' (January 24, 1076), 'Henry IV is deposed by Gregory VII' (1076), in Ernest F. Henderson, Trans., *Select Historical Documents Of The Middle Ages* (London: George Bell And Sons, 1905), 367–373, 376–77.

10.3 The Concordat of Worms (1122)
'The Promise of Calixtus II' and 'The Promise of Henry V', in Oliver J. Thatcher and Edgar H. McNeal, *A Source Book for Medieval History: Selected Documents Illustrating the History of Europe in The Middle Age* (New York: Charles Scribner's Sons, 1907), 164–166.

Primary sources

Gilchrist, John, editor, *The Collection in Seventy-Four Titles: A Canon Law Manual of the Gregorian Reform* (Toronto, 1980)

Gregory VII, *The Register of Pope Gregory VII,* translated by H. E. J. Cowdrey (Oxford, 2002)

Gregory VII, *The Correspondence of Pope Gregory VII,* translated by Ephraim Emerton, Columbia Records of Civilization, 14 (New York, 1932)

Humbert's *Three Books Against Simoniacs,* translated in Brian Tierney, *The Crisis of Church and State, 1050–1300* (Englewood Cliffs, New Jersey, 1964), pp. 40–2

Imperial Lives and Letters of the Eleventh Century, translated by Theodor E. Mommsen and Karl F. Morrison, Columbia Records of Civilization, 67 (New York, 1962)

Modern scholarship

Barstow, Ann Llewellyn, *Married Priests and the Reforming Papacy: The Eleventh-Century Debates,* Texts and Studies in Religion, 12 (New York, 1982)

Blumenthal, Ute-Renate, *The Investiture Controversy. Church and Monarchy from the Ninth to the Eleventh Century* (Philadelphia, 1988)

Chazan, Robert, *European Jewry and the First Crusade* (Berkeley, 1987)

Cowdrey, H. E. J., *Gregory VII* (Oxford, 1998)

Hay, David, *The Military Leadership of Matilda of Canossa, 1046–1115* (Manchester, 2008)

Lambert, Malcolm, *Medieval Heresy. Popular Movements from Bogomil to Hus* (London, 1977)

Moore, Robert I., *The Origins of European Dissent* (New York, 1977)

Robinson, Ian S., *Authority and Resistance in the Investiture Contest: the Polemical Literature of the late Eleventh Century* (Manchester, 1978)

Spike, Michèle K., *Tuscan Countess: The Life and Extraordinary Times of Matilda of Canossa* (New York, 2004)

Tellenbach, Gerd, *Church, State and Christian Society at the Time of the Investiture Contest,* translated by R. F. Bennett (Oxford, 1940)

Notes

1 Gregory VII, *Das Register Gregors VII,* book 8, letter 21, edited by Erich Caspar, Monumenta Germaniae historica, Epistolae selectae, 2/2 (Berlin, 1923), pp. 552–3; also translated in its entirety in Emerton, *The Correspondence,* pp. 166–75.
2 Gregory VII, *Das Register Gregors VII,* book 2, letter 55, edited by Erich Caspar, Monumenta Germaniae historica, Epistolae selectae, 2/1 (Berlin, 1920), pp. 201–8.

11

The rise of Christendom

Historians conventionally divide the Middle Ages into three phases: early, high or central, and late. The subdividing of the Middle Ages into smaller periods is more or less arbitrary, and the specifics of this practice are certainly contested. Whether an historian calls the middle part of the Middle Ages 'central' or 'high', and even the exact dates she or he uses for this period can, to the uninitiated, seem like little more than a matter of taste.

That being said, western society in the early Middle Ages (c.500–1050) was impoverished and relatively underdeveloped compared to the Byzantine or Muslim lands. Not much monumental architecture survives from that period because later, more prosperous generations replaced the buildings. Aside from liturgical objects and manuscripts, there is little from before 1100 that would impress the ordinary modern observer. In the modern popular imagination, the 'real Middle Ages' corresponds to what historians call the central Middle Ages (c.1050–1300), a period that fiction writers and film makers love for its crusades, knights in armour, tournaments, stone castles, cathedrals, stained glass windows, monasteries, illustrated manuscripts, heretics, inquisitors and universities. Because the popular media are weak on chronology, they occasionally confuse the phases of the Middle Ages: sometimes Charlemagne, who lived in the early Middle Ages, is shown in crusader's armour or standing on the turret of a fourteenth-century castle. The 'real Middle Ages' of the popular media – the historian's central Middle Ages – lasted only about five human lifetimes, from the First Crusade (1096) to the death of Pope Boniface VIII (1304). Because the cultural and religious accomplishments packed into such a relatively brief time were built on a foundation of remarkable growth in population and wealth, it is useful to look briefly at the economic rise of Latin Europe.

I. Population growth

Population growth was one key to the economic boom that enabled the transformation of medieval society. Faced with the burgeoning human population of the twenty-first century, we might find it hard to imagine a time when human populations barely held their own or even declined in the face of disease, famine and violence, but such was the case for a period of about

800 years in the later Roman Empire and the early medieval west. In the late tenth century, Viking, Muslim and Magyar invasions tapered off. In conditions of relative peace, with improved agricultural technology, a healthier diet and perhaps a more favourable climate, a growth in population began that continued until the late thirteenth or early fourteenth centuries. Precise figures are difficult to obtain. The situation in England can offer some sense of the magnitude of growth. *Domesday Book*, William the Conqueror's survey of his kingdom's resources in 1086, has been interpreted to imply a population of more than a million people. The records of the English poll tax of 1377, collected after the devastation of the **Black Death** (1349–51), point to a population of about 2 million, down from the pre-Black Death population of perhaps 3.7 million. If the English situation is comparable to that on the continent, we can estimate that the population of Latin Europe tripled or quadrupled between the eleventh and fourteenth centuries.

The growth of cities was proportionately even greater. Until the eleventh century, European cities were surprisingly small and unimportant both economically and socially. Economic and demographic growth changed that situation. Cities became centres of trade and industry, places of innovation and wealth, inhabited by new social classes created by the changing economy, including the merchant elite, craftsmen and artisans, and the urban poor. In 1100, there was probably no city in the Christian west with more than 10,000 inhabitants. By 1300, there were many cities of more than 10,000 people, and Paris, Milan, Venice and Florence exceeded 50,000.

Population growth without adequate means of support can create horrible human suffering, as it has done in some places in the nineteenth, twentieth and twenty-first centuries. But when the medieval European population began to grow, there were still vast uncultivated areas of forest, marsh and wasteland within Europe to accommodate all the new mouths to feed. For 250 years, western peasants and landlords conquered the internal frontiers of Europe. They filled in the spaces between the scattered early medieval villages. They cleared forests, drained swamps and founded thousands of new agricultural villages, some of which are still recognisable by their names: Newton, Villeneuve, Neuburg and Villanova, each of which means 'new town'. They raised livestock on marshy, dry, mountainous or infertile lands that were unsuitable for growing crops. By 1300, there was probably as high a percentage of the European landscape used for cultivation or grazing as was ever to be.

The growing population also spilled across the external frontiers and even overseas. The most important colonial expansion of Europe began with Christopher Columbus in 1492 and by the nineteenth century had affected the entire earth. It has overshadowed the earlier colonial experience of Europeans, which began in the eleventh century when knights, merchants and peasants colonised territory in Spain and eastern Europe, and temporarily in Syria, Lebanon and Palestine.

The crusades are the best-known episode of medieval expansion, but the least significant in terms of their lasting demographic effects. Most of the emigrants to the eastern Mediterranean were knights, clergy and merchants, who lived in the cities and dominated a native population of Muslims, Jews and eastern Christians. Few western peasants settled in what the French crusaders called *outremer* ('beyond the sea').

Southern Italy, Sicily, Sardinia and Corsica were also integrated by conquest into the Latin west during the eleventh and twelfth centuries. In 1000, those regions were subject to a tangle of overlapping and conflicting governments created by centuries of conquest and reconquest. Muslim emirs, Lombard princes and Byzantine functionaries struggled with one another for control, but no one was able to achieve more than temporary dominance. In the early eleventh century, knights from Normandy, who were returning from a pilgrimage to Jerusalem, saw in southern Italy a golden opportunity for themselves. Their grandfathers and great-grandfathers had been Vikings who settled at the mouth of the River Seine in north-western France in the early tenth century. The strong forces of cultural assimilation and intermarriage with the native population had made their descendants French-speaking Christians, but they were still formidable warriors. Normandy, as their homeland was called, was a rather small place and the knightly class, with its large families, sought outlets for its energy and surplus population. In the eleventh century, bands of Norman knights migrated to southern Italy, where they hired themselves out as mercenaries to whomever paid best. Soon they were conquering territory for themselves. In 1059, Pope Nicholas II gave legitimacy to Robert Guiscard (died 1085) by recognising him as duke of Apulia and Calabria. In return, Robert became the pope's vassal. By 1071, the last Byzantine stronghold in Italy, the city of Bari, had fallen to the Normans, who had become a serious threat to the Byzantine Empire itself. In 1072, the Normans began the conquest of Sicily from the Muslims. In 1130, the pope gave Roger II (1103–54), a nephew of Robert Guiscard, the title of king. Roger ruled a well-organised, multi-ethnic, and multi-religious state that included southern Italy and Sicily. Not many peasants migrated to the south, but the region became a part of western Christendom.

Other permanent colonial expansions were closer to the core of Latin Europe, in Spain and in eastern Europe, to which masses of peasant settlers could literally walk alongside carts containing their goods. Muslim armies had conquered Visigothic Spain in the early eighth century and had created a lively civilisation in which Muslims, Jews and Mozarabic (that is, Arabic-speaking) Christians participated. Small, independent Christian principalities survived in the rugged northern parts of the Iberian Peninsula. In the eleventh century, the Christian kingdoms of Leon, Castile and Aragon, later joined by Portugal, began a slow uncoordinated advance, called in Spanish history the *Reconquista* ('the Reconquest'), which reached Madrid in 1083, Toledo in 1085, Saragossa in 1118, Cordoba in 1236, Seville in 1248, and which conquered the final Muslim territory, Granada, in 1492. In the early stages of the *Reconquista*, knights from France, encouraged by Cluniac monks, took a leading role. Knights and peasants from northern Spain and southern France settled in the conquered territories. Until the forced conversions and expulsions of Jews and Muslims during the fifteenth and sixteenth centuries, Spain had large minorities of both groups, but the migrations of Christian peasants following military victories made the Iberian Peninsula a part of Latin Christendom. The opportunities to settle in central and southern Spain provided an outlet for the growing population of southern France and northern Spain.

The most significant medieval migration was probably that of German peasants and lords who moved east into modern Austria, the Czech Republic, Slovakia, eastern Germany, Lithuania, Latvia, Estonia and Poland. Some historians have called this medieval German expansion the *Drang nach Osten* ('drive to the East'), but the phrase has become contested because of its links to German expansion in modern times – the Nazis' 'drive to the East' into Poland and the Czech Sudetenland. Like its twentieth-century analogue, the medieval expansion came at the expense of Slavic peoples, who survived in considerable numbers but were dominated for centuries in the Middle Ages by an elite of German-speaking lords, townsmen, clergy and peasant farmers. The migration to the east had started and stopped several times in the ninth, tenth and eleventh centuries, as the western Germanic kingdom rose and fell. In the twelfth century, migrations began again on an ever-growing scale. These were not generally violent. Much of eastern Europe was thinly settled and economically backward. Slavic kings and princes often welcomed the migrants, whose skills in agriculture, mining and trade they valued as a way to 'modernise' quickly and avoid being overwhelmed politically by the aggressive German kings, dukes and counts to the west. The economic changes created by the German immigrants enriched the native Slavic upper classes even as they oppressed the native lower-class Slavs. Landlords enticed German-speaking peasants with low rents, the promise of personal freedom and the opportunity to exploit the untapped resources of a frontier region.

The movement into eastern Europe had many features in common with the settlement of the American West in the nineteenth century, including settlement agents, called 'boomers' in America and *locatores* in medieval Latin, who advertised the attractions of the Slavic frontiers, organised wagon trains, and helped the new arrivals to survive until their first crops were harvested. By the fourteenth century, the German colonists had remade much of eastern Europe. The area between the Elbe and Oder rivers, including Prussia, had been entirely Germanised. Further east there were large German peasant minorities and towns with a majority of German speakers. By bonds of language, religion, culture and trade, much of eastern Europe had been drawn into Latin Christendom. The conquests and migrations into southern and eastern Europe, coupled with the conversion of the Scandinavians, had at least doubled the land area of Latin Europe between 1000 and 1300, and had provided a crucial outlet for the growing population.

II. Economic growth

In modern experience, migration is one response to population growth, but internal economic growth is another. Without such economic growth, a rapidly increasing population can fall victim to abject poverty, even with some emigration. The central Middle Ages were marked by great economic growth, whose residue is still visible in churches, town walls, castles and luxurious objects surviving from the twelfth, thirteenth and early fourteenth centuries. However, trade and manufacturing were not evenly distributed, but were concentrated in two favoured regions. In the north, cities in Flanders (Belgium, Holland and a part of modern France) took the lead in uniting an economic zone that included the lands on the shores of the North and Baltic Seas. The German settlers in eastern Europe sold raw materials, particularly grain, lumber and salted herring, to feed the growing populations further west, buying manufactured goods in return.

The second region of significant manufacturing and commerce was located in northern and central Italy, whose cities were well situated to take advantage of the rich economic life on the coasts of the Mediterranean Sea. The Muslims and Byzantines had dominated the Mediterranean during the ninth and tenth centuries, but that changed in the eleventh century. In 1016, the Genoese and Pisans defeated a Muslim fleet and began the reconquest of Sardinia and Corsica. In the aftermath of the First Crusade (1096-9), the Mediterranean became a Christian lake, open to trading ships from Italy, southern France and the Spanish coast. The Italians were energetic economic imperialists, and gained great prosperity from their network of trading posts in the eastern Mediterranean, supported by economic privileges that they gained or extorted from the crusader states in the Holy Land and the Byzantine Empire. By the thirteenth century, the leading Italian city-states, Venice, Florence and Genoa, were rich, aggressive powers, using force and economic strength to dominate the trade of the Mediterranean and to pursue their economic interests in the rest of Europe.

There were many products bought and sold in the trade networks of the central Middle Ages, but just as steel, automobiles, and more recently electronics and computer chips have dominated economies in the modern world, so too medieval Europe had a dominant product that energised much of the economy: cloth. Italian entrepreneurs took the lead in that industry and grew rich in the process. The wet grasslands of England, the Low Countries and northern France provided the raw material, wool. Other regions provided the dyes and the alum needed to fix colours in the cloth. Thousands of skilled and unskilled workers in the cities of northern Italy and later of Flanders transformed the raw materials into cloth of every variety and value. By the thirteenth century, silk, linen and cotton cloth were also being produced in the cities of Italy. Cloth was shipped all over Europe, where only the most impoverished or backward people wore clothing made from home-made cloth. Cloth was also exported to the Muslim world: many inhabitants of Cairo, Tunis or Damascus wore western cloth. Alongside cloth, there was a growing local and regional trade within Europe in foodstuffs and manu-factured goods, as living standards rose and the growing urban populations needed to be fed. Most Europeans remained peasant farmers, but in the advanced commercial regions of Flanders and northern Italy, as much as 30 per cent of the population may have lived by non-agricultural pursuits in the late thirteenth and early fourteenth centuries.

III. The bonds of unity

Commerce did much to break down the regionalism that characterised the earlier Middle Ages. Buyers and sellers located at great distances from one another became economically interdependent: sheep disease in England could put thousands in Italy out of work, while a military defeat in the Near East could close trade routes and create shortages of dyes and spices. The bonds of commerce were reinforced by many other links. There is a stereotype that people in the Middle Ages were immobile, but in fact in the generations from the First Crusade to the Black Death (1096 to about 1350), there was much movement. We have discussed the peasant migrations to the growing towns and to the new lands, but the upper classes were on the move as well. Thousands of knights fought on crusade. Tens of thousands of men and women went on pilgrimage to Jerusalem as well as to the many local, regional and universal holy places, including the shrine of St Peter at Rome and the shrine of St James at Compostela in Spain. Monks, canons and **friars** were on the move for the business of their religious houses, for education, for the founding of new houses and for missionary work. Litigants came to princely, royal and papal courts to plead their cases. Papal legates were constantly on the move, representing papal interests, settling disputes with rulers and dealing with the religious problems of ordinary people. At universities, particularly

Paris and Bologna, both the teachers and the students were drawn from all over Christendom and often made careers far from their places of birth.

In an age of growing literacy, the letter became an instrument to bridge distance. Popes and kings issued hundreds or even thousands of letters each year. Students wrote to their parents, then as now, often to ask for money. Spouses kept in touch by letter. Merchants used letters to keep contact with their partners and employees. For example, in the business and family papers of the merchant Francesco Datini (1335–1410), which happened to survive in his native Italian town of Prato, there are about 150,000 letters, 500 account books and thousands of miscellaneous business documents. Europe was woven together by the movement of considerable numbers of people to buy, sell, study, visit or settle. There was even some travel beyond the bounds of Christendom. The book of the Venetian Marco Polo (*c*.1254–1324), which recounted his adventures during 20 years in Central Asia, China, India and the Near East, is a reminder of the small adventurous band of missionaries and merchants who journeyed to places that no one from the west had visited in centuries, or perhaps ever.

IV. Christendom

Latin Europe was united in the central Middle Ages not only by such tangible things as wool, papal legates and letters, but also by a new way of understanding itself. The eleventh-century reform movements stirred up the deeply held feeling that the Christian religion was more important, more real, than the other social groupings, such as regions or kingdoms, in which people lived. (See Figure 11.) In the struggles between popes and kings, many people were forced to examine their loyalties. For many the church seemed to demand their primary loyalty. There are analogies in the twenty-first century that may help to explain the medieval situation. The day-to-day reality of the modern western world is nationalism (or perhaps transnational capitalism), but many people in advanced countries feel an emotional tug toward 'humanity', which they regard as something greater than a particular country or other venture. Love of humanity is a vague notion, but occasionally it has real effects: money pours out to relieve a far-off famine; arguments about global climate change are couched in terms of one's duty to humankind and future generations; and there is a sympathetic interest in the art, music and literature of widely differing times and places. An even closer modern analogy is the religious revival that is taking place in the Islamic world, which puzzles many western secular observers. The countries of the modern Islamic world certainly fight with one other. But from Morocco to Pakistan, there is an emotional loyalty to the religion of Islam that can transcend political states. The emotions connected

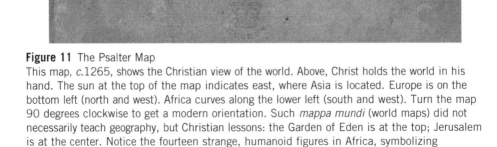

Figure 11 The Psalter Map
This map, *c.*1265, shows the Christian view of the world. Above, Christ holds the world in his
hand. The sun at the top of the map indicates east, where Asia is located. Europe is on the
bottom left (north and west). Africa curves along the lower left (south and west). Turn the map
90 degrees clockwise to get a modern orientation. Such *mappa mundi* (world maps) did not
necessarily teach geography, but Christian lessons: the Garden of Eden is at the top; Jerusalem
is at the center. Notice the fourteen strange, humanoid figures in Africa, symbolizing
European anxiety of the 'other'.

with belonging to and loving Islam can be so deeply felt that some people are willing to die and to kill for it. Something very similar to this swept over Christian Europe after the reform movements of the eleventh century. Many western Christians in the central Middle Ages felt that they were members of a church that transcended their regions and groups. It is important not to overstate the change. Since the mid-eleventh century, a growing **schism** between the eastern and western churches kept the whole church from being fully united – eastern patriarchs did not recognise the pre-eminence claimed by the western pope. Even in the west, warfare among Christians remained common. Local and regional loyalties persisted. Economic competition and class conflict were carried out in rough ways. But sometimes those forces retreated or paused in the face of the consciousness of belonging to something larger than one's region or kingdom, of belonging to the Christian people or, as we may call it, western Christendom.

V. The crusades

Like modern Islam, Christendom was not a single political entity. There were emperors and popes who dreamed of uniting it, but failed: it remained politically fragmented. In spite of this political fragmentation, the one institution that was in a position to benefit from the growing sense of Christendom was the papacy. The popes emerged from the eleventh-century as the visible heads of western Christendom. The success of the popes against the German rulers Henry IV and Henry V helped them to eliminate their chief rival for the leadership of Christendom, the German emperor. The crusades gave an early, concrete reality to the notion of the Christian people united under the pope for some great cause. The rise and decline of the crusading ideal roughly paralleled the rise and decline of the notion that Christendom could be led by the papacy.

In 1095, in the town of Clermont in central France, Pope Urban II (1088–99) preached on the need to aid fellow Christians in the east against the Seljuk Turks. Back in 1071, the Turks had defeated the Byzantines at Manzikert, and had seized much of Anatolia (modern Turkey), where the Byzantine Empire recruited soldiers and collected taxes. The Turks were Muslims, who were also in possession of the Holy Land, including Jerusalem. A generation earlier, Pope Gregory VII had tried to raise armies against the Muslims in Spain and the east, but with little popular response. Something had changed since the papacy of Gregory VII. The response to Urban's call was much greater and more emotional than he could have anticipated. A movement verging on mass hysteria swept the crowd of knights listening to his sermon. They cried out 'God wills it' and tore up cloth to sew crosses on their clothing, symbolising their resolve to rescue the Holy Land. In subsequent months, knights and ordinary people in much of France and the Rhineland were roused to a feverish activity by the call to arms against the foes of Christendom. The natural military leaders of the Christians would have been their kings, but Henry IV of Germany was excommunicated and other Christian kings were not willing or able to lead the crusade. Urban II did not go on the crusade, but he sent a bishop as his legate to represent him. By default, the pope became the head of the crusader army, the first immensely popular undertaking of Christendom.

Only the First Crusade (1096–9) was completely successful in military terms. In the late eleventh century, the Muslims along the eastern shore of the Mediterranean were internally divided and the westerners were able to conquer a strip of land from Edessa and Antioch in the north to Ascalon in the south, including the most desired prize, Jerusalem, which was taken by storm on 15 July 1099. (See Map 4.) Crusading armies planted small Christian principalities along the coasts of Syria and Palestine. The crusader states had long eastern borders that were difficult to defend. Subsequent crusades were prompted by the revivals of Muslim military strength that led to the reconquest of the crusader states bit by bit. Demographics (not enough western knights) and distance were major obstacles to the success of the later crusades, which were generally unsuccessful. The last crusader stronghold, the city of Acre, fell to Muslim armies in 1291.

That is the story of the crusades in a little more than 500 words! Of course, it was much more complicated than that. Our point here is that the history of the church in the central Middle Ages is incomprehensible unless one realises how the papacy tapped into a growing sense of loyalty to Christendom, of which the crusades were a concrete embodiment. The papacy did not create the sense of Christendom felt by so many medieval people, and when that sense faded in the later Middle Ages, the papacy could not revive it. The elaborate administrative structures of the church in the central Middle Ages would not have been possible without the willingness of millions of people to accept and pay for them. To be sure, there was lively debate about the details and the costs, but from Greenland to Jerusalem most western Christians accepted the spiritual authority of the papacy because they were convinced that it was a legitimate embodiment of Christendom in visible institutions.

VI. Hostility toward the 'other'

There was another side to the sense of Christian unity. As the awareness of a Christian 'us' sharpened, the awareness of a non-Christian 'them' sharpened as well. Scholars sometimes use the term 'alterity' (from the Latin *alter*, meaning 'other') to describe this phenomenon, in which one group constructs its own cultural identity by defining and spurning the cultural 'other'. In the presence

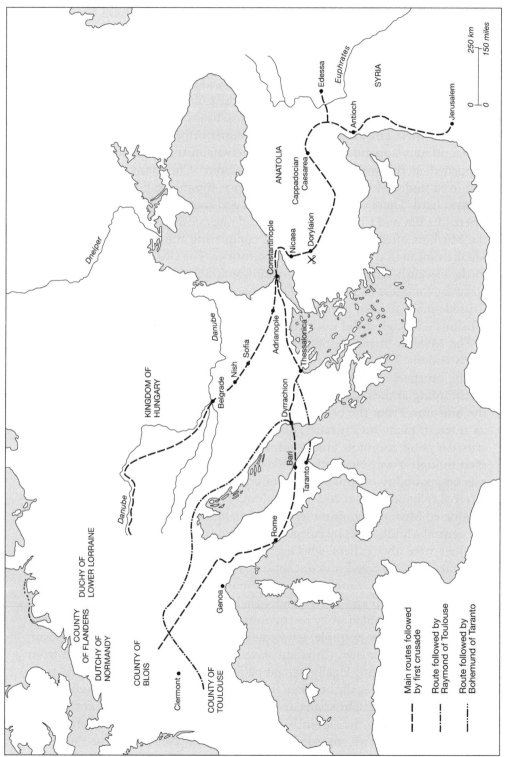

Map 4 The routes of the First Crusade

of deeply held feelings of group solidarity, some people have historically found it hard to live at peace with neighbours who differed from them in religion, language or race. We have seen in our own times how this is often accompanied by resentment, discrimination and even violence against people perceived to be outsiders, those 'others' who will not or cannot blend into the majority. Something similar happened in the central Middle Ages.

The most menacing 'others' were Muslims. From the seventh to the eleventh centuries, their cultural and economic superiority threatened to translate into a military superiority that would overwhelm the Christians. That never happened in the west, but millions of eastern Christians were conquered and lived under Muslim rule. Even the great Byzantine Empire was at times pressed hard. There was constant tension and frequent warfare in the regions where Muslim and Christian powers faced one another. In the early centuries, the Muslims often had the best of it, conquering the islands of the western Mediterranean in the ninth and tenth centuries. The situation began to change in the eleventh century. The Latin counterattack in the Mediterranean, the Norman conquest of Sicily, the *Reconquista* in Spain and the successful First Crusade made it seem possible to Christians that they would overwhelm the Muslims – though it did not entirely turn out that way.

The Muslim 'menace', both real and perceived, sharpened the sense of Christendom. The First Crusade showed how Christians could be energised by the prospect of defeating the Muslim 'infidels'. The subsequent failures of crusading armies dampened but did not end the enthusiasm for fighting the Muslims. From the twelfth to the fifteenth centuries, crusading retained its interest: plans for crusades, discussions of crusade strategy and calls for crusades were common and continued to touch the western imagination, even though it was less and less likely that they could succeed. Since there was no possibility of Muslim missionary work in the west, Islam was not an internal religious threat to Christendom. There were, however, a number of conquered Muslim communities in Spain and Sicily, which were protected in the central Middle Ages by rulers who valued them as law-abiding taxpayers.

There were also 'others' who lived inside Christendom: Jews and heretics. Contrary to widespread misconceptions, the Jews were not always persecuted in Christian states. Since the late Roman Empire, Jews had been legally allowed to worship and to live under their own laws within Christian lands. But they were hemmed in by restrictions that emphasised their second-class, outsider status. For example, Jews could not convert Christians to Judaism, marry Christians or own Christian slaves. Yet they were also protected from force. They could not legally be compelled to convert to Christianity, their children could not legally be taken from them and their synagogues could not legally be destroyed. Christians and Jews often did not like one another, but from the seventh to the eleventh centuries outright violence was rare. There were harsh anti-Jewish measures and some forced conversions in Visigothic

Spain during the seventh century and one such episode in sixth-century Frankish Gaul, but those were exceptional cases in the early Middle Ages. Otherwise, during the early Middle Ages, the Jewish minority lived in relative peace.

As the sense of unity within Christendom grew more intense, the presence of dissenting groups seemed more and more unacceptable. The popular feelings that made the crusades possible also worsened the situation of the Jews. In the atmosphere of expectation that God was going to give victory to the Christians, popular preachers said that, like the Muslims, the Jews were enemies of Christ – in fact, many perceived the Jews as being responsible for Christ's death. The organised crusader armies did not attack Jews, and both the civil and church authorities tried to protect them. But in 1096, mobs attacked Jewish settlements at Mainz, Worms and Speyer in the Rhineland and tried to force conversion under threat of death. Those three communities produced some apostates (people who renounced their religion, in this case Judaism), and many martyrs. Such violent outbursts were illegal and, in addition, threatened the financial benefits that rulers derived from protecting and exploiting the Jews. The authorities in church and state discouraged the violence, but the fact of popular violence highlighted the link between the growing sense of Christendom and the intolerance of the 'other'.

In the thirteenth century, there were efforts to convert Jews by persuasion. In France and Spain, Jews were forced to listen to sermons and debates with friars, some of whom were themselves converts from Judaism. Pope Gregory IX (*c.*1170–1241) ordered copies of the Jewish Talmud to be publicly burned. Popular animosity also grew more violent and the Jews were burdened with heavier economic and social restrictions. Many individual Jews did become Christians, though Judaism survived in the face of such pressure. By the late thirteenth century, the policy of some important rulers toward the Jews grew harsher. The Jews were expelled from England (1290) and France (1306) and their property was confiscated for the royal treasury. It is likely that the financial gain from expulsion was the rulers' main motive. Some of the Jewish refugees migrated east into German and Slavic lands, where there was also popular animosity, but local rulers protected them for their skills as craftsmen and usefulness as traders and moneylenders.

The intensifying sense of Christian unity also made the presence of Christian dissenters, called heretics, a problem. In the eleventh and twelfth centuries, the place in which heresy was detected determined how the heretics would be treated. In Germany, popular violence against heretics was common. They were seized by mobs and burned, presumably to cleanse the earth. In southern France and Italy, the dissenters found more tolerance and even some sympathy from townspeople and nobles. During the thirteenth century, the church and many governments declared a sort of martial law against heretics. They were either exterminated (for example, the **Cathars**) or driven into hiding in remote places (for example, the **Waldensians**). Chapter 15 treats heresy and heretics in more detail. The point here is that the growing unity of the Christian people left little room for outright dissenters.

VII. Western and eastern Christians

The rise of a sense of Christendom in the west also affected relations between the western and eastern churches. The westerners had ambivalent feelings toward the Orthodox Christians of the Byzantine Empire, who began as a part of 'us' and ended as 'them'. In the late Roman Empire, there was just one official church spread across imperial territory. Looking back, we can detect the beginnings of a process whereby eastern and western churches drifted apart, but contemporaries were not aware of it. In spite of quarrels and differences in language, the church of the late Roman Empire had virtually the same structures, creeds, sacraments and canon law. In the early Middle Ages, the Germanic and Muslim invasions disrupted life along the Mediterranean shores and made communication difficult. Eastern and western Christians were also cut off from one another by politics and by a growing inability to understand one another's language, but they did not formally repudiate one another: the church continued, at least in theory, to be one. In spite of periodic quarrels, eastern Orthodox Christians and western Latin Christians for centuries acknowledged their mutual legitimacy and harboured hopes for more cordial relations.

But during the generations of isolation from one another, their differences intensified. The difference between the Greek and Latin languages meant that they often, quite literally, could not understand one another. They also differed in what is called church discipline, that is, the rules for organising church life. For instance, Orthodox priests (but not bishops, who were often chosen from the ranks of monks) were permitted to marry; western priests were not. Orthodox priests were required to have beards; western priests were not. Orthodox Christians used leavened bread in the Eucharist; western Christians used unleavened bread, called azymes (ironically, from a Greek word, 'azymos', which means 'unleavened'). Such differences had no clear theological importance and, when relations were good, both sides generally accepted the differences as legitimate. But when for political reasons relations were strained, each side had a tendency to criticise and condemn the other for their differences in church discipline.

There was also at least one significant theological difference. In 381, the Council of Constantinople had issued a creed (called the Nicene-Constantinopolitan Creed), which stated that the Holy Spirit proceeded from the Father. Somewhere, probably in Visigothic Spain during the sixth century, one word (*filioque*) was added to that creed in order to declare that the Holy Spirit proceeded from the Father 'and from the Son'. The Frankish king

Charlemagne, who had Visigothic scholars at his court, adopted that version of the creed for recitation during mass. Popes of the ninth and tenth century did not use this creed because the Roman liturgy at the time contained no requirement to recite any creed during mass. Then in the early eleventh century, the papal liturgy at Rome adopted some practices that had originated north of the Alps, including the recitation of the expanded Nicene-Constantinopolitan Creed during mass. This creed was the occasion for what became known as the '*filioque* controversy' that drove the eastern and western churches apart on a point of theology. The implications of the *filioque* clause are complex. In simple terms, it concerns the nature of each member of the Trinity, and their relationships to each other. Eastern and western Christians argued with one another about this issue, but also about the legitimacy of adding words to the traditional creeds. As relations grew tense for political reasons, this point of theological controversy grew hotter as well. In 1054, things came to a head when two papal legates from the west marched into the great church of Hagia Sophia in Constantinople and delivered a papal bull that deposed and excommunicated the head of the Orthodox Church, the patriarch of Constantinople.

The deposition and excommunication of 1054 marked the beginning of what is called the Eastern Schism. Historians argue over the significance of these events, and whether they even registered with contemporaries. Yet between the eleventh and the fifteenth centuries, the two churches moved apart. Even then, the awareness of a shared heritage was not lost. The theological and disciplinary differences between eastern and western Christianity appear to a modern observer modest enough to have been worked out if both sides had wished to do so. In fact, the differences were occasionally put aside, but usually when the Byzantine state was in desperate need of western military help. For example, when the Byzantine emperor needed help against the Seljuk Turks, he asked the west for mercenaries. What he got instead were crusaders. Yet when Pope Urban II preached at Clermont in 1095, he based his appeal to aid the Byzantines on their plight as fellow Christians under attack by 'others'. Throughout the course of the crusades, the popes and other high-level planners believed that their success would mean reunion of the two churches and of Christendom. But to the papacy and to westerners in general, reunion would have to mean Byzantine acceptance of papal authority in the strong, activist sense given to it in the west after the mid-eleventh century.

The crusades brought eastern and western Christians into closer contact, but they found that they generally did not like one another. The westerners saw the easterners as treacherous and ungrateful. They regarded their sophistication as a sign of weakness and they resented their unwillingness to accept what westerners saw as correct Christianity. The easterners looked on in anger as the western crusaders kept for themselves territory conquered from the Muslims, which the Byzantines believed was rightfully theirs. Anna Comnena, daughter of the Byzantine emperor and historian of the First Crusade, described the 'Franks' (the eastern term for western crusaders) as 'insolent' and 'barbarous'.

In 1204, the Byzantines reacted in horror when a crusader army captured Constantinople. During this Fourth Crusade – which for economic and political reasons had been diverted from its original, papal goal of Jerusalem – western Christians did not attack the 'enemies of Christ', but their fellow Christians in the east. They looted Constantinople, including its churches and monasteries, substituted a westerner for the rightful Byzantine emperor, and created a Latin empire that lasted until 1261. This 'Latin Empire in the East', often replaced Byzantine clergy with Latins, who tried to romanise the Byzantine church in liturgy and discipline. The theologians might work out subtle compromises on the *filioque* issue and papal power, but in the thirteenth century ordinary Byzantines grew to hate the westerners, especially their attempts to force the Byzantines to trade their religious heritage for the military help they so desperately needed.

At the Council of Lyons (1274) and at the Council of Florence (1439), bishops, theologians and politicians on both sides agreed to a reunion between the churches, only to have it repudiated by the rank and file of Byzantine monks, lower clergy and laity. The rising fortunes of the west and the declining fortunes of the Byzantine Empire lay behind the Orthodox Church's repudiation of reunion on western terms. So long as the Byzantine Empire was the economically and politically superior culture, the eastern Christians viewed their western coreligionists with a mixture of pity and scorn. But as the west revived, beginning in the second half of the eleventh century, the Byzantine Empire went into a long-term decline. In the last, hopeless days of the empire, when during the fifteenth century it was reduced to little more than the city of Constantinople, there was a strong faction that preferred the Turks' turban to the pope's mitre. In 1453, Constantinople finally fell to Turkish forces.

The events of the Eastern Schism and the Fourth Crusade created long historical memories for the Orthodox Church, as well as continued tense relations between the eastern and western churches. In 1965, some 900 years after the start of the Eastern Schism, Pope Paul VI embraced Patriarch Athenagoras of Constantinople in a public ceremony in Jerusalem, rescinding the excommunications of 1054, in the hopes of future good relations between the churches. And in 2004, Pope John Paul II apologised for the Fourth Crusade, exactly 800 years after the fact.

The economic and demographic resurgence of the west, coupled with the growing sense of Christendom, had a profound impact on the western church in the central Middle Ages, making it more vigorous and expansive, but also more exclusive and more concerned to define and enforce boundaries. These developments must now be explored more fully in the following chapters.

Suggested reading

Companion website

www.routledge.com/cw/lynch

11.1   Urban II at the Council of Clermont
Excerpts from the accounts of the Council of Clermont by Fulcher of Chartres and Robert the Monk, in Oliver J. Thatcher and Edgar H. McNeal, eds., *A Source Book for Medieval History: Selected Documents Illustrating the History of Europe in the Middle Age* (New York: Charles Scribner's Sons, 1907), 513-521.

11.2   The Fourth Crusade and the Sack of Constantinople
Excerpts from Geoffrey de Villehardouin (1160 – c. 1212), 'The Sack of Constantinople', in Sir Frank Marziales, trans., *Memoirs of the Crusades* (New York: J.M. Dent & Sons, 1915), 58–66.

11.3   'Jacobus et Johannes', Codex Calixtinus (12th century)
Musical recording: The Rose Ensemble, *The Road to Compostela* (Saint Paul, MN, 2002)

11.4   'Vocavit Jhesus,' Codex Calixtinus (12th century)
Musical recording: The Rose Ensemble, *The Road to Compostela* (Saint Paul, MN, 2002)

Primary sources

Chazan, Robert, *Church, State and Jew in the Middle Ages* (New York, 1980)

Comnena, Anna, *The Alexiad*, translated by E. R. A. Sewter (London and New York, 1969)

Dawson, Christopher, *Mission to Asia* (London, 1956, as *The Mongol Mission*; reprinted Toronto, 1980)

Goodich, Michael, editor, *Other Middle Ages: Witnesses at the Margins of Medieval Society* (Philadelphia, 1998)

Harris, Peter, editor, *The Travels of Marco Polo* (New York, 2008)

Martin, Geoffrey and Ann Williams, editors, *Domesday Book: A Complete Translation* (London, 2004)

Medieval Trade in the Mediterranean World, translated by Robert S. Lopez and Irving W. Raymond, Columbia Records of Civilization, 52 (New York, 1955)

Origo, Iris, *The Merchant of Prato* (London, 1957)

Peters, Edward, editor, *The First Crusade: The Chronicle of Fulcher of Chartres and other source materials* (Philadelphia, 1998)

Shaw, Margaret, translator, *Joinville and Villehardouin: Chronicles of the Crusades* (New York, 1963)

The Jews and the Crusaders: The Hebrew Chronicles of the First and Second Crusades, translated by Shlomo Eidelberg (Madison, Wisconsin, 1977)

Modern scholarship

Bachrach, Bernard, *Early Medieval Jewish Policy in Western Europe* (Minneapolis, Minnesota, 1977)

Bredero, Adriaan H., *Christendom and Christianity in the Middle Ages: The Relations between Religion, Church, and Society*, translated by Reinder Bruinsma (Grand Rapids, Michigan, 1994)

Brown, R. Allen, *The Normans* (Woodbridge, Suffolk, 1984)

Chadwick, Henry, *East and West: The Making of a Rift in the Church, from Apostolic Times until the Council of Florence* (Oxford, 2005)

Chazan, Robert, *European Jewry and the First Crusade* (Berkeley, 1987)

Cohen, Jeremy, *The Friars and the Jews: The Evolution of Medieval Anti-Judaism* (Ithaca, New York, 1982)

Cohen, Jeremy, *Living Letters of the Law: Ideas of the Jew in Medieval Christianity* (Berkeley, 1999)

Duby, Georges, *The Early Growth of the European Economy*, translated by Howard B. Clarke (Ithaca, New York, 1974)

Epstein, Steven A., *An Economic and Social History of Later Medieval Europe, 1000–1500* (Cambridge and New York, 2009)

Erdmann, Carl, *The Origin of the Idea of Crusade*, translated by Marshall W. Baldwin and Walter Goffart (Princeton, 1977)

Haskins, Charles Homer, *The Normans in European History* (Boston, 1915)

Madden, Thomas, *Crusades: The Illustrated History* (Ann Arbor, Michigan, 2004)

Meyer, Henry Cord, *Drang nach Osten: Fortunes of a Slogan-Concept in German-Slavic Relations, 1849–1990* (Bern, 1996)

Moore, R. I., *The Formation of a Persecuting Society. Power and Deviance in Western Europe, 950–1250* (Oxford, 1987)

Muldoon, James and Felipe Fernández-Armesto, editors, *The Medieval Frontiers of Latin Christendom: Expansion, Contraction, Continuity* (London, 2008)

Pirenne, Henri, *Mediaeval Cities*, translated by F. D. Halsey (Princeton, 1925)

Pirenne, Henri, *Flemish towns, Belgian Democracy, its Early History*, translated by J. V. Saunders (Manchester, 1915)

Postan, Michael M., *The Medieval Economy and Society* (Harmondsworth, Middlesex, 1975)

Power, Daniel, *The Central Middle Ages: Europe 950–1320* (Oxford, 2006)

Pounds, Norman J. G., *An Historical Geography of Europe, 450 B.C.–A.D. 1330* (Cambridge, 1973)

Rörig, Fritz, *The Medieval Town* (Berkeley, 1967)

Runciman, Steven, *The Eastern Schism: A Study of the Papacy and the Eastern Churches During the XIth and XIIth Centuries* (Oxford, 1955)

Sedlar, Jean W., *East Central Europe in the Middle Ages, 1000–1500* (Seattle, 1994)

Waugh, Scott L. and Peter D. Diehl, editors, *Christendom and its Discontents: Exclusion, Persecutions, and Rebellion, 1000–1500* (Cambridge, 1996)

White, Lynn, Jr, *Medieval Technology and Social Change* (Oxford, 1962)

12

The age of the papacy

The major beneficiary of the growing sense of Christendom was the papacy, which used its position as the head of that body to translate long-standing claims into effective government. Indeed, the remarkable growth of papal power in the twelfth and thirteenth centuries is unimaginable without the prior existence of a sense of Christendom that the popes cultivated but did not create. Developments in the eleventh century had catapulted the sleepy and mostly ceremonial papacy into the leadership of reform movements that developed within the western church. When those reform movements were victorious, it gave the popes an immense reservoir of support and goodwill on which to draw.

Most institutions function effectively over long periods because the people involved accept their basic legitimacy, even if they disagree with specific policies. The papacy is a good illustration of this. The pope's authority was not based on his military power. He was the secular ruler of a few hundred square miles of central Italy, but the territory was turbulent and provided relatively few soldiers and only modest revenues. His authority was effective in the twelfth and thirteenth centuries because the rulers and opinion-makers in the west generally accepted him as the vicar of Christ, the successor of St Peter, and the head of Christendom, even as some of them may have opposed particular papal policies. Rulers, intellectuals and reformers criticised individual popes freely, but the fundamental legitimacy of papal power was unquestioned until the fourteenth century. On that base of goodwill, between about 1150 and 1350, the popes gathered into their own hands virtually all of the reins of church authority, building an imposing structure of laws, courts and financial resources. They made Christendom a visible reality.

I. The canon law

The twelfth and thirteenth centuries were an age of law. Merchants, townspeople and the church supported rulers who promoted orderly, rational legal procedures (instead of violence) for the settlement of life's inevitable quarrels. In Italy the rediscovered Roman law in the form of Justinian's *Corpus iuris civilis* (*Body of the Civil Law*) impressed the best minds of the age with its sophistication, its sense of justice and its rationality. In twelfth-century England, the judges of King Henry II (1154–89) began to create a 'common law' for that kingdom. Almost every grouping of human beings – towns, monasteries, religious orders, guilds and confraternities – began to make laws for itself in the search for order and rationality, and as a means to define the rights and duties of the group and its members. The church also had its own law, the canon law, which was key to the enhanced practical powers of the papacy.

The revived study of the canon law had been a major intellectual force for the eleventh-century reform movements. However, the multiplication of collections of canons, many of which were poorly organised and contained texts that were contradictory and of doubtful origin, created serious problems. By the twelfth century, the canon law desperately needed clarification and organisation if it was to function as an effective instrument of government. A jurist named Gratian, who may have been a bishop and was likely a law teacher at Bologna, carried out the most successful effort at reorganising the canon law in the 1120s, with revision and expansion of his work in the 1140s. Gratian's *Concordance of the Discordant Canons*, commonly known as the **Decretum**, began as a textbook he prepared for his students. It became the standard compilation of the traditional canon law, studied by generations of law students and used by judges. (See Figure 12.) The canon law regulated

Figure 12 The pope promulgating the law
This image from Gratian's *Decretum* shows the pope dealing with matters of law. The pope sits enthroned at the center, surrounded by cardinals (left), bishops (far left, wearing pointy mitres), and kings (right, wearing crowns). Seated in the front row are likely theologians and lawyers.

all aspects of church life and a great deal that in modern times is the responsibility of the state, including every sort of vow, wills, marriage, divorce and the legitimacy of children. The importance of canon law as the law of Christendom intensified in the twelfth and thirteenth centuries, during which an international system of church courts was developed to enforce it. Canon law became a university subject that prepared ambitious men for dignified, lucrative careers in the church.

In general, law must grow and adapt if it is to remain a living force. As medieval society became more sophisticated, wealthy and urban, the canon law had to confront new problems or provide more exact solutions to old ones. In modern America or Britain, an elected legislature creates new laws and abolishes outmoded ones, but Christendom had no legislature. In fact, aside from infrequent ecumenical councils, it had only one visible institution, the papacy. The papacy provided a mechanism of orderly change and, building on earlier practices, it assumed the function of legislating for Christendom. Since the fourth century, popes had been consulted on theological, liturgical and disciplinary matters and had often rendered their judgements in the form of letters, called decretals. Such documents had been issued only rarely in earlier times, but in the twelfth and thirteenth centuries papal decretal letters became the normal way to legislate for all of Christendom. Hard cases reached the papal court on appeal and ecclesiastical judges subsequently applied the judgement given there in similar cases. The canon law grew and adapted to 'modern times' by means of papal decisions recorded in decretals. This is not to say that the pope's legislation was automatic, or that it went ahead uncontested. For example, the Archbishop Stephen Langton (1150–1228) believed in the pope's 'plenitude (fullness) of power', but he also argued that any law decreed by the pope should be judged against the Scripture: 'Even though the bishop or the pope should forbid [something], he would not be bound to obey, for a matter of this kind is contrary to the Decalogue [i.e. the Ten Commandments].'[1]

Papally authorised compilations and canon law manuals became a second element of the canon law, alongside Gratian's *Decretum*. In 1210, Pope Innocent III (1198–1215) approved the *Compilatio tertia* (third compilation), in which the Cardinal Petrus Beneventanus had compiled documents from Innocent's pontificate. In 1226, Pope Honorius III (1216–27) approved the *Compilatio quinta* (fifth compilation), of the canonist Tancred. In 1234, Pope Gregory IX (1227–41) approved Raymond of Pennaforte's carefully organised collection of papal decretal letters. In 1298, Pope Boniface VIII (1294–1303) issued another authoritative collection of papal decretals, the *Liber Sextus*, and in 1317 Pope John XXII (1316–34) added yet another official collection, the *Constitutiones Clementis V*, which his predecessor Pope Clement V had started but had not finished before his death. Taken together, this formidable volume of laws was the *Corpus iuris canonici* (*Body of the Canon Law*), which could be compared favourably to the Roman law or to any secular law because of its breadth and sophistication. In the universities, scholars called decretists, who studied and commented on Gratian's *Decretum*, and decretalists, who worked on the papal decretals, created a well-developed body of commentary and legal theory. The canon law became a creation of the pope, issued by him or at least sanctioned by him for inclusion in the official collections.

Anyone reading the canon law is aware of how stern the punishments were. In fact, they were often so harsh as to be mostly symbolic, an expression of indignation toward the offence. In practice they were rarely exacted in their full vigour, particularly if the offender was penitent. For centuries the eastern and western churches had acted on the principle that if the strict application of a law would do more harm than good, it could be softened or, as the lawyers expressed it, 'dispensed'. As a simple example, the canon law said that mass was to be celebrated in a church by a priest who was fasting. But if in an emergency a priest had to say mass in the open air (for instance, with troops in the field), or if he had eaten because he did not expect to celebrate, then for necessity and common sense he could be dispensed from the law. Similarly, in their efforts to enhance the dignity of the clergy, the eleventh-century reformers had forbidden the ordination of illegitimate children, especially those of priests. However, if the young man was otherwise suitable for the clergy, and if there was no danger of seeming to approve of the fornication or adultery of his parents, or of the priest in question imitating his parents' fornication, then it became quite ordinary to dispense him from the law. As the papacy assumed a more central position in the life of the western church, dispensations in important matters were sought from the popes. In a pattern that repeated itself often in the twelfth and thirteenth centuries, the popes gradually became the sole source of dispensations from the full rigour of the law in such important matters as hitting a clergyman, marrying within the prohibited degrees of kinship, ordaining illegitimate persons and a host of other matters – though bishops could also grant some dispensations on their own authority. There were theoretical limits on the pope's power to dispense. He could not dispense from direct divine commands, such as the biblical prohibitions concerning idolatry. But almost every law touching on church discipline was the occasion for some sort of dispensation. Marriage cases alone brought thousands of lay people into direct contact with papal courts, which emphasised the pope's authority to exercise justice or mercy, to bind or to loose as he saw fit.

II. Papal exercise of power

The pope was not only the chief legislator of the church, but also the chief appeals judge, comparable perhaps to the American Supreme Court. As with the issuing of decretals and granting of dispensations, this was not entirely new in the central Middle Ages. In 382, the Roman emperor Gratian (375–83) had authorised the bishop of Rome to judge cases involving metropolitan bishops and to hear appeals from western bishops who had been convicted of wrongdoing by their fellow bishops. The popes had long maintained that they should have jurisdiction over important cases (*causae maiores*). During the early Middle Ages, the losers in some important cases, often theological arguments or marriage disputes, had appealed to the pope. What was new in the central Middle Ages, however, was the range and volume of such appeals. There was a complex apparatus of lower church courts, presided over by arch-priests, archdeacons, bishops and archbishops. As the prestige of the papacy grew, many litigants were unwilling to accept the decisions of such lower courts as final. From all over Christendom, aggrieved parties in disputes over marriage and divorce, church offices and elections, wills and inheritance, and a host of other issues brought their appeals to Rome. The popes welcomed the appeals, but the decision to appeal was that of the litigants. Litigants complained about expense and delays, but they came in ever-increasing numbers to the papal court because the justice dispensed there was perceived to be rational and fair.

The papal court was reorganised to handle the expanding business. From the later twelfth century, the pope and the cardinals, to whom he delegated much of the work, spent a significant part of each day hearing cases. Most decisions were routine, based on the law and its interpretation by the canonists. The more interesting and novel decisions became precedents for the future and were included in the official collections of papal decretals to be studied by lawyers and judges. The magnitude of business can be measured in the output of letters. R. W. Southern has calculated that under Pope Benedict IX (1033–46), one of the low points of the pre-reform papacy, we know of an average of only one letter per year. From Pope Leo IX (1048–56) until the 1130s, the average number of papal letters rose to 35 a year. The pace quickened in the later twelfth and thirteenth centuries: an annual average of 179 letters for Hadrian IV (1154–79), 280 letters for Innocent III (1198–1216), 730 for Innocent IV (1243–54) and 3,646 under John XXII (1316–24).[2] By the mid-twelfth century, the sheer volume of appeals to Rome made it necessary for the pope to appoint judges delegate to hear cases on the papacy's behalf in the provinces where they originated.

The popes also exercised practical authority through their legates, usually cardinals, who were empowered to act on their behalf in specific places or for specific purposes. The popes did not travel far, except when forced to flee the violence of Rome or threats from political enemies – which happened often enough. Legates carried the pope's presence and authority to all parts of Christendom, presiding over councils, negotiating with rulers, investigating important legal cases on the spot, organising crusades, collecting money owed the pope and mediating national and international disputes. They often referred complex or politically sensitive cases back to the pope. As a consequence of the activity of legates, the popes of the central Middle Ages were not distant, passive figures, as their predecessors had been before the eleventh-century reform. The papal court was the centre of a complex web of activity that reached the whole of Christendom through legates, appeals and letters.

The main rivals to papal power *within* the church were the archbishops and bishops, who in the early Middle Ages had traditionally acknowledged papal precedence but had retained a wide freedom of action within their dioceses. In the central Middle Ages, the popes maintained their traditional precedence among the bishops and in addition gained substantial control over them. Things that in the year 1000 local bishops would have felt free to do were increasingly subject to approval by the papacy or were removed from the bishops' control entirely. Canonisation of saints is a good example. Eternal life in heaven was the point of Christianity for the individual. It was taken for granted that many anonymous, ordinary dead Christians were in heaven, that is, they were saints. But the Christian community believed that it knew some of the saints by name. There were the New Testament saints (for example, the Virgin Mary, St Peter or St Paul) and the martyrs of the Roman persecutions. Saints from the earliest days of Christianity had not been canonised, a process by which the church formally declares a deceased person to be a saint and lists them in the canon of saints. Most early saints were simply acknowledged by the communities that remembered their stories, and commemorated them in the liturgy on certain days of the year. The ranks of the saints were not closed. Every Christian was a potential saint and the community continued to believe that God sent signs to reveal who some of the saints were. In the strong localism of the early Middle Ages, there were some people who were honoured as saints only in a particular region, or diocese, or monastery, or even in a single village.

Because the signs of the sainthood of any particular person had to be gathered and judged, the bishops began to take a leading role in canonisation. Before the twelfth century, the local bishop supervised the cult of saints in his diocese, as he did almost everything else touching on religion. Procedures were developed to judge whether a person was a saint. Usually there was a written life of the saint and accounts of miracles, often healings, at the saint's burial place. The bishop's approval of a saint began by moving or, as it was called, 'translating' the saint's body into a church. Next the bishop recited the saint's name in the canon of the mass – after the Offertory, when the bread and wine are offered for consecration, and before Communion, when the consecrated bread and wine is consumed by the faithful. For centuries, bishops authorised these acts on their own authority. In the Carolingian period, it became common to translate the saint's body during a council of bishops in order to lend increased dignity and authority to the proceedings. In 993, that search for dignity and assurance led to the papacy, when for the first time a pope canonised a saint, Bishop Ulrich of Augsburg (died 973). There was not yet an obligation to involve the pope, though his participation did add to the solemnity of the proceedings. Pope Alexander III (1159–81), a vigorous pope with training in canon law, insisted that canonisations be carried out in a formal way, with the pope presiding. In 1200, Pope Innocent III confirmed Alexander's canonisation procedure, and henceforth canonisations became the prerogative of the papacy: only the pope could declare a person to be a saint. In this and other decisions, the freedom of bishops to act was restricted by the pope's growing competence to do everything.

III. Church councils

The rise of papal authority also changed the nature of church councils, in which bishops had historically exercised their collective authority. In the twelfth and thirteenth centuries, there were more councils than there had ever been in the past. Bishops met with their priests in diocesan councils, archbishops met with their bishops in provincial councils, and papal legates met with regional groups of prelates. In earlier centuries, diocesan and provincial councils had taken initiatives, wrestled with serious problems of belief and discipline, and had made new canon law. The recognition of the popes as the proper source of new law largely stripped them of that function. They continued to be important for publicising law and policy, but they rarely made new law or new policy. Their canons were not supposed to be original. Usually they informed the local clergy and people of the reform ideas emanating from the papacy, and they repeated the important provisions of the canon law, with adaptations for local conditions.

The greatest theoretical rival to papal authority was the ecumenical or general council. The first general council, that of Nicaea (325), had been summoned and paid for by the Roman emperor Constantine. Pope Sylvester I (314–25), who was too old and ill to attend, sent two legates to represent him. Both precedents were followed for the first seven ecumenical councils: emperors summoned the councils and popes were not personally present but sent representatives. The series of ecumenical councils whose authority was recognised both in the east and the west ended with the Second Council of Nicaea (787). The reformed papacy of the twelfth century exercised its leadership of Christendom by summoning what it called 'general councils', though the eastern Orthodox churches rarely sent representatives and never acknowledged the ecumenical character of the councils. In 1123, Pope Calixtus II (1119–24) summoned the first western ecumenical council, which met in the Lateran Basilica at Rome. Successive popes summoned general councils in 1139, 1179 and 1215 to meet in the Lateran Basilica, in 1245 and 1274 at Lyons, and in 1311–12 at Vienne on the River Rhone.

As just one example of the work of councils, the Fourth Council of the Lateran (1215) was arguably one of the most influential of the central Middle Ages. Convoked by Pope Innocent III, the Fourth Lateran, also called the 'Great Council', was attended by 71 patriarchs and metropolitans, 412 bishops, 900 abbots and priors, and several representatives of kings. It issued canons which, among other things, condemned heresy, exhorted the eastern church to reunite with the western church, proclaimed papal primacy, forbade the establishment of new religious orders, urged every Christian to confess their sins annually, and required that Jews and Muslims within Christendom wear special dress to distinguish them from Christians. Such ecumenical councils were fully under the control of the pope, who summoned them, set their agenda, presided in person or by legates, and ratified their decisions. Even the ecumenical council had become an instrument of papal authority.

IV. Papal appointments to church offices

Papal appointment to church offices was an effective instrument of control, which did much to narrow the gap between theory and practice. In 1050, Pope Leo IX could appoint no one to church office outside central Italy; in 1342, Pope Clement VI nominated candidates for 100,000 church offices, a truly astonishing increase in effective power. Papal control of appointments was highly contested because it directly threatened the cherished and sometimes lucrative rights of lay and clerical patrons, cathedral chapters, monks, nuns and canons, who normally made such appointments. It was achieved only in the early fourteenth century, rather late in the process of papal growth.

Papal control of appointments grew incrementally, building on precedents. The most fruitful source of authority to appoint was a disputed election, which was normally appealed to the pope. The potential for disputes was built into the complicated and sometimes ambiguous way that prelates were elected. The eleventh-century reformers had opposed the power of laymen in ecclesiastical appointment, and had made 'election in accordance with the canons' one of their important aims. In the effort to eliminate the influence of powerful laymen, they generally eliminated all lay control and tried to place authority to elect in some defined group of clergy: monks in a monastery elected their abbot; the chief clergy of the diocese, organised into the cathedral chapter, elected the bishop. In the effort to make elections orderly and fair, the rules governing them grew more complicated, and therefore violations, whether intentional or unintentional, were common. The losing candidate frequently appealed the decision to the pope on legal grounds: for instance, that the election was too soon after the death of the former bishop or abbot, or that it was delayed too long after his death; that some electors had not been summoned; that some persons participated who should not have; that candidates had committed simony; that outsiders had pressured the electors; that the person elected was unsuitable in morals or learning; and so on. When the case came to the pope, he could choose one of the contenders or dismiss them all as unfit and impose his own candidate. In the thirteenth century, when virtually every election to a bishopric or an abbacy was disputed, the popes eventually chose most bishops and many abbots and abbesses as a consequence of appeals.

There were tens of thousands of other positions in the church, including the rectorship of parishes and membership in cathedral chapters. These positions, called benefices, were desirable because they had an endowed income connected to them. The holders of benefices were not elected but appointed. Historically such appointments had not been the business of the pope. Many people, including bishops, abbots, lay patrons and town councils, had the right to appoint or, as the technical term said, to 'provide' men to benefices. But precedent by precedent, the popes gained control over the filling of many benefices.

In its simplest form, a person petitioned the pope for a benefice. The sorts of people who needed to do this were often those who had no strong ties to a local patron. They might be university graduates, officials at the papal court or poor clergymen without a position. Such people enthusiastically supported the growth of papal power because it benefited them. In the twelfth century, popes began to respond to such petitions by requesting benefices from patrons. In the thirteenth century, they commanded that their nominees be given benefices, superseding the right of the traditional patron. Since these papal **provisions** threatened the rights of lay patrons, they were criticised in the 1240s in both England and France, but their numbers were at that time still very small. Popes often avoided awarding benefices whose patrons were laymen, so as not to alienate kings and princes. It was harder for a bishop to refuse an order to provide a benefice for a papal nominee - though they sometimes did.

For about a century, papal provision to benefices was sporadic and, compared to the number of benefices in Christendom, quite modest. In 1265, Pope Clement IV declared that a particular category of benefices, those that were vacated (for example, by death) while the holder was at the papal court, were reserved for the pope to fill. Over the next 50 years, the papacy continued to create new categories of benefices reserved for his appointment. Within a human lifetime, the popes came to provide the majority of benefices in Christendom, a fairly sudden change in traditional practice.

Papal provision was not an arbitrary procedure, but was carried out according to careful rules. A petitioner had to prove that he had the required age, education and good character to be granted a benefice. Many petitioners were refused on those grounds. If the petition was successful, the cleric received a letter of provision and went to take possession of the benefice. If a patron or a cathedral chapter refused to admit the person who had been provided, there was a legal proceeding to weigh the objections, since there had to be legal reasons for refusing a papal provision. It has been estimated that in the fourteenth century only about half of those who petitioned for a benefice received a papal provision and only about half of them actually succeeded in gaining the benefice to which they had been provided.

There are some things to take into account in assessing the significance of papal provision to benefices. First, by the late thirteenth century, the sheer numbers of provisions meant that no pope handled the business personally. The papal bureaucracy received requests for benefices and acted on them in an orderly fashion, according to precise rules and regulations. The vast majority of provisions were routine and carried out according to rules. If a provision had some extraordinary feature, for example, the person wanted to hold more than one benefice or was too young, the pope himself had to dispense from the rules. Papal bureaucrats, cardinals and papal nephews benefited from dispensation of the rules, but they received only a small portion of the thousands of benefices in Christendom, though often some of the most richly endowed. Second, the rules for papal provisions were progressive. For instance, they favoured university graduates over the choices of local patrons. Third, the system had checks and balances in it. If the candidate had some serious flaw he would often fail to gain possession of the benefice. Local patrons and cathedral chapters had many ways to resist. They used the law to foil the law, by appealing and delaying. Papal universalism was often frustrated in practice by ties of kinship, class and local patronage. For instance, many cathedral chapters in late medieval Germany took only noble members. If a commoner was provided to a church position, these chapters appealed or even accepted excommunication rather than yield. Their tactics could stall the entry of the commoner for years, or even thwart it all together. But even with the limits on it, the system of papal provisions made real the pope's claim to power. By the fourteenth century, many of the church's personnel, in one way or another, owed their positions to the pope.

In the twelfth and thirteenth centuries, the trajectory of papal power was upward. The papal court was the nerve centre of Christendom, which made every major decision and thousands of minor ones (though probably not regarded as minor by the participants). But even at its high point, the papacy had problems that we can probably see better than contemporaries could.

V. Papal finances

The greatest long-term weakness of the papacy was financial. It was an axiom of medieval political life that rulers should live from their own income. Ideally, a ruler would own landed estates that produced income and he would supplement that with traditional, limited payments from his subjects. Every ambitious ruler strove to increase his income, but normally he had to do it in ways his more powerful subjects regarded as legitimate. For example, King John of England (1199–1216) attempted to use his rights over his feudal vassals to raise revenue, but his barons saw the efforts as abusive and contrary to custom. They rebelled, defeated him and forced him to agree to the famous *Magna Carta*, which limited his rights to milk them financially. If a thirteenth-century ruler needed money for an emergency, for example, to conduct a war or to ward off an invasion, he often had to negotiate with the richest groups in his territory, usually the nobles, the townsmen and the clergy, who might grant him temporary taxes in return for privileges and concessions on his part. The surest way for a ruler to gain the resentment of his subjects and to arouse their resistance was to tax them arbitrarily.

Until the late thirteenth century, the pope had to live by the same rules. He had the landed wealth of the Roman church, from which he collected the rents, dues and payments in kind owed to any landlord. He ruled a little state in central Italy that paid him tolls, dues and tribute. Monasteries, such as Cluny, sought exemption from local bishops by placing themselves under the direct protection of the pope, and they paid a modest sum annually to acknowledge that protection. For political reasons, some lay rulers placed their territory under papal protection and paid an annual tribute to acknowledge it. In the thirteenth century, these tribute payers included the kings of England, Sicily, Castile, Portugal and Aragon, as well as many lesser lords. England, Poland and the Scandinavian countries paid an annual gift called Peter's Pence, which was theoretically one penny per household. As the custodian of the relics of Saint Peter and as the most dignified bishop of the church, the pope received gifts and legacies from the pious. Pilgrims made offerings in the many historic Roman churches, which offerings the pope shared with the individual church. His traditional sources of income were many, but people at every level of medieval society were notoriously reluctant to pay taxes, rents, dues and tribute. The sums owed to the papacy were often in arrears. The pope was not poor, but as the papacy became more active, like so many modern governments, its expenses often outran its income. The modern practice of adding the deficit in income to the long-term national debt had not yet been invented. Like other medieval rulers, the pope had to pay his bills in cash or to borrow from Italian bankers at high interest rates and against solid assets.

Traditionally the pope had no right to tax directly the other churches of Christendom. But that obstacle was overcome in indirect ways during the central Middle Ages. For example, the popes turned their leadership of the crusades to financial advantage. In 1187, the Muslim ruler of Egypt, Saladin (1169–93), reconquered Jerusalem, which had been in Christian hands for 88 years. Christendom was swept by indignation and launched the Third Crusade (1188–92). Contemporaries regarded the loss of Jerusalem as one of those emergencies that justified extraordinary taxes. The kings of England and France, who went on the crusade, demanded a subsidy from their lay and clerical subjects. The precedent of the crusade tax, which both clergy and laity paid, was set.

The papacy imposed direct crusade taxes on the clergy, but not on lay people. In 1199, Pope Innocent III levied a crusade tax of 2.5 per cent on every cleric's benefice. The situation in the Holy Land continued to worsen and crusade taxes on the clergy's income became common in the thirteenth century, often at a rate of 10 per cent for a period of one to six years. Once the precedent was set that the pope could tax clerical incomes, the revenues were in fact used for all sorts of purposes. In 1228, Gregory IX levied a 10 per cent tax to fight the Emperor Frederick II. By the later thirteenth century, the burdens and needs of the Roman church were a sufficient reason to levy taxes on the income of clergy throughout Christendom.

The popes of the thirteenth and fourteenth centuries also raised revenue by doing what other rulers did: charging fees for services. In one way or another, those who received a benefice from the papacy paid a tax proportional to its value, although the poorest category of benefices was exempted from fees. When the pope and cardinals confirmed the appointment of archbishops, bishops and abbots in a formal session, the newly appointed office-holders agreed to pay the *servitia*, which was a third of their first year's income. Benefices that did not pay the *servitia* paid *annates*, also a portion of the first year's income. Litigants in the papal courts paid for the cost of justice. Every proceeding conducted and every piece of parchment issued cost a sum of money to pay the judges, scribes and other officials. Recipients of dispensations, privileges and exemptions paid for the labour and materials involved in drawing up and registering the necessary documents. Papal authority generated considerable revenues, though often not enough to cover costs, and at the price of considerable resentment from those who paid, some of whom accused the papal court of simony.

In the later thirteenth and fourteenth centuries, the papacy's role as the head of Christendom and a major participant in European politics peaked. So, too, did the pope's need for money to support his upper-class lifestyle – popes and cardinals were overwhelmingly noble and expected to live as such. They also needed money to support the papal bureaucracy, crusades, building projects and armies to protect papal possessions in Italy. 'Crusade' taxes were levied regularly; fees for services were raised in amount and extended to cover almost everything. Still, the papacy ran a deficit, although contemporaries did not know that because the papal accounts were secret.

In response to these developments, there was a chorus of criticism that the papacy was greedy, that the fees were too high and that the popes were over-stepping traditional bounds. Some of this criticism took satiric form. The *Tractatus Garsiae Tholetani (Treatise of Garcia of Toledo), or The Translation of the Relics of Saints Albinus and Rufinus*, written in the eleventh century, addresses corruption at the papal court: a churchman travels to Rome to offer Pope Urban II the relics of two saints in exchange for a posh job in the church. The sin of simony is highlighted and ridiculed by the names of the saints, Albinus and Rufinus, which were code for silver and gold.

It is important to keep the criticism in perspective. In modern western democracies, many individuals and groups criticise their governments, but they do not hesitate to use their services and seek their aid when they need it. Like-wise, criticism did not prevent thirteenth- or fourteenth-century people from seeking provisions to benefices, marital dispensations and other papal services. Over the long run, however, the growing perception that the papal court was too interested in money and power undermined the foundation of goodwill on which the papal structure had stood at least since the Gregorian Reform.

VI. Pope Joan

Criticism of the papacy might also appear in mythic form. It is not difficult to imagine a 'worst case scenario' for the male-dominated medieval church: what if the highest cleric in the land were actually a woman disguised as a man? This is the theme of an interesting legend that first appeared in the thirteenth-century chronicle of a Dominican Friar named Jean de Mailly:

> Concerning a certain Pope or rather female Pope, who is not set down in the list of Popes or Bishops of Rome, because she was a woman who disguised herself as a man and became, by her character and talents, a curial secretary, then a Cardinal and finally Pope: One day, while mounting a horse, she gave birth to a child. Immediately, by Roman jus-tice, she was bound by the feet to a horse's tail and dragged and stoned by the people for half a league, and where she died, there she was buried, and at the place is written: '*Petre, Pater Patrum, Papisse Prodito Partum*' [Oh Peter, Father of Fathers, Betray the childbearing of the woman Pope]. At the same time, the four-day fast called the 'fast of the female Pope' was first established.[3]

This version of the legend does not name the pope, though later authors called her Pope John (when she was in disguise), and then Pope Joan (once her true identity was revealed). Authors throughout the Renaissance and Reformation retold the legend. In 1353, the poet Boccaccio published a version of the legend in his work 'Concerning Famous Women'.

Historians and other scholars generally dismiss the tale of Pope Joan as a medieval legend, but it is interesting to analyse it as a primary source of its own time, to see what it can tell us about the medieval mindset. The legend tells us a lot about attitudes toward women. Men continued to view them as deceptive (Joan disguises herself), manipulative (Joan works her way to the top) and lustful (even as the highest cleric, Joan cannot remain celibate). The legend may also be commenting on attitudes toward the church. During periods of reform, the fact that a woman could rise to the office of pope might be evidence of corruption (the church should not allow this), or at least incompetence (the church should have known). We can see how anti-clerical Protestants might use the legend as political satire. If the legend were true, it would mean a disruption in the continual laying on of hands from one pope to the next since the time of Peter. Since Joan, as a woman, could not legitimately be ordained, then the succession of the pope who followed her, and all popes thereafter, would not be valid. Great for the Protestants; not so great for the Catholics.

Even in our own time, the legend of Pope Joan continues to excite the interest of many. In 2009, German filmmakers produced, *Die Päpstin* ('The Female Pope'), with the English title, *Pope Joan*. Such interest can tell us something about the modern mindset. One scholar has argued that the desire to prove the Pope Joan legend true, in spite of the historical evidence against it, is little more than feminist wishful thinking blended with a renewed anti-Catholic, anti-papist sentiment.[4] It could also be that people are just curious about stories that do not fit the norm, whether they are historically true or not.

Let us return to the 'non-legendary' popes. By the mid-fourteenth century, the papacy had attained a position of practical, working authority in the church that would have been unimaginable three centuries earlier. On the basis of an accumulation of precedents, the papacy had firm control of the personnel of the church, and legislated for and judged Christendom, which meant lay people as well as clergy. Some canonists and theologians had sharpened the theoretical basis of papal power as well. From the pope's traditional roles as vicar of Christ, successor of Peter and head of the church, papal champions argued that the pope had full power (*plena potestas*) to manage the church and even lay society. He was the universal bishop of the church and all other clergy were merely his assistants, who could be put aside if he chose. In a succinct and extreme formulation, some canonists said that 'the pope is the church' (*papa est ecclesia*). The reality was less than that: long-standing tradition, financial restraints and the resistance of lay rulers to papal tampering in what they regarded as their sphere of power limited the popes. But papal power was greater in the early fourteenth century than it had ever been in the past, or ever would be.

Suggested reading

Companion website
www.routledge.com/cw/lynch

12.1   The Canonization Elizabeth of Thuringia
'Pope Gregory IX's bull canonizing Elizabeth of Thuringia' (1235), in Count de Montalembert, *Life of Saint Elizabeth of Hungary: Duchess of Thuringia*, Francis Deming Hoyt, trans., (New York: Longmans, Green, and Co., 1904), 414–420.

12.2   The Saladin Tax
'Henry II, Ordinance of the Saladin Tax (1188), in George Burton Adams and H. Morse Stephens, eds., *Select Document of English Constitutional History* (London: MacMillan and Co., Ltd., 1916), 27–28.

12.3   Antiphon: 'O Gloriosissimi lux', Hildegard von Bingen (1098–1179)
Musical recording: The Rose Ensemble, *Seasons of Angels, Harmony of the Spheres* (Saint Paul, MN, 2001)

12.4   Responsory: 'O nobilissima viriditas', Hildegard von Bingen (1098–1179)
Musical recording: The Rose Ensemble, *Seasons of Angels, Harmony of the Spheres* (Saint Paul, MN, 2001)

Primary sources

Bernard of Clairvaux (1090–1153), *Five Books of Consideration*, translated by John D. Anderson and Elizabeth T. Kennan, Cistercian Fathers series, 37 (Kalamazoo, Michigan, 1976)

John of Salisbury (1120–1180), *Historia Pontificalis, Memoirs of the Papal Court*, translated by Marjorie Chibnall (London, 1956)

Lunt, William E., *Papal Revenues in the Middle Ages*, two volumes, Columbia Records of Civilization, 19 (New York, 1934)

The Book of St Gilbert, edited by Raymonde Foreville and Gillian Keir (Oxford, 1987)

Modern scholarship

Barraclough, Geoffrey, *Papal Provisions* (Oxford, 1935)

Boureau, Alain, *The Myth of Pope Joan*, translated by Lydia G. Cochrane (Chicago, 2001)

Brundage, James, *Medieval Canon Law* (London, 1995)

Cheney, Christopher R., *Pope Innocent III and England*, Päpste und Papsttum, 9 (Stuttgart, 1976)

Duffy, Eamon, *Saints and Sinners: A History of the Popes* (New Haven, 1997)

Hughes, Philip, *The Church in Crisis. A History of the General Councils, 325–1870* (New York, 1961)

Jedin, Hubert, *Ecumenical Councils of the Catholic Church*, translated by E. Graf (Edinburgh, 1960)

Kemp, Eric W., *Canonization and Authority in the Western Church* (London, 1948)

Kuttner, Stephan, *Harmony from Dissonance: An Interpretation of Medieval Canon Law*, Wimmer Lecture, no. 10 (Latrobe, Pennsylvania, 1960)

Morris, Colin, *The Papal Monarchy: The Western Church from 1050–1250* (Oxford, 1989)

Tillmann, Helena, *Pope Innocent III*, translated by Walter Sax (Amsterdam, 1980)

Ullmann, Walter, *Law and Politics in the Middle Ages: An Introduction to the Sources of Medieval Political Ideas* (Ithaca, New York, 1975)

Ullmann, Walter, *The Growth of Papal Government in the Middle Ages*, 3rd edition (Cambridge, 1970)

Ullmann, Walter, *Medieval Papalism: The Political Theories of the Medieval Canonists* (London, 1949)

Waley, Daniel P., *The Papal State in the Thirteenth Century* (London, 1961)

Winroth, Anders, *The Making of Gratian's Decretum* (New York, 2000)

Yunck, John A., 'Economic Conservatism, Papal Finance, and the Medieval Satires on Rome', *Mediaeval Studies* 23 (1961), 334–51, and reprinted in abbreviated form in *Change in Medieval Society*, edited by Sylvia Thrupp (New York, 1964), pp. 72–85

Notes

1 Frederick M. Powicke, *Stephen Langton: Being the Ford Lectures Delivered in the University of Oxford in Hilary Term 1927* (Oxford, 1928), p. 16. The matter at hand was the restitution of ill-gotten funds.

2 R. W. Southern, *Western Society and the Church in the Middle Ages*, Pelican History of the Church, 2 (Harmondsworth, Middlesex, 1970), pp. 108–9.

3 Jean de Mailly, *Chronica Universalis Mettensis*, *Monumenta Germaniae Historica*, SS, xxiv, p. 514, published in Herbert Thurston, 'Pope Joan', *The Month*, vol. 123 (London, 1914) p. 451.

4 Philip Jenkins, *The New Anti-Catholicism: The Last Acceptable Prejudice* (New York, 2003), p. 89.

13

············

The New Testament revival

The papacy shaped the central medieval church, but it was not the only force at work. A religious revival affecting all levels of the church occurred simultaneously with the rise of the papal monarchy, sometimes supporting it, sometimes in conflict with it, and sometimes quite independent of it.

Religion can be a force for stability, legitimising the status quo. That was to a large degree the role of early medieval Christianity, when disorder was a constant danger and the weak institutions of society benefited from religious support. Religion can also be a force for change, challenging the status quo. That was sometimes the role of central medieval Christianity. The new critical stance of Christianity grew out of the eleventh-century reforms, which set in motion developments that not only stimulated the sense of Christendom and enhanced papal authority, but also unleashed a long-lasting religious revival, which one scholar has called 'the Medieval Reformation'.[1]

I. The Old Testament

To understand the nature of the religious revival, it is necessary to describe briefly the importance of the Old Testament in early medieval Christianity. From a certain perspective, the intellectual history of Christianity can be viewed as an effort to cope with the Old Testament. Since the very beginning, Christians have expended an immense amount of intellectual energy to tame the Old Testament and to make it compatible with the theological worldview of the New Testament. Some Christian Gnostics of the second and third centuries decided that the task was hopeless and simply rejected the Old Testament as the product of an evil or inferior god. However, the main stream of Christian development, the Catholic Christians, believed that the same God spoke both in the Old and in the New Testaments, and that the two collections of documents were in fundamental harmony. Such a formal belief could not hide the fact that the Old Testament was a complex and occasionally troubling book. The Latin Vulgate translation of the Old Testament, done mostly by Saint Jerome (347–420) in the late fourth and early fifth centuries, consisted of 46 items written in different times, places and literary genres. The New Testament, translated from Greek by Jerome, had 27 items, written within a century of one another, but differing in genre and sometimes in their views. Even a superficial comparison of the New Testament with the Old Testament reveals great differences. The Christian Gnostics attacked the worthies of the Old Testament, such as the patriarchs, some of the prophets and King David, for cruelty, lying and sexual immorality; they attacked the God of the Old Testament for ignorance, bloodthirstiness and pettiness. This contrasted to the New Testament God, especially as seen through the teachings of Jesus, who was loving and forgiving.

Other early Christian scholars set out by various techniques of interpretation, particularly typology and allegory, to find acceptable Christian meanings in Old Testament texts. For much of the poetry and prophecy in the Old Testament, that was easy enough, since they were filled with uplifting maxims and calls to repentance. The legal and historical books posed greater problems, since they depicted a God whom many thought was violent, arbitrary, ignorant, cruel and strict about petty rules. Much of the vast body of sermons and biblical commentaries from the ancient church was stimulated by the desire to defend the Old Testament against criticism and to harmonise it with the theology and morality of the New Testament. By the fifth century, the Catholic Christians had outlasted their Gnostic rivals and the Old Testament retained a secure place in the Christian Bible. In fact, for cultural reasons, its importance grew greater in the early medieval west.

Any sacred text, including the Bible, must speak to believers in ways they can understand. A people's socio-economic situation and cultural values will influence what they find relevant or irrelevant, comprehensible or incomprehensible in the Bible. Across history, some portions of the scriptures have had great importance in one era and almost none in another. For instance, during the European witch-craze of the sixteenth and seventeenth centuries, the text of Exodus 22:18 ('You shall not allow a sorceress to live') was cited to justify the burning alive of tens of thousands of people. In the twenty-first century, it is unlikely that this text is even mentioned by preachers. The biblical passage remains the same, but the values and outlook of the readers have changed.

The Germanic and Celtic barbarians who were converted to Christianity in the early Middle Ages were different from the literate urban populace that set the tone for Christianity in the fourth- and fifth-century Roman Empire. The newcomers were better suited by their culture and experience to understand the Old Testament than the New. The Germanic and Celtic Christians and their clergy certainly accepted, in so far as they understood it, the authority of the New Testament and the importance of the God-man Jesus. But they saw a reflection of their own lives in the earthy descriptions of the Jews of the Old Testament, wandering and fighting under the leadership of warrior-kings. The Old Testament deeply influenced early medieval Christianity. Early medieval rulers found models for themselves in the kings of Israel, who fought their wars under the protection of Yahweh. Like the Old Testament kings, the

Frankish kings disciplined their people and protected the unity of religion, by force if necessary. The Frankish elite saw itself as the new Israelites: it was no accident that Charlemagne's nickname was David, the great Israelite warrior-king, and his son Louis's nickname was Solomon, David's wise and wealthy successor. Some of the moral teaching of the New Testament that was highly prized in later times was almost incomprehensible in a violent world. 'Turning the other cheek' and 'going meekly like a lamb to the slaughter' were hard notions for an early medieval warrior to appreciate. An eighth-century chronicler reported that when Clovis (481–511), the first Christian Frankish king, was told of Jesus's crucifixion, he said, 'If I and my Franks had been there, I would have avenged the wrong.'[2] The *Heliand* ('Saviour'), a ninth-century poem based on the Gospel of Mark, depicts Jesus as the war chief and the apostles as his warrior companions. The Germanic peoples of the early Middle Ages understood God as the Lord God of Hosts who led them in battle and also as the strict Judge who would eventually repay everyone according to his deeds. The belief in Jesus's loving Father was not denied, but it apparently made less sense in a violent warrior culture.

The elaborate moral and ritual regulations of the Old Testament also appealed to some early medieval clergy, who were trying to introduce order into a very disorderly society. They found the religious spirit of the Old Testament, with its adherence to rules and obedience to prohibitions, understandable and attractive. Between the seventh and tenth centuries, intellectuals, particularly among the Irish and those influenced by them, eagerly read the Old Testament, and tried with varying success to introduce Old Testament practices into contemporary Christianity. The Carolingian imposition of tithes – the mandatory payment of one-tenth of one's income – on the whole Christian society was perhaps the most spectacular and long-lasting revival of an Old Testament practice, but not the only one. Old Testament prohibitions of work on the Sabbath, that is, Saturday, were transferred with some success to Sundays and holy days. Old Testament notions of ritual cleanness and uncleanness were also revived: menstruating women were to avoid contact with anything holy; women who had recently given birth had to be purified; and married couples who wished to receive the Eucharist had to abstain from sexual relations for a time to make themselves worthy. There were efforts to reintroduce some of the food prohibitions of the Old Testament: for three 40-day periods a year, the faithful had to reduce their intake of food by fasting and abstaining from meat. Old Testament models of worship were imitated in the Christian liturgy, which borrowed the use of incense and anointing with oil as means to sanctify people and things. It is necessary to repeat that early medieval people read and revered the New Testament, but they placed relatively greater weight on the Old Testament, probably because it made cultural sense.

II. The New Testament

A major shift in Christian perceptions and feelings occurred between the eleventh and the fourteenth centuries, when western Christians in great numbers discovered the emotional power of the New Testament, especially the gospels. The Old Testament remained authoritative as sacred scripture. The imagery of the psalms, the exhortations of the prophets and the rich lore of the Old Testament heroes kept their prominent place in art, liturgy, preaching and theology. However, the relative weight shifted from the Lord God of Hosts, who triumphed over the enemies of Israel, to the loving God, who sent his son to live in poverty, to die in great suffering on behalf of humankind, and to rise in glory. This was not a new story in western Christianity, but more people began to feel it more deeply.

Important changes in religious life are not easy to explain. The most immediate cause seems to have been the eleventh-century reform movement, which marked a turning point in so many aspects of religious and political life. Sacred kingship had been built in part on the model of Old Testament kings. The papal monarchy was built in part on the New Testament promises from Christ to Peter. Hence the papal party downplayed and undermined the appropriateness of Old Testament models, which were interpreted less literally and more figuratively. The debates accompanying the reforms took place in public and engaged many people. Clergy and highborn lay people found themselves forced to choose sides in controversies about the basic foundations of society. In the growing urban areas, some townspeople also threw themselves into the struggle for and against particular reforms. For more than fifty years, western Christians had been mobilised around religious issues. The energetic concern with change in religion survived even after the particular issues had subsided.

Shifts in socio-economic conditions may also have played an important role in religious change. The growth of towns provided a new context for a complicated debate over the best way to live as a Christian. For 700 years, the church had laboured in and adapted to a rural society with small villages, endemic poverty and illiteracy. The rapid rise of towns in the twelfth and thirteenth centuries challenged the church to develop ways of ministering to human types that were new or at least much more numerous in the west: the urban merchant, the artisan and the urban poor. Towns were not just a way of concentrating more people in a smaller area: they comprised a new social universe. The spread of literacy, the growth of the urban social hierarchy, the great contrast between rich and poor living side-by-side in small towns, the needs of self-government, the struggle to gain a living from commerce or artisanship, the competition among urban factions and the demands of survival in a world hostile to commerce, all nourished a mentality that questioned, probed and judged inherited traditions, including religious ones. The institutional church found no easy solution to the problems that urban life posed for it.

Even among the traditionally dominant social groups, religious change was visible. Some nobles internalised the message of the New Testament. The semi-literate pious among them began to use simple prayer books for their private devotions. They sought closer ties with monastic houses and adopted some monastic practices for their own piety. Their choice to join monastic life in large numbers sometimes led to the extinction of noble families.

Whatever the mix of causes, a new religious outlook that centred on the gospels flowed through the central medieval church in ways that are both obvious and not so obvious. We can probably best gain immediate access to the intense reaction to the New Testament through medieval art. Early medieval depictions of the crucifixion generally showed a serene Jesus, sometimes crowned, who had overcome death even on the cross. Beginning in the eleventh century, artists (and the patrons who paid them) generally laid greater stress than before on the emotional and human aspects of Christianity, particularly on Jesus and his mother, Mary. In pondering the traditional belief that God became a man, the artistic emphasis shifted to Jesus's humanity. Central medieval depictions of the crucifixion emphasised more clearly Jesus as he suffered: unconscious, chest sunken, head tilted, wounds bloody. (See Figure 13.) Artists wanted viewers to understand what Jesus had endured on their behalf. In a similar way, early medieval depictions of Mary and the child Jesus showed a dignified woman, a queen perhaps, with a child who was often just a man in miniature, looking out at the viewer, sometimes making a gesture of blessing or teaching. In contrast, many central medieval paintings and sculptures showed a young mother, pretty, with a realistically portrayed baby who might be playing with a ball or sucking at the breast. The viewer was reminded of the reality of Jesus's humanity: he had been a baby, just as they all had been. The twelfth and thirteenth centuries also saw a kind of Marian obsession, with churches and monasteries being founded and endowed in Mary's name. Devotion to Mary increased, and her feast days (the Annunciation and the Assumption) took on greater importance.

Of course, the new religious emphasis found expression in ways other than art, though these other forms also emphasised the gospels and Christ's humanity. Pilgrimage became a common practice, by which hundreds of thousands of westerners went to Palestine between the eleventh and the fifteenth centuries, drawn in part by a desire to see for themselves the actual places where they believed Jesus had been born, lived, preached, died and rose from the grave. For medieval people, even the practice of crusade – which we generally associate only with warfare – was a kind of pilgrimage. In theological terms, Easter was the main religious festival of the church, because it

Figure 13 Suffering Christ
The crucifix of Archbishop Gero of Cologne (*c.*970) shows Christ suffering on the cross: head hanging down, hands twisted, knees bent. Earlier depictions of Christ's crucifixion showed him in a more triumphant pose, posture erect, head held high, looking straight ahead. The different depictions of Christ, 'in majesty' or 'suffering for humanity', reflect the historical contexts in which the artists created them. The Gero Crucifix is life size. The halo and crosspieces are original, but the sunburst in the background was added during the Baroque period (1683), again showing a different context and attitude toward the crucifixion.

celebrated the resurrection of Jesus. But in the central Middle Ages, Christmas grew in importance because it commemorated the humanity of Jesus with its rich images of a virgin conceiving a child, a birth in a humble stable, wise men from the east, shepherds and a baby boy with his mother. It might have been Francis of Assisi (1180–1226) himself who created the first manger scene, with its straw and live animals, to bring home vividly to Italian urban dwellers the reality of Jesus's birth and humanity. Francis was also the first in a long tradition of followers who identified so strongly with the sufferings of the human Christ that he and his followers believed he was given Christ's wounds, called the *stigmata*, on his hands, feet and side.

This '**evangelical** revival' (from the Latin word for gospel, *evangelium*), reached all levels of society, including some peasants, lower-class urban people and especially women, whose roles in religious life in the early Middle Ages are almost invisible to us. For lay people, religious activism was quite new, and there were few models for them to follow. Traditionally, very pious lay people had become monks or nuns to provide an ordered setting in which to intensify their religious practices. For a minority of people that practice continued, but something new happened in the central Middle Ages: many lay people sought a more intense and personal religious life while remaining in the secular world, perhaps married, and even earning their own living.

The institutional church often did not know how to react to such people but it generally welcomed the development. It attempted to reinforce and also to channel the evangelical revival by teaching the orthodox faith to the laity through the media at its disposal. For the literate, this was the beginning of the age of personal prayer books, which eventually developed into splendidly illustrated books of hours. Literate, pious lay people imitated the prayer life of monks, reciting simple Latin prayers or the psalms at regular intervals during the day and praying for the dead. In that way, there was a flow of devotions and practices out of religious houses into the elite of the laity. For instance, every day the exceptionally pious French king Louis IX (1226–70) heard the canonical hours sung by a full choir and attended a mass specifically for the dead. In addition, he also attended the mass of the day, if he could. During his afternoon siesta, he and a chaplain recited the office for the dead. King Louis was unusual, but he does represent the widespread tendency to internalise religious practices by imitating the monks and friars. For many people, particularly pious women, knowledge of even simple Latin was unavailable. For them, prayers and pious reading were translated into the vernacular languages. Beginning in the late twelfth century, favourite prayers, simple sermons, materials for meditation and portions of scripture (psalms and gospels) were translated or paraphrased into the European vernaculars to be read by pious individuals, or to be read to them. The translation of the scriptures into the vernacular languages made the church authorities uneasy because in their view most lay readers and uneducated clergy were incapable of understanding the texts in accordance with traditional beliefs. In some instances, the church found unauthorised scriptural translations to be heretical, for example, with the Waldensians. Yet, vernacular translations were not absolutely forbidden by any pope or council, and did circulate among the literate and semi-literate.

The majority of people, however, were illiterate, unable to read either in Latin or in their native tongue, yet some of them were also touched by the evangelical revival. The church sought to teach them by means of communications that were auditory and pictorial rather than written. The consequences of the church's urge to teach are still visible in the decoration of churches built in the central Middle Ages. Before 1050, the exterior of a church was ordinarily quite plain, with neither statues nor carvings. The interiors were ornate, even splendid, with carvings, frescoes and tapestries showing religious scenes, but much of the decoration (leaves and vines, heads of fanciful beasts) had no obvious teaching purpose. In the twelfth century, growing prosperity made possible a massive surge of church building, often in a new style that we call Gothic. It has been calculated that between 1050 and 1350 in France alone, 80 cathedrals, 500 large churches and 10,000 parish churches were built. The new churches were consciously designed as teaching devices. Their outer walls, visible to passers-by, were covered with sculpture that depicted recognisable stories from the Old Testament, the New Testament or the lives of the saints. Their interior walls were hung with tapestries or painted with religious scenes. Their windows were filled with stained glass in which the basic Christian message was proclaimed in pictorial narratives and allegories. Some of the art was filled with such complex symbolism that lay people could not easily decipher it without the help of clergy. Yet in many of the new churches, accessible images of Jesus, his mother and his apostles were the focal points of art designed to teach.

Knowledge of biblical stories and saints' lives also reached wide audiences through the ears. Between the eleventh and the fourteenth centuries, the sheer volume of preaching to lay audiences grew enormously, particularly from the orders of friars, founded in the thirteenth century for the express purpose of preaching and teaching. For the first time since antiquity, dramas were staged that depicted the central points of Christian belief. In some areas, town councils and guilds of merchants and craftsmen annually sponsored plays in the squares and streets (the modern Passion play at Oberammergau is a late descendant of such efforts). At York, where the actual texts survive from the fifteenth century, the cycle of Christian belief from the fall of Lucifer before creation to the Day of Judgement was depicted in lively plays, performed in the streets on wagons used as stages, during the festival of *Corpus Christi* ('Body of Christ'), which celebrates the real presence of the body and blood of Jesus in the Eucharist. Street performers, called *jongleurs* in French, had in their repertory religious poems in the vernacular, particularly about the saints. Through such means, the pious partially quenched their thirst for religious knowledge.

III. The apostolic life

Christianity is complex, but in any period the intelligent man or woman in the street can sum up, almost in slogans or bumper stickers, what seems most important to them. It should be no surprise that the emphasis would vary considerably across space and time. In twenty-first century America, that man or woman might say 'God is love' or that the message of Christianity is 'Peace'. In sixteenth-century Germany, a Lutheran might have said 'We are saved by faith alone' and a Catholic might have said 'Faith without works is dead.' In twelfth-century Europe, many pious and spiritually sensitive laymen and clerics said that they were called to live the *vita apostolica*, 'the **apostolic life**'. This imitation of Jesus and the apostles was a powerful model that attracted adherents and generated controversy about how it was to be carried out. One influential description, which the reader may recall from Chapter 2, is from *The Acts of the Apostles*, 4:32–5:

> The whole group of believers was united, heart and soul; no one claimed for his own use anything that he had, as everything they owned was held in common. The apostles continued to testify to the resurrection of the Lord Jesus with great power, and they were all given great respect. None of the members was ever in want, as all those who owned land or houses would sell them, and bring the money from them, to present it to the apostles; it was then distributed to any members who might be in need.

The main elements of the apostolic life, as it was understood in the twelfth and thirteenth centuries, are in this biblical passage: renunciation of personal wealth, sharing with one's spiritual brothers and sisters, life in a community and preaching the message of personal salvation.

This could be summed up in two words: poverty and preaching. Of course, poverty due to birth or misfortune was not regarded as meritorious in itself, because such poor people often envied their betters and wished to be rich. The most admirable poverty was voluntary, like that of the apostles who had abandoned their homes, lands and families for the sake of the gospel (Mark 10:29–30), or that of St Paul, who worked with his hands as a tentmaker to earn his living. In that sense, people who had some wealth adopted voluntary poverty like that of the apostles. It is no accident that voluntary poverty for religious reasons was praised in an age of economic expansion and increasing material success. The growing urban life of Europe created sharp divisions among the few rich merchants, nobles and clerics (who were regarded as proud and showy), the artisans and craftsmen (who often had a precarious livelihood) and the truly poor (who struggled to make ends meet). The renunciation of personal wealth in favour of apostolic poverty must often have been a dramatic repudiation of the values of a commercial society.

There was also an influential description of how the apostles behaved when they preached. When Jesus sent his disciples to preach to the Jews, Mark (6:7–13) described the scene thus:

> Then he summoned the Twelve and began to send them out in pairs giving them author-
> ity over unclean spirits. And he instructed them to take nothing for the journey except a
> staff – no bread, no haversack, and no coppers for their purses. They were to wear sandals
> but, he added, 'Do not take a spare tunic.' And he said to them, 'If you enter a house
> anywhere, stay there until you leave the district. And if any place does not welcome you
> and people refuse to listen to you, as you walk away shake off the dust from under your
> feet as a sign to them.' So they set off to preach repentance; and they cast out many
> devils, and anointed many sick people with oil and cured them.

By contrast, in Matthew 10:10, the apostles were told *not* to take sandals or a staff on their preaching trips, a difference that caused friction among some of the preachers. But the model of penniless, wandering, apostolic preachers (some with shoes and some without shoes) was a powerful one in the society of the central Middle Ages.

Many people felt the attraction of the apostolic life, but the responses were varied, depending on which of its main features one emphasised: poverty or preaching. The majority of people could not adopt such a way of life. But many did what we in the twenty-first century do when we encounter an admirable (but for us impossible) ideal: they gave money and support to those who did adopt it. Abbots and bishops, whose lives were filled with lawsuits and visits to the royal court, supported hermits, who lived a life of poverty. The kings of England annually gave silver pennies to anchorites walled up in churches. Townspeople gave alms and protection to the grubby preachers who passed through their region. Admirers also adopted those bits and pieces of the apostolic way of life that could fit into ordinary life. Thomas Becket (1118–70), archbishop of Canterbury, a man who dressed and ate well and hobnobbed with the elite of England, wore a rough, scratchy and lice-ridden garment called a hair shirt under his fine robes. Some Italian merchants set aside part of their profits for the account of the 'Lord God' and gave the money to the poor.

So far, the influence of the evangelical revival among lay people has been stressed, but the clergy were, if anything, even more influenced by the high value given to poverty and preaching. Clergy had always taken an active role in religion – it was their occupation – but the new evangelical ideas touched the core of what they did. Since Carolingian times, great weight was put on the role of the priest as a liturgical intermediary with God. He was the dispenser of sacraments, the intercessor with God, and the custodian of holy things that were important to the wellbeing of individuals and the community. That liturgical role continued, but the ideal of the apostolic life added an emphasis on the priest's personal poverty and fervent preaching. Even though the new ideal was powerful, many secular clergy resisted the call to poverty, and few could preach adequately because of lack of training.

Other clergy, particularly regular clergy, did attempt to live the apostolic life, often combining it with traditional ways of monastic life. There was a lively debate among the regular clergy about which of them best lived the apostolic life. Monks and nuns, who renounced personal wealth and lived in communities of prayer and work, believed that they lived the apostolic life, with the added virtue of sexual abstinence. Regular canons argued that they were closer to the apostolic ideal because they embraced poverty and chastity as monks did, and also taught and preached to lay people. In the twelfth and thirteenth centuries, reform movements continuously agitated religious life in one way or another, always attempting to push reality closer to the ideals of the apostolic life. It was symptomatic of the low status of ordinary parish priests that no one thought they lived the apostolic life, or that they ordinarily could.

IV. Wandering preachers

In the long run, the most important result of the pursuit of the apostolic life was that intense religious behaviour was no longer a monopoly of monks, nuns and canons. It had burst out into society with many consequences. In the twelfth century, unauthorised travelling preachers appeared for the first time on a large scale in the medieval west. They were mostly priests, but some were laymen. They differed among themselves, but almost all were promoting a variation on the apostolic life of poverty and preaching. Many tried to live a biblically literal version of the life of Jesus and the apostles, impoverished, barefoot or sandalled, and preaching repentance to all who would listen. They posed a great problem for the authorities. Their message was often religiously orthodox, but the consequences of applying in a literal way Jesus's hard sayings about property and family were socially disruptive: men and women abandoned their occupations and families; bands of men and women travelled together, slept out of doors and begged for food; occasional sexual scandals encouraged suspicion about such people; and charlatans took advantage of the situation. Try to imagine such things happening in a modern, prosperous suburban congregation and you will have some sense of the uproar that an effective preacher of the apostolic life could cause in a medieval city.

Christian moral theology had long distinguished between biblical commands that bound everyone (for instance, Exod. 20:15, 'You shall not steal'), and biblical counsels that were pieces of advice that the individual could choose to follow for the sake of gaining merit (for instance, Matt. 19:21, 'Sell all you have, give to the poor, and come follow me'). In the view of the church, the call to adopt the apostolic life was a good thing, but it was a counsel rather than a command. If a preacher encouraged hearers to adopt the apostolic life voluntarily, that was quite acceptable. But if in his zeal he said they must, and that those who did not were damned, that was unacceptable. When authorities in the church or the government resisted these 'unauthorised' preachers, they often became more extreme. Some verbally and even physically attacked the secular clergy, who did not impose such a lifestyle on themselves or on the laity. The many churches, monasteries and other institutions that made up the church had benefited from the growing prosperity of Europe, and some were wealthy. That wealth provoked criticism and resentment from many quarters, including these new preachers of poverty. The wandering preachers drew support from the evangelical revival and nourished it in many places, but with mixed results for the institutional church.

V. Hermits

Seemingly quite distinct from these mobile, popular preachers – but in fact responding to a similar urge for simplicity of life, poverty and personal religious experience – were the hermits who became prominent on the religious scene in the eleventh and twelfth centuries. A rich literature from fourth- and fifth-century Egypt extolled the virtues of the great hermits of the desert, particularly Saint Anthony (c.250–355). These stories depicted the early desert hermits living lives of ferocious self-denial, going without food, sleep, adequate clothing and human companionship. In the eleventh and twelfth centuries, hermits seemed to embody the poverty side of the apostolic life and to live out another slogan of the age, 'naked to follow the naked Christ'. In England, association with hermits became almost fashionable: nobles retained them on their lands; small town parishioners supported local hermits; and almost everyone undertook pilgrimages to the hermit's remote dwellings, called hermitages, seeking prayers, advice and wisdom. In the mountains of southern Italy and the forests of western France, a hermit's much-admired way of life could also draw disciples in loose groupings that sometimes became unstable. The death of the hermit often forced a change:

either a scattering of the group or a move to a more ordered life. It is perhaps ironic that many strict religious houses and orders arose out of a hermit's individualistic strivings in the wilderness.

The religious revival, with its emphasis on the New Testament, marked the central Middle Ages between the late eleventh and the early fourteenth centuries. Subsequent chapters will study this revival in more detail.

Suggested reading

Companion website

www.routledge.com/cw/lynch

13.1 Francis of Assisi and the first Nativity scene
Excerpts from Brother Thomas of Celano, *The Lives of S. Francis of Assisi*, trans. A. G. Ferrers Howell (London: Methuen & Co., 1908), 82–85.

13.2 Francis of Assisi and the Stigmata
Excerpts from Brother Thomas of Celano, *The Lives of S. Francis of Assisi*, trans. A. G. Ferrers Howell (London: Methuen & Co., 1908), 92–95.

13.3 The Piety of King Louis IX
Excerpts from the Sire De Joinville, *Saint Louis, King of France*, trans. James Hutton (London: Sampson Low, Marston, And Company, 1892), 199, 205–207, 208–210.

13.4 Cantiga #252, Cantigas de Santa Maria (13th-14th century)
Musical recording: The Rose Ensemble, *Rosa das Rosas* (Saint Paul, MN, 2006)

Primary sources

Beadle, Richard and Pamela M. King, editors, *York Mystery Plays: A Selection in Modern Spelling* (Oxford, 1999)

Brooke, Rosalind B., *The Coming of the Friars*, Historical Problems: Studies and Documents, 24 (New York, 1975)

Habig, Marion A., editor, *St. Francis of Assisi. Writings and Early Biographies*, 3rd revised edition by John R. H. Moorman (London, 1973)

Jean de Joinville, *The Life of Saint Louis*, translated by M. R. B. Shaw in *Chronicles of the Crusades* (Harmondsworth, Middlesex, 1963)

Murphy, G. Ronald, editor and translator, *The Heliand: The Saxon Gospel* (New York, 1992)

Schenkkan, Robert and Kai Jurgensen, editors, *Fourteen Plays for the Church* (New Brunswick, New Jersey, 1948)

Modern scholarship

Bolton, Brenda, *The Medieval Reformation* (London, 1983)

Boyle, Leonard E., 'Innocent III and Vernacular Versions of Scripture', in *The Bible in the Medieval World. Essays in Memory of Beryl Smalley*. Studies in Church History, Subsidia, 4 (Oxford, 1985), pp. 97–107

Chenu, Marie-Dominique, 'Monks, Canons, and Laymen in Search of the Apostolic Life', in *Nature, Man, and Society in the Twelfth Century*, translated by Jerome Taylor and Lester K. Little (Chicago, 1968), pp. 202–38

Constable, Giles, *The Reformation of the Twelfth Century* (Cambridge, 1996)

Duby, Georges, *The Europe of the Cathedrals, 1140–1280*, translated by Stuart Gilbert (Geneva, 1966)

Grundmann, Herbert, *Religious Movements in the Middle Ages*, translated by Steven Rowan (South Bend, Indiana, 1996)

Kelly, J. N. D., *Early Christian Doctrines*, 2nd edition (New York, 1978), pp. 64–78

Leyser, Henrietta, *Hermits and the New Monasticism. A Study of Religious Communities in Western Europe, 1000–1150* (New York, 1984)

Licence, Tom, *Hermits and Recluses in English Society, 950–1200* (New York, 2011)

Little, Lester K., *Religious Poverty and the Profit Economy in Medieval Europe* (Ithaca, New York, 1978)

Mâle, Emile, *The Gothic Image. Religious Art in France of the Thirteenth Century*, translated by Dora Nussey (New York, 1913; reprinted 1958)

Warren, Ann K., *Anchorites and Their Patrons in Medieval England* (Berkeley, 1985)

Woolf, Rosemary, *The English Mystery Plays* (Berkeley, 1972)

Notes

1 Brenda Bolton, *The Medieval Reformation* (London, 1983).
2 Pseudo-Fredegar, *Chronicarum quae dicuntur Fredegarii libri quatuor*, book 3, ch. 21, edited by Bruno Krusch and reprinted in *Quellen zur Geschichte des 7. und 8. Jahrhunderts*, Ausgewählte Quellen zur Deutschen Geschichte des Mittelalters, vol. 4a (Darmstadt, 1982), p. 108.

14

Monastic life in the twelfth century

I. Cluny

In 1095, Pope Urban II, a former grand prior at the Abbey of Cluny, returned to that monastery to consecrate the main altar of the new church being built there, the largest church in Christendom. The contemporary abbot of Cluny, Hugh the Great (1049–1109), was second only to the pope in prestige and had considerably greater economic resources. He presided over an empire of approximately 1,000 monasteries, containing perhaps 20,000 monks. The monastery of Cluny itself had more than 300 monks, many of whom were the sons of important aristocratic and even royal families. In the impressive church at Cluny, long and elaborate liturgical services in magnificent surroundings were performed at regular intervals, both night and day. In 1095, Cluny was at the height of its influence, the very model of how a fervent Benedictine monastic life should be carried out. Aristocrats sent gifts, offered their sons as oblates, and sought the monastic habit in serious illness or old age so they could die as Cluniac monks. But the Cluniac interpretation of the monastic ideal was already under criticism by individuals and small groups, whose influence was minor in 1095 but grew in the twelfth century as the ideal of the apostolic life of poverty and preaching gained adherents. Some critics sought to redefine the Benedictine ideal; others sought to replace it entirely. Even as Pope Urban and Abbot Hugh were presiding over the ceremonies at Cluny, about a hundred miles away at Molesme, Abbot Robert was attempting to persuade his monks to adopt a more austere, simpler version of the Benedictine rule. About 750 miles away in southern Italy, one of Urban II's teachers, Bruno of Cologne (c.1030–1101), had abandoned the Benedictine rule altogether and was living the harsh life of a hermit, praying in simple, isolated surroundings and earning his bread by the work of his hands. The ideal of the apostolic life of poverty, preaching and personal religious experience was beginning to challenge the solid Cluniac structure and the religious ideal that it represented.

Hugh the Great was the last abbot of Cluny who could legitimately think that his monastery was unchallenged in its position as the leading monastery in Christendom. His successors had to deal with serious practical problems as well as with a shift in religious ideals. The practical problems had to do with supervision and money. Benedictine monasteries had traditionally depended on a vigilant abbot to maintain the quality of religious life. By 1095, the

Cluniac order had expanded far beyond any abbot's ability to supervise the hundreds of houses subject to his rule. Because of distance and numbers, many Cluniac monks never saw the abbot of Cluny. The consequences were a slackening of observance in some houses, which was reflected in violations of the rules against eating meat, in accepting unsuitable candidates, in internal quarrels and in a lifestyle that was sometimes more worldly than monks should live.

Cluny's financial problems were also rooted in its success. In its early days, the house had fed and clothed the monks and servants from the produce of estates in the vicinity of Cluny. In the later eleventh century the flow of gifts in gold and silver, which reflected both the prestige of Cluny and the economic revival of Europe, encouraged the monastery to buy more of what it needed and to run into debt for building projects, including the construction of its huge new church. As religious ideals shifted in the twelfth century, the monetary gifts on which the house had become dependent began to dry up. The stormy abbacy of Pons de Melgeuil (1109–22) damaged Cluny's internal discipline, finances and reputation. Abbot Peter the Venerable (1122–56) reformed the customs and finances of the house, but retrenchment was painful and created internal dissent.

Cluny had originated before the eleventh-century Gregorian reforms. It embodied important ideals of that period: an orderly and dignified lifestyle; an emphasis on corporate liturgical prayer; and cooperation with the lay world from which the monks received support and for which they interceded with God. Cluniac monasteries supported themselves as lay lords did, from income derived from estates, serfs and lucrative rights to tolls and mills and such. Without apology, Cluniac monks and abbots played an important role in church and state. They attended councils, advised kings and were chosen as bishops, even as popes. As the new ideal of the apostolic life took root, first in fringe groups and then in the heart of religious society, the Cluniac ideal looked more and more out of step. In spite of problems with internal discipline, the Cluniac order was not morally corrupt, but it was not in touch with the new religious currents. After the middle of the thirteenth century, no new Cluniac houses were founded, but the massive weight of institutional inertia and landed wealth kept most of the existing houses in business. Cluniac monasticism did not finally disappear until the French Revolution, when in 1790 the French Republic suppressed Cluny. However, Cluniac monasticism had already begun to lose its leading role in society during the middle decades of the twelfth century.

II. The reformed Benedictines: Cistercians

Cluny remained important, but a new interpretation of Benedictine monasticism replaced it as the vigorous, growing part of that way of life. The **Cistercian** monks put forward a competing and highly successful interpretation of Benedict's *Rule*. They were called white monks because their habits were made of undyed wool, a sign of less pretentiousness than other Benedictines, who were called black monks from the colour of their dyed habits. The Cistercians began in 1098 when Abbot Robert of Molesme failed to persuade the monks of his house to adopt a more austere and literal version of the Benedictine life. He withdrew from his monastery with 21 monks and founded a new monastery at Cîteaux in Burgundy, about 60 miles north of Cluny. (See Map 5.) For 20 years the new foundation struggled to survive in difficult conditions: Abbot Robert was forced to return to Molesme; some monks died at Cîteaux; and no new recruits were attracted to the impoverished, harsh life. It appeared that Cîteaux would be one more failed experiment in monastic life, a not-uncommon occurrence. Then in 1112, a 22-year-old Burgundian noble named Bernard (1090–1153) sought admission to Cîteaux. He had with him about thirty men, including two uncles, two cousins and four of his five brothers. The fifth brother was too young, but became a Cistercian later, as did Bernard's father. By age 25, Bernard had become the abbot of Clairvaux, a daughter house founded from Cîteaux. In spite of lifelong illness brought on by his austerities, Bernard of Clairvaux was a persuasive preacher and a man of great energy in an order marked by energy. Bernard was the force that launched the Cistercian order on its period of impressive growth.

The Cistercians sought to strip away from Benedictine monasticism the additions made since the Carolingian period, and to live the monastic life according to the letter of St Benedict's *Rule*. Such a return to origins fits well with the contemporary admiration for the poverty and simplicity of the apostolic life. The Cistercians were the upstart challengers of the existing situation, while the Cluniacs were its main representatives. Many Cistercian actions were explicit or implicit criticisms of the Cluniac way of living the *Rule* of Benedict. Unlike the Cluniac pattern of a single abbot for the entire order, each Cistercian house had its own abbot, who was elected by the local monks. The Cistercians reintroduced the yearlong probationary period, called a novitiate, which Benedict demanded, but which had fallen into disuse in many Cluniac houses. Even though they generally followed Benedict's rule literally, the Cistercians rejected Benedict's (and Cluny's) practice of admitting children. They set a minimum age of 15 years for admission, later raised to 18, because they valued personal choice in religious life and because they saw the problems that unhappy, unsuitable recruits posed for the internal discipline of Cluniac houses.

As new recruits came, the Cistercians developed an orderly process for founding new monasteries. They sent an abbot and 12 monks to the new site, which was chosen with care to avoid excessive entanglements with the secular world. Growth was rapid. In 1119, there were five houses. In 1150, there were about 350 houses, including 68 founded from Bernard's monastery of

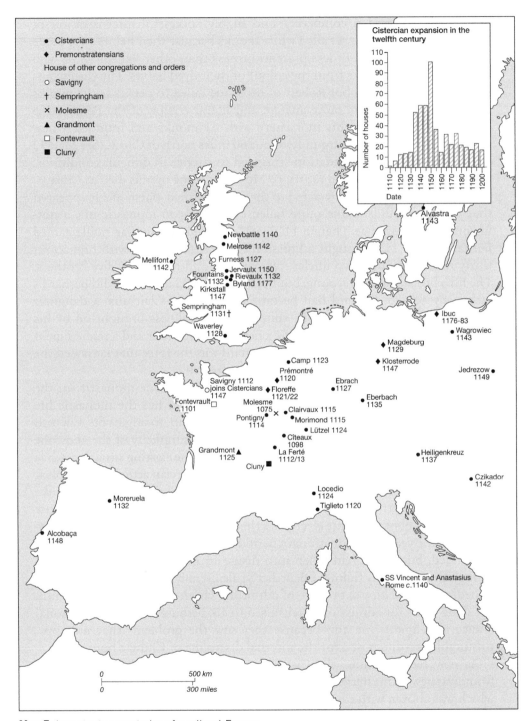

Map 5 Important monasteries of medieval Europe

Clairvaux, which had in their turn founded other houses. In 1200, there were 525 houses all across Christendom and by 1250 there were 647. In 1500, the order had 738 houses of men and about 650 houses of women.

Benedict's balance of prayer and work, which Cluny had tipped decisively toward prayer, was restored. Cistercian monks followed the more manageable daily round of prayers laid out in Benedict's *Rule*, and performed physical labour to support themselves by their own hands. Even after the completion of prayer and work, the Cistercian day had more time than the Cluniac day for personal religious devotions, reflection and meditation, which were central to the new monastic spirituality of the twelfth century.

The Cistercians' preference for solitude made them important actors in the internal settlement of Europe in the twelfth and thirteenth centuries. When they could, the white monks chose to settle in wild places, without villages and serfs, where they were pioneers who cut trees, moved rocks, built buildings, and planted and harvested crops. To aid in the hard farm work they accepted lay brothers, called *conversi*, who were real monks but with simplified liturgical duties and a heavy responsibility for the agricultural work. The lay brothers were generally illiterate and had no voting rights in the house, which were reserved for the choir monks, that is, those who performed the more complicated liturgy. The land holdings of a Cistercian house were organised in farms called granges, where groups of lay brothers lived and worked, though they returned to the main monastery regularly for prayers and discipline. This was the first time since monastic origins in the Near East that large numbers of lower-class men were welcomed into monastic life and the response was enthusiastic. In 1300, at the house of Les Dunes in Flanders, there were about 180 monks and 350 lay brothers, a significant labour force. Les Dunes was extraordinary, but many houses had the labour of 50 or more lay brothers to cultivate the fields and perform other manual labour.

The Cistercians also returned to the letter of Benedict's *Rule* on the conduct of daily life, interpreted in the light of the contemporary ideal of apostolic poverty. They dressed in rough, undyed woollen habits; they ate an austere vegetarian diet; they built churches without sculpture, stained glass, paintings, ornaments or bell towers, preferring simple stone, whitewashed interior walls and plain glass windows; they celebrated the liturgy in simple vestments, with painted wooden crosses and iron chalices (though lined with precious metal to honour the Lord's blood). In their desire for solitude and simplicity, they sought to minimise those contacts with the lay world that were characteristic of Cluniac monasticism. They did not welcome outsiders into their churches; they did not own parish churches or administer sacraments to lay people; they did not accept oblate children; they did not accept dying men who wished to become monks on their deathbeds; they did not permit women to enter the cloistered areas; and they permitted laymen and secular clerics to visit their monasteries only in special circumstances. They did not always persevere in these measures, but that was what they wanted.

The twelfth century was distinguished by experimentation in many forms of government. For example, the papacy, the kingdom of England and the north Italian city-states responded to the favourable economic conditions by creating workable governments, though they differed from one another in almost every way. The Cluniac order at its height in the late eleventh century was still a rather undeveloped, primitive structure, which depended on the personality and energy of the abbots of Cluny. To a large degree the Cluniacs were slow or unable to adapt to changing views of monastic life. In contrast, the Cistercians were pioneers in the creation of a workable, international religious order. In the early days, no one could have foreseen the explosion of the Cistercian order, but they made decisions that proved durable. The Cistercian order was a federation of equal monasteries with the five earliest houses, Cîteaux (1098), La Ferté (1113), Pontigny (1114), Clairvaux (1115) and Morimond (1115), having some privileges and responsibilities. Over the course of two generations (1119–65/90), the Cistercian order worked out a written constitution, called the 'Charter of Charity' (*Carta caritatis*), which regulated relations within the far-flung federation of monasteries. The purpose of the 'Charter' was to maintain uniformity in liturgy and discipline and to prevent deviations from strict norms. It combined a large degree of local autonomy with central supervision. In accordance with Benedict's *Rule*, every Cistercian house was a complete monastery: it had its own abbot, admitted its own recruits and managed its own economic life. However, the individual houses were integrated into an international structure, something Benedict had not contemplated.

The discipline of the Cistercian order was rooted in three remarkable institutions: connections of 'mother' and 'daughter' houses, called filiations; annual visitations; and annual meetings of all the abbots, called general chapters. The Cistercian order was divided into five great families of houses, descended from the original five foundations. In the model of a human genealogy, each monastery that sent out a colony was the mother of that daughter house. Each year, every daughter monastery was visited by the abbot of its mother house. The visitors inspected the financial and spiritual health of the house. Some minor problems were corrected on the spot, but others were reported to the general chapter meeting. Each September, hundreds of abbots of the order gathered at Cîteaux in what was called a general chapter, where they undertook policy decisions, reported any serious breaches of discipline visitors had found, disciplined or even deposed offending abbots, and conducted all sorts of business touching the order. The general chapter at Cîteaux was the only time, aside from infrequent ecumenical councils, that representatives from every corner of Christendom met to discuss not only the specific business of the Cistercian order, but also the religious and secular politics of Europe.

Although individual houses occasionally fell on hard economic times because of a poor site, a natural calamity or bad management, the Cistercian order was a great economic success. The Cistercian decision to live an austere life on lands that they worked with their own hands was religiously motivated, but it had important economic consequences. Without peasants or villages bound by custom, the Cistercians could respond more easily to market forces in an expanding European economy. For instance, the English Cistercians prospered by producing wool to meet the demand of the cloth industry in Flanders and Italy. The consciously simple Cistercian lifestyle discouraged superfluous spending, especially heavy investment in elaborate buildings and precious objects to adorn the liturgy. Surplus wealth was reinvested in productive enterprises, when it was not taxed away by kings and popes. The Cistercian monks, who led personally austere lives, were members of monasteries that by the late twelfth and early thirteenth centuries were often quite wealthy and sometimes resented by their lay and religious neighbours for their skill in business.

III. Bernard of Clairvaux

The height of Cistercian influence was reached in the complicated career of Bernard of Clairvaux (1090–1153). He was a shy, sickly man who said that if he had his choice he would have withdrawn into a life of contemplation. But his talents and the needs of the order and of the wider church drew him into an active career. For 30 years, he was the leading abbot of the Cistercian order, a vigorous founder of new houses (the filiation descended from Clairvaux was the largest in the order). He was renowned as a preacher both to popular audiences and to monks. His sermons to the monks of Clairvaux on the Song of Songs, a biblical love poem, were a classic of Cistercian spirituality, with its emphasis on personal mystical experience. (See Figure 14.) Bernard may also have had his own mystical experiences. According to one legend, while Bernard prayed before a statue of the Blessed Virgin, the statue came alive and nursed the monk from her breast.

Bernard was also a skilful debater and writer, whose talents were put to use defending the fledgling order from its many critics in traditional Benedictine circles. He believed a good offence was the best defence. In about 1124, he directly attacked traditional Benedictine monasticism, including Cluny, in a letter to William, abbot of St Thierry. He disapproved of many things that he saw as deviations from Benedict's *Rule*, including their diet, their clothing, their churches decorated with paintings and sculptures, their proud abbots travelling with a large entourage of horsemen and servants, in short all their

Figure 14 Bernard of Clairvaux preaching
This manuscript detail shows an historiated initial (the first letter of a word that contains a story), in this case Saint Bernard of Clairvaux preaching one of his 86 sermons on the *Song of Songs* to his fellow Cistercian monks. The figures are contained in the initial 'V', first letter in the phrase '*Vobis, fratres . . .*' ('To you, brothers . . .').

'vanities and superfluities'. His open debate with the abbot of Cluny, Peter the Venerable (1122–56), gained him European-wide notice and put Cluny on the defensive.

Bernard was primarily an abbot, but he soon gained a reputation as a bold critic of contemporary society. He was the embodiment of what twelfth-century Christendom admired in a holy man: personally austere and without apparent personal ambition, he refused all efforts to promote him to higher office. That reputation gave him influence in the wider world of bishops, popes and lay rulers. There have been figures in the Christian church who were compared to the prophets of the Old Testament, fearless denouncers of the sins of their contemporaries. Bernard was one of those 'prophetic' figures, who wrote and said to popes and kings things that might have brought other churchmen or laymen into serious trouble. The prophetic figure was tolerated in medieval society because he or she seemed so obviously holy that public admiration supported them.

In 1130, Bernard was drawn out of monastic affairs and into European politics by a disputed election to the papacy. Innocent II (1130–43) was pitted against Anacletus II (1130–8), whose Jewish ancestry became an issue in the struggle. Bernard championed Innocent as the better man and travelled through France, Germany and northern Italy to rally the support of important churchmen and laymen for his candidate, who eventually won. His success pushed him into the limelight for the last 20 years of his life. Without a significant material power base, but with personal integrity and eloquence, he became a major force in church life, intervening in monastic reform and disputed episcopal elections, engaging in political struggles and theological debates (particularly with the radical scholar Peter Abelard). More than four hundred of his letters survive, full of advice to all sorts of people. A former monk of Clairvaux was elected pope as Eugenius III (1145–53), for whom Bernard wrote his treatise *On Consideration*, which warned that the growth of secular and legal business at the papal court threatened to overwhelm the papacy and to endanger Eugenius' soul. Bernard was the chief preacher north of the Alps for the Second Crusade (1145–9), and a key supporter of new military orders like the Templars. His eloquence enlisted many northern aristocrats, including the king of France, but the failure of the crusade tarnished Bernard's image. When Bernard died in 1153, he was the most famous churchman in Christendom, and the Cistercian order was still growing rapidly as the model of reformed Benedictine monasticism.

IV. Beyond the Benedictine rule

The Benedictine tradition, divided among Cluniacs and Cistercians and independent monasteries, as well as numerous nunneries of each type, recruited thousands of men and women in the twelfth century and received material support from tens of thousands more. However, the ferment among monks and nuns sometimes broke out of the boundaries of Benedictine tradition, broad as they were. In the later eleventh and twelfth centuries, Christendom was dotted with experiments in religious life, some of which collapsed, some of which survived as independent houses and small religious orders. Only a few of these became highly successful, though in size and appeal none could compare to the Cistercians. It is not possible to survey all of the new choices in religious life, but a description of important types will illustrate the range and novelty of developments.

V. The Carthusians

Benedictine life of whatever sort was always lived in a community, although Benedict had allowed for the possibility that mature monks after many years of community living might choose to live as hermits. In the eleventh and twelfth centuries, the total self-deprivation of the hermit found admirers and practitioners. The hermits of the distant past who had lived in the Near Eastern deserts had long fascinated the imagination of Christians. There had been some hermits in the early medieval west, but in the eleventh century they appeared in larger, though still very small, numbers. The life of a hermit was quite unlike that of a Benedictine monk, because it encouraged individualism, loneliness and severe austerities, which Benedict had advised his followers to avoid. The church authorities admitted the validity of the hermit's life, but were troubled by practical problems: the eccentricities, instability and unauthorised preaching of individual hermits.

In the eleventh century, several attempts were made to institutionalise the life of the hermit, the most successful of which is associated with Bruno of Cologne (*c*.1030–1101) and his order of Carthusians, so named from their chief monastery at La Grande Chartreuse in the Alps of eastern France. After some experimentation, the Carthusians created a small but remarkably stable religious order (38 houses in 1200, 200 houses in 1500). Communities were compact, limited to 12 monks and a prior, and lay brothers who lived in their own little community. They avoided accumulating more land than was necessary to survive, and were very strict about admitting members, who had to undergo a long trial period. The Carthusian way of life was like that of a hermit in some ways and that of a Benedictine monk in others. During the week, the monk-hermits lived alone in small apartments called cells, eating, working, praying and sleeping in solitude and absolute silence. On Sundays, they gathered for mass, a common meal and some conversation. The Carthusian monks were relieved of material concerns by the community of lay brothers, who lived nearby in their own quarters and took care of all the tasks connected with farming, raising livestock and construction. In the twelfth century, the Carthusians borrowed from the Cistercians the use of visitations and the annual general chapters, which met at La Grande Chartreuse. This combination of the life of the hermit and the monk was much admired and was generally acknowledged by contemporaries to be the most difficult form of religious life, open only to a few men.

VI. The warrior monks

Early Christianity had a strong current of pacifism, which was largely submerged in the fourth century when the Roman Empire became Christian and the need to defend its borders intensified. However, Christianity remained uneasy about the shedding of human blood. In the early Middle Ages, the church was negative about the occupation of soldiering. For instance, killing in any circumstances rendered a man ineligible to be ordained a priest. Lay warriors were expected to do penance for their violent deeds, particularly killings. During the eleventh century, the crusades and the rise of chivalry changed those attitudes. The career of the knight was Christianised, though never to the extent the church wanted. Bearing arms under a legitimate ruler for a good cause was not merely tolerated, but even came to be sanctioned by blessings and liturgical ceremonies that were intended to transform a warrior into a crusader or a knight.

Some knights became monks, but when they did they put aside their weapons forever. In the 1120s, a French knight residing in the crusader Kingdom of Jerusalem, Hugh of Payen, sought to combine monastic life with military service. He and eight companions founded the first military religious order, the Knights of the Temple, so named because their headquarters were on the Temple Mount in Jerusalem near the Mosque of Al-Aqsa and the Dome of the Rock. They swore to the patriarch of Jerusalem that they would be poor, obedient and chaste, traditional monastic virtues. Their innovation was that they would use their military skills to be a sort of police force, protecting pilgrims on the dangerous road from the coast to Jerusalem. They gained the enthusiastic approval of Bernard of Clairvaux, who wrote a tract *In Praise of the New Knighthood* (1128), and composed a written rule for the group. The widespread popular support for the crusades benefited the Templars, who grew rapidly in numbers and wealth. They created a network of estates in Europe donated by admirers to support their work in the crusader states. Within a generation, they had become a religious order of an unprecedented type, dressed in a white habit with a red cross, headed by an official called the master and divided into three groups: the knights who fought, the sergeants who aided them and the chaplains who provided religious services. With the failure of the crusades, the Templars fell in reputation. They were victims of a sham trial that accused them of heresy and worse. In 1312, their order was disbanded.

In the Holy Land, the Templars and the other major military order, the Knights of the Hospital of St John, were crucial to the protection of the crusader states, since they constituted the only standing army to defend the Christian principalities between crusades. The Templars soon found imitators. Between 1100 and 1300, about twelve military orders were created to defend and expand the borders of Christendom. The Knights of Calatrava, a branch of the Cistercians, took on the Moors in Spain, while the Teutonic Knights were active in eastern Europe along the Baltic Sea.

VII. The secular and regular canons

There were, of course, tens of thousands of clergy who were not monks: the priests serving in rural churches, in the chapels of kings and princes, in urban and cathedral churches. The eleventh-century reformers thought that the spiritual, moral and intellectual level of those men would be raised if they were to some degree monasticised. The reformers enforced celibacy on them and in addition encouraged or forced more of them to live a communal life, pooling their wealth, eating together, praying the liturgy on a schedule and sleeping in common dormitories. It was utterly impractical to impose such a structure on the large numbers of isolated rural priests, who were always near the bottom of the ecclesiastical hierarchy: ill-trained, ill-paid and often ill-behaved. In wealthier churches there was a long tradition of organising the clergy into a corporate body, called a canonry, which chose officers, administered income, performed liturgical services and carried out pastoral work among the laity. Such secular canons, as they were called, were different from monks. Their way of life was less severe. For instance, they could eat meat and wear linen clothes, which monks could not. They could retain their own income and their own residences, where they ate and slept. Often against bitter opposition, eleventh-century reformers struggled to impose a monastic style of life on secular canons, to make them live the apostolic life of sharing goods in a community that was called a *regular* canonry, that is, a canonry living under a written rule (from the Latin *regula*, 'rule').

Benedict's *Rule* was inappropriate for such men because they often had pastoral duties. In lieu of this, eleventh-century reformers 'discovered' a *Rule of Saint Augustine* that they thought applicable to guide the lives of secular clerics living in a community. This Augustinian 'rule' was actually a composite of extracts from works by or attributed to Saint Augustine. It was more flexible than the Benedictine *Rule* and, when supplemented by other legislation to fill in its gaps, could accommodate both the needs of cloistered communities and those who worked in the world as preachers or nurses. Those canons who agreed (or were forced) to live under the *Rule of St Augustine* were called regular or Augustinian canons. The movement to organise secular clergy in communities was most successful in southern France and Italy, where regular canons became common, but the movement had some success everywhere in the twelfth and thirteenth centuries. There were, for instance, 274 houses of regular canons in England, many of them small (six canons was considered a reasonable number), and independent. There were also orders of regular canons, including one centred at St Victor in Paris (the Victorines), and another at Prémontré (the Premonstratensians), founded by Norbert of Xanten (c.1080–1134). The diversity among regular canons was very great. Some maintained a pastoral outreach by preaching, running schools and serving as confessors to lay people. The Premonstratensians were active missionaries in eastern Europe and along the Baltic Sea. But other Augustinian canons chose a more cloistered life, carrying the imitation of monastic life so far as to become contemplative and liturgical communities, with no pastoral duties among lay people.

VIII. The servants of the sick

At a much humbler level of society, the religious ferment led to the creation of hospitals and leper houses, many of which were organised as small religious houses. Charity to the poor and ill was nothing new to Christianity. Well-off laymen had for a long time put some of their hope for salvation on the phrase 'Charity covers a multitude of sins' (1 Peter 4:8). There was also a long tradition of monks providing charity to those in need. Chapter 53 of Benedict's *Rule* said that monks should receive travellers as they would receive Christ. For centuries monasteries had maintained hostels where travellers could stay the night and where a sick person might recover. Monasteries and nunneries paid for the hostel out of the community's income as a form of charity, but they usually hired lay workers to serve the hostel under the direction of a monk or nun. Monasteries also distributed food, usually bread, to the poor who came to their gates.

   In the rural and thinly populated society of the earlier Middle Ages, relatives and neighbours cared for most of the sick, the aged, the blind and other unfortunates, with help from the alms of the more prosperous. The growth of urban life created more unfortunates, or at least concentrated them in cities, where the older, personal forms of charity continued but were inadequate to meet this need. New institutions were created to serve the poor and ill. In the twelfth century, the hospital became a common feature in the urban landscape. The word hospital, with its modern images of doctors and drugs and healing, is misleading. The medieval hospital, often called in contemporary language 'God's House' (*Domus dei* in Latin or *Maison-dieu* in French), was a rest home for the aged, a place for the temporarily ill to recover, a final bed for the terminally ill or a residence for the blind. Some patients recovered, but that was usually not due to medicine and doctors. The founders of hospitals were drawn from a wide group in society, sometimes the towns themselves, sometimes bishops or abbots, sometimes kings or princes, sometimes even rich townspeople. They made provision for the endowment, the buildings and the staff. There were also religious orders devoted to hospital work, including those of the Holy Spirit and St Anthony of Vienne. In many places, the hospital personnel was organised as a small religious community, living under the Augustinian *Rule*, calling one another brother and sister, wearing a simple habit and carrying out a simple round of daily prayers that was intentionally designed not to interfere with the care of the patients.

Leprosy (Hansen's disease) probably existed in southern Europe and the Near East for centuries, but seems to have spread after the crusades began. Its victims were disfigured and eventually crippled. There was no cure and the only protection for the healthy was lifelong segregation of the ill. Some lepers, using bells or clappers to signal their presence, lived by begging. Others lived in the leper houses or leper communities that dotted Christendom. In the thirteenth century, there were about 325 leper houses in Britain and more than 2,000 in France. Many leper settlements were squalid rural shantytowns, but some were organised as religious houses in which the lepers themselves took vows that obligated them to chastity and prayer. They lived on alms.

Such direct work among the sick and poor was new in organised religious life, but was not as prestigious as the cloistered life of prayer and austerity practised by traditional monks and nuns. The desire to organise religious houses to do practical good in such places as hospitals or leper houses grew in the central Middle Ages, but it was overshadowed by the monastic communities whose primary purpose was worship and intercession with God.

One thing that did not happen in medieval monasteries is worth noting. In the nineteenth and twentieth centuries, religious orders have devoted great energy and resources to running schools. But that was not true for the central Middle Ages. Religious houses never undertook the education of the young in a systematic way, though some boys and girls learned the rudiments of reading in monasteries or convents. Children of the rich and of the prosperous urban dwellers were educated by tutors or in private grammar schools, but that was usually outside religious houses.

IX. Women in religious life

Laywomen often expressed their piety by endowing churches and monasteries with economic gifts. This was obviously more common for women of the nobility, who had the economic means to make such endowments, but even this expression of faith became difficult as changes in inheritance and marriage laws made the position of women weaker. In the mid-eleventh century, the emerging popularity of primogeniture – where the eldest son inherits everything from the father, as opposed to sharing the inheritance among all siblings – may have been one reason for the declining economic status of women during this time. Younger sons, without inheritance, had to marry rich heiresses, whose dowries – once disposed of as the woman saw fit – became the husband's property and responsibility. Yet even though women had less and less direct influence over property, they could still influence their husbands' economic decisions, often to the benefit of monasteries and other church institutions. Donation charters to monasteries often listed women as co-donors. The language in these charters reflected how even gifts from men came at the 'inspiration' or 'admonition' or 'request' of their wives.

In spite of their donations to male monasteries, with rare exceptions, lay-women were forbidden entry into their monastic churches. Male monasteries were partially defined by their exaggerated fear of female sexuality, and avoidance of women altogether. The goal of monks was to deny the outside world, which included 'fleshly' temptations. These restrictions on women carried over into other sacred spaces, until almost every aspect of church life was at least partially limited to its male members. In parish churches, women were often restricted to sitting on the left side of the church, and sometimes denied access to cemeteries and holy wells. In the weeks after giving birth, a woman was regarded as unclean because of the flow of blood; for health reasons, she was held to a temporary period of less work and better food. Her re-entry to normal life was marked by a religious ceremony, sometimes called 'churching', which was inspired by the Purification of the Virgin Mary (Luke 2:22–38). One rich area in recent scholarship has been the study of physical space and its relationship to medieval women. How people placed themselves and were placed in space, how people moved and were moved through it, can tell us a lot about certain members of society and their relationship to others. Women's physical designation within sacred space (where they were allowed to enter or sit) put them at a disadvantage when it came to practising their religion, and speaks volumes about their position within medieval society. For the most part, it confirmed their position as the 'ostracised Eve'.

While this was the case for most laywomen, those women who entered religious life had a slightly different experience. In the nineteenth and twentieth centuries, approximately three-quarters of the people in Roman Catholic religious orders were women. But in the Middle Ages, men dominated monastic life in numbers, wealth and prestige. In the wake of the evangelical revival, the number of women seeking to live some form of the apostolic life grew considerably and in ways that contemporaries often thought unmanageable.

The new religious climate, which opened monastic life to many groups not represented earlier, had much to do with the surge of women's interest. In 1000, recruitment into Benedictine monasteries was largely aristocratic and male. Even in the nunneries, of which there were relatively few, the recruitment was from aristocratic families. For instance, in England in 1066, there were only 13 nunneries compared to about 48 Benedictine houses for men. In the course of the twelfth century, new social groups found a place in the burgeoning religious houses, though nobles were still dominant in the older, richer foundations. The great success that the Cistercians, Carthusians and other orders had in recruiting lay brothers from the humbler groups in agricultural society reflected the desire of such people for the apostolic life. Some wealthy townsmen broke the traditional noble monopoly by putting their children into monastic life. Brothers and sisters who staffed hospitals, as well as hermits, were often people of modest social standing who might not have been admitted to any Benedictine house.

Women also participated in the remarkable increase in the numbers and kinds of people living in religious communities, or in the more loosely organised apostolic life. Some reasons for this may have been particular to women, including demographics. In the early Middle Ages, there were apparently relatively few women who did not marry. There may have been more men than women in the population, perhaps because of female infanticide or because young married women died from the infections and other hazards connected with childbirth. In any case, the relatively modest number of nuns in the early Middle Ages probably reflects the fact that the demand for marriageable women was high and their families responded by giving them to husbands rather than to God. That situation seems to have changed in the general demographic boom of the central Middle Ages. There may have been a surplus of unmarried women for whom society offered few alternatives. Between the twelfth and fourteenth centuries, the interaction of religious revival and demographic change fuelled an unprecedented increase in the number of women seeking the apostolic life.

The growth in the number of women seeking some form of religious life posed a major problem because resources did not grow quickly enough to meet the demand for places in convents. The major barrier was economic. Male religious could earn part of their expenses in many ways: by working with their hands in agriculture as the Cistercians did, or by saying mass for donors who had given endowments as the Cluniacs did, or by collecting tithes given for pastoral services as canons did, or by managing the estates of the monastery as any monk might. Societal norms made it difficult for women to do almost any of those things. Since the honour of women was bound up with their chastity, canon law proposed for nuns a general ideal of strict enclosure within the convent walls. Consequently, a convent of nuns needed a staff of men, such as stewards to manage estates, labourers to do agricultural work and chaplains to provide religious services.

The economic problems of nunneries were compounded because they often lacked the prestige that might attract large donations. Most nunneries received smaller initial endowments than their male equivalents and subsequent gifts were mostly dowries for new entrants, which were seldom generous. Nunneries were in competition for gifts with the male houses, but they were at a great disadvantage because nuns could not say mass for the dead, a major reason why patrons donated to religious houses. There were some notable exceptions, but it is generally true that female religious houses were poorer than male ones.

Another problem posed by increasing numbers of women wishing to lead a religious life was the lack of suitable chaplains and spiritual advisers. Nuns needed religious services, especially mass, confession and preaching, which the church only allowed men to provide. They also needed spiritual advisers who were educated in theology, canon law and the traditions of spiritual life. In the twelfth century, many new convents of nuns tried to affiliate with the burgeoning orders of men, particularly the Cistercian monks and the Premonstratensian canons. The orders of men were reluctant to take on the religious direction of women and even resisted papal commands to do so (or did so grudgingly). From the perspective of the monks and canons, there were disadvantages in such work. The main disadvantage was that a male **religious** who lived in or near a nunnery had to give up communal life, one of the very reasons he had chosen one of the new orders. In addition the male religious houses might find themselves burdened by the economic problems of the nunneries. The monks and canons also saw moral danger in the proximity of men and women. There were enough sexual scandals to make the new orders, which already had many critics among the older orders, reluctant to endanger their reputations by counselling nuns. Of course, convents could hire secular priests as chaplains and some sympathetic abbots did dispatch monks to aid them, but the spiritual direction of nuns was a continual problem in the central Middle Ages.

There were many more nunneries in 1200 than there had been in 1100, but even then they could not meet the demand and were often not open to women of the lower strata of society. Some women, especially in towns, created unofficial communities of their own. Such '**beguines**', as they were called, often lived in small groups in private houses, took no vows and could leave to marry if they wished. They lived from handiwork (for example, lacemaking), occasional alms and the assets of their families. They sought religious services and spiritual advice from sympathetic priests. Because of their unofficial and unregulated character, they and their less numerous male counterparts, called '**beghards**', were suspected of heresy and sexual disorders by the church authorities. In spite of such suspicion and occasional attempts to suppress them, the beguines flourished in northern, urban Europe in the thirteenth and fourteenth centuries because they provided an outlet for female piety that more conventional convents could not meet.

Beyond these demographic and economic considerations, what was the experience of medieval women who entered religious life? In spite of the clergy only grudgingly wanting to deal with nuns, for all the reasons noted above, their idealised perception of nuns was better than their perception of laywomen. The ideal nun was sexless, unmarried, virginal and therefore closer to Mary than to Eve. In the context of the generally negative social views of women, nuns were better off. By all accounts, they also enjoyed (at least within the confines of the convent) more opportunities for personal freedom and education than laywomen.

One member of the convent who would experience these opportunities to the fullest was the abbess. When the nuns of a convent elected one of their sisters as abbess, she underwent a change in status virtually unknown to women outside of the church. Ceremonies for investing newly elected abbesses were often extravagant. In a society in which women had little power or influence, an abbess' had a considerable amount of both, as well as great responsibility for her community. The fact that nuns got to elect their leader – though it was only the leader of their small community – was a powerful right and responsibility, not achieved in many countries until the twentieth century.

X. Hildegard of Bingen

Women in religious orders also contributed to the history of Christian thought through their writings. Nuns in convents learned Latin, but only rarely with the fluency achieved by their male monastic counterparts. This may have been because nuns were generally not allowed to attend cathedral schools as children (a privilege most commonly exclusive to boys). The emergence of devotional and mystical writing brought women's writing to the forefront of medieval Christian literature. Mysticism depended more on inner experience, rather than textual authority. This new style of writing and experiencing Christ may be due to, or at least related to, the decrease of Latin learning by religious women, and is the only medieval literary genre where women were more prolific than men. The works of Hildegard of Bingen (1098–1179) provide a good example.

Hildegard produced visionary and theological works, natural histories and medical treatises, musical compositions, and a corpus of letters in which she offered advice to all manner of nobles and clergy, including kings and popes. The tenth child of a noble family, she was dedicated to the church and entered monastic life at the age of 8. She apparently had visions all through her childhood, but kept these to herself until she finally confessed them to her teacher, an anchoress named Jutta. An anchoress (anchorite in the masculine form) was a kind of hermit who lived in a walled-off section of a church or monastery. They were literally cloistered off from the rest of the physical world, receiving their meals through a small slot in the wall (not unlike a prison cell), through which they could also hear the church services. Jutta taught Hildegard to read and chant the Psalms in Latin, and together they listened to the chanting of the Benedictine monks of Disibodenberg, the monastery to which Jutta's anchorage was attached. When Jutta died, Hildegard was 38 years old, and her sisters respected her so much that they elected her abbess.

Hildegard continued having visions (possibly caused by migraines), but up to that point, she had confessed this only to Jutta, and a monk name Volmar. She refused to write her visions down until she 'heard a voice from Heaven, saying to [her]: "Tell these wonderful things and write them."

'It happened in the year 1141 of the Incarnation of the Son of God, Jesus Christ, when I was forty-two years and seven months old, that a fiery light of the greatest brilliancy coming from the opened heavens, poured into all my brain, and kindled in my heart and my breast a flame, that warms but does not burn, as the sun heats anything over which he casts his rays. And suddenly I knew and understood of the explanation of expositions of the Psalter, the Gospels, and other Catholic books of the Old and New Testaments, but not the interpretation of the texts of the words, nor the division of the syllable, nor did I understand the cases and the tenses.'[1]

Apparently, Hildegard was one of those nuns who learned Latin, but did not master all the intricacies of its grammar, for she 'understood the explanation' of the Scripture, but not 'the cases and the tenses'. Because of this, the monk Volmar became her lifelong secretary, and images of Hildegard's visions often show her dictating to him. Concerned that her visions might be considered schismatic or even heretical, Hildegard wrote to Bernard of Clairvaux, who brought the abbess' visionary writings to Pope Eugenius III. The pope gave his permission, and Hildegard completed her *Scivias*, a work that described 26 of her visions, complete with illustrations. The title *Scivias* is from a Latin phrase '*scito vias Domini*', which means 'Know the Ways of the Lord'.

Hildegard also wrote medical treatises that drew on the Greek understanding of the four elements (earth, air, fire and water), and Galen's theories of the four humours (blood, phlegm, black bile and yellow bile). Like the best practitioners of her time, she believed that keeping the humours in balance was the key to health, and her writings reflect her own experimentation with the medicinal applications of plants and other objects to that end. Remarkably, for a celibate woman who had spent her entire life in a convent, she ventured to write on human sexuality. Unlike so many of her male monastic counterparts, she seems to have had a positive view on this topic. Here is Hildegard's description of sex from the female perspective:

When a woman is making love with a man, a sense of heat in her brain, which brings with it sensual delight, communicates the taste of that delight during the act and summons forth the emission of the man's seed. And when the seed has fallen into its place, that vehement heat descending from her brain draws the seed to itself and holds it, and soon the woman's sexual organs contract, and all the parts that are ready to open up during the time of menstruation now close, in the same way as a strong man can hold something enclosed in his fist.[2]

Music was also an important part of Hildegard's life. She composed many works dedicated to saints and virgins, especially the Blessed Virgin Mary. Her most famous composition (text and lyrics), was the 'Order of the Virtues' (Latin: '*Ordo Virtutum*') in which 17 virtues – Hope, Chastity, Innocence, etc. – struggle with the Devil for the human soul. Perhaps with a sense of irony, Hildegard wrote the roles of the virtues for women's voices, while the Devil's part was written for a man. Near the end of her life, her monastery became involved in a scandal over the burial of a man in their cemetery. Church officials believed the false rumours that the man had been excommunicated, and ordered the nuns to exhume the body. When Hildegard refused, the officials forbade her and her nuns from singing the Divine Office. What could be worse than to ban a musician from singing? Hildegard fought this ban and eventually won. She died a few months later in 1179.

The changes in monastic life between 1050 and 1200 were remarkable. There was an explosion both in the numbers of religious and in the variety of ways to live a religious life. Even taking into account the general growth of population, there were probably proportionately more men and women living some form of organised religious life in 1200 than there had been in 1050. The increase in the kinds of religious life was striking as well. In 1050, the Benedictines, some of whom were Cluniac but many of whom were not, held the monopoly on the monastic ideal. In 1200, the Benedictines still existed, enriched by the Cistercian interpretation of the *Rule*, but there was a wide variety of other choices: from aristocratic nunneries to regular canonries to military orders to hermitages.

Suggested reading

Companion website
www.routledge.com/cw/lynch

14.1   Bernard of Clairvaux performs a miracle
Excerpts from the *Acta Sanctorum*, transl. in Edward L. Cutts, *Scenes and Characters of the Middle Ages* (London, 1872), pp. 11–12.

14.2   The Lactation of Bernard
Rendering by Phillip C. Adamo of the 'Lactation of Bernard', based on the image at Oxford, University of Oxford, Bodleian Library, MS. Douce 264, fol. 038v, 16th century.

14.3   The Origin of the Templars
Excerpts from William Of Tyre, *History Of Deeds Done Beyond The Sea*, in Oliver J. Thatcher, Edgar H. McNeal, eds., *A Source Book for Mediæval History: Selected Documents Illustrating The History of Europe in The Middle Age* (New York: Charles Scribner's Sons, 1907), 492–494.

Primary sources

Berman, Constance H., editor, *Women and Monasticism in Medieval Europe: Sisters and Patrons of the Cistercian Reform* (Kalamazoo, Michigan, 2002)

Bernard of Clairvaux, *Apology to Abbot William*, in Bernard of Clairvaux, *Treatises I*, Cistercian Fathers Series, 1 (Spencer, Massachusetts, 1970)

Bernard of Clairvaux, *In Praise of the New Knighthood*, in Bernard of Clairvaux, *Treatises III*, Cistercian Fathers Series, 19 (Kalamazoo, Michigan, 1977)

Bernard of Clairvaux, *The Letters of St. Bernard of Clairvaux*, translated by Bruno Scott James (London, 1953)

Carthusian Spirituality: The Writings of Hugh of Balma and Guigo de Ponte, translated and introduced by Dennis D. Martin (New York, 1997)

Idung of Prüfening, 'Dialogue between a Cluniac and a Cistercian', in *Cistercians and Cluniacs: The Case for Cîteaux*, translated by Jeremiah F. O'Sullivan, Cistercian Fathers Series, 33 (Kalamazoo, Michigan, 1977), pp. 3–141

The Life of Saint Douceline, a Beguine of Provence, translated by Kathleen Garay and Madeleine Jeay (Woodbridge, Suffolk, 2001)

The Meditations of Guigo I, Prior of the Charterhouse, translated by A. Gordon Mursell (Kalamazoo, Michigan, 1995)

Modern scholarship

Barber, Malcolm, *The New Knighthood: A History of the Order of the Temple* (Cambridge, 1995)

Berman, Constance H., *The Cistercian Evolution: The Invention of a Religious Order in Twelfth-Century Europe* (Philadelphia, 2001)

Brooke, Christopher, editor, *The Monastic World*, with photographs by Wim Swaan (New York, 1974)

Dickinson, John C., *The Origins of the Austin Canons and their Introduction into England* (London, 1950)

Evans, Joan, *Monastic Life at Cluny, 910–1157* (London, 1931)

Gribbon, Joseph A., *The Premonstratensian Order in Late Medieval England* (Suffolk, 2000)

Hamburger, Jeffrey F. and Susan Marti, editors, *Crown and Veil: Female Monasticism from the Fifth to the Fifteenth Centuries* (New York, 2008)

Hunt, Noreen, *Cluny under Saint Hugh, 1049–1109* (Notre Dame, Indiana, 1968)

Knowles, David, *Cistercians and Cluniacs: The Controversy between St. Bernard and Peter the Venerable*, Friends of Dr Williams's Library, 9th lecture (Oxford, 1955)

Knowles, David, *From Pachomius to Ignatius. A Study in the Constitutional History of the Religious Orders* (Oxford, 1966)

Lawrence, C. H., *Medieval Monasticism: Forms of Religious Life in Western Europe in the Middle Ages*, 3rd edition (London, 2001)

McDonnell, Ernest W., *The Beguines and Beghards in Medieval Culture* (New Brunswick, New Jersey, 1954)

Power, Eileen, *Medieval English Nunneries* (Cambridge, 1922)

Raguin, Virginia Chieffo and Sarah Stanbury, editors, *Women's Space: Patronage, Place, and Gender in the Medieval Church* (Albany, New York, 2005)

Richards, Peter, *The Medieval Leper and His Northern Heirs* (Cambridge, 1977)

Riley-Smith, Jonathon, *The Knights of Saint John in Jerusalem and Cyprus, 1050–1310* (London, 1967)

Rubin, Miri, *Charity and Community in Medieval Cambridge*, Cambridge Studies in Medieval Life and Thought, 4th series, 4 (Cambridge, 1986)

Seward, Desmond, *The Monks of War: The Military Religious Orders* (London, 1972)

Schmitt, Miriam and Linda Kulzer, *Medieval Women Monastics: Wisdom's Wellsprings* (Collegeville, Minnesota, 1996)

Thompson, E. Margaret, *The Carthusian Order in England* (London, 1930)

NB: To get a taste of modern Carthusian life, which must have been similar to that of medieval Carthusians, see the amazing documentary 'Into great silence', directed by Philip Gröning (Zeitgeist Films, 2007), which records life in the monastery of The Grande Chartreuse. The film has no interviews or voiceovers, and no music other than the monks' own chanting. We also recommend the music of Hildegard of Bingen, available on numerous music labels.

Notes

1 Hildegard of Bingen, 'The Visions of St. Hildegarde: Extracts from the *Scivias*' translated by Francesca Maria Steele, in Elizabeth Alvilda Petroff, *Medieval Women's Visionary Literature* (Oxford, 1986), p. 151.
2 Excerpt from Hildegard of Bingen, *Causae et Curae*, in Peter Dronke, *Women Writers of the Middle Ages: A Critical Study of Texts from Perpetua (d. 203) to Marguerite Porete* (Cambridge, 1984).

15

The heretics

Reform movements, religious enthusiasm and social needs stimulated the creation of several kinds of quite different religious houses. By 1200, the inherited network of monasteries, nunneries, chapters of regular and secular canons, commanderies of the military orders, hospitals, leper-houses and hermitages was a powerful force in European life. Their collective membership was drawn mainly from the upper and middle groups in society, though some humbler social strata were represented as well, especially among the Cistercian *conversi*. Their buildings and landed endowments represented a significant portion of Christendom's wealth. Although the Benedictine tradition had reached a point of saturation, other sorts of religious houses continued to attract recruits, gifts and new foundations. But the forces that invigorated organised religious life also pushed in other directions.

I. From wandering preachers to monastic communities

In 1200, many of the newer houses owed their existence to a hermit or a wandering preacher of the previous century. Such holy men gathered laymen and laywomen into small, unconventional groups that believed they were living as Jesus and the apostles had lived.

These groups were inherently unstable because they depended on the charisma of the leader and the enthusiasm of the members. The pattern of development that occurred often, though not always, was that a loosely structured group pursuing the apostolic life was transformed into a more conventional religious community. Sympathetic bishops and abbots encouraged such groups to adopt the patterns of religious life sanctioned by centuries of tradition: a written rule; a fixed residence; a stable income; a hierarchical organisation; a regular pattern of worship; and separation from secular life. The transformation was prompted by various means: sometimes the charismatic leader died; sometimes bishops who were uneasy about potential or actual disorder and scandal pressured such groups to settle down; and sometimes the group itself sought a more stable, conventional way of life.

The experience of Robert of Arbrissel (*c*.1047–1117) can represent that of many other twelfth-century apostolic preachers. He was an important cleric in a bishop's household who became a hermit in the woods of western France about 1095, when he was approximately 50 years old. He spent much time in isolation and prayer, but emerged occasionally as a wandering preacher, travelling barefoot and in rags, with long hair and a beard. He was a powerful popular preacher, but his criticisms of the clergy before audiences of lay people irritated local bishops. However, in 1096, Pope Urban II gave him special permission to continue his preaching. He attracted a following of men and women who abandoned their families and possessions to live as 'Christ's Poor', which was the name they took for themselves. His success created the practical problems of supplying the group with food and shelter. Contemporaries were suspicious about the unsegregated living of his male and female followers. About 1100, a council of bishops apparently convinced Robert to found a Benedictine nunnery at Fontevrault in France for his female followers, where the women were in charge of the spiritual and material aspects of the house. Robert and his male followers became canons who were chaplains to the nuns, although he himself continued to travel widely to preach. In one human lifetime, Fontevrault became the favoured nunnery in north-western France for royal and aristocratic ladies. Robert's popular movement dissipated after his death, but it left as a residue the order of Fontevrault, with about one hundred houses in 1200.

The traditional monastic pattern of organisation, based on the rules of Benedict or Augustine, was tested over centuries and it worked. The apostolic groups that made the transition to stability often survived for a long time, some to the present day. Some became indistinguishable from traditional cloistered monastic communities, but others retained particular features from their origins, including pastoral work among the laity and an openness to the spiritual needs of women.

The church's success at domesticating some apostolic groups left the field open to other groups that resisted domestication. When groups became more sedate, structured and conventional, they lost much of their appeal to the broad popular audience that admired the literal observance of the apostolic life of wandering and preaching in poverty. As some apostolic groups were transformed into organised religious congregations, the groups that resisted efforts to tame them retained their hold on the claim to live like the apostles, and had a popular following that admired them for it. Using terms like 'tame' and 'domesticate' is problematic. It suggests that these other groups were the opposite: undomesticated, uncontrollable, wild. To some extent, mainstream church authorities may have seen them this way. By 1200, the institutional church found it difficult to tolerate or to co-opt such groups – though Innocent III had some success in this vein. Whatever the institutional church's reception of these groups, whether they became 'domesticated' or not, they were all part of the same religious ferment. Groups that refused to accept the traditional monastic patterns increasingly monopolised the broad yearning for the apostolic life. When the transition to a more conventional monastic life did not occur, the group might vanish, might be suppressed by the authorities, or might develop in directions that led it out of the church. New monasteries, nunneries and hospitals were a consequence of the religious revival of the eleventh and twelfth centuries, but it is important to realise that the widespread admiration for apostolic poverty and preaching could also lead to heresy.

The word heresy comes from a Greek word, *haireisthai*, meaning 'to choose'. A heretic, then, was someone who had chosen a religious belief other than orthodoxy. It is important to keep in mind the tension between orthodoxy (which literally means 'right teaching') and heresy (which came to mean wrong teaching). Orthodox authorities decided what was heresy. Heretics believed themselves to be orthodox, and often accused their orthodox accusers of heresy. Point of view played a huge role in defining both heresy and orthodoxy.

II. The Waldensians

To understand heresy in the twelfth century, the case of the Waldensians is instructive. Their leader, Valdes (his followers later called him Peter), was a wealthy merchant in the southern French city of Lyons. He was married with at least two daughters. Like so many others in the twelfth century, Valdes' life was thrown into a crisis of conversion by the attraction of apostolic poverty. In the 1170s, he embraced the apostolic life after hearing a street performer sing in French the story of St Alexius, who had abandoned his bride on their wedding night to live in poverty, returning years later to die unrecognised in his father's house. Valdes consulted a theologian who approved of his decision to abandon wealth and the world. Valdes was not well educated, but he did want personal contact with the scriptures. He commissioned from sympathetic priests vernacular translations or paraphrases of some of the scriptures, which confirmed him in his decision to adopt a life of apostolic poverty and preaching.

Valdes divided his wealth with his wife and gave his daughters dowries to enter Fontevrault, the nunnery founded by Robert of Arbrissel. He distributed his share of the family wealth by throwing it into the streets of Lyons. He might have become a monk himself, but instead he gathered a band of followers, who lived the life of apostolic poverty in the world, basing their actions literally on Jesus's sending of the 12 apostles on a missionary journey (Matt. 10:7–13):

> And as you go, proclaim that the kingdom of heaven is close at hand . . . You received
> without charge, give without charge. Provide yourselves with no gold or silver, not even with
> a few coppers for your purses, with no haversack for the journey or spare tunic or footwear
> or a staff, for the workman deserves his keep. Whatever town or village you go into, ask
> for someone trustworthy and stay with him until you leave . . . Remember, I am sending
> you out like sheep among wolves; so be cunning as serpents and yet harmless as doves.

Lyons, with its few thousand people, was not a modern New York or London, where eccentrics of every sort abound. Valdes shocked many of his more conventional neighbours by abandoning his considerable wealth, by begging for his food and, before his definite conversion to apostolic preaching, by refusing to eat meals with his wife. In the eyes of church authorities, he had a right to do these things: conversion of mind and body was a good thing and the apostolic life, however disruptive, was a meritorious choice.

Preaching was the twin to voluntary poverty in the twelfth-century view of the apostolic life. Valdes felt called to preach as the apostles had, which led to a confrontation with the archbishop of Lyons and ultimately to a break with the church. Apostolic poverty, adopted by an obviously sincere group whose members had given up a great deal, might pose severe practical problems, but did not violate the canon law. However, the canon law reserved the right to preach for ordained clergy (and not all of them). For a century, the church authorities had dealt with apostolic groups by tolerating their way of living while discouraging their preaching. A few leaders, such as Robert of Arbrissel, had been given permission to preach, but most, particularly those who were laymen, were forbidden from doing so. The reasons for reluctance to permit preaching were obvious. Some priests and almost all lay people were, to use the contemporary term, *idiotae*, that is, ignorant of the Latin that would have given them access to the scriptures, the canon law and the writings of the church fathers. Without access to the traditions of scriptural interpretation, such people often could not navigate the complexities of theology. In spite of the canon law's prohibition of unauthorised preaching, many advocates of the apostolic life preached anyway. By the later twelfth century, as a result of three generations of experience with the preachers' theological errors and unbridled criticism of the church, the authorities were convinced that the ban on unauthorised preaching was correct.

When Valdes began to preach in the streets of Lyons, reciting and interpreting the vernacular scriptural texts he had probably memorised, the archbishop told him he could not continue to do so. In a pattern common in the twelfth century, Valdes appealed to the pope. He went to the Third Lateran Council (1179) at Rome, where he showed his translations and asked to be permitted to preach. The great danger was not necessarily the translations, but that they might lead Valdes to unorthodox, even heretical interpretations of the scripture. Valdes and his followers were examined on their knowledge and beliefs, but their answers only convinced the learned theologians that these sincere enthusiasts were not fit to preach. Walter Map, an English chronicler attending the Third Lateran Council, gave this description of the Waldensians' humiliation there:

> [The Waldensians] most urgently requested [the pope] to authorize them to preach because they saw themselves as experienced persons, although they were nothing more than dabblers . . . Shall pearls, then, be cast before swine? Shall the Word be given to the ignorant, whom we know to be incapable of receiving it, much less of giving in their turn what they have received? . . . Let waters be drawn from the fountains, not puddles in the street.[1]

In the end, Pope Alexander III approved their way of life, but forbade preaching unless local priests gave them permission. That compromise proved unworkable since the clergy at Lyons were not about to give free rein to people it regarded as illiterate enthusiasts and vigorous critics. But with equal conviction, the Poor Men of Lyons, as Valdes' followers called themselves, were not going to give up their call to live as the apostles, which in their view included public preaching. They fell back on that biblical text beloved by so many religious dissidents in western history: 'We must obey God rather than men' (Acts 5:29).

It is important to stress that though Valdes might have been an eccentric or an enthusiast, he was not heretical in his core beliefs, which did not differ significantly from those of the church. But he would not yield on the issue of public preaching and neither would the church authorities. In 1184, Pope Lucius III issued the bull *Ad abolendam* ('On abolition'), which, among other things, condemned anyone who preached without the pope's authorisation. This included Valdes, who became a heretic because of his disobedience to the pope. Valdes broke with the church. He lived into the early thirteenth century, and he and his barefoot preachers fanned out across southern France and northern Italy, where they found some converts and many sympathisers who approved of their moral life, their poverty and their preaching. They embodied the apostolic life in a very concrete and literal way.

The Waldensians were not alone in their reluctance to accept the ground rules laid down by the church. There were other apostolic groups active in the late twelfth and early thirteenth centuries. The 'humble ones' (*humiliati*) in north Italian towns included clergy, unmarried laity and married couples. They earned their living, perhaps by manual work in the cloth industry, dressed in simple undyed garments, refused oaths and litigation on biblical grounds (Matt. 5:33–42), and gave away all income beyond what was necessary to satisfy their basic needs. They did not wander or beg, but they too wanted to preach to their members, a desire that was generally refused by the church authorities. In 1201, Pope Innocent III approved most *humiliati*, especially those who had agreed to obey the church authorities, but others remained on the fringes of orthodoxy or outside it. The church had an uneasy relationship with these people who were living in a grey area between the laity and the monks. It could generally cope with the poverty element in the apostolic life, however extreme the practices adopted, but it often could not cope with the desire of laymen to preach. Fervent but illiterate lay preaching seemed from experience to lead to attacks on the church itself and to outright heresy.

The groups emphasising apostolic poverty and preaching were primarily an outcome of developments that had arisen within western Christianity, which had praised religious poverty and had held up for admiration the example of the primitive church of the apostles. In the aftermath of the eleventh-century reforms, western Christianity bubbled with large and small groups attempting not merely to admire but also to imitate that primitive church, as they understood it. The apostolic preachers can best be understood as part of a broad spectrum of interrelated religious movements that included such groups as hermits, Carthusians and Cistercians. Diversity did not imply heresy, though the refusal of individuals to obey the church hierarchy, particularly on the issue of preaching, often led to splits and occasionally led to heresy.

III. The Cathars

For 500 years, Christianity had faced no serious religious rivals within the boundaries of western Europe. The earlier religions of the Romans and the Germans survived tenaciously in folk practice, in half-remembered stories, and in the continued veneration of sacred wells, stones and groves. However, the pagan gods had no priests, no temples, no written theology and no missionaries. They had retreated to out-of-the-way corners of society where they posed no threat to the dominant Christianity, though their remnants annoyed zealous clergy. Judaism was tolerated but encapsulated. Now and then a Christian became a Jew, but the ensuing uproar usually forced him to flee or to reconvert to Christianity. In fact, the flow of converts was quite the other way: far more Jews became Christians than Christians became Jews. This happened from coercion, but also from personal conviction. Finally, centuries of antagonism had erected significant barriers between Islam and Christianity. In Spain and southern Italy, conquest put Islamic populations inside Christendom, but their religion was not attractive to significant numbers of Christians. Here and there, a Christian converted to Islam, but usually that happened overseas with almost no impact at home.

The appearance of the Cathars, a new, sophisticated, aggressively missionary sect, challenged Christianity's comfortable dominance within western Europe. The term 'Cathar' comes from the Greek word meaning 'pure ones', though they often called themselves the 'good men' or the 'good Christians'. The group is also known by the term '**Albigensian**', named from the city of Albi in southern France, one of their strongholds. Some modern scholars think the Cathars practised a version of Christianity, but others see Catharism as a distinct religion that merely used some of the external trappings and language of Christianity. Scholars also debate about when the Cathars first appeared in the west. They originated in the eastern Mediterranean or perhaps in the Balkans. We have already mentioned, in Chapter 9, Ademar of Chabannes' claim of Manichean dualists in Aquitaine in the early eleventh century, who may or may not have been Cathars. Hildegard of Bingen recorded Cathar heretics along the Rhine around 1140. The monk Eckbert of Schönau had encountered Cathar heretics in the 1150s and preached against them in a series of sermons in 1163. The Cathars, highly organised, with their own dioceses, clergy, ascetics, theology and rituals, posed a challenge to Catholic Christianity that had not existed for centuries.

There is even scholarly argument over what the Cathars believed, since the writings of inquisitors inform many of our assumptions about the Cathars, and not the Cathars themselves. With that caveat in mind, here is a description of Cathar theology. The Cathars were dualists: they believed that there were two conflicting powers in the universe, a good one identified with all that is spiritual, and an evil one identified with the material world, including the human body and sexuality. Adherents attempted to escape from the evil material realm to the good spiritual one. Failure to escape meant that the person would be reborn, perhaps as a lower creature, to struggle again for release from matter. This rejection of the material world led some Cathars to reject the incarnation of Jesus (since this was the spirit becoming flesh). Some rejected the Eucharist on similar grounds (bread and wine becoming the body and blood of Jesus).

Cathar leaders were called 'perfects', since they adhered fully to the strong ascetic requirements of the group, including severe fasting, vegetarianism and abhorrence of sexual intercourse. In their simple clothes and ascetic lifestyles, the Cathar perfects looked like exceptionally zealous monks or preachers of apostolic poverty, but the theology that prompted such behaviour had little in common with the imitation of the apostles. The majority of adherents were called 'believers', who supported the perfects but did not fulfil the ascetic requirements in their own lives. Their hope was that on their deathbeds they would have time to summon a perfect, who would carry out a ritual (the *consolamentum*) to make them perfects. Some seriously ill believers were starved to death (the *endura*) after they had become perfects to prevent a relapse into the world of matter.

The Cathar pattern of organisation was actually quite familiar to Catholics. Their equivalents of the perfects were monks and nuns, who lived a life of poverty, vegetarianism, fasting and chastity. Ordinary Catholics, including many clergy, were the equivalent of the believers in that they admired the monastic life though they did not embrace it themselves. Like the Cathar believers seeking the *consolamentum*, many Catholic men and women repented or even made monastic vows on their deathbed so that they could die with their sins forgiven, or even die as monks or nuns.

By the later twelfth century, Catholic theologians were aware that in spite of some outward resemblances, the Cathars' **dualism** made them quite distinct from the Waldensians and other poverty preachers, who were substantially in agreement with the beliefs of their Catholic critics. The Catholic theologians categorised the Cathars as Manicheans, the dualist Gnostics against whom Augustine had written in the fifth century. Like many Gnostic groups, the Cathars revealed their entire theology only to fully initiated members. To the man or woman in the street of a southern European town, such details about belief were not readily available. To them, Cathar perfects could seem to be practitioners of a higher Christianity, an apostolic Christianity. Many people who were neither Cathar perfects nor believers admired the self-denial of the perfects and supported them by their alms and especially toleration. In fact, in spite of the church's concern that any heresy had the potential to infect all of Christendom, many Cathars and Christians lived side by side for decades in relative peace.

The Cathars in western Europe were divided in their theology and organisation along lines that had originated in the Balkans, from which their missionaries came. Some were modified dualists, who believed that Satan, the creator of the material world, had once been subordinate to the good God. Others were radical dualists who held that the principle of evil was an independent power, equal to the principle of good. Such internal divisions probably impeded their spread, which was impressive nonetheless. In about 1167, a Cathar bishop named Nicetas came from the Balkans to preside over a council at St-Félix-de-Caraman in southern France, at which three native Cathar bishops were reconfirmed in office and smaller communities without bishops were represented. By 1200, there were 11 Cathar bishops in western Europe: 1 in northern France, 4 in southern France and 6 in Italy. In the late twelfth and early thirteenth centuries, with protection from important people and a segment of public opinion, Cathar perfects travelled, preached and held public debates with Catholics in southern Europe. The Waldensians, who were active in the same regions, opposed the spread of Cathar dualism, even as they opposed the institutional church. The church authorities from the pope down to the bishops of the affected regions were alarmed by the spread of Catharism as well as of Waldensianism, but had found no effective way to deal with them.

Thus, in the early thirteenth century, southern Europe was alive with religious dissent verging on or already in an open break with the church. No counter-measures seemed to work. Austere Cistercian abbots were sent to preach and debate publicly with the Cathars, but they proved unable to compete successfully against their lifestyle of personal poverty and preaching. The church authorities tried compromise. Some small groups of Waldensians, called the Poor Catholics and the Poor Lombards, were received back into the church on terms favourable to their desire for poverty and preaching, but they made little headway in convincing their former companions to do the same. Violent repression of the heretics was not possible in much of southern Europe because of circumstances. Many southern bishops and clergy were slow to oppose the heretics, in part because of fear of their supporters and in part because of laxity and indifference to the problem. The lay aristocracy and the urban authorities of southern France and northern Italy protected or at least tolerated the religious dissenters, perhaps as a way to bring pressure on local church authorities. Neither persuasion, nor accommodation, nor repression worked, and the Catholic Church was rapidly approaching a crisis in southern France and northern Italy in the first decade of the thirteenth century.

IV. The Albigensian Crusade

From the church's point of view, the spread of heresy seemed to threaten the very foundations of society. Contemporaries described heresy in negative images: as a contagious disease or as treason against God. Traditional measures such as preaching and local investigation had almost no success in halting its spread. In the first half of the thirteenth century, the church authorities, supported by many rulers and much of the populace, moved to more systematic and violent means to repress heresy.

In southern France, the Cathars found sympathy and support among the native nobility and a tolerant attitude among the clergy. Some nobles were attracted by Cathar doctrine and life, but others saw Catharism as a way to weaken the influence and financial control of the institutional church. Most noble men were at least formally Catholic, but some of their relatives, often the women, were sympathisers or activists. For instance, the count of Foix, an important noble, was a formal Catholic, but his wife and sister were Waldensians and another sister was a Cathar – what a religiously complicated family that must have been!

In the early thirteenth century, the young, energetic Pope Innocent III decided to intervene in southern France. He needed the cooperation of local rulers if heresy was to be checked, but they were unresponsive. Innocent had tried to pressure Count Raymond VI of Toulouse to take measures against the heretics in his important principality, but Raymond refused. In 1208, a papal legate was assassinated under circumstances that threw suspicion on Count Raymond. Innocent called a crusade against the Cathars and their sympathisers in the south of France. Although Philip Augustus (1180–1223), the king of France, declined to lead the crusade, it found a successful leader in a northern French noble, Simon de Montfort. The Albigensian Crusade was both religious and political, directed against Cathars and against their political protectors.

Crusading had originated as an instrument directed against external foes, primarily the Muslims in control of the Holy Land. Innocent turned the crusading idea for the first time against enemies inside Christendom. This caused difficulty in identifying the enemy, as shown in this passage from the contemporary Cistercian chronicler, Caerarius of Heisterbach:

> When they discovered, from the admissions of some of them, that there were Catholics mingled with the heretics they said to the abbot [who was also the papal legate], 'Sir, what shall we do, for we cannot distinguish between the faithful and the heretics.' The abbot, like the others, was afraid that many, in fear of death, would pretend to be Catholics, and after their departure, would return to their heresy, and is said to have replied 'Kill them all, for the Lord knoweth them that are His' (2 Tim. 2:19).[2]

Wherever the crusaders were successful, they slaughtered Cathars and suspected Cathars. (See Figure 15.) The papacy replaced the southern lords and bishops sympathetic or indifferent to the Cathars with more trustworthy northern allies. The situation of the Cathars grew more desperate: their organisation was disrupted; their sympathisers were terrorised; and their leaders were hunted down and killed. By the 1230s, the Albigensian Crusade had changed the political and religious situation in southern France. The king of France, Louis VIII (1223–6), who had taken charge of the crusade, was in the process of consolidating his control of the region and the Catholic Church was reasserting its control as well.

V. The inquisition

In the aftermath of the Albigensian Crusade, the papacy utilised a new institution, the inquisition, to root out the surviving heretics in a systematic way. The ordinary canon law was a legal system that respected the rights of the accused and allowed for appeals, delays and other processes that favoured the defendant. Because heresy was regarded as a serious offence against God and society, a kind of infectious disease that, if left untreated, threatened the whole of society, no measure seemed too extreme to protect society and individuals. Traditionally, local bishops were in charge of dealing with heresy inside their dioceses, but they had failed in the twelfth century. Some were

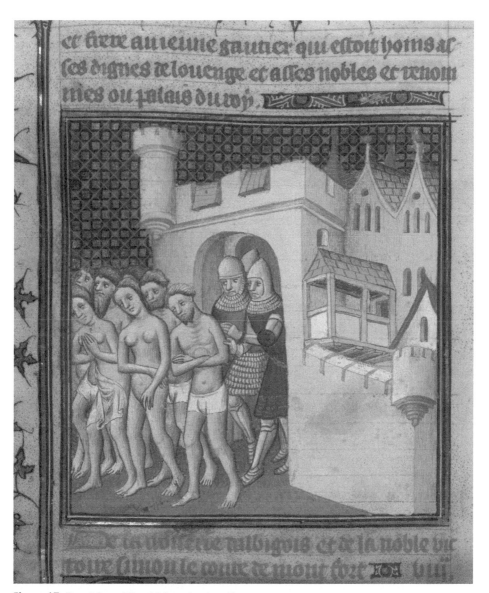

Figure 15 Expulsion of the Albigensian heretics
This image from the *Grandes Chroniques de France* (*c*.1415) shows the expulsion of the Albigensian (Cathar) heretics from the walled city of Carcassone in southern France in 1209. Notice their shame at their nakedness, perhaps referencing the expulsion of Adam and Eve from Paradise.

not diligent in pursuing heretics and in general the procedures of the canon law were too cumbersome to deal with secret, mobile groups that could move from diocese to diocese. The inquisition, from the Latin word for 'inquiry', was a special court, which had originally been established to discipline clergy who fell short of reform ideals. It was independent of the local bishop and operated under a sort of martial law. The inquisition gradually set aside the normal canon law in order to deal with what the church regarded as a real emergency. It was entrusted with the duty of uncovering and punishing heretics and those who supported them.

In 1232, the Emperor Frederick II of Hohenstaufen had created an inquisition within the Holy Roman Empire. Pope Gregory IX (1227–41) feared such an increase in Frederick's power and created a papally controlled inquisition, staffed mostly by Dominican friars. The papal inquisition was a powerful instrument for repressing heresy. As we shall see in Chapter 16, the friars were educated, zealous and tireless pursuers of heresy. The popes gradually gave them startlingly wide powers to carry out their task. In order to save heretics or, if that was not possible, to prevent them from infecting others, the inquisition adopted ruthless measures, many of them borrowed from the ancient Roman law. Inquisitors encouraged anonymous informers to denounce suspects, which the accusers might have done for any number of reasons, including personal gain. The accused were interrogated without the opportunity to confront those who had informed against them. If they could explain their behaviour, they would be released. If they voluntarily confessed, they were given a severe penance and deprived of their property. After 1252, if the accused could not explain and would not confess, the inquisition could use torture to extract a confession. The penalty for stubborn heretics or for those who returned to heresy, who 'relapsed', was to be handed over to the secular authorities, who generally burned the heretic at the stake and took for themselves all or part of the heretic's property.

There were inquisitions wherever there were heretics and where local rulers would permit them to function. The inquisition in the south of France functioned for a century. Without political protectors, subjected to efficient pursuit and challenged by the orthodox but popular friars, the Cathars disappeared from all but the most backward places by 1330. Other heretics, such as the Waldensians, survived in hiding in remote places beyond the reach of the inquisition.

If we put ourselves in the minds of church authorities, tasked with saving Christendom from wrong teaching, we can see how they might justify the inquisition's methods. Yet, as with most human institutions, there could also be abuses, for example, inquisitors going after people who were not really heretics but were falsely accused of it. We have already mentioned the trial against the Templars, which is a case in point. For political and financial reasons, King Philip IV of France conspired against the Templars and in 1307 had them arrested and brought to trial. Pope Clement V cooperated with the king on this trial, but perhaps more to rehabilitate the reputation of the papacy after Philip's clashes with Clement's predecessor, Boniface VIII. While bishops in France generally went along with the trial of the Templars, many outside of France rejected the charges. Templars were arrested in England, Aragon and Cyprus, but not on the same scale as in France. Under severe interrogation and torture, the Templars admitted to heresy, blasphemy and sodomy. Many of the Templars, including their leader, Jacques de Molay, later recanted their confessions. In 1310, 54 Templars were burned at the stake. In 1314, Jacques de Molay would meet that same fate.

A beguine named Marguerite Porete (died 1310) presents another case of the inquisition probably going too far. Porete, a French mystic, wrote a book called *The Mirror of Simple Souls*, a dialogue about the progress of the soul through higher and higher levels of God's grace. The church might have allowed such writings, most of them orthodox and traditional, had they come from a cloistered nun. Coming from a woman living as a beguine, without vows, without a rule, etc., they caused the inquisition to respond in the worst way. They burned *The Mirror of Simple Souls* and ordered Marguerite to stop distributing it. She refused, and in Paris in 1310 was burnt at the stake for heresy.

Brutal repression was only part of the response to heresy. There were also important efforts to compete with the Cathars and Waldensians for the loyalties of the vast majority of Christians. The Catholics did not cease to claim that they had the true tradition of apostolic poverty and preaching, as we shall see with the advent of the friars.

Suggested reading

Companion website
www.routledge.com/cw/lynch

15.1   Waldo of Lyons
'Waldo Of Lyons' (1218), in James Hervey Robinson, ed., *Readings in European History: A Collection of Extracts from the Sources Chosen with the Purpose of Illustrating the Progress of Culture in Western Europe since the German Invasions* (Boston: Ginn and Company, 1904), 380–381.

15.2   The Albigenses or Cathars
Excerpts from Bernard of Gui, *Inquisitor's Guide* (early 14th century), in James Hervey Robinson, ed., *Readings in European History: A Collection of Extracts from the Sources Chosen with the Purpose of Illustrating the Progress of Culture in Western Europe since the German Invasions* (Boston: Ginn and Company, 1904), 381–383.

Primary sources

Biller, Peter, with Caterina Bruschi and Shelagh Sneddon, editors and translators, *Inquisitors and Heretics in Thirteenth-century Languedoc: Edition and Translation of Toulouse Inquisition Depositions, 1273–1282* (Leiden and Boston, 2011)

Peters, Edward, editor, *Heresy and Authority in Medieval Europe: Documents in Translation* (Philadelphia, 1980)

Porete, Marguerite, *The Mirror of Simple Souls*, translated from the French with an introductory interpretative essay by Edmund Colledge, J. C. Marler and Judith Grant, and a foreword by Kent Emery, Jr (Notre Dame, Indiana, 1999)

Wakefield, Walter L. and Austin P. Evans, translators and editors, *Heresies of the High Middle Ages*, Records of Civilization: Sources and Studies, 81 (New York, 1969)

Modern scholarship

Audisio, Gabriel, *The Waldensian Dissent, Persecution and Survival c.1170–c.1570* (Cambridge, 1999)

Barber, Malcolm, *The Trial of the Templars* (Cambridge and New York, 2006)

Hamilton, Bernard, *The Medieval Inquisition* (New York, 1981)

Hollywood, Amy, *The Soul as Virgin Wife: Mechthild of Magdeburg, Marguerite Porete, and Meister Eckhard* (Notre Dame, Indiana, 2001)

Lambert, Malcolm, *Medieval Heresy: Popular Movements from the Gregorian Reform to the Reformation*, 3rd edition (Oxford, 2002)

Lambert, Malcolm, *The Cathars* (Oxford, 1998)

Le Roy Ladurie, Emmanuel, *Montaillou: Catholics and Cathars in a French Village, 1294–1324*, translated by Barbara Bray (London and New York, 1978)

Moore, R. I., *The Formation of a Persecuting Society: Power and Deviance in Western Society, 925–1250* (Oxford and New York, 1987)

Pegg, Mark, *The Corruption of Angels: The Great Inquisition of 1245–1246* (Princeton, 2005)

Smith, Jacqueline, 'Robert of Arbrissel, *Procurator Mulierum*', in *Medieval Women*, edited by Derek Baker and Rosalind M. T. Hill, Studies in Church History, Subsidia, 1 (Oxford, 1978), pp. 175–84

Strayer, Joseph R., *The Albigensian Crusades* (New York, 1971)

Sumption, Joseph, *The Albigensian Crusade* [London, 1978]

Notes

1 'Walter Map's account of the Waldenses, 1179', in Walter Wakefield and Austin Evans, translators and editors, *Heresies of the High Middle Ages*, Records of Civilization: Sources and Studies, 81 (New York, 1969), pp. 203–4.

2 Caesarius of Heisterbach, *The Dialogue on Miracles*, translated by H. von E. Scott and C. C. Swinton Bland, with an introduction by G. G. Coulton (London, 1929), ch. 21.

16

The friars

The crisis provoked by the spread of heresy led to a major change in the religious life of Christendom, a change that occurred initially in southern urban Europe where the Cathars and Waldensians also found their strongest support. To put the matter simply, Catholicism found its own wandering poverty preachers. The friars, from the Latin *fratres*, for 'brothers', were religiously orthodox; their living of the apostolic life was sincere and believable; and they challenged the heretics for the admiration and loyalty of many ordinary Christians.

I. Francis of Assisi and the Franciscans

Francis of Assisi (*c*.1181–1226) had many points in common with Valdes. He was the son of a prosperous Italian cloth merchant and was inspired in his twenties by the ideal of the apostolic life. He was a layman with little formal education, though he probably could read simple Latin. After his conversion to the apostolic life, Francis had no elaborate plans to combat heresy or to educate people. For several years he searched for a personally satisfying way to live out his commitment to poverty and preaching. He loved vivid parables and symbolic gestures. For instance, he signified his break with his family by stripping naked in the main square of Assisi, casting off clothes given to him by his father and receiving a simple cloak from the bishop. For a time he ministered to lepers, among the most despised people in medieval society, and repaired dilapidated churches in the vicinity of Assisi. By 1208 he had gathered a group of lay followers that must have looked like many of the contemporary apostolic groups, including the Waldensians. He and his band of laymen, who called themselves 'little brothers' (*fratres minores*), wandered in central Italy, begging for a living or working for food, sleeping in barns or out of doors, and preaching a simple message of peace and repentance. In about 1209, Francis and his 11 followers walked to Rome and requested to see Pope Innocent III (1198–1216). It must have been a remarkable meeting. Innocent was a Roman aristocrat, trained in theology at Paris, with experience in canon law. He was made a cardinal-deacon at 19 and elected pope at the unusually early age of 37. Francis and his companions were semi-literate laymen, *idiotae* in the clergy's view, enthusiasts dressed in rags. Francis asked the pope to approve his way of life. That was not a serious problem, because the church accepted as good a life of voluntary poverty. He also wanted permission to preach, the point of contention with so many similar groups. But Francis was unlike the Waldensians in his conscious loyalty to the institutional church and his devotion to the two church practices so widely criticised by other groups: the validity of holy orders, even if exercised by a sinful priest, and the reality of Christ's presence in the eucharistic bread and wine. He was unlike the Cathars in his affirmation of the goodness of material creation and the legitimacy of the church. He affirmed the dignity of priests and the reality of the Eucharist when he dictated his *Testament* in the autumn of 1226, when he was dying:

> Afterward the Lord gave me and still gives me such faith in priests who live according to the form of the holy Roman church, on account of their [priestly] order, that if they should persecute me, I wish to hasten back to them. And if I should have as much wisdom as Solomon had and I should meet poor priests of this world, I am unwilling to preach against their will in the parishes where they dwell. I wish to fear, to love and to honour them and other [priests] as my lords. I do not wish to consider the sin in them, since I see the Son of God in them and they are my lords. I do this because in this world I see nothing physically of that most high Son of God, except for his most holy Body and Blood which [the priests] receive and they alone administer to others. Above everything else, I want these most holy mysteries [i.e. Christ's body and blood] to be honoured and venerated and gathered in precious places.[1]

Friar Thomas of Celano, Francis's first biographer, reported that the night before the meeting with Francis, Pope Innocent had a dream in which the walls of the Lateran basilica were collapsing and a little man in rags propped them up on his own back and prevented the fall. (See Figure 16, lower left image.) Thomas said that the pope identified Francis as the man who had literally saved the church from collapse. Perhaps weighing more heavily in the pope's decision was the recognition that serious mistakes had been made in dealing with Valdes on several occasions during the preceding 20 years. Innocent did not want to drive Francis, an obviously sincere man, and his followers out of the church by flatly refusing permission to preach. He gave Francis verbal permission to preach, hedged with some conditions. The permission was restricted to moral preaching; the friars were to stay away from the complications of theology that were reserved for the learned among the clergy. That was acceptable to Francis, and Innocent's decision paid great dividends.

Francis's interpretation of the apostolic life was attractive to many, but proved unworkable in the long run. While there are still Franciscans

Figure 16 Saint Francis of Assisi
This painting by Giotto (*c*.1267–1337) shows St Francis receiving the stigmata, the wounds
Christ received during the crucifixion. The *predella* (bottom row of images) shows the vision of
Pope Innocent III, in which Francis props up the church (left); the Pope approving the
establishment of the Franciscan order (center); and Saint Francis preaching to the birds (right).

today, their way of life has been greatly adapted from Francis's practice. Yet Francis's example had a powerful hold on the emotions and imaginations of later generations of medieval people. Aside from a few New Testament saints, such as St Peter or the Virgin Mary, Francis became the most popular saint of the Middle Ages. It is useful to understand his views before the pressures of hard reality modified them.

Sometimes modern scholars describe the friars as just another variety of monk, but in fact they intended to be something very different. Like so many in the twelfth and thirteenth centuries, Francis wished to imitate the life of Christ and the apostles as literally as possible. He particularly emphasised the precariousness and poverty of their lives. He wanted to embrace real poverty, without any rationalisations or modifications. His band of followers would beg for their daily food, would take no care for tomorrow, and would own nothing - really nothing. For almost a thousand years, monks had committed themselves to personal poverty, but the monastery as an institution always had some property and might even be very wealthy. Francis embraced both personal and group poverty: no fixed residences, no buildings, no books, no extra clothes, no reserve of cash for emergencies, no endowments. Dressed in their threadbare cloaks with a piece of rope for a belt, the little brothers would beg door to door (hence the name '**mendicants**', from the Latin word for begging), or work in return for food (Francis would not even touch coined money), or go hungry. Without structures or rules except for the simple precepts of the gospel, the friars would spontaneously do what came their way. They prayed, but not in the structured, regular way of traditional monasticism. They preached in public on God's love and mankind's need for repentance, but not on complicated theological points. They reconciled enemies in the violent, factionalised cities of Italy, cared for lepers, and even dreamed of converting the Muslims. In 1211 Francis set out for the Holy Land but was shipwrecked on the Croatian coast and came home. In 1219 he joined the Fifth Crusade in Egypt. He went with Brother Illuminato to the sultan's camp and preached before him. Although the sultan was not converted, he treated the holy man courteously and sent him back to the crusaders' camp. It must be stressed that the friars were not just another form of monasticism; they were something quite new in western Christianity.

Francis did not approve of heretics, of which there were many in Italy, but he did not set out to combat them. However, the friars soon proved to be effective rivals to the religious dissidents. They lived like apostolic groups such as the Waldensians, but combined with that way of life a firm loyalty to the Catholic Church. Unlike the Cathars, they did not attack the goodness of creation, sexuality or human life. In his famous *Canticle of Brother Sun*, Francis reaffirmed in a way no Cathar could his links to the created world that praised God by its goodness:

... All praise be yours my Lord, through all that you have made,
And first my lord Brother Sun,
Who brings the day; and light you give to us through him.
How beautiful is he, how radiant in all his splendour!
Of you, Most High, he bears the likeness.
All praise be yours, my Lord, through Sister Moon and Stars
In the heavens you have made them, bright
And precious and fair.
All praise be yours, my Lord, through Brothers Wind and Air . . .[2]

The followers of Francis offered the possibility that the widespread popular devotion to the apostolic life could find a focus in an orthodox group. The popes of the early thirteenth century, particularly Honorius III (1216–27), recognised the friars' potential and promoted them as a counterweight among the people to the heretical devotees of poverty and preaching.

Francis touched a need in contemporary Christendom. The numbers of friars began to explode in the decade between 1215 and 1225. When the friars met at the church of the Portiuncula in 1217 in an open field, Francis's little band of 12 had grown to perhaps 5,000. The Italian movement soon became international as groups of friars set out for Spain (1217), France (1218), Germany (1221), England (1224) and Hungary (1228). In many places they encountered initial resistance because they could not speak the local language and looked like heretics, but they soon attracted local members and patrons. Within a century of Francis's death, his order numbered about 28,000 members and was active all over Christendom and even beyond its borders.

II. Clare of Assisi and the Second Order Franciscans

Women as well as men were attracted to the life of the friars. But it was socially unacceptable for respectable women to live by begging or to sleep in barns or to preach in public. Unconventional as Francis was in so many ways, even he did not affront such deeply held opinions of his society. In the thirteenth century, women could not live the spontaneous life of the male friars. However, Francis was sympathetic to the spiritual needs of women and began the long tradition of friars providing spiritual guidance to nuns, to beguines and to pious lay women. Clare of Assisi (1194–1253) founded the second order of St Francis (the first order was that of the male friars) in 1212. She was an aristocratic woman who fled from the prospect of an arranged marriage at the age of 18 to become a follower and close friend of Francis. Since she could not live as a friar, she was forced by circumstances to create a cloistered community of nuns at the church of San Damiano in Assisi. If the nuns could not preach then she wanted them at least to adopt the other pole of the apostolic life as interpreted by Francis, absolute poverty. For years she fought pressure from the papal curia to adopt the rule of Benedictine nuns and to seek a reliable source of income for her convent. Two days before she died, Pope Alexander IV approved the rule that Clare had composed, which emphasised the Franciscan principle of personal and corporate poverty, but carried out in a cloistered environment.

III. The Third Order Franciscans

As Francis's original movement separated into the first order for men and the second order for women, there was a large group of sympathetic lay people who could not join either of the orders because of marriage, children or other responsibilities. By the 1220s such lay people were organised into a third order whose members lived in the world, scrupulously observed the fasts and other regulations of the church, and led a life of penance, that is, sober devotion, under the direction of friars who served as their spiritual advisers and guarded their orthodoxy. The third order of St Francis offered an alternative to pious urban lay people, who might otherwise have patronised the Waldensians or the Cathars. The Franciscans had an immense following and impact on contemporary society.

IV. Development of the Franciscan Order

The Franciscans' loose, spontaneous way of life was suitable for a dozen laymen in 1209, but became less workable as numbers grew into the hundreds and then the thousands. Although he could inspire, Francis had never been a planner or organiser. When he was in his late thirties, he became chronically ill; perhaps he had contracted an eye disease in Egypt. Even as his following was growing rapidly, he and a few companions withdrew to a hermit's life, and were increasingly preoccupied with mystical experiences. Francis had an intense devotion to the humanity of Jesus. As his own health deteriorated, he increasingly meditated on Jesus's suffering and death. In 1224, his body was marked with wounds in his hands, feet and side that were interpreted as the five wounds of Christ, called the *stigmata*. (See Figure 16.) As Francis became less involved in the direction of the little brothers, Pope Honorius III and some leading friars sought to structure the group and to channel its remarkable energies and popular appeal. Even during Francis's lifetime, his group was being transformed into a religious order, though of a type never seen before since it vigorously embraced work in the world.

Francis and his earliest companions had been laymen, some of them rich and others poor, before their conversion; none of them was ever ordained a priest, though Francis was ordained a deacon later in his career. The lay character of the friars changed as educated men joined the group. Within a generation, ordained clergy were preferred for leadership posts. The spontaneity of the early days gave way to planning. The Franciscans soon had buildings and officers, called ministers ('servants'), yet they retained features that distinguished them from other religious orders. Above all they continued Francis's impulse to do good in the world. The friars resisted the attraction of the cloistered life, which had drawn so many twelfth-century apostolic groups into conventional monastic practice. They built their residences, called friaries, not in rural isolation but in the cities of Europe, and ministered actively to the laity, particularly as preachers and confessors. Despite Francis's spontaneity and lack of interest in matters of organisation, a workable arrangement was in place by the 1240s. The order was organised to provide the flexibility to do whatever needed doing. Friars belonged to the order as a whole and not to any particular house, as Benedictine monks did. They were transferred from place to place as needed and might do any work to which they were assigned. The governance of the order was in the hands of the minister-general, although there was a democratic element: friaries elected representatives to provincial meetings and provincial meetings elected representatives to the general meeting of the Franciscan Order, which was held every three years. For the first time in monastic history, a religious order had burst forth from the cloister walls to work in the world for the spiritual and material welfare of their fellow Christians.

The most difficult legacy that Francis left to his friars was his uncompromising ideal of poverty, which was so complete as to be not only an abandonment of possessions but also an emptying of the self of all selfish impulses. Even though Francis's extreme poverty was not sustainable in the long run, the main body of friars remained devoted to a workable poverty, a plain and humble life. They needed churches and residences, but they used a legal fiction to avoid owning property: they vested the legal ownership of the buildings in lay friends of the order and, after 1245, in the papacy. Francis's immediate companions, several of whom survived for decades after his death, and some of their successors were never reconciled to the relaxation of rigorous personal and group poverty. Some were bitter about what they saw as a betrayal of Francis's ideals.

The internal history of the order in the later thirteenth and fourteenth centuries was marked by a sort of guerrilla warfare of the 'Spiritual' Franciscans, who wanted a return to the uncompromised past, against the dominant 'Conventual' Franciscans, who accepted the new state of affairs. In the early fourteenth century, the Spirituals became more radical in their practice of poverty, and joined legalistic debates on the differences between 'use' and 'ownership' and 'dominion' of property. They criticised the pope, whose wealthy, aristocratic lifestyle was not at all like that of the poor Christ and his apostles. The Spiritual Franciscans inspired and associated with other groups who practised radical poverty, like the Apostolic Brethren and the Dolcinites. In 1317, the pope suppressed the Spiritual Franciscans along with these other groups. Some of them persisted, and evolved into new groups, like the Fraticelli. The debate over the Franciscan relationship to their property continued. In 1323, Pope John XXII (1316–34) issued a bull that made it heresy to preach the absolute poverty of Christ. In 1324, Emperor Ludwig of Bavaria took the side of the friars and accused the pope of heresy. (He also happened to be arguing with the pope over who had ultimate authority in Christendom: pope or emperor.) In 1328, the emperor invaded Italy and installed the Franciscan Pietro Rainalducci as the Anti-Pope Nicholas V. The pro-papal party was later restored, though John XXII lived out his papacy in Avignon. For centuries, the tension between Francis's ideal and his order's compromise with reality continued to haunt the Franciscans.

V. Dominic de Guzman and the Dominicans

During the thirteenth century, at least nine orders of begging friars were founded. Dominic de Guzman (*c.*1170–1221), a regular canon from Castile in Spain, founded an order of friars that was contemporary with and became equal in importance to the Franciscans. As he travelled in southern France in the early thirteenth century, Dominic was shocked at the spread of heresy, particularly Catharism. Unlike Francis, Dominic was a planner. He envisioned an order devoted to preaching and combating heresy. The members of Dominic's Order of Preachers (*Ordo Praedicatorum*), as it was called, would be highly trained in theology and preaching, and would adopt a way of life as austere as that of the Cathar perfects in order to gain credibility with the heretics' sympathisers. For Dominic, a life of poverty and begging was a means to an end, whereas for Francis, it was an end in itself.

The increase of new religious orders and monastic rules troubled church authorities, particularly the bishops, who believed such proliferation invited confusion and competition. The Fourth Lateran Council (1215) mandated that new orders adopt one of the traditional monastic rules, and forbade the creation of new rules. Since Pope Innocent III discouraged Dominic from writing a new rule, he adopted the *Rule of St Augustine*, which was adapted to contemporary needs with the addition of written constitutions. Pope Honorius III formally authorised the Order of Preachers in 1216.

From the beginning, Dominic recognised that learning was essential for training preachers. The Order had internal schools and sent its most promising members to the new universities. Some of the greatest thinkers of the Middle Ages were Dominicans, including Albertus Magnus (*c*.1193/1206–80) and Thomas Aquinas (1225–74). Many in the Order used their education to fight heresy, which was the main reason Dominic had created it. A friar named Jordan of Saxony wrote a brief life of the founder, in which Dominic's mother:

> saw in a vision that she would bear in her womb a dog who, with a burning torch in his mouth and leaping from her womb, seemed to set the whole earth on fire . . . her child would be an eminent preacher who, by 'barking' sacred knowledge, would rouse to vigilance souls drowsy with sin.[3]

This story most likely surfaced, or was constructed, when the Order began to be called the Dominicans, after Dominic's name. It also created a nice pun for a fighter of heresy: the Latin *Dominicanus* sounded a lot like *Domini canis*, 'Hound of the Lord'. One of the most famous Dominican inquisitors was Bernard Gui (*c*.1262–1331), who convicted over 900 heretics in 15 years, and also wrote a famous manual for inquisitors, which included descriptions of the Cathars, Waldensians and Beguins, as well as Jews, sorcerers and 'those who invoke demons'.

VI. Friars in the world

Because of their numbers, education and energy, the friars quickly gained great prominence in the church and in society. (See Map 6.) The success of the friars was won in part at the expense of bishops and parish priests. Structurally, the church had long been a linking of relatively independent dioceses. The canon law said that no one could preach or minister in a diocese without the permission of the church authorities. That policy had been a major point of contention with groups devoted to the apostolic life. Many bishops and parish priests would have refused to welcome the friars, just as they had refused to permit Valdes and others like him to preach. However, the thirteenth-century popes valued the energy, the zeal and the learning of the friars, and were unwilling to see their effectiveness curtailed by the vested interests of the local clergy. In the thirteenth century, the papacy was reaching its highest point of authority. Popes overrode the traditional canon law and the local authorities in order to grant the friars privileges, that is, exemptions from normal legal requirements, especially local episcopal control. The friars gained a sort of

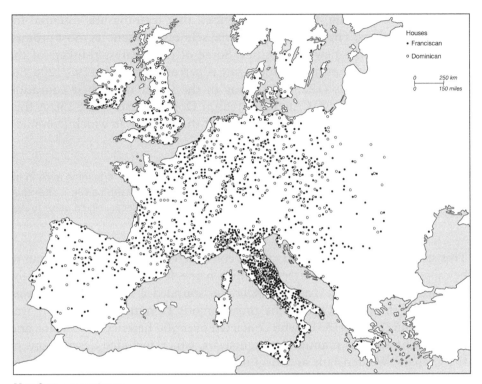

Map 6 The mendicants

extraterritorial status, not answerable to the local bishop, but only to their order and to the pope. The friars built churches, preached, heard confessions, buried the dead in their cemeteries and gave other sacraments, sometimes to the annoyance of the local clergy, who saw their own prestige and income diminished. The secular clergy tried in the mid-thirteenth century to curb the friars, whose alliance with the popes proved too strong. However, by the 1270s the pope and bishops judged that there were too many orders of begging friars. At the Council of Lyons (1274), all but the Franciscan, Dominican, Carmelite and Austin friars were suppressed or forced to give up begging and live in a more conventional way.

In spite of skirmishes or outright struggles with the local clergy, the friars gave new life to the Catholic Church. Traditional monks, such as Cluniacs and Cistercians, had ministered to lay people only reluctantly because they judged that such ministry was contrary to the spirit of withdrawal that characterised monastic life. The friars chose as their main duty service to the universal church and willing ministry to lay people. They were activists, particularly in the burgeoning urban world where the church had previously had such difficulty in finding effective ways to minister. Although there were some aristocratic and learned recruits, the friars, particularly the Franciscans, retained a more socially diverse recruitment than the traditional religious orders. By choice, their houses were in cities and their presence was very visible. Their churches were designed above all for preaching and they cultivated a lively, interesting preaching style. They ministered to lay people in many ways: as mediators in feuds and quarrels; as confessors; as advisers to members of the third order or to pious women; as popular preachers; as teachers in the theology faculties of the new universities; as bishops; and even as popes. They were missionaries as well, though their efforts to go into Muslim lands probably created more martyrs than converts. They were active in the Byzantine Empire, Armenia, Persia and India. When the religiously tolerant Mongols ruled the vast expanse from Russia to China, friars went to such exotic places as Beijing, where the Franciscan John of Monte Corvino (died 1330) laboured for 40 years as archbishop, building a church staffed with Chinese slave boys who sang the liturgy in Latin, much to the delight of the Great Khan, or so John tells us.

Without the Albigensian Crusade and the inquisition, the friars probably could not have eliminated heresy – though most inquisitors were friars, especially Dominicans. But all friars challenged heresy on its own terms, offering a believable orthodox alternative to the poverty and preaching of the Cathars and Waldensians. By their positive activism, they co-opted a large part of the movement for apostolic poverty, though not all of it. They dominated church life in the thirteenth century and helped to stave off for 150 years the divisions and disillusionment that the crisis of 1200 seemed to threaten.

Suggested reading

Companion website
www.routledge.com/cw/lynch

16.1   The Franciscans receive Papal approval
Excerpts from Brother Thomas of Celano, *The Lives of S. Francis of Assisi*, trans. A. G. Ferrers Howell (London: Methuen & Co., 1908), 31–33.

16.2   Clare of Assisi
Excerpts rom Charlotte Balfour, transl., *Life and legend of the Lady Saint Clare* (London and New York: Longmans, Green and co., 1910), 41–46.

16.3   'Sia laudato San Francesco' Anonymous (13th century)
Musical recording: The Rose Ensemble, *Il Poverello* (Saint Paul, MN, 2009)

16.4   'Beatus Franciscus' Jeronimo de Aliseda (1548–1591)
Musical recording: The Rose Ensemble, *Il Poverello* (Saint Paul, MN, 2009)

Primary sources

Clare of Assisi, The Lady: Early Documents, edited and translated by Regis Armstrong (New York and London, 2006)

Mission to Asia, edited by Christopher Dawson (Toronto, 1980); first published as *The Mongol Mission* (London, 1955)

Saint Dominic: Biographical Documents, edited by Francis Lehner (Washington, DC, 1964)

St. Francis of Assisi: Writings and Early Biographies, edited by Marion A. Habig and translated by Raphael Brown, *et al.*, vol. 1, 4th revised edition (Quincy, Illinois, 1991)

The Coming of the Friars Minor to England and Germany; being the chronicles of Brother Thomas of Eccleston and Brother Jordan of Giano, translated by E. Gurney-Salter (London and Toronto, 1926)

Modern scholarship

Brooke, Rosalind B., *Early Franciscan Government: Elias to Bonaventure* (Cambridge, 1959)

Brooke, Rosalind B., *The Coming of the Friars* (London, 1975)

Brooke, Rosalind B. and Christopher N. L. Brooke, 'St. Clare', in *Medieval Women, Dedicated and Presented to Professor Rosalind M. T. Hill on the Occasion of her Seventieth Birthday*, edited by Derek Baker (Oxford, 1978), pp. 275–87

Hinnebusch, William A., *The Early English Friars Preachers* (Rome, 1952)

Lambert, Malcolm, *Franciscan Poverty* (London, 1961)

Lawrence, C. H., *The Friars: The Impact of the Early Mendicant Movement on Western Society* (London, 1994)

Le Goff, Jacques, *Saint Francis of Assisi*, translated by Christine Rhone (London and New York, 2004)

Little, Lester K., *Religious Poverty and the Profit Economy in Medieval Europe* (Ithaca, New York, 1978)

Moorman, John R. H., *A History of the Franciscan Order from its Origins to the Year 1517* (Oxford, 1968)

Vicaire, Marie-Humbert, *Saint Dominic and His Times*, translated by Kathleen Pond (New York, 1964)

Notes

1 *Testament of St Francis*, edited by K. Esser, *Françoise d'Assise. Ecrits*, Sources chrétiennes, 285 (Paris, 1981), pp. 204–6; the complete *Testament* is in Habig, *St Francis of Assisi*, pp. 65–70.
2 Excerpt from *The Canticle of Brother Sun*, quoted from Habig, *St. Francis of Assisi*, pp. 130–1.
3 *Saint Dominic: Biographical Documents*, edited with an introduction by Francis C. Lehner, O. P., (Washington, DC, 1964), ch. 5; translation by R. F. Larcher, from the Latin text edited by H. C. Scheeben in *Monumenta Ordinis fratrum praedicatorum historica* (Istituto storico domenicano S. Sabina, Rome), vol. 16, pp. 25–88.

17

The schools

Since virtually everything in western Christendom was reshaped by the economic and demographic growth of the eleventh to the thirteenth centuries, it is no surprise that education was transformed as well. In 1000, advanced learning was concentrated in a few monastic and cathedral schools. In 1300 the leading institutions of advanced learning were the universities, of which there were perhaps twenty. At a humbler level, in 1300 a growing network of lower schools, often called grammar schools, taught the basics of literacy in Latin to the children of those willing to pay. In those three centuries there were massive increases in the number of students and teachers. There were also significant changes in the organisation and curricula of the schools.

Basic literacy in Latin and in the many vernacular languages increased dramatically between 1000 and 1300, especially in urban areas. As the complexity of society increased, so too did the usefulness of literacy for many lay people and clergy. Bailiffs, clerks, merchants and government functionaries, indeed anyone who needed to read a contract, balance a ledger, or issue or carry out a written order had to be literate, which meant reading and writing in Latin. Expanding lay and ecclesiastical governments encouraged the emergence of a new elite group, consisting of judges, lawyers, notaries, bureaucrats and others whose stock-in-trade was not just literacy, but knowledge. In the struggle for political power, forward-looking rulers, including popes and bishops, relied on the law and written records to defend their rights and to supplement their military strength. In kingdoms, principalities and cities, as well as in the households of bishops and abbots, educated men found employment keeping written financial records and mastering complex legal systems to defend the rights of their employers. The papal court was a pioneer in record-keeping and legal activity: by 1200 it had the most sophisticated governmental apparatus in Europe. Other rulers attempted to create effective governments, with varying degrees of success. Of course, thirteenth-century bureaucracies were minuscule when compared to the gargantuan bureaucracies of the modern world, but when compared to the rudimentary structures available to a pope or a king in the year 1000, they appear very impressive. They enabled many rulers to exercise far more power and to collect far more revenue than their predecessors. It was this need for educated men and the prospects for a good career that fuelled the growth of schooling at every level.

The development of medieval schools was organic, with new departures growing out of existing institutions. Until the second half of the twelfth century, literacy was practically a monopoly of the clergy. Before there was any significant number of educated laymen, rulers employed clergy for record-keeping, writing, diplomacy and advice. From 800 to about 1150, those clergy-bureaucrats, as well as bishops, abbots, leading clerics, monks and some ordinary clergy, were trained in schools attached to monasteries or to cathedrals.

I. Monastic schools (800–1150)

From the Carolingian Renaissance to the middle of the eleventh century (800–1050) the monastic schools were the most prestigious and influential. The nature of monastic life made some sort of school a necessity. Proper monastic life was inconceivable without books, including Benedict's *Rule*, the scriptures, the church fathers (such as Augustine or Gregory), and the liturgical books that laid out the elaborate prayers of the monastic day. Monasteries reproduced themselves from one generation to the next by recruiting members, often children, from an outside world that was mostly illiterate. Monasteries often developed a special spiritual and intellectual culture that monks and nuns had to learn in every detail. The recruits did not know the rich, complicated intellectual culture based on the Bible and the church fathers. They did not know the chants, prayers, rules of behaviour, dietary restrictions and folklore of the particular monastery they entered. Some form of schooling was indispensable to prepare male and female recruits to participate in the religious life.

In the violent, impoverished society of tenth- and eleventh-century Europe, some Benedictine monasteries used their resources to support teachers and students, to copy books, and to create libraries. Adults were welcome as converts to monastic life. If they were literate clerics, they could quickly take their place in the community. If they were illiterate laymen, they might learn to read, but it was not necessary: salvation was not thought to depend on literacy. Many illiterate lay men and women would be accepted as they were and spend their monastic lives employed in the many agricultural and artisan tasks in the monastery that did not require literacy.

Children offered by their parents to be monks or nuns, called oblates, were numerous from the ninth to the early twelfth centuries. They were the usual students in the monastic schools. Since the boys were shielded from life's temptations, particularly sexual ones, they were thought exceptionally suitable to be prepared for the priesthood, which was conferred according to canon law after the twenty-fifth year of age. A child who entered the monastery at age 10 could spend more than fifteen years under the tutelage of his monastic teachers before his ordination as a priest. The same would be true for female oblates, who were not educated for ordination, though they might become educated abbesses.

II. Monastic culture

The purposes of monastic culture were primarily religious, centred on the worship of God and the meditation on his words in scripture. The means to achieve those purposes included an education that was primarily literary, intended to give students the ability to read, write and think in a dead language, Latin, the language of the medieval Bible and the church fathers. Grammar and rhetoric, the first two subjects of the liberal arts *trivium*, absorbed the most attention. Logic (called 'dialectic') and the more technical subjects of the *quadrivium* (arithmetic, geometry, astronomy and music) were relatively neglected between 800 and 1100.

In the twenty-first century, originality in art and literature is highly valued, sometimes with absurd consequences. To the monastic scholar of the two centuries following the collapse of the Carolingian Empire, 'originality' in our sense of something that has never been said, written, seen or thought before was to be avoided. Monastic scholars saw themselves following in the great tradition of the church fathers, and stuck to the tried paths whenever they could. The twelfth-century theologian John of Salisbury (c.1120–80), in an oft-repeated phrase, compared scholars to dwarves standing on the shoulders of giants. They could see a bit further, but only because the giants had left them their heritage. The best monastic students mastered the literary models placed before them, which included the Bible, the fathers, and even some of the more chaste pagan writers of ancient Rome. They imitated the language and thought of admired texts from the past, sometimes so closely that we might call it plagiarism.

Not only did monastic culture prize faithfulness to tradition, it also taught students to expect to find signs of God's presence in the created world. The monastic writers of the tenth, eleventh and twelfth centuries saw the universe as an elaborate system of signs and symbols that, when correctly understood, pointed to God's creative power and moral judgements. The monk, theologian, and poet Alain of L'Isle (1128–1203), put it this way:

Omnis mundi creatura	Every creature of the world,
quasi liber et pictura	like a picture or a book,
nobis est in speculum.	is to us as a mirror.[1]

War, plague, and personal suffering were interpreted as God's punishment of sinners, while peace and abundance were generally understood as blessings on those who honoured him. The monastic scholar was encouraged to contemplate with feelings of religious awe God's wonders as revealed in scripture, history and nature. He was not inclined to probe them too deeply, to attempt to unravel how they actually worked, or to argue about them according to the rules of logic. The characteristic literary products of monastic culture were aimed toward proclaiming God's power and encouraging the individual to think about it for his own spiritual growth: saints' lives, sermons, histories, meditations, poetry, letters and liturgical works, all of them heavily dependent for language and ideas on the Bible, the fathers and the pagan classics.

Monastic schools existed primarily for the education of monks and nuns. But some boys who wanted to be secular priests and even some boys, usually nobles, who had no intention of being clergy but wanted an education, might mingle with the oblates. A few rich monasteries educated their monastic students separately from the outsiders, but ordinarily there were not enough students to justify that, and all were taught together. Since many bishops came from the ranks of the monks, important secular clergy of the tenth and eleventh centuries honoured monastic intellectual values outside the monastery.

III. Cathedral schools

Even in the best of times the education of all of the secular clergy was beyond the resources of the medieval church. In the impoverished conditions of the tenth and eleventh centuries, the educational attainments of many secular clerics were humble indeed, though secular clerics of upper-class birth often had access to a good education. The rural clergy, recruited from peasant families, might not be different in outlook and education from their lay kinsmen. They had only minimal formal schooling and generally learned their job during an apprenticeship to a local priest, whom they assisted and imitated. Many had only enough literacy in Latin to carry out the indispensable religious services such as baptising a baby or singing mass. Some probably memorised the Latin words without understanding them. We know almost nothing about how such humble priests saw themselves, though we know that their social and religious superiors, especially the bishops and religious reformers, were very critical of their level of learning and their personal behaviour.

It was not impossible for a talented man of humble birth to rise in the church hierarchy, but it was unusual before the thirteenth century. The important churchmen, including bishops, archdeacons, cathedral canons and abbots, were usually born to knightly or aristocratic families. Between the ninth and twelfth centuries, the training of the elite of the secular clergy was carried out in cathedral schools, which were usually located within the complex of buildings surrounding the cathedral. Sometimes a learned bishop taught the advanced students himself, but ordinarily a member of the cathedral chapter, called the *scholasticus*, instructed the young clerics. Like monastic education, cathedral school education was pious, literary and rooted in tradition, though it had the added feature of training clergy to minister to the laity.

We are accustomed to thinking in terms of educational 'systems', but that idea falsifies the loose, scattered and localised character of tenth- eleventh- and twelfth-century schools. Vital as monastic and cathedral schools were to the intellectual life of post-Carolingian Europe, they were, in a material sense, rather modest affairs. Ordinarily there were no separate buildings: the school was conducted in some part of the monastic or cathedral complex. There was ordinarily only one teacher or *magister* ('master'), as contemporaries called him, and he and perhaps an assistant taught everyone from beginners to mature men. There were no formal degrees. A student progressed as he could, or until other interests, for example ordination to the priesthood or a lack of money, called him to do something else.

The framework of the curriculum had been set in the Carolingian period, though it owed much to Roman thinking about education. Augustine of Hippo advocated for the seven liberal arts – the *trivium* of grammar, rhetoric and dialectic, and the *quadrivium* of geometry, astronomy, arithmetic and music. According to Augustine, these were the ideal preparation for the mastery of scripture, which only the most advanced students could attain. In practice a school's curriculum depended on the interests and skills of the local master. By necessity almost every school concentrated on grammar and rhetoric in order to teach Latin, a difficult foreign language. Some cathedral schools had masters with reputations for being especially good in particular advanced subjects. In the early twelfth century, the cathedral school at Laon was renowned for the study of theology, that at Orleans for the study of the Latin classics, and that at Chartres for the study of the scientific subjects of the *quadrivium*. Ambitious students travelled from one cathedral school to another to pursue their advanced interests. But the death or departure of a master could change the situation quickly.

Even though monastic and cathedral schools shared ideas about curriculum and teaching, they began to diverge from one another in the eleventh century. Their differences became even sharper in the twelfth century. Cathedral schools were urban institutions whereas monastic schools, even if located physically in a town, were cloistered and rural in spirit. Already in the late eleventh century, the energetic urban life of north-western Europe was being reflected in the cathedral schools. In particular, a new approach to learning was developing, which is often called scholasticism (from *scholasticus*, the word for a teacher).

Scholasticism can be understood in part by describing its differences from monastic culture. The students differed. Oblates and young monks were quite unlike boys in cathedral schools who had received the tonsure and were technically clerics, but in fact had more choices to make about their behaviour and career. The teachers were different. A Benedictine monk or nun took a vow to remain forever in the monastery, with its traditional pattern of work, study and prayer. He or she lived within an endowed community and did not directly have to earn a living. A monastic teacher might become an abbot, an abbess or a bishop, but ambition was regarded as a vice. In a paradoxical way, the road to an abbacy or a bishopric might best be travelled by not seeming to want it. In contrast, the masters in the cathedral schools were often wanderers without firm roots, who had sought their training and their employment in many places. They often had to scramble to gain a living. Some received paid positions in cathedral chapters to support them, but others lived at least in part from student fees. They often did not see it as desirable to grow old teaching Latin grammar to young boys. They were openly ambitious, and might seek to gain a reputation by attracting large numbers of students or by participating in the theological debates of the day. Most cathedral schoolmasters wanted to move on to a bishopric or a good job in the bureaucracy of church or state. Finally, the intellectual atmosphere in the two sorts of schools grew more different. Monastic schools remained more contemplative, more leisurely, more wedded to tradition. Cathedral schools were more open to intellectual innovation, in particular to the use of Aristotle's logic to solve intellectual problems in all fields of knowledge, including theology.

Advanced training was a great career asset and ambitious families sought it for their sons. Few students went on to become schoolmasters. After their money ran out or their interest waned, most students sought a living in the service of a church or a prince. But many of them adopted the bold new attitude of logical inquiry that remade the face of European culture and religion.

As the twelfth century progressed monastic schools lost their dominance, in part because monastic reformers wished to separate monasteries more completely from the world. The new orders, including the Cistercians, forbade the acceptance of children and hence a major reason for schools within monasteries disappeared. The traditional Benedictines eventually followed their lead and generally raised the age for entry to monastic life to 18. Some monasteries retained an internal school for the younger monks, but such schools cultivated strictly monastic interests and resisted the advance of Aristotelian logic, which became an important subject of study in many cathedral schools. By the mid-twelfth century, outsiders were no longer common in monastic schools, partly because the reformed monks wanted to cut ties with the world and partly because ambitious students had more attractive choices.

For a couple of generations (*c*.1120–80) cathedral schools asserted their dominance in advanced education, particularly in the heartland of Christendom, the region that included southern England, northern and central France, and western Germany. But the demand for education outstripped the supply provided by the cathedral schools alone. In the lively environment of growing cities, regular canons opened schools, as did independent masters. Such schools were often international, with students drawn from more remote places, including Scotland, Ireland, and much of Germany and eastern Europe. The Latin language, shared by the educated, made such border crossings feasible. Latin had been an unspoken language, but among the intellectual elite trained in the twelfth-century schools it became a living language again, both written and spoken, much like Hebrew has been revived in modern Israel.

IV. Peter Abelard

The career of Peter Abelard (1079–1142) illustrates the growing importance of the cathedral schools in the first half of the twelfth century. Abelard was the eldest son of a knight in Brittany, a culturally backward place, and as a young man of about 15 he set out to acquire an education. He did not see his career as a leisurely search for truth. It was an intellectual combat, comparable to the physical warfare practised by his knightly kinsmen:

> My father had acquired some knowledge of letters before he was a knight, and later on his passion for learning was such that he intended all his sons to have instruction in letters before they were trained to arms. His purpose was fulfilled. I was his first-born, and being specially dear to him had the greatest care taken over my education. For my part, the more rapid and easy my progress in my studies, the more eagerly I applied myself, until I was so carried away by my love of learning that I renounced the glory of a military life, made over my inheritance and rights of the eldest son to my brothers, and withdrew from the court of Mars [god of war] in order to be educated in the lap of Minerva [goddess of wisdom]. I prefered the weapons of dialectic [logic] to all the other teachings of philosophy, and armed with these I chose the conflicts of disputation [debate] instead of the trophies of war.[2]

Abelard made his career in north-western France, which was a lively centre of the new intellectual currents. He was both physically and intellectually on the move, a wandering scholar and teacher for most of his life. He studied logic at Loches and at Paris and he taught logic at Melun and Corbeil. The economic revival of the twelfth century made it possible for an independent teacher to make a living from student fees, though he needed the approval of the local bishop to teach. Abelard returned to Paris to study logic with William of Champeaux, but quarrelled so violently with him over a philosophical point (and apparently forced his master to concede that Abelard was correct) that he was compelled to withdraw to Melun, where he again opened a school. He returned to Paris to teach outside the city walls at Mount St Geneviève, where students flocked to hear him. At about age 35, he decided to study theology at the cathedral school of Laon with the renowned master Anselm. With his skill in logic, Abelard found Anselm vague and wordy and he was not reluctant to say so:

> I therefore approached this old man, who owed his reputation more to long practice than to intelligence or memory. Anyone who knocked at his door to seek an answer to some question went away more uncertain than he came. Anselm could win the admiration of an audience, but he was useless when put to the question. He had a remarkable command of words, but their meaning was worthless and devoid of all sense. The fire he kindled filled his house with smoke but did not light it up; he was a tree in full leaf, which could be seen from afar, but on closer and more careful inspection proved to be barren.[3]

Understandably Anselm of Laon and Abelard soon parted ways. Abelard returned to Paris where he taught at Notre Dame, the city's cathedral. He taught logic and theology to throngs of students and, as he tells us, won both financial gain and glory.

Abelard's relationship with a young woman named Heloise temporarily derailed his academic career. Heloise's uncle, a canon of Notre Dame named Fulbert, saw great academic promise in his niece, and invited Abelard to become her tutor. According to Abelard, 'In looks [Heloise] did not rank lowest, while in the extent of her learning she stood supreme. A gift for letters is so rare in women that it greatly added to her charm and had made her most renowned throughout the realm.' As for his own attributes, Abelard says that he 'had youth and exceptional good looks . . . and feared no rebuff from any woman [he] might choose to honour with [his] love'.[4]

The story of Abelard and Heloise is one of the most famous love stories in history. Abelard's seduction turned to love, though some scholars maintain that he never felt more than lust. For her part, Heloise loved Abelard, as her later letters to him show. Heloise became pregnant, and – through a series of missteps on the part of Abelard, and misunderstandings leading to outrage on the part of Fulbert – Abelard was castrated. In the 1120s, the former lovers both entered monastic life. Abelard became a monk, but the purely contemplative life did not suit him, so he returned to teaching in a hermitage he built called the Paraclete (from a Greek word for the Holy Spirit). Heloise had become a nun and then a prioress in a convent in Argenteuil, north-west of Paris. When her nuns were evicted from Argenteuil, Abelard gave Heloise the Paraclete, where she became abbess for the rest of her life. In the 1130s, she undertook a correspondence with Abelard, which offers further evidence of her intellect. Some of the letters dealt with her continued affection for Abelard, but most of them concerned spiritual guidance, which Abelard offered to Heloise.

Abelard is the model, exaggerated to be sure, of the emerging scholastic culture that challenged and eventually triumphed over monastic culture. He was combative, ambitious, ready to go where he could learn or teach, and devoted to the study and use of Aristotle's logic, even in theology. The latter created problems for Abelard, especially in his encounters with Bernard of Clairvaux. Bernard, arguably the most powerful man in the church in those days, found Abelard's teaching troubling, especially his writings on the Trinity. The two took part in a to-and-fro of admonition and defiance, until finally, in 1141, a council was called at Sens so that they might discuss their theological differences. On the night before the council, without Abelard's presence, Bernard and the bishops condemned Abelard's writings. The next morning, with charges of heresy raised against him, Abelard refused to defend himself, choosing instead to appeal to Rome. Before Abelard could make it to Rome, Bernard had the papal curia confirm the condemnations of Abelard's writings. The issue was only resolved when the Cluniac Abbot Peter the Venerable had Abelard's case mitigated by Rome, and reconciled him with Bernard. Abelard became a monk at Cluny, and lived out his days there, teaching in the monastery school.

Even though conservatives, such as Bernard, criticised the cathedral schools' irreverent, public debates on the traditional beliefs of the church, they could not prevent the triumph of logic in the cathedral schools and in the later medieval universities.

V. The universities (1180–1300)

The dominance of the cathedral schools was relatively brief, although many continued to train clergy right to the end of the Middle Ages. But the growth of knowledge and the increasing specialisation of learning soon left them behind. In the late twelfth and early thirteenth centuries, the most advanced and 'modern' education was concentrated in a few cities, particularly Paris, Bologna and Oxford, where a new educational institution was emerging: the university. (See Map 7.)

The earliest universities grew spontaneously, responding to local conditions. Thanks in part to Abelard and his rivals, twelfth-century Paris had a continuous tradition of advanced education, conducted in several independent schools concentrated in a relatively small area on the left bank of the River Seine and the island in the Seine on which stood the cathedral of Notre Dame. The cathedral school at Notre Dame, a school at the regular canonry

Map 7 The universities of medieval Europe

of St Victor, a school at the monastery of St Geneviève, as well as independent masters attracted a steady flow of students from elsewhere. The city of Paris welcomed the growth since the numerous students and teachers enriched the economy by renting lodgings and buying food, books, and other goods and services from the townspeople.

But several schools side by side do not make a university. The earliest universities, including that at Paris, were born in strife rather than in books. The basic meaning of the word 'university' is instructive. In modern times it refers exclusively to educational institutions. But in the Middle Ages it had a broader meaning. It meant 'the whole of something', and was primarily a guild term, or as we might say, a labour union term. It was one of the words for a group – like a corporation or community – that might organise to protect its interests, usually economic interests. There could be a 'university' of goldsmiths or shoemakers, who had organised themselves to deal with the political authorities, to control competition and to guarantee the quality of their product.

The scholars at Paris had good reasons, not primarily academic reasons, to organise a union. Most students and teachers at Paris were foreigners in the eyes of the citizens of Paris, even if they came from a village only a few miles away. Citizenship in medieval towns was jealously guarded because citizens had economic and legal rights that outsiders did not. In modern times, there is often a love–hate relationship between a town and its college students: the merchants and townspeople love the money students bring in, but hate the students because of their loud partying and other behaviour. That was also true in medieval Paris. The city was crowded and the students, most of whom were teenagers, were rowdy. Student pranks, riots and serious crimes were common enough to disturb the citizens of Paris. It was especially annoying to them because the students had received the tonsure and were legally clergy. This meant that, even for very serious crimes, they were answerable to the relatively mild justice of the church. For their part, the students and masters thought they were abused by the locals, treated roughly by the civic authorities, denied what we would call due process of law, and cheated over the cost and quality of housing, food, drink and books. As individuals, the students and masters were at a great disadvantage when dealing with the corporate power of the Parisian citizenry.

The masters also had their own grievances against the church authorities in Paris. The schools at Paris were located within a mile of the residence of the bishop and his chancellor, who had the canonical right to license teachers (for a fee), to oversee the content of their teaching, and to confer degrees, which were licences to teach (*licentia docendi*). In the late twelfth and thirteenth centuries, as the schools burgeoned, the masters' growing desire for autonomy led to attempts to escape the chancellor's supervision.

Neither the city of Paris nor the chancellor of Notre Dame cathedral was willing simply to hand over what the masters and students wanted. The central Middle Ages were prolific in creating voluntary groups for religious, economic, political and social purposes, such as religious orders, guilds, communes and confraternities. Like so many of their contemporaries, the masters and students at Paris united in self-defence, and the medieval 'university' of Paris was born.

The guild of scholars had two weapons at its disposal: appeal to higher authorities and strike, both of which they used in the thirteenth century to gain protection and independence. In 1200 there was a tavern brawl in the student quarter. In a counter-attack by Parisian citizens and royal officials, many students were injured and several killed, including a young man who had been elected but not yet consecrated as a bishop. The masters appealed to King Philip II Augustus (1180–1223). The king took the side of the masters and students, issued a document to protect them in the future from the jurisdiction of the city of Paris, and, to strengthen the point, had the provost of Paris, the chief royal official in the city, imprisoned for his transgression of student rights.

In 1229, drunken students initiated a violent brawl that led to the arrest of some students and the execution of one of them, in violation of the scholars' privileges. King Louis IX (1226–70) was only 15 and the regent was his Spanish mother, advised by an Italian cardinal. In such a state of weakness, the monarch did not dare to come to the aid of the scholars against the powerful city of Paris. In response the masters went on strike (*cessatio*). They suspended teaching and left the city, taking their money with them. For two years the university was out of business, and important people became concerned. By 1229, the University of Paris had become a fixture of Christendom, the indispensable training ground for the prelates and preachers of the church and for the right-hand men of the king. Pope Gregory IX (1227–41) was alarmed at the collapse of the greatest centre for theological training in Christendom; the French king was distressed that a source of prestige and expertise for his kingdom was lost; and the citizens of Paris missed the money. In 1231, king and pope granted the masters the self-government they wanted. In the course of the thirteenth century, successive French kings and popes heaped privileges on the university masters and students, who were quite willing to use violence to protect what they had. They effectively neutralised the power of the city of Paris and of the bishop. The masters formed a self-governing corporation that made its own rules, admitted members to its ranks, and gave the equivalent of degrees to its students.

Medieval guilds not only protected their members from outsiders but also regulated the production of goods. A well-entrenched guild of craftsmen prevented non-members from competing with them and had written statutes that set such conditions as hours of work, the number of assistants a guild member could have and even prices. The university, that is, the guild of masters and scholars at Paris, operated much as a guild of butchers did, though their product was different. They instituted what look to us like degrees, but were in fact the stages of initiation into the guild. The beginners, who would be apprentices in an ordinary guild, were the students who paid fees to attend the masters' classes. In the butchers' guild the more advanced workers were called journeymen, because they worked by the day (*jour* in French). Their equivalent in the scholars' guild were the bachelors, advanced students who helped to instruct younger students while they completed their own studies. In the butchers' guild, the full members who had passed through all the stages of training and initiation were the masters. In the scholars' guild, the same word was used. The masters in arts or theology or any other subject were the fully trained members of the guild. Like the masters in any guild they met regularly to deal with guild business and to vote on the rules of the guild. The masters at Paris agreed among themselves what books they would read in class, how they would examine students, and how long they would require a student to attend lectures before he would be permitted to become a master. Most of the students at Paris were young – roughly the age of students in modern secondary schools. Consequently the masters at Paris took the lead in organisation. The University of Paris was a guild of teachers, and it was their tradition of faculty dominance that was adopted and modified in northern and eastern European universities, and later in American and Canadian universities.

At Bologna in northern Italy, different conditions produced different university structures. In the twelfth century, Bologna developed a strong reputation for the teaching of canon and civil law. Many of the students were already masters in arts and were generally older than the students at Paris. The citizens of Bologna valued the teaching of law, which was a practical subject in urban Italy and an economic asset for the city. They treated the masters well: it helped that some masters were Bolognese citizens. It was primarily the students at Bologna who needed to protect themselves from the rent gougers, the food mongers and the booksellers. At Bologna, the students formed the guild; in fact they formed two 'universities', one for Italians and one for students from north of the Alps. The student universities elected officers, negotiated with the city authorities and with the masters, who in turn formed a guild to protect themselves. The Bolognese model of a student-governed university was widely adopted in southern Europe (and later in Latin America).

VI. Teaching

Scholasticism was not only a new spirit of inquiry based on the study of Aristotelian logic, but also a method of teaching. In every field of medieval learning, the starting point was written texts, called *auctoritates* ('authorities'), which had usually been composed centuries before. For instance, in theology the authorities were the scriptures; in Roman law, the *Corpus iuris civilis* (*Body of the Civil Law*) of the Emperor Justinian (528–65); in canon law the *Decretum* of Gratian and the decretal letters of the popes; and in logic, the works of Aristotle. Some authoritative texts presented intellectual challenges at many levels. Although some were originally written in Hebrew or Greek or Arabic, they were read in Latin translations of varying quality; they occasionally contradicted themselves, or one another, or common sense, or even the faith of the church. Scholasticism sought to harmonise these conflicting authorities. The scholastics were convinced that logic, as developed by the Greek philosopher Aristotle (384–322 BC), could deal with the problems presented by the authoritative texts. In the twelfth and thirteenth centuries, intellectuals were optimistic about the capacity of the human mind to work out intellectual problems by using Aristotelian logic, either to harmonise conflicting authorities or to choose among them. For example, Abelard created a kind of workbook for his student in which he juxtaposed apparently contradictory quotations from the church fathers concerning theological topics. Entitled *Sic et Non* (Latin for 'yes and no'), the book outlined a logical method for Abelard's students to reconcile these seeming contradictions. Thomas Aquinas (1225–74) – a Dominican friar who studied at the University of Paris and was arguably the greatest theologian of the Middle Ages – used Aristotelian logic to prove, among other things, the existence and nature of God, the nature of the Trinity, problems of ethics and the purpose of human existence.

Just as the study of grammar had dominated early medieval education, so during the twelfth century logic was adopted in every facet of the central medieval university curriculum. The mastery of Aristotle's logical texts was the undergraduate's major intellectual task. This interaction of authoritative texts and logic shaped all university teaching, even in advanced fields such as medicine or theology. The masters in the recognised fields – the seven liberal arts (mostly logic), canon law, civil law, medicine and theology – agreed among themselves on a list of authoritative texts and subjected them to an intensive analysis. The master read the books word by word to his students, a technique called *lectio*, from which the modern 'lecture' comes. In the course of the *lectio*, difficult words were defined, general points brought out and obscurities clarified. (See Figure 17.) The master also posed questions arising from the text and then tried to resolve them, a technique called the *quaestio*. Finally, medieval university education placed high value on the ability to carry out an orderly oral argument, called the *disputatio*. Masters had students dispute with one another as part of their training. On holidays masters might dispute publicly with one another on controversial topics in their field. A hard-working student in a medieval university was imbued with the principles of logic, which he applied in detail to the authoritative texts. Educated men were skilled in oral and written combat, in logic and in the careful analysis of written texts.

In the early thirteenth century there were only three universities: Paris, Bologna and Oxford. Since the usefulness of universities to the church and

Figure 17 A medieval classroom
This illustration shows the famous teacher Henricus de Alemannia (at the podium) lecturing to his students in the mid-fourteenth century. Notice how the interest of the students seems to change as you move from the front row (attentive) to the middle rows (distracted and even sleeping) to the back row (talking). Perhaps some things never change?

the state was clear, places that did not have a university tried to steal or found one. During the strike at Paris in 1229–31, the city of Toulouse successfully coaxed some unemployed masters to come there to teach. According to tradition, Cambridge University came into being in 1209, when striking students and masters from Oxford withdrew to Cambridge and stayed there. The more normal way to acquire a university was to found one. As the benefits of universities grew more evident, particularly the training of potential bureaucrats, governments sought to encourage them. The German Emperor Frederick II (1215–50), as king of Sicily, was the first ruler to found a university, that at Naples in 1224. A modest wave of foundations continued until in 1500 there were about seventy universities throughout Christendom, although some so-called universities never amounted to much in the Middle Ages, and the oldest universities kept their pre-eminence.

By modern standards, medieval universities were small. Paris had between 5,000 and 7,000 students in the central Middle Ages. Oxford had between

1,500 and 2,000. Most other universities were much smaller. They fell well below those numbers after the Black Death of 1348. In spite of modest numbers, their cultural impact was great. Noble birth continued to give even an ignoramus an advantage in the later Middle Ages, but a university degree was the next best thing for a man of middling birth to gain a lucrative career in church or state. Training in law was the surest route to a good career, but even a master in arts or in theology could do well. By the thirteenth century, such training was almost obligatory for a man to be chosen for a high post in the church or state.

Universities also had an impact on society as a whole. University graduates wrote a great deal and their surviving works, which are complex and sophisticated, may make us forget for the moment that they were not typical. The vast majority of people in medieval society were illiterate peasants or semi-literate town dwellers, who had their own tenacious beliefs, customs and values, which we find difficult to understand because such people left few written records. However, university graduates constituted one of the elites of medieval society, that of the pen and the book. They controlled the learned professions of theology, medicine and above all law, without which medieval society would have been very different. In spite of modest numbers, university graduates had a great impact on society and especially on the church. The tone of later medieval church government was set by men trained in logic and law, a fact that helps to account for some of the church's strengths, such as its efficient and enduring structures, and some of its weaknesses, including its mediocre success in dealing with emotional popular religion, especially with the ardent advocates of the apostolic life.

Suggested reading

Companion website
www.routledge.com/cw/lynch

17.1 Peter Abelard, The Story of his Misfortunes
Excerpts from Peter Abelard, *Historia Calamitatum: The Story of My Misfortunes*, Henry Adams Bellows, trans. (Saint Paul: Thomas A. Boyd, 1922), 1–2, 10–13.

17.2 Life of Students at Paris
Excerpts from James of Vitry, *Historia Occidentalis*, in Dana Carleton Munro, ed., *Translations and Reprints from the Original Sources of European History: The Mediæval Student* (Philadelphia: The Department of History of the University of Pennsylvania, 1895), 18–19.

17.3 Privilege of Philip Augustus in favour of the students of Paris
'Philip Augustus, Chartularium universitatis Parisiensis I', in Dana Carleton Munro, ed., *Translations and Reprints from the Original Sources of European History: The Mediæval Student* (Philadelphia: The Department of History of the University of Pennsylvania, 1895), 4–6.

Primary sources

Abelard, Peter, *History of my Calamities* (*Historia Calamitatum*), in *The Letters of Abelard and Heloise*, translated by Betty Radice (Harmondsworth, Middlesex, 1974)

Aquinas, Thomas, *Thomas Aquinas: Selected Writings*, edited by Ralph McInerny (New York, 1999)

Augustine, *On Christian Doctrine*, translated by D. W. Robertson, Jr (Indianapolis, Indiana, 1958)

Thorndyke, Lynn, *University Records and Life in the Middle Ages*, Records of Civilization, Sources and Studies, vol. 38 (New York, 1944; reprinted 1975)

Modern scholarship

Baldwin, John W., *The Scholastic Culture of the Middle Ages, 1000–1300* (Lexington, Massachusetts, 1971)

Cobban, A. B., *The Medieval Universities: Their Development and Organization* (London, 1975)

Daly, Lowrie J., *The Medieval University* (New York, 1961)

Haskins, Charles Homer, *The Rise of the Universities* (Providence, RI, 1923; revised edition Ithaca, New York, 1957)

Kibre, Pearl, *Scholarly Privileges in the Middle Ages* (Cambridge, Massachusetts, 1962)

Leclercq, Jean, *The Love of Learning and the Desire for God*, translated by Catharine Misrahi (New York, 1961)

Leff, Gordon, *Paris and Oxford Universities in the Thirteenth and Fourteenth Centuries. An Institutional and Intellectual History* (New York, 1968)

Rashdall, Hastings, *The Universities of Europe in the Middle Ages*, revised edition by F. M. Powicke and A. B. Emden, 3 vols (Oxford, 1936)

Southern, R.W., *Scholastic Humanism and the Unification of Europe*, 2 vols (Oxford and Cambridge, Massachusetts, 1993)

Van Steenberghen, Fernand, *Aristotle in the West*, translated by Leonard Johnston (Louvain, 1955)

Wagner, David L., editor, *The Seven Liberal Arts in the Middle Ages* (Bloomington, Indiana, 1983)

Notes

1 Alain de Lille, *De Incarnatione Christi*, in Jacques Paul Migne, *Patrologiae latinae*, vol. 210, 579a. In 2001, the German darkwave/electro-medieval band Helium Vola set these words to music with a haunting, driving melody, available on Chrom Records.
2 Peter Abelard, *Historia calamitatum*, in *The Letters of Abelard and Heloise*, translated with an introduction and notes by Betty Radice, revised by Michael Clanchy (New York, 2003), p. 3.
3 Abelard, *Historia calamitatum*, p. 7.
4 Abelard, *Historia calamitatum*, p. 10.

18

The sacramental life

As much as the Parisian masters might argue the finer points of theology, the Christian account of the universe was more than just an abstract intellectual exercise. It was woven into a structured way of life for the church's members. Through the sacraments and other forms of the liturgy, the major Christian beliefs were re-enacted or even recreated for individuals and groups. Medieval Christianity appealed to the senses as well as to the mind. Water, bread, wine, oil, music, stained glass, statues, incense, candles and distinctive clothing were among the visible features of the medieval Christian church. In modern times, the words 'ceremony' and 'ritual', particularly when joined with the word 'mere', take on a negative connotation. 'Mere ritual' is generally regarded as empty and without much connection to reality. But in the medieval world, ritual was central to religion and society. The ceremonialisation of life went far beyond what is ordinary in the twenty-first century. Ceremonies were not just symbolic displays, but were believed to be transformational, that is, they changed persons and things to make them what they had not been before. It was not just good but indispensable that every baby be baptised, that every priest be ordained, that every king be anointed or crowned and that every chalice be consecrated. In short, rituals brought about changes to the essence of things and persons.

In medieval society, there was also a strong sense of the 'holy', as anthropologists might call it. Persons, places and objects were set aside by ceremony for God's use, so that they could not legitimately be employed again for ordinary purposes. Through rituals and blessings, a man became a priest, a woman became a nun, a cup became a chalice, a piece of ground became a cemetery, a building became a church. Contemporaries believed that those consecrated people and things had really changed. Because they had become holy, misuse or disrespect was sacrilege, an offence against God, which could have serious consequences in this world and in the next.

Some ceremonies were more important than others because they were rooted in the New Testament and the long-standing practice of the church. Seven ceremonies became identified as sacraments from among the welter of church rituals. (See Figure 18.) They were the chief rituals of the church for individuals, though some had social consequences as well. They were used at the crucial moments in human life, as critical passages from one stage to another. They made the Christian explanation of the universe concrete

Figure 18 The seven sacraments
This woodcut shows the seven sacraments emanating from Christ's sacrifice. In the top-center image, the blood of Christ flows symbolically from the wound in his side to all the other sacraments. We see baptism (top left), confirmation (middle left), penance (bottom left), Eucharist (bottom center), holy orders (top right), marriage (middle right), and extreme unction (bottom right). Notice in the image of penance the angel and demon lingering behind the person confessing.

through words, smells, tastes and gestures. Most importantly, the sacraments were the chief means for the church to mediate 'grace', that is, God's favour, to its members.

I. Baptism

The sin committed by Adam in disobeying God had been disastrous for him because it cost him residence in paradise, health and immortality. It was also a hereditary taint among his descendants. Every baby was born with the sin of Adam, and consequently was doomed to pain, to a tendency to commit personal sins, to physical death and to eventual damnation. Augustine of Hippo (354–430) was the most influential theologian in the Middle Ages, particularly on the doctrine of original sin. He taught that because of Adam's sin, which was transmitted by the act of sexual intercourse, every human had lost God's favour, was incapable of any thought or act that was good in God's sight, and was justly damned. However, from God's infinite goodness and for reasons known only to him, he chose to save certain human beings out of the 'lump of sin' that was humanity. Others were left in their deserved fate and so were lost to hell. Augustine believed that there was no way in this life to know who was saved and who was damned, since God's will was absolutely free. Some of the outwardly pious could be damned and some of the outwardly sinful could be predestined to salvation. Augustine's powerful and frightening assessment of the human predicament was neither repudiated nor fully accepted by the church in later centuries, though it exercised a fascination on theologians, including Luther and Calvin, well into modern times.

Since the church did not know who was damned and who was saved, it pursued a more optimistic pastoral approach to its members than Augustine's views on predestination might have suggested. Even though theologians were fascinated by the subtleties of predestination, the vast majority of the clergy performing pastoral work among the laity ignored it and took a more practical approach to salvation. They acted as if most could be saved, particularly through a combination of the individual's own efforts and the ministrations of God's instrument on earth, the church.

The sacraments were the chief means for the church to mediate grace to its members – though 'her' members might be more accurate, since they actually thought of the church as female, hence 'Mother Church'. Baptism was the first sacrament that any person received. Since it made a permanent change in the recipient, it could be taken only once. Baptism was the gateway to membership both in the church and in society. Unbaptised Jews and Muslims and the heretics who were thought to have repudiated their baptism were not just outside the church, but they were also incapable of full membership in society.

Every Christian was baptised, which was understood as a washing away of the original sin inherited from Adam. The overwhelming majority of those baptised were infants, who had committed no personal sins. In the interval between baptism and the age of reason (usually the age of 7, when medieval canonists believed children understood right from wrong), children were sinless and incapable of committing a personal sin. If they died during those years, they were thought to go directly to heaven. If as sometimes happened adults were baptised, all of their personal sins were forgiven as well as the original sin with which they had been born. Baptism undid the spiritual damage of Adam's sin and gave the human being a clean slate in God's eyes, though the physical consequences of pain and death remained.

Precisely because baptism was so crucial, the Christian church developed a complex case law that provided for all sorts of exceptions. If we put those exceptions aside momentarily, the usual baptism in the central and late Middle Ages was carried out more or less in the following way. Since the worst thing that could happen to a child was to die in original sin, infants were carried to church as soon as possible after birth, which often meant somewhere between the first and third days of life. The mother was unable to go because of her physical condition and because she was religiously unclean due to the flow of blood following birth. A group consisting of the midwife, the baptismal sponsors and perhaps the father went to the parish church. Centuries earlier the church in the Roman Empire had created baptismal ceremonies that were intended to bring adults into the Christian community by stages. The ceremonies of the fourth and fifth centuries had been complex, sometimes taking a month or more to complete. During the very different conditions of the early Middle Ages, the baptismal ceremonies evolved toward compactness and simplicity, especially in response to the predominance of infant baptism and the desire to baptise soon after birth. Ceremonies that had been carried out during the 40 days of Lent in ancient Rome were completed in a half hour in medieval Europe. The prayers were in Latin, but the vernacular language might be used to instruct the sponsors, who were traditionally three in number, two of the same sex as the child.

The priest met the baptismal party at the door of the church or, in parts of southern Europe, at the door of the baptistry, which was a building used exclusively for baptisms. He asked the child's name and that became the moment when a child formally received a name. He exorcised the child to expel unclean spirits and made him or her a **catechumen**, which in the ancient church was the probationary status of an adult preparing to receive baptism. The baptismal party then entered the building and went to the font of water. The priest asked the child questions based on the creed and the sponsors answered on her or his behalf 'I believe'. The child was then stripped naked and plunged into the baptismal font three times (symbolically referencing the

Trinity), while the priest said 'I baptise you in the name of the Father and of the Son and of the Holy Spirit'. In some places full immersion had been replaced by a sprinkling or pouring of water. The sponsors received the child from the priest's hands and clothed it in a white garment or perhaps a white headband, as a symbol of its new sinlessness and innocence. The child received its first communion immediately after baptism in the form of a sip of wine and, if a bishop was present, it might be confirmed as well. At some point the father or the sponsors might pay the priest a small fee for the baptism. The baptismal party then retired to a tavern or returned home where there was a celebration and the offering of gifts to the mother and the child.

The consequences of baptism were not just religious. When infants were snatched from Satan's realm and made children of God, they also became members of society. In addition, baptism extended the circle of kinsmen by creating a new spiritual family that consisted of the child, the parents and the sponsors. Because the sponsors had become parents-in-God, or godparents, to the child, they were incorporated into his or her family. They became spiritual relatives of the child and of the child's parents, all of whom were bound to one another by mutual obligations of trust and help. Spiritual kinship was an important social glue which created networks of friends and allies beyond those provided by common ancestry and marriage. Since the spiritual kin were regarded as real relatives, they were bound by incest taboos and could neither marry nor have sexual relations with one another.

During the period when there were active missionary areas on the expanding medieval frontiers, baptism of adults was common. Even in Christianised lands, the conversion and baptism of a Jew or Muslim happened now and then. In those circumstances, the adult convert spoke on his own behalf, but otherwise the rituals for baptising an adult were like those for an infant, though the social consequences were less significant because the baptisee's parents, if they remained Jewish or Muslim, did not enter into the new spiritual family.

Infant death rates were very high in the primitive sanitary conditions of all pre-modern societies. Since the death of a child without baptism was a serious matter with eternal consequences, the church's canon law allowed important exceptions to the general rules. Priests were warned to be ready and willing to baptise in a life-threatening emergency, with a ceremony reduced to the minimum of words and acts. If a priest was absent from his church, he had to make provisions for a substitute to baptise in such emergencies. If a birth was difficult or an unbaptised infant so seriously ill that there was no time to summon a priest, any man, woman or child, whether Christian or not, could baptise. In such a case the ritual was reduced to its essential points: the child was sprinkled with water while the baptiser said a brief formula 'I baptise you in the name of the Father and of the Son and of the Holy Spirit'. Midwives and other women who attended childbirth were instructed in the words of baptism in Latin or in their native tongue, and were encouraged to baptise in an emergency.

Augustine's view that anyone, including an infant, who died in original sin was damned seemed harsh to many, particularly as the human and humane aspects of Christianity came to be stressed. In the thirteenth century, some theologians proposed the notion of limbo, a place in the underworld to accommodate unbaptised infants and other unbaptised persons, such as the mentally ill or retarded, who had not personally sinned because they did not have the capacity to do so; they did not have the free will to choose between good and evil. The theologians argued that those in limbo did not suffer, but also did not enjoy the vision of God, which they thought was the essence of salvation. The idea of limbo did not entirely relieve the anxiety of parents who wanted the best for their babies. Baptism soon after birth remained the ideal and was the usual practice.

Baptism saved the recipient from the inherited sin of Adam and from all personal sins that had been committed before baptism, but the human inclination to sin, also inherited from Adam, was not fully removed. Even after baptism, life was perceived to be a struggle to adhere to good and to avoid evil, a struggle that drew the participation of the good and evil personalities that peopled the universe. Through sermons, exhortations and the other sacraments, the church attempted to guide the minds and strengthen the wills of her baptised members.

II. Confirmation

In the ancient church, the rituals of initiation into Christianity had included an anointing with oil after the baptism itself, which was thought to impart the Holy Spirit to the candidate, to strengthen or 'confirm' him or her. This ritual of **confirmation** was linked to Pentecost, when in the New Testament the apostles received the gift of the Holy Spirit. In the eastern Orthodox churches and in some places in the early medieval west, the anointing could be performed by any priest, but at Rome it was reserved for a bishop. As the Roman liturgy spread across the west, confirmation by a bishop became normal. In the central and late Middle Ages, only a bishop could 'confirm' a baptism by anointing the candidate on the forehead with oil while saying a brief prayer such as 'I sign you with the sign of the cross and confirm you with the chrism of salvation, in the name of the Father and of the Son and of the Holy Spirit'. If a bishop happened to be present at a baptism, a person could be confirmed immediately. However, since most infants were baptised in a local church soon after birth, it was highly unlikely that such would be the case. Hence the anointing of confirmation, which had originally been part of the complex rituals that included baptism, gradually came to be separated in time from baptism and emerged as a distinct sacrament.

Even though confirmation was a sacrament, practical considerations made it a rather peculiar one. In the modern churches that have retained some form of confirmation, it has become associated with adolescence. It is viewed as an occasion for young people to reaffirm the commitment made for them as infants by their parents and sponsors. That is a rather late development in the history of confirmation. In the Middle Ages, the confirming of baptism was not linked to a particular age or to any clear practical purpose. Many people, in some times and places perhaps most people, did not receive confirmation, because there were only 500 to 600 diocesan bishops in the whole of the western church. To compensate for that shortage, many large dioceses had assistant bishops, called auxiliaries, who carried out such liturgical functions as confirmation for absent or busy bishops, but even the assistant bishops could not reach everyone. Conscientious bishops announced days for confirmation, but the occasions for conferring the sacrament were often haphazard and not very solemn. Bishops on visitation of their dioceses might confirm crowds of people at their stops. We have accounts of bishops travelling on other business who confirmed from horseback without so much as dismounting. Some particularly conscientious bishops who encouraged confirmation were exhausted by the stream of people of every age who came to be confirmed.

Theologians reacted to the fact that many people lived and died unconfirmed by arguing that all baptised persons should be confirmed, but if they were not, it made little difference because baptism alone was sufficient to forgive sins and convey the Holy Spirit.

III. Eucharist

Baptism and confirmation were given only once to each person, since their consequences were believed to be permanent. The sacrament of the Eucharist, which was ordinarily distributed during the mass, was repeated uncountable times in settings ranging from the most ornate cathedrals to humble dirt-floor chapels. Every Christian above the age of reason took the Eucharist at least once a year and some people did so more often. The Eucharist, from a Greek word meaning 'to give thanks', had its origin in the New Testament accounts of Jesus's final meal with his apostles (Matt. 26:26–8; Mark 14:22–4; Luke 22:17–19; and I Cor. 11:23–5). In Matthew's version, while they were eating, 'Jesus took some bread, and when he had said the blessing he broke it and gave it to the disciples. "Take it and eat," he said, "this is my body." Then he took a cup, and when he had returned thanks he gave it to them. "Drink all of you from this," he said, "for this is my blood, the blood of the covenant, which is to be poured out for many for the forgiveness of sins." ' Already in the church of the Roman Empire, the eucharistic meal was embedded in an elaborate ceremony consisting of formal processions, singing, fixed and variable prayers, and readings from scripture, which are collectively called the mass, a term which derives from the formula of dismissal at the end of the service, *Ite, missa est*, 'Go, it is finished'.

Aside from a small number of heretics, every thirteenth-century Christian agreed that Christ was present in the consecrated bread and wine. That was the faith of believers and must not be confused with the theologians' attempts to explain *how* that presence occurred. There was one theological tendency that explained Christ's presence as somehow symbolic, but that was decisively rejected by the victory of the competing theological tendency that emphasised the physical reality of Christ's presence. At the Fourth Lateran Council (1215), the presence of Christ in the bread and wine was explained according to the science of the day, which was that of the Greek philosopher Aristotle (384–322 BC), whose works were in the process of being recovered and understood. In Aristotelian physics, all existing things, called substances, were composed of matter and form. The underlying matter is without characteristics until it is shaped into a thing by a particular form, a particular 'somethingness'. As a simple example, featureless matter could be a tree if it received the form of 'treeness' or a bird if it received that form. The Fourth Lateran Council defined as doctrine that when a priest consecrated the bread and wine, their form, that is their outer appearances, remained: they still looked, smelled and tasted like bread and wine. However, the underlying matter had been transformed into the real body and the real blood of Christ. The bread and wine changed their substance, were 'trans-substantiated', as the theological formula put it: Christ was really present under the outward appearances of bread and wine.

In the ancient church, the Eucharist had retained some aspects of a communal meal, but that had faded across the centuries. The conviction grew that the Eucharist was an awesome mystery and the liturgy was reshaped to reflect that view. By the thirteenth century, the priest stood with his back to the congregation, often behind a screen that partly or wholly blocked their view. He spoke in Latin and lowered his voice so as to whisper at particularly solemn moments in the mass. Lay people were encouraged to adopt an attitude of reverence in the presence of so awesome an event as the physical presence of the saviour.

Already in the seventh and eighth centuries, the church required people to prepare themselves carefully to receive the consecrated bread and wine, an act called communion. The details of the preparation varied by place and time, but usually involved the confession of sins, sexual abstinence for several days, fasting from food, the forgiving of one's enemies and perhaps even a bath. Some authorities recommended that women who were menstruating or had recently given birth should avoid communion because they were unclean in the Old Testament sense of ritual uncleanness. There were other prestigious authorities, including Pope Gregory I, who rejected that view. The implication of a demand for such rigorous preparation was that people were unworthy to approach communion without a major break with their day-to-day lives. As reverence for the Eucharist increased, so did anxiety about receiving communion unworthily; it became rare for lay people to take communion. Many attended Sunday mass but few dared to approach the altar for communion. Sometimes the priest gave them bread, called *eulogia*, which had been blessed but not consecrated, as a sign of love and as a substitute for the awesome 'bread of life'. Even in religious houses it was not unusual for the monks or nuns to receive communion only rarely, perhaps three times a year, although they went to mass daily. Only very pious laymen and religious, a distinct minority, took communion more often.

It is paradoxical that even as the mass became the most exalted ceremony of the church it also became the sole responsibility of the priest; it was poorly understood and passively witnessed by the laity. The consequences of that development are not surprising. The clergy complained of talking and milling around in church during mass. It was not unusual for men to stand outside the church until the consecration of the Eucharist, when they rushed in to see the priest lift the consecrated bread and wine so that they could quite literally behold Christ. The Eucharist remained the focus of much popular piety, but many lay people supplemented their mass-going with other religious practices and devotions that more directly responded to their emotional, intellectual and spiritual needs.

At the Fourth Lateran Council, the western church adopted a policy on the reception of the Eucharist that had a significant and long-lasting impact. All Christians above the age of reason had to receive the Eucharist at least once a year at Easter in their own parish churches, unless their parish priest advised against it or there was a reasonable excuse. In preparation for Easter communion, all had to confess their sins to their own parish priest and to perform the penance that he imposed. This became the norm for lay people: confession and communion once a year, with the hope that they would also receive communion on their deathbed as a *viaticum*, literally a 'provision for the journey' to the next life. Since the obligation of confession and communion could normally only be fulfilled in one's own parish, the parish priest knew who had not complied. Those who did not, and lacked an adequate excuse, could be forbidden to come to church and could be denied Christian burial if they had not corrected the situation before they died. The obligation to confess and take communion at least once a year became a cornerstone of the church's pastoral care of lay people.

The growth in reverence for the Eucharist accords well with the growing reverence for the human Jesus that was so prominent in popular piety after the eleventh century. Artistic representations of the crucifixion reminded believers of Christ's sacrifice for them, and the mass made Jesus's body and blood really present to be worshipped directly. Two developments – the recounting of eucharistic miracles and the creation of a religious festival to honour the Eucharist – point to the centrality of the eucharistic bread and wine in popular piety. The presence of evil in the world was a fact of life and a prominent part of faith. Since the Eucharist was the awesome presence of the saviour of the world, it was obvious that Satan would seek to undermine the faith of believers and to profane the sacrament. Beginning in the twelfth century, there was a recurring pattern in the miracle literature that reflected the new emphasis on the real presence of Christ. A person, often a priest, doubts Christ's real presence in the bread and wine. His faith is restored by some very physical manifestation: he sees Christ made visible in the bread and the wine or when he lifts the consecrated bread, called the host, it begins to bleed. Such bleeding hosts sometimes became the focus of a local pilgrimage or shrine.

Another recurring pattern in the miracle literature was disrespect for the host. There was a widespread fear that the outsiders and dissenters, such as witches, heretics or Jews, would profane the holy bread. There was probably some basis for such popular anxieties. It was in fact easy to obtain a host, usually by receiving it in church but not swallowing it. Witches and practitioners of folk healing did perhaps want such a powerful object for their rituals. Some heretics, particularly the dualists who condemned all material things, did hold the Eucharist in contempt. Yet, some of them went to church regularly and even received communion at Easter in order to protect themselves from detection. The rumour that the Lord's body was in the hands of unbelievers could provoke riots and attacks on individuals or, in the case of the Jews, groups.

The multiplication of miracle stories and horror stories about the Eucharist testified to the importance of the sacrament. But the growing popular reverence for the Eucharist was relatively new in the twelfth and thirteenth centuries and was just beginning to find adequate expression in ritual and pageantry. The religious festival of *Corpus Christi* ('the Body of Christ') was created in the thirteenth century to honour the Real Presence of Christ in the Eucharist. A female visionary convinced the bishop of Liège to authorise what was at first a local festival in honour of the Eucharist. In 1264 Pope Urban IV, who had been archdeacon in the diocese of Liège, extended the observance of the festival to the entire western church. The Dominican friar and theologian, Thomas Aquinas (1225–74), helped to compose the liturgical service for the festival.

The feast of *Corpus Christi*, which was observed on the Thursday after Trinity Sunday, could fall between 23 May and 24 June, when the weather in most of Europe had become warm and pleasant. *Corpus Christi* became one of the major holidays of the church, with a degree of popular participation rivalling that of both Easter and Christmas. In addition to the liturgical activities, the consecrated host was carried in procession through the streets. Every rank in society marched in the parade in their finest clothes. City streets and squares were decorated for the passage of the Lord's body. By the fifteenth century, the *Corpus Christi* festival was the occasion for public performances of religious dramas, called mystery plays, often staged by the urban guilds to teach vividly the Christian story of salvation.

IV. Penance

Sin loomed large in the Christian view of the world. Adam's legacy to his descendants was the original sin that in itself made them worthy of damnation. No baptised person lived entirely free from sin, though the seriousness of sins varied. All sin required a remedy, which needed to include heartfelt regret (contrition), confession and a reparation to the person wronged as well as to God (satisfaction).

In the early church, the relatively minor transgressions of everyday life, such as unjustified anger, envy, greed and gluttony, were cleansed by prayer and confession to God, fasting and charity to the needy. There was no confession to a priest as later Catholicism practised it, though many people did talk privately to a priest or bishop about the right course to follow in reacting to their sins. But the remedy for serious sins, which were later called 'mortal', including such things as murder, blasphemy, idol worship, adultery and sodomy, posed bigger problems. The earliest Christian congregations simply expelled members who committed such sins. In the second century, some argued that serious sins were unforgivable or, to be precise, they held that the church community should never readmit people who committed them, though the merciful God might forgive them. Others proposed a milder policy that was widely adopted: serious sinners might be allowed to repent and be readmitted to the church, but only once and not easily. It was not sufficient in the early church merely to say that one was sorry for one's serious sins. A severe public penance was required. Serious sinners confessed their fault before the entire church congregation, then spent considerable time, perhaps years, in the status of a penitent. Only God could know the secrets of the heart, but the community could judge the sincerity of internal repentance by the penitent's visible patience and willingness to endure severe requirements, including hard fasting, frequent prayers, sexual abstinence even for the married and unavoidable public shame. After a suitable time, penitents were reconciled by the bishop and readmitted to the church, but even then they continued to live as persons set apart: they could never receive public penance again and could not be ordained to the clergy.

Changes in the social framework of Christianity made public penance increasingly unpalatable to many. Between the fourth and sixth centuries, Christianity absorbed almost the whole of the Roman Empire's population. One consequence of the increase in numbers was the decline of rigorous public penance. Bishops continued to recommend it for those who created public scandal by gross, publicly known sins. However, because its consequences were both severe and lifelong, many serious sinners avoided public penance until old age or illness led them to set their lives in order. Many must have hoped that circumstances would allow them to seek public penance on their deathbed, when its benefits would be gained without its severe personal consequences. It was a gamble that many must have lost.

As the use of public penance declined in continental Christianity, sixth-century Irish monks on the western fringes of the Christian world created an alternative which was private, adaptable to the penitent's circumstances, and repeatable as often as needed. When the Irish were active on the continent as missionaries and pilgrims during the seventh, eighth and ninth centuries, they spread many of their customs, including private penance. Sinners confessed privately to a priest whatever they wished, including minor sins. The priest imposed a penance fitted to the sin and to the circumstances of the sinner (for example, male or female, young or old, married or unmarried, healthy or ill). By twenty-first-century standards, the early medieval penances were demanding, including 40-day-long fasts on bread and water, long periods of prayers, long pilgrimages, and even corporal punishments such as whippings. If the penitent could not perform a severe physical penance because of age, illness or some other reasonable cause, the priest might 'commute' it to something manageable, such as prayers or the giving of alms to the poor. Handbooks, called penitentials, were composed to offer advice and suggest appropriate penances to priests for their dealings with sinners, in what was described as the 'medicine of souls'.

Under this system of penance, any sin could be handled privately, and even minor faults were supposed to be confessed to one's 'soul-friend'. Serious sin was still a problem but an important distinction was made. If the sin was not widely known, it could be confessed privately. But if it was a public scandal, a public penance was needed to expiate it. Such a dual system became normal in the Middle Ages. Most people went to private confession where they received private penance. Notorious sinners, including the excommunicated, were compelled to perform a public penance if they wished the priest's absolution. When knights of the English king, Henry II, killed Archbishop Thomas Becket in 1170, there was public outrage at this crime. Although the king had not directly ordered the assassination, his anger and verbal outbursts at the archbishop made him partly responsible. To satisfy public opinion and the church's penitential system, Henry II performed a public penance at the door of Canterbury Cathedral in addition to the private penance imposed on him by Pope Alexander III. For lesser persons than a king, public penance could be both humiliating and painful. In 1299, the archbishop of York ordered Lady Cecilia de Stanton, who had been convicted of adultery, to do public penance for a public scandal. She was to be beaten while walking around the outside of the church of Stanton on six Sundays and was to be beaten on six days at the public markets at Nottingham and Bingham. If she refused the penance, she was to be excommunicated and forced to comply.

By the thirteenth century, private confession had become one of the central sacraments of the church. The theological basis for the priest's role in confession lay in Matthew 16:19, where Jesus said to Peter, 'I will give you the keys of the kingdom of heaven: whatever you bind on earth will be considered bound in heaven; whatever you loose on earth shall be considered loosed in heaven.' Theologians attempted to define the conditions under which a confession was properly carried out. Penitents had to be in a mental state of contrition, which is sorrow for their sins; they had to confess candidly to a priest; and they had to perform satisfaction for the sin, which was the penance that the priest imposed on them. If penitents fulfilled those conditions, the theologians taught that they were forgiven.

During the thirteenth century, two developments occurred that enhanced the regularity of this private or auricular confession, so named because the penitent confessed quietly in the ear (*auris*) of the priest. First, the Fourth Lateran Council required all Christians above the age of reason to confess annually to their parish priest in preparation for the obligatory Easter communion. Annual confession became a central fact of the ordinary Christian's life. Second, the rise of the friars, educated activists who were eager to minister to the religious needs of lay people, and who became skilled at hearing confessions. To guide their dealings with those confessing, some friars composed and many used theologically and psychologically sophisticated manuals of confession, quite different from the relatively primitive early medieval penitentials. These manuals for confession were also disseminated to the parish clergy who heard confessions annually during Lent, as canon 21 of the Fourth Lateran required.

The English theologian Thomas of Chobham wrote one such confessor's manual around 1215. Chobham had a nuanced and subtle understanding of human nature and how it related to sin. For example, he seemed to believe that women could use the tempting ways of Eve for good, and not evil, in order to change the sinful ways of their husbands:

No priest is able to soften the heart of a man the way his wife can. For this reason, the sin of a man is often imputed to his wife if, through her negligence, he is not corrected. Even in the bedroom, in the midst of their embraces, a wife should speak alluringly to her husband, and if he is hard and unmerciful, and an oppressor of the poor, she should invite him to be merciful; if he is a plunderer, she should denounce plundering; if he is avaricious, she should arouse generosity in him, and she should secretly give alms from their common property, supplying the alms that he omits. For it is permissible for a woman to expend much of her husband's property, without his knowing, in ways beneficial to him, and for pious causes.[1]

This is a complicated passage indeed. If original sin came about because Eve was a temptress, one would think that medieval women should try not to act like Eve. Yet here is a confessor saying that if a married man sins, even those sins are his wife's fault if she does not correct him. Then the wife is told to behave like Eve 'in the bedroom', and tempt her husband away from sin. It is also interesting that Thomas of Chobham encourages wives to 'secretly give alms from their common property' and 'expend much of her husband's property ... for pious causes', since much of that alms giving would have been directed toward the church.

Of course, many people observed only the minimum demand for annual confession to their parish priest. But the pious and some in the upper classes sought penance often; some mystics and visionaries even confessed daily. Skilled confessors, many of them friars, became the advisers of those who came regularly for penance. If the richly detailed manuals reflect what actually happened, even those who came once a year received a thorough grilling.

V. Marriage

Traditionally, marriage in medieval Europe was a private matter between two families, particularly those with property, since the choice of a spouse was intended to gain heirs and to regulate the transmission of property from generation to generation. Human feelings were always involved but medieval marriage was not ordinarily romantic in the modern sense of that term. Because marriage was tied closely to the values, anxieties and practical needs of differing societies, it varied considerably in details from one part of Christian Europe to another. In the early Middle Ages, there was a bewildering variety of marriage practices, deriving from the mixed cultural and religious heritage of the west. There were marriage rituals deriving from Roman, Germanic, early Christian and biblical sources.

Not every cohabiting couple was married. There were sharply conflicting views of what constituted a valid marriage: was it parental consent to the union?

Was it the consent of the man and woman? Was it sexual consummation? Or was it some combination of consent and sexual relations? Was a religious ceremony necessary to a valid marriage? Or could two families or even the two individuals arrange a marriage without outside participants? There were also conflicting views in the earlier Middle Ages on the termination of marital unions. The church authorities generally held that if a marriage had been valid to begin with (and in the uncertainties of the era that was a significant 'if'), then the union was dissolved only by the death of one partner. However, Roman law and some Germanic laws had recognised divorce by mutual consent or at the initiative of the husband. Pre-Christian Germanic societies had practised polygamy and concubinage. Even after the Germanic peoples had accepted Christianity, older practices survived by custom. Nominally Christian men in the early Middle Ages repudiated wives and remarried or took concubines and, in effect, practised a form of polygamy. Thus, in many ways long-standing social customs differed considerably from the church's norms on marriage.

Under the church's complex rules, not just any man and woman could marry. There were impediments to marriage, that is, existing conditions that prevented the formation of a marriage that was valid in the eyes of the church. In medieval society, as in our society, a man and woman cannot legally marry if either has a living, legally recognised spouse. In our society people who are closely related, for example brother and sister, cannot marry. In medieval society impediments arising out of kinship were much more broadly defined. The church was deeply concerned about marriages of relatives – called incest – and forbade unions among even relatively distant kin. When such unions were detected, the church demanded (not always with success) that the partners end what canonists regarded as incestuous unions rather than valid marriages. There were also marital impediments arising out of sponsorship at baptism and confirmation: godparents and godchildren generally could not marry one another.

The church's efforts to encourage exogamy, that is, marriage outside one's kin group, ran counter to some customs and practical considerations. Certain western societies actually preferred marriages between persons who were close kin, particularly first cousins, because it kept property within the extended family. In a rural society, it must often have been very difficult to find a marriage partner with whom one did not share a common ancestor. As the church's norms for a valid marriage were developed in detail, it was probably true that many unions could not have withstood close scrutiny according to the strict requirements of the canon law. In recognition of that fact, the Fourth Lateran Council reduced considerably the number of blood relatives who could not marry. The intention was not only to make marriage easier, but divorce more difficult: many twelfth-century nobles had exploited rules on marriage restriction in order to secure easy divorces. Even with these changes, the creation of a valid marriage remained a complex legal issue.

The church's efforts to impose its rules on marriage grew considerably after the eighth century and achieved a great deal, but marriage was never as completely under the control of the church as the other sacraments were. The chief competitor for control of marriage was the family, whose finances and future were bound up with good marriage alliances. By the thirteenth century, however, canonists and theologians had created a synthesis of the mixed heritage of western marriage practices, rejecting some, modifying others and allowing a great deal of variety in the way people carried out a marriage. The church's marriage law became the set of rules within which lay people sought to carry out their agenda of making alliances, obtaining heirs and transmitting wealth. The rules were important because failure to observe them might bring a family's plans crashing down.

The church *recommended* many things for a proper marriage: the observance of a betrothal ceremony; the provision of a dowry; the prior notification of the marriage, which was called 'proclaiming the banns'; and the presence of a priest and other witnesses to the exchange of consent. During the twelfth century, theologians and canonists had agreed decisively that the consent of the man and the woman was the act that made a valid marriage. The sacrament of marriage was unusual in that it was regarded as administered to the couple by their own consent; the priest was only a witness to the vows and a guardian of the rules. Parents still thought that their permission was necessary and in practice it usually was, but theologically only the free consent of the couple was needed, provided that there was no impediment to their consent, such as a pre-existing marriage or a close degree of kinship.

The stress on consent as the key to the creation of a valid marriage had important social consequences that generated frequent litigation and made many parents angry. In simple terms, a boy and a girl out in the garden with no one else around could say to one another something like 'I take you as my wife/husband', and if there was no impediment they were legally married. Thus marriage was a sacrament between husband and wife, with no priest needed. From the thousands of court cases that arose out of such 'clandestine marriages', it is clear that frequently the couple found a comfortable place to consummate their union, but consent alone had been sufficient in the eyes of the church to create a true marriage.

The secrecy and spontaneity of such marriages gave rise to frequent problems. Sometimes one party, often the man, denied that a free consent to marriage had occurred while the woman asserted that it had. The man might even admit that he had had intercourse with the woman, but denied that he had consented to take her as his wife, that is, he admitted to fornication but denied marriage. Sometimes parents, who had plans for their child, were furious that he or she had married without their consent and they tried to undo the union by pressuring their child to deny that he or she had consented.

A trial in a church court was often necessary. If the circumstantial evidence (ordinarily that was the only evidence there was) supported the contention that both parties had consented to marriage, the court would order them to live together as husband and wife.

Clandestine marriage is the extreme case that defines the essence of marriage as the medieval church understood it: the consent of a man and a woman to live together as husband and wife. However, most people followed social convention and married in a more public, formal way. To see what this looked like, let us follow a proper marriage in an English setting in the thirteenth or fourteenth century. The participants had some property, since the marriages of the poor could be made with less formality, and for love, precisely because they had no property to transmit and no one cared about their heirs.

Boys and girls and their families were presumably always on the watch for suitable partners, but nothing was official until the parents agreed on the contract to marry, which was called the betrothal. The contract might be made when one or both future partners were very young. Since wealth was usually in the control of the couple's respective fathers, it was they who carried out the negotiations. They had to agree on the dowry to be brought to the marriage by the woman as well as the property to be brought by the man. The betrothal was sealed in England with a public 'troth-plight' or 'handfasting', when the couple solemnly joined hands and exchanged rings and promises to marry. If the couple were of the proper age, they might give their consent and be bedded down together that same evening, making the marriage complete. For various reasons, they might also wait until a later date to turn the betrothal into a marriage.

Such a marriage was public and quite normal, even though the church did not necessarily have anything to do with its creation. Public opinion did not frown seriously on the couple living together after the handfasting. In fact, in some social strata the provision of an heir was so important that the couple might delay a church ceremony until the woman was pregnant or even until the child was born. The church encouraged people to add to the secular rituals of marriage a religious service performed by a priest before witnesses after proper publication of the proposed union, but it was not until 1563 that the Catholic Church required marriages take place in a church. Canon law required that on three successive Sundays, the banns, that is, the proposal to marry, be announced from the pulpit of every parish church where either person had lived. This was to ferret out impediments, such as a pre-existing marriage or a close kinship. After 1215, when the Fourth Lateran required wedding banns to be read, secret marriages remained valid, but were considered illegal, and any children born of them were illegitimate. Eventually most married couples had their union blessed 'in the face of the church', and church participation in weddings gradually became the custom, though it was never completely observed.

VI. Holy orders

There was a fundamental division within Christian society between the unordained, called the laity, and the ordained, called the clergy. The clergy were those set apart for God's service by special ceremonies which conferred the sacrament of holy orders.

The clergy had a legally privileged position in society and were organised in a hierarchy of grades or steps. The lower clergy or, as they are sometimes described, those in minor orders (doorkeepers, acolytes, lectors and exorcists), had fewer rights and responsibilities than the men in major orders (subdeacons, deacons, priests and bishops). The lower clergy were not bound by celibacy. Many were married men who worked for a church. Entry to the clergy at the lowest rank was by means of tonsure, that is, a cutting of the hair. The tonsured person was set aside by that visible symbol for God's service, though in fact the obligations were not serious. Students, child oblates, little boys intended for clerical careers and others were marked out by their haircut, which was short with a bald spot on top. They shared in the valuable legal privileges of clerical status, including the right to be tried in church courts, but they could leave the clerical state rather easily, simply by letting their hair grow out.

The major orders (subdeacon, deacon, priest, bishop) were more serious because the candidate had to promise lifelong celibacy to receive them. The central ritual of the major orders was a laying on of hands, which could be administered only by a bishop. The higher clergy were expected to behave as if they were set apart from ordinary life. They were to be recognisable by their tonsure and their clothing, which was to be sober and appropriate. They were to be set apart in that they lived without wives or children. They were also set apart by the way they earned their living. In the ideal, they should live from tithes, fees and other revenues from the altar, but that was not always possible. If they needed to do something else to earn a living, it should be honourable, for example, a chaplain or a teacher, and certainly not disreputable, such as being an innkeeper, a money lender or the assistant of some secular lord.

From the standpoint of most people, celibacy was the distinguishing mark of the higher clergy, though this rule was rarely enforced before the early twelfth century. The sacraments of baptism, confirmation, Eucharist, penance and **extreme unction** were available to all Christians, whether clergy or laity. However, by the central Middle Ages the sacraments of matrimony and holy orders could not be held simultaneously. That had not always been so. In the early church many clergy had been married. After the fourth century, the western clergy were required to be sexually continent, but even then married men were ordained as priests or bishops under certain conditions. If the clergyman's wife was still living, he was expected to support her but as a condition of ordination he was also expected to give up sexual relations with her, that is, he was to be sexually continent. That legal requirement persisted but was ignored in practice in many early medieval dioceses, in which much of the clergy, especially in rural areas, was married.

The church reformers of the eleventh century opposed all forms of sexual activity by the higher clergy, that is, the subdeacons, deacons, priests and bishops. Some of the more radical reformers encouraged lay people to refuse to receive the sacraments from married clergy, whom they tried to force to choose between spouses and careers. Within a few generations the reformers succeeded in bringing the marriage of the clergy into disrepute. Usually only unmarried men or widowers were ordained to the higher grades of the clergy. Thus, marriage marked one state of life and holy orders marked another: the same person could not lead both simultaneously.

VII. Extreme unction

Death was also embedded in rituals. In the Letter of James 5:14–16, believers were told 'If one of you is ill, he should send for the elders of the church, and they must anoint him with oil in the name of the Lord and pray over him. The prayer of faith will save the sick man and the Lord will raise him up again; and if he has committed any sins, he will be forgiven.' This text was the basis for the sacrament of extreme unction or final anointing. It became associated with dying, in prayers and actions sometimes called the last rites. The terminally ill were instructed to confess their sins, be reconciled by a priest, be anointed with oil, and finally receive the Eucharist in preparation for death. Like confirmation, extreme unction never rooted itself so deeply in the popular religious consciousness as baptism, penance and the Eucharist did.

VIII. Beyond the seven sacraments

The seven sacraments certainly did not exhaust the possibilities of expressing religious life and feeling through words, objects and gestures. At least two of the sacraments, confirmation and extreme unction, were marginal to the religious life of most people. There were other eagerly sought rituals that were not classified as sacraments because they were thought to have been established by the church rather than by Christ. As the theologians gradually restricted the number and sharpened the definition of sacraments, they called the other rituals 'sacramentals' to distinguish them from sacraments.

The medieval church created or just accepted many practices that responded to the needs of a complex society. One was the anointing of kings, a grand and solemn religious occasion modelled on the anointing of Hebrew kings in the Old Testament. In the tenth and eleventh centuries, which were the high points of sacred kingship, some intellectuals had proposed that royal anointing was a sacrament, but ecclesiastical reformers, struggling to reduce the power of lay rulers in the church, repudiated the idea. However, the anointing of a monarch remained a ceremony rich in religious and political symbolism, which few rulers would dare or want to omit.

IX. Purgatory and prayer for the dead

Concern about and care for the dead shaped both popular piety and church organisation, especially in the later Middle Ages. The medieval church optimistically assumed that most Christians would not go to hell, but it did not therefore assume that they would go to heaven, at least not directly. Many of the not-too-good but not-too-bad would go to an intermediate place called purgatory where they would, through real suffering that was intense and could last a very long time, settle their account for the penance they should have performed while they were on earth. In a society where kinship was a major social bond, the fear that one's relatives were suffering was a heavy psychological burden. There was considerable variety in how the afterlife of such 'undamned' sinners was imagined. The scriptural basis for prayer on behalf of the dead was in II Maccabees 12:43-5, in which it was recounted how Judas Maccabeus sent money to pay for a sin offering in the Temple on behalf of his fallen comrades: 'This was why he had this atonement sacrifice offered for the dead, so that they might be released from their sin.' Historian Jacques Le Goff argues that the doctrine of purgatory did not appear in western theology until the late twelfth century – which was when we find the first appearance of the word *purgatorium* – and links the growth of belief in purgatory to social changes in the Middle Ages, both intellectual and popular. There was no official teaching on purgatory until the Council of Florence (1438-45) defined it, in response to Byzantine objections, and the Council of Trent (1545-63) reasserted the view in response to Lutheran criticisms. However, popular faith in purgatory had long preceded precise theological definitions about it.

The conviction that sinners suffered in the afterlife but could be helped by the living was firmly held and vigorously acted upon. Since it seemed natural to pray for an ill parent or child, it also seemed natural to pray for a deceased parent, spouse, friend or child who might be suffering in purgatory. Such convictions were strengthened by visionaries and mystics who said or wrote that they saw the souls in purgatory crying out for help. Some theologians were puzzled about how prayer could change God's eternal will, but the Christian population was convinced that it did and acted accordingly. The living on earth and the dead in heaven and purgatory (but not hell) remained part of the same society, the people of God, the church. Their solidarity was expressed in part by praying for one another. The holy dead, called the saints, could pray to God on behalf of the living. For instance, in a prayer of the mass, Mary and other saints were asked to pray to God on behalf of the living. The saints did not need the prayers of the living, but the latter could pray to God on behalf of other living persons and the suffering in purgatory. The impulse to aid the suffering was strengthened by a long-standing belief that it was possible to offer one's own good deed to benefit someone else. For instance, it was not uncommon for a living person to recite the psalms, to fast or to go on a pilgrimage for another living person who could not or would not do so. Penance that a person had not fulfilled while alive was regarded as a debt that still needed to be paid. If the one who owed it died before paying it, then his surviving friends and relatives could pay it and gain some benefit for her or him in purgatory.

Such debt in purgatory could also be wiped clean by papal indulgence. The idea of indulgences was based on the pope's power to 'bind and loose', that is, to forgive sins. In 1095, Pope Urban II began the practice of issuing plenary (full) indulgences as a kind of recruiting tool for the First Crusade. Knights who felt contrition and confessed their sins would be automatically freed of any suffering in purgatory – their going on crusade was their penance. While a plenary indulgence took care of all sin committed up to that point in a person's life, one could never be sure how many indulgences and how much penance would be enough to satisfy God. At first, indulgences were written up on parchment, but with the advent of the printing press in the fifteenth century, they were produced in bulk and sold to raise funds for the church. This latter practice, the selling of indulgences, caused a bit of a furore known as the Protestant Reformation.

Since the tenth century, the church had set aside a day, the feast of All Souls (2 November), on which all the Christian dead were remembered in prayer. Some altruistic persons prayed that the sufferings of all souls in purgatory might be shortened. But most people wanted prayers for themselves and their relatives – they wanted to be named in the prayers. It was common to make provisions while living, or in a written will, to obtain intercessory prayer, especially masses, for oneself and specific relatives. Although almsgiving, fasting, pilgrimage, prayer and other good deeds were believed to help the dead, increasingly the mass, which was regarded as the most perfect form of prayer because it re-enacted Christ's atoning sacrifice to his Father, rose above the others as the best way to provide help to those in purgatory.

The status of the dead created anxiety. The living could never be sure how much prayer for the suffering dead was enough. In the later Middle Ages, there was an inflation in the number of masses for the dead. Some wealthy people arranged for scores, hundreds and even thousands of masses. The will of John Ferriby, made on 18 September 1470, was not extraordinary. He paid his chaplain twelve and one-half marks to sing mass daily for a year. He gave the priests at Beverly a silver saltcellar and 40 shillings, and the vicars at Beverly the same gift, on condition that after supper forever they would recite the penitential psalm *De profundis* (Psalm 130) for his soul, his parents' souls and all Christian souls. He promised 10 shillings to every friar at Beverly and Hull who would sing mass for him each day for 30 days. He gave four pence to each priest, chanter and sacristan at the high mass in Beverly minster on the day of his burial and in addition he requested a hundred masses at Beverly minster.

The growing demand for masses for the dead influenced the entire church. Monks and friars offered masses annually for the salvation of benefactors and members of the house's fraternity. Guilds and confraternities hired priests to offer masses for deceased members. The wealthy often made provision by will for an endowed foundation, called in England a chantry, to support a priest to say mass daily for a specified number of years or even forever. The number of chantries multiplied everywhere in Latin Christendom in the later Middle Ages as anxiety about the afterlife intensified.

Concern for the dead and actions to lessen their suffering took deep root in popular religious culture. But there were serious, unanticipated consequences that flowed out of the conviction that the living should help the dead by offering masses. There was ordinarily a fee, fixed by custom or by statute, for the celebration of private masses for special intentions, such as for the dead. Although a rich family might be lavish in its gifts for its dead, the usual fee was not large. However, the cumulative effect of hundreds of thousands of fees each year had a discernible impact on the clergy. For instance, the character of monasticism was changed by the apparently insatiable demand for masses for the dead. When monasticism began in the later Roman Empire, most monks were laymen, who sang the psalms and other prayers in the divine office at fixed hours and earned part of their living by manual labour within the monastery or in its nearby fields and orchards. Because of monks' reputation for holiness, requests grew for their intercession with God for the living and the dead. By the ninth and tenth centuries, the proportion of monks who were ordained as priests grew larger, probably in response to the need for priests to say the many masses that outsiders requested. Over the centuries religious houses accumulated a large, sometimes overwhelming burden of masses for the dead, which were regarded as a contract that must be observed. There were some efforts to lighten the load, for example by combining the benefactors' masses on the anniversary of their deaths. But in many religious houses, every suitable monk was ordained a priest in order to fulfil the obligation of masses. Even church architecture changed in response to masses for the dead. Monastic churches often had multiple altars where simultaneously several priests said mass privately or with a single assistant. The earlier tradition of manual labour by monks generally shrank or vanished as monk-priests earned their keep by saying mass. The balance of prayer and work which Benedict had laid out in his *Rule* tipped decisively toward prayer for the dead.

The growth in the number of private masses for the dead also influenced the secular clergy. The priest in charge of a parish church, called the rector or **vicar**, could sing only a small portion of the masses his parishioners might want. In response to the excess demand, there grew up a lower class of priests, without permanent positions, who supported themselves by saying masses for fees. Such 'mass-priests' were generally poorly educated, poorly paid, underemployed and often not particularly pious or well-behaved. The most fortunate of them were appointed to an endowed chantry, where they carried out the wishes of the founder. In the later Middle Ages some of them ran schools – chantry schools – to teach children how to read or write. They charged a small fee or even taught for free if the chantry endowment provided sufficient income. But some priests without steady employment were comparable to day labourers, living from the meagre fees for masses.

The yearning of the laity and clergy for masses to aid their beloved dead (and themselves) created an unintended but nonetheless troubling situation for the church as a whole. Much, though not all, of the clerical immorality and disorder of the later Middle Ages arose in this potentially embittered clerical proletariat who lived in relative poverty from mass fees. In the later Middle Ages, heretics would challenge the validity of some sacraments and masses for the dead, as well as the authority or necessity of the clergy to perform them. The context for these changes and their consequences are the subject of the following chapters.

Suggested reading

Companion website
www.routledge.com/cw/lynch

18.1 St. Augustine of Hippo on Sin
Excerpts from Augustine, *A Treatise on the Merits and Forgiveness of Sins, and on the Baptism Of Infants*, in Peter Holmes, trans., *The Anti-Pelagian Works of Saint Augustine, Bishop of Hippo*, vol. 1 (Edinburgh: T & T Clark, 1872), 10–13.

18.2   Caesarius of Heisterbach on Confession and Trial by Ordeal
Excerpts from Caesarius of Heisterbach, *Dialogus Miraculorum*, in G.G. Coulton, ed.,
Life in the Middle Ages (New York: Macmillan, c.1910), vol 1, 73–74.

Primary sources

Shinners, John and William J. Dohar, editors, *Pastors and the Care of Souls in Medieval
England* (Southbend, Indiana, 1998)

Whitaker, Edward C., editor, *Documents of the Baptismal Liturgy* (London, 1960)

Modern scholarship

Brooke, Christopher N. L., *The Medieval Idea of Marriage* (Oxford, 1989)

Brundage, James A., *Law, Sex and Christian Society in Medieval Europe* (Chicago, 1987)

Deane, Herbert, *The Political and Social Ideas of St. Augustine* (New York, 1963),
pp. 13–77

Duby, Georges, *Medieval Marriage: Two Models from Twelfth-Century France*, translated
by Elborg Forster (Baltimore, 1978)

Goody, Jack, *The Development of the Family and Marriage in Europe* (Cambridge, 1983)

Le Goff, Jacques, *The Birth of Purgatory*, translated by Arthur Goldhammer (Chicago,
1984)

Lynch, Joseph H., *Godparents and Kinship in Early Medieval Europe* (Princeton, 1986)

Moorman, John R. H., *Church Life in England in the Thirteenth Century* (Cambridge,
1955)

Paxton, Frederick S., *Christianizing Death: The Creation of a Ritual Process in Early
Medieval Europe* (Ithaca, New York, 1990)

Notes

1   Quoted in Sharon Farmer, 'Persuasive Voices: Clerical Images of Medieval Wives', *Speculum*
61 (1986), p. 517.

19

Crisis and calamity

The fourteenth century witnessed famine, plague, warfare, social violence, economic contraction, religious anxiety and other threats to the survival of Christendom. Things were so bad that historians have labelled the fourteenth century an extended period of 'crisis'. The subtitle of Barbara Tuchman's popular book, *A Distant Mirror*, even called the fourteenth century 'calamitous'.

Since the year 1000, three centuries of growth had transformed the demographic, economic, cultural and religious landscape of Europe. Everything in 1300 was on a bigger scale. Christendom had many more human beings, and had added more territory in the east, the north and the south. Sophisticated institutions, including the papal monarchy, bishoprics, international religious orders, universities, guilds and especially the network of parishes, effectively structured the lives of Christendom's inhabitants. Although the majority of people lived from farming and herding, a lively regional and international trade sustained hundreds of cities, which housed a prosperous and assertive merchant class and a large working class. All of that growth and development came under attack in the fourteenth century.

I. Famine and plague

Thomas Malthus (1766–1834), a pioneering English economist and demographer, theorised in his *Essay on the Principle of Population* (first published in 1798) that unchecked population growth would inevitably outrun the resources available to support it. When a population reached the limit that could be supported, it would be held at that limit by famine, war, disease and general misery for the poor. Malthus was not a student of the developments in late medieval Europe, but they seem to confirm several of his observations. In the first half of the fourteenth century, Europe may have suffered a classic 'Malthusian crisis', where unchecked population growth outran the resources available to support it. For several centuries, western European population growth had been accommodated in three ways: putting more land into cultivation, some surplus peasants moving to the growing cities, and others migrating to the fringes of Christendom, especially to the Slavic lands in the east and to Spain. Those outlets began to close in the later thirteenth century, and the living conditions of the peasantry and the urban poor deteriorated, especially in the heavily populated regions. When European population began to outstrip the capacity of the cultivated land, the owners of the land gained the economic upper hand. Most peasants did not own land, and those who rented land paid heavy rents and fees to landlords, reducing their living standard. There had been localised famines throughout the Middle Ages, but beginning in 1300, famines were more frequent and more severe, often resulting in a temporarily higher death rate and outbreaks of infectious disease.

Overpopulation was exacerbated by climate change. As we write these pages, the media and many citizens in the twenty-first century are troubled by the threat of a modern climate change, sometimes called global warming. In the later Middle Ages, the population crisis was made worse as the weather in northern Europe apparently cooled. Climatologists have identified a 'little ice age' that began in the late twelfth century and reached its most severe point in the mid-fourteenth century; it probably lasted until the late sixteenth century. The change in average temperature may have been slight but its effects in northern Europe were significant: more rain, shorter growing seasons, late frosts in the spring and early frosts in the autumn, each of which contributed to crop failure, famine and death. Northern Europe suffered severely when crops failed on a wide scale for three years in a row, 1315–17. Prices rose steeply and the poor, who were most vulnerable to famine, died in great numbers.

Then came a severe epidemic known in European history as the plague, or the Black Death, which brutally resolved the overpopulation crisis in no time. The evidence is ambiguous, but there had likely been outbreaks of the plague in the sixth century, contributing to population decline during the late Roman Empire. After the late eighth century, Europe was generally free from plague, though certainly not free from all epidemics, until it reappeared in the fourteenth century. Historians have traditionally attributed the Black Death to bubonic plague, though recent scholarship has challenged this idea. For example, Samuel Cohn, an historian of medicine, has argued that what we know today as bubonic plague did not even exist in the Middle Ages, and that the medieval plague was a distinct disease, with a different epidemiology. The noted medievalist Norman Cantor has speculated that the Black Death was really a combination of several pandemics, including anthrax. Historian Michael McCormick has offered counter-arguments to these claims, to uphold the older tradition. This debate can be followed through the suggested readings at the end of this chapter. For now, we offer the traditional narrative.

Bubonic plague is a bacterial disease transmitted by fleas that live on rodents, especially rats. Where human beings and rodents come into contact, as in crowded cities, the disease can spread to the human population. The bacillus *yersinia pestis* was common in the rodent populations of central Asia, which was perhaps disturbed by the changes that were occurring in the climate. In the late 1340s and 1350s an epidemic of bubonic plague ravaged human populations from China and India to Greenland and Morocco. The disease was apparently carried to Europe on shipboard from southern Russia or the Middle East, where the plague struck earlier than in western Europe. There is a plausible account of how the disease reached the west. The Genoese had a trading post called Caffa in southern Russia on the Black Sea. While Caffa was under siege by the Tartars, the plague broke out in the besiegers' camp. They catapulted dead bodies into Caffa. Subsequently, infected crews or perhaps infected rats set out on shipboard for Italy. When the ship reached Sicily in October 1347, the crew was dead or dying and the plague had made its entry into a population with little immunity to it. In the course of three years (1348–51), the epidemic swept across Europe, leaving few places untouched.

When the plague appeared, mass terror followed. People withdrew to their homes or fled elsewhere, carrying the plague with them. Suffering and death were so extensive that even such basics as the burial of the dead ceased for a time. After several months in a particular locality, the epidemic would subside, leaving a high proportion of the population dead and life seriously disrupted. The terror that the Black Death inspired is revealed in Boccaccio's *Decameron*, whose literary framework was that of a group of wealthy people hiding out from the disease and telling stories to pass the time:

> In the year 1348 . . . the deadly plague came upon famous Florence, more beautiful than any other Italian city. It began some years earlier in the east either through the influence of heavenly bodies or because God's just anger with our wicked deeds sent it to mortals. In a few years it killed an uncountable number of people. . . . Against this plague all human wisdom and foresight were useless. The city had been cleansed of much filth by the authorities; entry by any sick person was forbidden; much advice was given for the preservation of health. At the same time humble supplications were made over and over to God by pious persons in processions and otherwise. And yet in the beginning of the spring of the year mentioned above, its painful results began to appear in a horrible way.[1]

For Europe as a whole it is estimated that between one-third to one-half of the population died in three years. In the crowded and unsanitary cities, the percentage was often higher. Even when outbreaks subsided, the plague bacillus survived in the rodent population of Europe. For centuries the plague returned periodically. At each new outbreak, the death rate rose for those who had no immunity, which normally meant children and young people born since the last outbreak. Thus even after the massive death tolls of 1348–51, population in many places continued to decline throughout the fourteenth and into the first decades of the fifteenth century.

The Black Death solved the Malthusian crisis. Abruptly, the epidemic brought the population back into balance with resources. The long-term consequences of a rapid and drastic contraction of the population were so complex that economic and social historians continue to debate about them. The peasants and workers who survived were generally better off. There was an abundance of good land and a shortage of takers. In some places there were more jobs than workers. The economic law of supply and demand led to a fall in the cost of living and a rise in wages. For a time the living standards of the lower classes probably improved in such practical ways as more abundant food, more meat in the diet and better clothing.

The Black Death did not respect social status. (See Figure 19.) Many clergy died, since their ministry to the dead and dying made them vulnerable to the disease. The rich died as easily and horribly as the poor. In some noble families, the few surviving heirs were made wealthy by inheriting the property of their dead kinsmen. But the aftermath of the plague was not entirely favourable for the upper classes – including much of the institutional church – who lived off tithes and income from landed estates. Plunder from the frequent wars of the fourteenth and fifteenth centuries sustained many of the lesser nobles whose estates could no longer support them. Threatened economically, nobles took measures to protect their privileges and restrict the entry of outsiders into their ranks, particularly the wealthy merchants, who were better able to adapt to and profit from the new economic conditions.

The Black Death had serious consequences in commerce, industry and urban life as well. Warfare between rich and poor or between rich and middling broke out in many parts of late fourteenth-century Europe. In 1358, peasants in northern France, exhausted by plague, the Hundred Years' War, taxation, the demands of their landlords, and marauding bands of soldiers, rose up in a desperate, unorganised attempt to throw off their oppressors. The rising was called the Jacquerie, from the common peasant personal name 'Jacques'. The peasants, joined by some townspeople and priests, stormed castles and murdered every upper-class man and woman who fell into their hands. For two months they terrorised northern France. When the nobles and their social allies regained the initiative, they attacked with massive bloodshed, crushing the rebellion.

More often the rebels were not the very poor, but the middle groups in society, such as artisans and lesser landowners, whose rising expectations of economic improvement were frustrated by the political power of the nobles and urban elites. In England, a series of poll taxes, which fell equally on the rich and the poor, fanned social antagonisms into a rebellion in 1381, in which the grievances of a wide spectrum of people, including peasants, were expressed. This 'Peasants' Revolt' lasted only about a month, but frightened the ruling classes. In London, rebels looted for two days, killed the archbishop of Canterbury and other nobles, and attacked foreign merchants, whom they regarded as oppressors. In 1378, unskilled Florentine wool workers, called the *Ciompi*, aided by some of the middle class, seized control of the city for three years from the wealthy merchant class and attempted to restructure it in their favour. In 1382, the Florentine oligarchs regained control by political skill and force. Everywhere in late medieval Europe the upper classes reasserted their control, but they remained nervous and often took measures to co-opt, overawe or repress their opponents.

Figure 19 The dance of death
This miniature from a Book of Hours shows the so-called 'dance of death'. A skeleton carries a bier over his shoulder with one hand, and at the same time tugs at the vestments of the pope with the other. The pope, wearing his triple-crowned tiara, crosses his arms on his breast, perhaps acknowledging that not even he can escape death. Behind the pope is a king, also with arms crossed, and the indication of a large group following the procession. Notice how the grim message is juxtaposed against the lovely floral border. The text 'Dilexi quoniam exaudiet Dominus vocem orationis meae' ('I love the Lord, because he has heard my voice and my prayers') is the first line of Psalm 116, which is about death and salvation.

II. Warfare and violence

Although there is no precise way to measure social violence, there are good reasons to believe that it grew in later medieval Europe. We have already described the lower and middle class rebellions that inflicted violence on the upper classes and were in turn put down violently. Armed conflict between political units certainly increased as well. The Hundred Years' War, fought off and on from 1337 to 1453 between England and France, is only the best known example of the almost endless fighting during the fourteenth century, which included conflicts among Italian city-states, between Scotland and England, between Spanish Christians and Muslims, between Christian Slavs and Muslim Turks in the Balkans, and between crusaders and pagan peoples, especially the Lithuanians, along the Baltic Sea. War became an important industry, from which powerful people derived a significant portion of their income, and in which they had a vested interest. The life of a professional soldier attracted many nobles. Bands of soldiers, called companies, fought on behalf of those who hired them. When pay was slow or they were unemployed, they lived by extortion or looting the local population.

Medieval society had never been gentle to criminals, rebels or religious dissenters, but it seems that measures against them became both harsher and more widespread in the hard times of the later Middle Ages. In England the penalty for treason, inflicted on the Welsh prince David in 1283 and on Sir William Wallace in 1305, was the public spectacle of drawing and quartering. The traitor was dragged by a horse to the site of execution; he was hanged by the neck until almost dead and then cut down; his intestines were cut out and burned; he was then beheaded and his body cut into four parts that were sent as a warning to places where he had supporters. In the political violence of the fourteenth and fifteenth centuries, even anointed persons, kings and bishops, were not spared. From the mid-eleventh to the fourteenth century, kings captured in battle or by rebellious sons were treated relatively gently. However, of the eight kings who ruled England between 1284 and 1485, four were deposed and killed. Being part of the clergy was no guarantee against violence. People criticised clergy for all sorts of failings, and the resulting anticlericalism occasionally burst into violence. Some rural and urban uprisings left bishops and other high clergy dead, and peasant rebels often attacked wealthy ecclesiastical landlords, like abbeys.

The treatment of the Jews also worsened in the later Middle Ages. Since at least the twelfth century, the church had attempted to limit Jewish-Christian contacts for religious reasons. The merchant and craft guilds had supported such measures for economic reasons. However, for generations the practical measures to achieve separation were sporadic and porous. The unfavourable economic conditions of the late Middle Ages increased pressure to reduce economic competition from Jews. Those efforts were reinforced by growing religious intolerance and the search for someone to blame for the hard times. From the late twelfth century, Jews were occasionally expelled from particular cities or small regions and their goods confiscated. As times grew worse, the scope of the expulsions increased. Edward I (1272–1307) seized the wealth of Jews in England in 1290 and expelled the entire community. Similar expropriations of property and expulsions were carried out in France in 1306, in much of Germany in the fourteenth and fifteenth centuries, and in Spain in 1492, with lesser expulsions in between. Where the Jews were not expelled, as in most of Italy, they were placed under heavier social and economic burdens. Their segregation from Christian society was vigorously pursued, especially by creating compulsory residences for Jews, walled-in districts of the city, called ghettos.

The Black Death itself worsened social relations between Christians and those perceived as 'others'. The plague demanded an explanation. It was only in the 1850s that Louis Pasteur formulated the germ theory of disease. In the mid-fourteenth century, some intellectuals and physicians sought to explain the plague by the concept of contagion in the air, but others were just as satisfied with astrological explanations. Even Pope Clement VI (1291–1352) consulted astronomers, who explained the Black Death's causes as a conjunction of Saturn, Jupiter and Mars. Some believed the plague was a punishment from God and organised great processions of **flagellants** (from Latin *flagellare*, to whip), who inflicted wounds on themselves as satisfaction for human sin. Initially, the church tolerated the flagellants, but in 1349, Pope Clement VI condemned the practice. Many terrified people believed that it had to be the consequence of poisoning and sought scapegoats among the marginal people in society. In parts of France, lepers were blamed and killed. In Germany, suspicion fell on the Jews, who were widely believed to have poisoned the wells. A wave of bloody attacks in 1349–50 prompted many of the German city authorities to create walled-in Jewish streets (*Judengassen*) to protect but also to control the Jews. Pope Clement VI issued papal bulls condemning this violence, saying anyone blaming the Jews for the plague had been swayed by the devil, and urging clergy to protect the Jews.

In a society that saw itself under siege and in danger of disintegration, the position of outsiders, including Jews, lepers, heretics and suspected witches, deteriorated.

III. The church in turmoil

The church was not immune from the interlocking crises of the fourteenth and fifteenth centuries – far from it. In the second half of the thirteenth century, the papacy probably reached the high-water mark of its uncontested authority. Most individual popes of the period are not generally memorable, but they presided over the most sophisticated institution in Christendom. Their authority rested on almost universal, voluntary acceptance of the view that they were the successors of St Peter, to whom Christ had entrusted the headship of the church. Several generations of canon lawyers had given that theological belief a legal definition, which made the pope the 'universal bishop' of the church. The lawyers developed the position that all other clergy were the pope's assistants, entrusted by him with their specific role in the ministry of the church. The papal bureaucracy helped to make the pope's theoretical authority effective to the far corners of Christendom. The papal law courts, the inquisition, crusades, interdicts, excommunications and above all the cooperation of many lay rulers were used at various times in the thirteenth century against religious dissenters, heretics, political opponents and even those who were unwilling to pay their bills to the church. In spite of widespread support and a generally effective exercise of power, the pontificates of the 14 popes from Innocent IV (1243–54) to Boniface VIII (1294–1303), which averaged about four years, were not placid. The inhabitants of the city of Rome were turbulent. Elsewhere in Europe, rulers and popes periodically opposed one another in the many grey areas where secular and religious claims overlapped. The frequent papal elections were sometimes bitterly contested by cardinals and candidates motivated by personal, familial or national rivalries. The political ambitions of some popes outran the resources available to pay for them. In particular, the financial pressures of war and diplomacy were a constant source of anxiety and debt.

The theological underpinnings of the papal monarchy were rarely attacked directly in the thirteenth century, although there was a steady stream of criticism about how it functioned in practice. Aside from scattered groups of heretics, who were dismissed by the overwhelming majority of Europeans and successfully countered by the friars and repressed by the inquisition, no serious person in the thirteenth century could imagine the church without the pope. Some thought the papal institution needed changes, but no western Christian advocated abolition. Although lawyers and theologians debated about the outer limits of papal power and rulers resisted some papal claims that had financial effects on their domains, there was no alternative theory to that of the divinely established papal monarchy. Both on a practical and a theoretical level, in 1300 papal control over the church seemed complete.

The papal monarchy was certainly strong, but it did have two long-term weaknesses which were already visible in the later thirteenth century. The first was its finances. As the papacy asserted itself during the eleventh century, its need for money grew and so too did criticism of papal finances. In a society that was already heavily burdened by taxes, the papacy's growing income provoked a steady stream of comment. By the thirteenth century, the papacy's interests and responsibilities were international but its income was derived from a patchwork of traditional dues, income from the Papal States, fees for services and granting offices, sporadic gifts and crusade taxes. Income often did not meet expenses, but the taxes themselves alienated many quite religiously conservative people. One did not need to be a heretic to resent what seemed to be high taxation and inappropriate spending. The recipients of services or offices from the papacy often reacted with anger to what seemed to be excessive financial demands. They complained about simony, the selling of holy things. Even at its height, the papacy was dogged by a growing undercurrent of criticism centring on its insatiable need for money.

The other long-term weakness was the pope's governance of the city of Rome and the surrounding territories in central Italy. The pope was the secular ruler of the Papal States and as such could not escape the grubby realities of Italian politics. Northern and central Italy were divided among independent or would-be independent city-states and feudal lords who brawled with one another. All resisted outsiders who tried to govern them. The emperors of Germany, who had a historic claim to be the kings of Italy, attempted repeatedly between the eleventh and the fourteenth centuries to exercise power in Italy, but they finally failed, frustrated by the intense localism of the peninsula. From the later thirteenth century, the French and Aragonese monarchies struggled for control of Sicily and southern Italy. The popes thought they had to play a dangerous, expensive diplomatic game to prevent any political entity from becoming so powerful in Italy that it could threaten the papacy's independence.

The popes had only modest success in governing their territories, which shared the contemporary desire for independence. The inhabitants of the Papal States, turbulent and rebellious, did not want to pay taxes or obey laws imposed from above. The disorder in the papal territories forced successive popes to try to find ways to deal with the mess. Often they had to flee the city. They made political alliances, they compromised with rebels, they hired mercenaries and used brute force, they invited kings to protect their interests, and they used religious weapons such as excommunication to punish secular offences such as non-payment of taxes. None of the solutions worked for long, and they were expensive, time-consuming and corrosive of the spiritual prestige of the papacy. It was damaging to the pope's reputation across Christendom to be seen as just one more ruler engaged in the unspiritual business of war and diplomacy. In the best of times, the Papal States barely paid for their own defence and administration. Often they ran a considerable deficit that had to be made up from revenues derived from the pope's spiritual headship of Christendom. The other side of the coin was the papal court's belief, probably quite correct, that if it did not have its own independent territory, it would lose its freedom of action and be subjected to whatever secular ruler governed the city of Rome and controlled the election of popes. The possession of secular territories was perhaps unavoidable for the papacy, but it damaged its reputation and worsened its financial problems.

With the advantage of hindsight, we can see that medieval society was changing in the thirteenth and fourteenth centuries in fundamental ways that undermined the papal monarchy, though that edifice had considerable staying power. Perhaps the most profound cultural change was the spread of literacy. At the highest levels of society, the universities, so favoured by the papacy, trained intellectuals who used their skills in the interests of whoever hired them, often kings, city states and other lay rulers. In 1000 the elite of the clergy was the only learned profession, at ease with words and abstract ideas. But in an increasingly complex society the church gradually lost its monopoly on learning; intellectuals in its employment were no longer the only people with the skills needed to theorise and to explain the world. In 1300 lawyers, notaries, judges and others were autonomous professionals, proud of their social status, jealous of their income, and quite capable of defending the claims of their employers against the theoretical and legal claims of the church.

In the middling levels of society the spreading literacy among merchants, townspeople and bureaucrats, stimulated by the evangelical revival and by the needs of business and government, created groups of people who were capable of formulating criticisms of the moral failings, financial demands and political positions of the church, including the papacy. Such people were not necessarily opposed to the church or the papacy, but they were increasingly independent and apt to be troubled by the gap between the gospel ideals and the contemporary reality.

In the later thirteenth and fourteenth centuries, the most immediate threat to the papal monarchy came from a few secular governments that were consolidating their hold over the loyalties and purses of their subjects. Rabid nationalism is so deeply rooted in the twenty-first century and is assumed to be so natural that we may forget how recently it developed. The French Revolution (1789–99) and Napoleon's conquests of continental Europe (1799–1814) stimulated modern forms of intense national feeling in France as well as among her enemies. In earlier centuries the growth of national feeling had been gradual and not at all automatic or natural. In the twelfth century, the loyalties of elite groups were divided among Christendom, local and regional powers, and kingdoms, roughly in that order. The twelfth-century popes were the first medieval rulers to harness widespread loyalty to Christendom for practical purposes. By 1200, the papacy was the most advanced government in Europe, with legislative power, law courts, bureaucracy, formal procedures, written records, considerable income from fees, taxes and gifts, and firm loyalty among Christians. Secular governments were less developed, but during the thirteenth century several of them caught up with the papacy, creating their own mechanisms to make laws, exercise justice, keep peace and collect money. Since the same human beings were answerable both to the church and to the secular governments, all of which were expanding aggressively in the thirteenth century, there were bound to be conflicts over their respective rights, jurisdictions and claims to revenue. During the twelfth and thirteenth centuries the church was often the winner in such struggles, although they often had to strike compromises.

The most successful secular governments were monarchies, smaller and more manageable than the empire in Germany, but larger and more populous than city-states in Italy or Flanders. By the late thirteenth century the kings of England and France had become powerful rivals to the papacy within their respective kingdoms, with efficient bureaucracies, considerable income and a solid base of loyalty among their subjects. Their practical power was supported by theorists, mostly lawyers, who defended their king's authority over the church in his realm against the traditional rights of the pope. Two great examples of such theorists are John of Paris, whose *On Papal and Royal Power* (1302) argued that kings existed before popes, therefore kings did not derive their power from popes, and Marsilius of Padua, whose *Defender of the Peace* (1324) argued that popular consent created government (whether ruled by kings or popes), and therefore popular consent could even depose the pope.

IV. Boniface VIII and Philip the Fair

Pope Boniface VIII (1294–1303) was at the centre of the first serious defeats for the mature papal monarchy at the hands of the rising national monarchies. Boniface was trained in canon law and made his career as a papal bureaucrat and diplomat. He was about 60 when elected pope, an intelligent but rude and ill-tempered man, or at least that is what his critics said. He held a strong view of the extent of papal authority, but in that he was merely following the common opinion of the theologians and canon lawyers of his generation.

His first clash with King Edward I (1272–1307) of England and King Philip IV the Fair (1285–1314) of France came over money. The kings were preparing for war with one another over their conflicting claims to rule the south-western parts of what became modern France. Each king expected the church in his kingdom to support the war by paying taxes. According to canon law, the common law of Christendom, the church was exempt from taxation by lay rulers. But the rising tide of national feeling made it difficult for churchmen to escape taxation in a 'national emergency', such as war. During the thirteenth century, a ruler wishing to tax his clergy had usually obtained the approval of the pope, who might receive a share of the money. But both Philip and Edward were taxing their clergy directly, without papal authorisation and in clear contradiction to canon law. In 1296 Boniface issued a papal letter, known by its first words as *Clericis laicos*, which restated the traditional legal position that taxation of the clergy without permission of the pope was forbidden. The clergy of England and France were forced to choose between the pope and their respective kings. Popes could excommunicate clerics who disobeyed them but kings also had effective ways to bring pressure. Edward I 'outlawed' the clergy, that is, he denied them access to his courts for the defence of their property and persons. They quickly agreed to give him 'gifts'. Philip IV reacted decisively, forbidding the export of wealth from France to the papacy, thus cutting off a major portion of Boniface's income. The French clergy, pressured by the monarch and much of lay society, agreed to royal taxation. Pope Boniface had to back down, revealing clearly that in a direct confrontation, the kings of England and France had the practical power to tax their clergy, whatever the canon law said.

In 1301 Philip IV breached a second of the legal foundations of the church's position in society. According to the canon law, the clergy had a privileged status: no matter what a clergyman's crime, he was subject to the jurisdiction of the church, not of the state. In what became a test case, the bishop of Pamiers, who had fallen out of royal favour, was arrested, tried, imprisoned and tortured. He appealed to the pope, as was customary, but the royal authorities refused to recognise the pope's jurisdiction. Boniface was furious, but while he was deciding on retaliatory measures, Philip and his chief adviser, William of Nogaret, seized the initiative. In order to arouse public opinion against the pope, they circulated forged papal letters insulting to the French. They summoned representatives of the clergy and important laity of the kingdom to the first meeting of the Estates General, similar to a parliament, and publicly accused the pope of serious crimes, including an illegal election, heresy and sodomy. They demanded that Boniface be tried before a church council. The king was successful in playing cynically on the growing sense of national feeling among his subjects. The French laity supported the king vigorously, although the French clergy did so reluctantly. Nogaret went to Italy with a military force to stir up troubles for Boniface, who was residing in Anagni, in central Italy, the town of his birth. With the help of the Colonna cardinals, who were Boniface's bitter enemies, Nogaret captured the pope and held him prisoner for two days, apparently physically maltreating him. Nogaret intended to take Boniface back to France for trial, but the local Italians freed the pope, who died soon after. According to one tradition, Boniface died of 'extreme embarrassment' at his ill treatment. Even though the pope was dead, Philip continued to press for a posthumous trial and condemnation.

The papacy did not collapse after its humiliation by Philip IV. It remained one of the leading institutions in Europe; its bureaucracy and income even grew in the fourteenth century prior to the Black Death (1348). Once the immediate crisis over Boniface's humiliation subsided, things returned to a semblance of normality. But in fact a watershed had been crossed. In a direct confrontation between a pope and a king, people who were subjects of both chose to support their king. In the future they did not always do that, but popes had to tread more cautiously, even though their rhetoric remained the same as it had been when they really did lead Christendom.

As the national monarchies increased in strength, their rulers took an increasing role in the governance of the churches within their territories. Popes continued to issue the documents that appointed bishops or ordered the collection of taxes, but behind the scenes the kings of France and England in particular demanded and usually won a major role in the decisions and a major share in the revenues. Although the universal church united under the leadership of the pope remained a powerful ideal, and to some degree a reality, national feeling was a growing factor in church affairs. During the fourteenth and fifteenth centuries, the dominance that civil rulers gained over religious institutions during the sixteenth century was foreshadowed in many places.

V. The popes at Avignon (1309–78)

Boniface VIII was succeeded by Benedict XI (1303–4) and then by Bertrand de Got, the archbishop of Bordeaux, who took the name Clement V (1305–14). The new pope found himself in a difficult situation, particularly because the French king pressed his advantage over the papacy. Philip IV demanded that Boniface VIII be tried posthumously for his alleged crimes. Rather than condemn his predecessor, Pope Clement cooperated with the French king's political plans. In particular, he gave the College of Cardinals a majority of French members, which guaranteed a succession of French popes; and he acquiesced, probably reluctantly, in Philip's destruction of the military order of the Templars.

The French king was not the only cause of Clement V's problems. The city of Rome was more turbulent than usual. To avoid the disorder of the city and to prepare for the Council of Vienne (1311–12), Clement settled the papacy in 1309 in Avignon, in an enclave of papal territory on the south-east border of the French kingdom. In 1348, Pope Clement VI (1342–52) bought Avignon from the countess of Provence and it remained a papal possession until the French Revolution. Legally, Avignon was in the German Empire, but just across the Rhone river from the kingdom of France. This location hurt the papacy's reputation for independence and fairness: a French pope, only a river's width away from France, surrounded by a majority of French cardinals, living in a French-speaking territory, and often supporting the political and diplomatic aims of French kings. This angered France's political enemies, particularly England, who saw the papacy as playing favourites. The popes' abandonment of the traditional chair and tomb of St Peter in Rome troubled the pious throughout Christendom. The Italian humanist Petrarch (1304–74), who lived occasionally at Avignon and held lucrative benefices from the popes, was critical of the situation, comparing the residence of the popes at Avignon to the forced exile of the Jews in Babylon (585–536 BC). He gave it a nickname, whether deserved or not, that has stuck: 'the Babylonian Captivity' of the papacy.

The popes, who remained the bishops of Rome, never intended to stay permanently in Avignon, but the years rolled on. The move to Avignon was expensive. The pope and the cardinals built elaborate residences because, in an aristocratic society, the leaders of the church lived a lifestyle appropriate to their social class. The palace of the popes at Avignon, which is still standing, is an impressive monument to the cost of the move. Such an expensive standard of living drew constant criticism. In addition, the papal bureaucracy needed offices for its work. The bureaucracy itself grew during the years at Avignon and so did the expense of maintaining it. Expenses in Italy continued even after the transfer to Avignon because the popes did not give up their claim to the Papal States in central Italy. However, their absence from Rome strengthened the tendency to local independence, and there was a danger that the Papal States would be permanently lost. For much of the fourteenth century, the popes spent heavily on diplomacy and mercenary troops to try to regain control of their Italian territories. Some of the popes at Avignon tried to escape or decrease the control of the French king, but that too meant heavy spending on diplomacy and on financial support or bribes for potential protectors. The response of the Avignonese popes to their crushing expenses was to pull out all the stops in their search for revenue, turning every traditional right and loophole to financial advantage. Building on thirteenth-century developments, church authority became even more centralised at Avignon. Fairly routine matters that in earlier generations would have been handled locally were referred to the papal court. The papal bureaucracy expanded to handle an increase in the volume of business and expenses rose accordingly. In rapid evolution, earlier precedents that had been used occasionally were generalised to the entire church. The Avignonese papacy set fees for everything from a dispensation for a marital impediment to a confirmation of a document.

The change that had the most direct impact on local churches was the papal appropriation of the right to appoint to almost every office in the church. Local election or local appointment to bishoprics, abbacies and other church positions virtually ended, replaced by a system of papal appointment, called provision, in return for fees roughly proportional to the income of the position. Taken individually the measures to raise money were both legal and generally justified by the papacy's expenses, but their cumulative effect was disastrous for the reputation of the papacy, since the spectacle of greed and high living alienated many clergy and laymen, who also resented the loss of control over local church offices.

For the thousands of ordinary transactions handled at Avignon each year, the papal bureaucracy gave even-handed treatment according to rational rules. The bureaucracy was not arbitrary and the criteria it applied were generally high-minded. When local authorities appointed churchmen, favouritism for relatives or clients weighed heavily: an aristocrat's underaged brother might be preferred over a commoner with a degree in canon law. The papal bureaucracy favoured university graduates and men of proper age and accomplishment. On objective grounds, papal appointees were probably more qualified than those that local appointment would have produced. But in an era in which the traditional localism of medieval society was reinforced by growing national feeling, papal exercise of the power to appoint often ran counter to local preferences. Some of those who opposed papal power to appoint were motivated not by high ideals but by anger at their own loss of power and income. Yet, their voices contributed to the rising chorus of criticism.

The Avignonese popes used their power of appointment to solve the pressing problem of how to support the cardinals and bureaucrats on whom the papal monarchy depended. They conferred some of the most lucrative benefices in Christendom on their cardinals, bureaucrats and relatives. For instance, a benefice with a good income, perhaps in Germany or England, would be granted to a cardinal whose residence and duties were at Avignon. The cardinal would appoint a salaried priest, called a vicar, to carry out the duties of the benefice and would take for his own use the surplus income, often a considerable sum. Since one benefice could hardly support a cardinal and his household, this would be done several times, a practice called **pluralism** of benefices.

There were legal safeguards to guarantee that the benefice was not defrauded of its rights. Many of the wealthiest benefices were in cathedral chapters and collegiate churches, where the duties were mostly liturgical, such as saying mass and singing the daily divine office. In such a situation, a hired priest could fulfil the duties quite well. But when a benefice required pastoral duties among lay people, which was called 'care of souls' (*cura animarum*), hired priests were sometimes less satisfactory. Local people were angered that the benefice was held by a non-resident foreigner who might rarely or never see the church that supported him. Furthermore, the non-resident often skimped on the customary donations for local charity or the upkeep of the church building, thus further alienating the parishioners. As the power of lay rulers grew, they too saw in church benefices a handy way to support those of their bureaucrats who were also clergymen. They demanded that the popes confer benefices on their favourites, who were often non-resident pluralists employed full time in the service of the ruler.

When we look at the seven popes who lived at Avignon between 1309 and 1378 individually, they appear to be decent men, sometimes even committed to reform. But their need for money and the sheer inertia of the bureaucracy prevented any substantial change in the growth of papal fiscalism. Throughout Europe, the papal court was criticised for greed, pomp and a lavish way of life. England and its allies, which were political enemies of France, also criticised the papacy for its pro-French bias. The national origins of the cardinals reflected French dominance. From 1316 to 1375, there were 90 French cardinals, 14 Italians, 5 Spaniards and 1 Englishman. Increasing popular anti-papal feeling expressed itself in ways that had been muted or unusual in the thirteenth century. During the first stage of the Hundred Years' War, the English parliament issued the Statute of Provisors (1351) to prevent the Avignonese popes from providing foreigners to English benefices. In the Statute of *Praemunire*, issued in 1353 and revised in 1365 and 1393, the English parliament forbade subjects of the English king to litigate without royal permission in the papal court on any matter that the royal judges thought to be under their jurisdiction. English kings enforced the statutes only sporadically, particularly when they wanted to pressure the pope for a political purpose. Ordinarily they dealt with the pope by diplomacy and shared behind-the-scenes control of appointments. But such anti-papal measures were a sign of the intersection between growing national feelings and resentment of papal authority.

The Avignonese period produced major changes both in the functioning of the papacy and in the way the rest of the church perceived it. Never had the papacy done so much or with such effectiveness. Never had the papacy possessed a greater income or a greater impact on the furthest reaches of Christendom. But simultaneous with this growth in power was a decline in reputation. In the mid-eleventh century, the papacy had emerged as the leader of the reform movements in the western church. For more than two centuries the popes gave direction and inspiration to zealous reformers and pious believers. They protected many reforming groups, including the friars, against the stodgy defenders of the status quo, and championed the unity of Christendom against narrow-minded local tendencies. In the fourteenth century, the conviction grew that the papacy itself needed reform. Some popes conceded that much had gone astray in the church. Reform proposals, ranging from modest adjustments in the fees at the papal curia to total confiscation of the property of the clergy, flew thick and fast. However, no substantive reform occurred. The conflicting interests (mostly having to do with income and power) of popes, cardinals, bureaucrats and secular rulers produced a sort of gridlock. Those who benefited from the situation preserved it, even as they roundly criticised others. Among the educated and the pious, the frustrated aspiration for reform grew more intense. The evangelical ideals of poverty and preaching took more radical forms in the face of papal fiscalism, ecclesiastical pomp, pluralism and absentee priests. Much of the spontaneous affection for the papacy slipped away under such circumstances, although the papal institution was so deeply rooted that no alternative could win substantial approval.

VI. The Great Schism (1378–1417)

Even though residing temporarily at Avignon, the pope was by his very definition the bishop of Rome, a city hallowed in the eyes of the pious by its treasure trove of relics and great churches, and in the eyes of the growing movement of Italian humanists by its associations with the classical past. Reformers of every sort argued that if only the popes returned to Rome, the financial and moral problems so evident at Avignon could be solved. Pope Urban V actually went back to Rome in 1367, but the political situation was so disturbed there that he returned to Avignon in 1370. Against the advice of many cardinals, Pope Gregory XI (1370–8) returned to Rome in 1377, moved in part by the impassioned pleas of the mystic, Catherine of Siena (1347–80).

Rome had deteriorated badly in the 70 years since the papal court had left. Its main industry had been the church and the move to Avignon had, in a figurative sense, closed the factories in Rome. The city was impoverished, with a reduced though still turbulent population. Many of the former papal buildings and residences were in disrepair.

Gregory died in March 1378 and the first papal election at Rome in more than seventy years took place in an atmosphere of politicking among the cardinals and mob scenes in the streets. Fearing that the papacy would return to Avignon if a Frenchman were elected, the Roman populace clamoured for an Italian pope. The cardinals (4 Italians, 12 Frenchmen and 1 Spaniard) elected a high official of the curia, Bartolomeo Prignano, who was the archbishop of Bari in southern Italy. Urban VI (1378–89), as the new pope called himself, was an experienced administrator and had a reputation as a pious man. After he became pope, he revealed a side of his personality that he had apparently kept hidden. He turned out to be an ardent reformer. He started his reform with the cardinals, whose greed, lavish cuisine, personal morals and failure to reside in their benefices he publicly and rudely criticised. On one occasion he even struck a cardinal. Within a few months after his election, when Urban flatly refused to return to Avignon, the non-Italian cardinals withdrew to Anagni and declared his election null and void because, as they now said, they had acted under fear of the Roman mob. They elected Cardinal Robert of Geneva, a cousin of the French king, as Clement VII (1378–94), who returned to Avignon. Urban VI did not accept the legitimacy of his deposition.

The two popes excommunicated each other, and created rival colleges of cardinals and rival bureaucracies intent on filling offices and collecting dues. Christendom was in schism, a word that means a split or tear. (See Map 8.) From 1378 to 1409, there were two lines of popes. In such a situation, secular rulers exercised great power by their choice of whom they would support as the legitimate pope. They could prevent one or both papal claimants from collecting money and appointing church officials within their territory. The political antagonisms of Europe were soon reflected in the papal schism. France and England were locked in the Hundred Years' War. The French king opted for the Avignonese line of popes and so did his allies, which included the duchy of Burgundy, the kingdom of Scotland and the kingdom of Naples. The English king and his allies, including Flanders and Portugal, supported the Roman line of popes, as did the Hungarians, the Poles, the Bohemians, the Scandinavian kingdoms, and most of the numerous German and Italian rulers. Each secular ruler convinced (or forced) the clergy of his domains to accept his choice. International religious orders were split, as the members in one country chose a different papal line from the members in another. Christendom was bitterly divided.

There had been earlier papal schisms, some quite long-lasting. But in the political conditions of the fourteenth century, this schism threatened to become permanent, as national political rivalries were transferred openly into church government. The intelligentsia and politicians of Christendom debated how to end the schism, a delicate matter since the papacy had become the nerve centre of the church and few wanted to damage it seriously in the process of settling the dispute. The many proposals for ending the papal schism can generally be categorised under three headings. Some proposed that the rival popes resign simultaneously. In spite of negotiated promises to resign, those efforts finally proved fruitless, since each pope was convinced that he was the rightful pope. Others proposed that the secular rulers of Christendom withdraw their support (and money) from both popes, thus forcing them to yield. Diplomacy could not achieve such a universal withdrawal of support because many rulers were pleased with a situation that increased their control over the church in their own domains. The third proposal, which grew in appeal as the schism dragged on and the lines of division hardened, was to summon a general council. It was widely hoped that such a council would end the schism, reform the church 'in head and members', as the contemporary phrase put it, and deal with the spread of heresy in Bohemia.

The conciliarists, proponents of summoning a general council to end the schism, knew that they had to do this in a legal way – any illegality would make

Map 8 The Papal Schism, 1378–1417

the situation worse by undermining confidence in the council. According to canon law, only a pope could summon a general council, but neither the Avignonese nor the Roman claimant would jeopardise his situation by summoning a council that he could not control, and which might judge him out of office. In 1408, both colleges of cardinals withdrew support from their respective popes and summoned the Council of Pisa, which in 1409 deposed both the Avignonese pope, Benedict XIII (1394–1423/24), and the Roman pope, Gregory XII (1406–15). The council elected Alexander V (1409–10), but neither of the rival popes would accept the legality of their depositions. Each had enough secular support to hang on. There were now three claimants to the papacy, the Roman, the Avignonese and the Pisan!

The conciliar solution to the schism was tried again, with success, at the Council of Constance (1414–18). The emperor Sigismund (1410–37) pressured the new Pisan pope, John XXIII (1410–15), to summon the council, a move later ratified by the Roman pope, Gregory XII. With the backing of Sigismund, the council accepted the voluntary resignation of Gregory XII, who was made cardinal-bishop of Porto; it deposed and imprisoned the Pisan pope, John XXIII; and it deposed the Avignonese pope, Benedict XIII, who defied the conciliar decision until his death in 1423/24. In 1417, the council elected Martin V (1417–31) as the definitive pope, and the Great Schism was success-fully ended.

Suggested reading

Companion website
www.routledge.com/cw/lynch

19.1   Boccaccio on the Plague
Excerpts from Giovanni Boccaccio, *The Decameron of Giovanni Boccaccio: including forty of its hundred novels*, trans. Henry Morley (London: G. Routledge and Sons, 1886), 10–14.

19.2   Pope Boniface VIII, Clericis Laicos (1296)
Excerpts from Henry Gee, William John Hardy, eds., *Documents Illustrative of English Church History* (London: MacMillan and Co., 1896), 87–89.

Primary sources
Boccaccio *The Decameron*, translation by G. H. McWilliam (New York, 2003)

Crowder, Colin, editor, *Unity, Heresy, and Reform, 1378–1460: The Conciliar Response to the Great Schism*, Documents of Medieval History, 3 (New York, 1977)

The Council of Constance, documents translated by Louise Ropes Loomis, edited and annotated by John Mundy and Kennerly Wood, Columbia Records of Civilization, 63 (New York, 1961)

Modern scholarship

Barraclaugh, Geoffrey, *The Medieval Papacy* (New York, 1968)

Boase, T. S. R., *Boniface VIII* (London, 1933)

Cantor, Norman, *In the Wake of the Plague: The Black Death and the World It Made* (New York, 2001)

Cohn, Samuel K., 'The Black Death: End of a Paradigm', *The American Historical Review* vol. 107 (2002), pp. 703–38

Dobson, R. B., *The Peasants' Revolt of 1381*, 2nd edition (London, 1983)

Hay, Denys, *Europe in the Fourteenth and Fifteenth Centuries*, 2nd edition (London, 1989)

Jordan, William Chester, *The Great Famine: Northern Europe in the Early Fourteenth Century* (Princeton, 1996)

McCormick, Michael, 'Rats, Communications, and Plague: Toward an Ecological History', *Journal of Interdisciplinary History*, vol. 34 (2003), pp. 1–25

Mollat, Guillaume, *The Popes at Avignon, 1305–1378*, translated by Janet Love (London, 1963)

Mollat, Michel and Philippe Wolff, *The Popular Revolutions of the Late Middle Ages*, translated by A. Lytton-Sells (London, 1973)

Partner, Peter, *The Lands of St Peter: The Papal State in the Middle Ages and the Early Renaissance* (Berkeley, 1972)

Renouard, Yves, *The Avignon Papacy, 1305–1403*, translated by Denis Bethell (Hamden, Connecticut, 1970)

Strayer, Joseph R., *The Reign of Philip the Fair* (Princeton, 1980)

Tuchman, Barbara, *A Distant Mirror, The Calamitous 14th Century* (New York, 1978)

Ullmann, Walter, *The Origins of the Great Schism* (London, 1948)

Waley, Daniel P., *The Papal State in the Thirteenth Century* (London, 1961)

Wood, Charles T., *Philip the Fair and Boniface VIII: State vs. Papacy*, 2nd edition (Huntington, New York, 1976)

Note

1 Giovanni Boccaccio, *Decameron*, edited by Vittore Branca (Florence, 1976), pp. 9–10.

20

The church in the fifteenth century

In spite of serious disruptions brought on by the plague, by social conflicts, by chronic warfare, and even the papal schism, the basic structures of medieval society proved resilient enough to survive. Government, politics, education and economic life were buffeted by abrupt changes but they continued to develop more or less along the lines laid down in the thirteenth century. Within a generation after the plague, the traditional institutions of Christendom had adapted with varying degrees of success to the new conditions. The problems of the fourteenth-century church were severe, but contrary to what one might expect, Christianity as a lived religion flourished into the fifteenth century, in spite of hard times.

I. Conciliarism

The Great Schism saw not only a reduction of the pope's real power, but also the development of a coherent theory of church government, which challenged that of the papal monarchy. The new view, worked out by university-trained lawyers and theologians, is called **conciliarism** because the centrepiece of their theories was the overriding authority of a general council. In the twelfth and thirteenth centuries, the canon lawyers had created a body of legal opinions and laws dealing with the problems of corporate bodies, an important issue since so many of the church's institutions, including monasteries, cathedral chapters, hospitals and even the College of Cardinals, were corporations that chose members, elected officers, administered income, owned property, and could sue and be sued. A key element of the canon law of corporations was that the interests of the corporate group should not be damaged by the actions of its officers. The officers held their authority for the good of the group and the corporate body could protect itself from incompetent or malicious officers, as a last resort by deposing them.

In the effort to end the Great Schism in an acceptable way, some intellectuals argued that the church itself was a corporate body whose executive in ordinary times was the pope. But when the executive could not or would not act in the interests of the corporate body, then the church could defend itself, just as any corporation could. Some theorists argued from a different angle that the cardinals were the corporate body of the Roman church and hence could discipline or depose an erring pope. However, the view that generally prevailed was that Christendom itself was the corporate body, of which the pope was the head. Conciliarists argued that Christendom, represented in a general council, could protect its interests even against the pope, who was subject to the council's authority. In the context of the times, those were radical ideas, but as the Great Schism persisted and other solutions failed, they gained respectability. Conciliarism was put into action at three councils in the fifteenth century, Pisa (1409), Constance (1414–18) and Basel (1431–9). The method of representation in the general councils was not based on the modern idea of one person/one vote. But the councils embodied remarkable political experiments. Important elements or interest groups in Christendom were represented. Some, such as the bishops, cardinals and abbots, came in person. But other important individuals and groups chose representatives to act for them, including religious orders, cathedral chapters and the universities. Christian rulers such as kings, princes and city-states were also represented. At the Council of Constance (1414–17), the participants were organised into the Italian, German, French and English 'nations' (later a Spanish 'nation' was added). The members of the 'nations' met among themselves to decide how to cast their one collective vote.

The Council of Constance issued two decrees embodying the essential views of the conciliarists. In the canon that began with the words *Sacrosancta* or *Haec sancta* (1415), the Council of Constance declared its superiority to the pope:

> This holy council of Constance . . . declares, first that it is lawfully assembled in the Holy Spirit, that it constitutes a General Council, representing the Catholic Church, and that therefore it has its authority immediately from Christ; and that all men, of every rank and condition, including the Pope himself, are bound to obey it in matters concerning the Faith, the abolition of the schism, and the reformation of the Church of God in its head and its members. Secondly it declares that any one, of any rank and condition, who shall contumaciously refuse to obey the orders, decrees, statutes or instructions, made or to be made by this holy Council, or by any other lawfully assembled general council . . . shall, unless he comes to a right frame of mind, be subjected to fitting penance and punished appropriately; and, if need be, recourse shall be had to the other sanctions of the law.[1]

Most conciliarists at Constance accepted the view that the routine but vital business of running the church would have to be carried out by a pope and his bureaucracy: the services were needed and government by committee seemed unwieldy and unworkable. However, the Council of Constance wanted to make the summoning of councils at regular intervals a part of the constitution of the church. In the canon *Frequens* (1417), the Council of Constance ordered another council to be summoned in five years, then in seven years, and every ten years thereafter. If it had been successful, this ambitious experiment in constitutional monarchy would have radically redefined the papacy's position in the church. The Council of Constance was the high-water mark of the conciliar movement, which issued revolutionary decisions about church government, removed the three men who claimed to be pope, and elected Martin V, thus ending the Schism.

The council scheduled for 1423 was put off because of an outbreak of plague. But in 1431, in accordance with the provisions of *Frequens*, Pope Martin V summoned a council to meet in the city of Basel (in modern Switzerland). Conciliarism was in its prime, although neither the pope nor his supporters accepted its claims. Almost from the beginning, a new pope, Eugenius IV (1431–47), sparred with the council. In 1431, he ordered the dissolution of the council, which successfully defied him and remained in session. By 1434 the council set out to reform the papacy in a radical direction: it tried to cut off all the pope's income from outside the Papal States and to set up committees of its own members to exercise the judicial, administrative and executive functions of the pope. The conciliar committees granted such things as benefices and dispensations and attempted to manage the church directly.

Pope Eugenius sought to undermine the council by direct negotiations with important rulers. In the struggle for public opinion, he capitalised on the centuries-old hope for reunion with the Greek Orthodox Church. By the 1430s, the situation in the Byzantine Empire was desperate. The Ottoman Turks had conquered all but the city of Constantinople and some scattered possessions on the Greek mainland and islands. In hopes of gaining western aid, the emperor John VIII Paleologus (1425–48) proposed negotiations to reunite the eastern and western churches, as some of his predecessors had done in the face of earlier Muslim military threats. The crucial point was that the emperor preferred to deal with the pope rather than with the council sitting at Basel. Pope Eugenius summoned the council from Basel to Ferrara (and subsequently to Florence in 1439) to meet representatives of the Greek Orthodox Church. Most of the bishops left Basel, but the dedicated conciliarists, many of whom were lawyers and university teachers, held out. The small remnant at Basel, with only seven bishops present, deposed Eugenius in 1438 and elected the duke of Savoy, a pious layman, as Pope Felix V (1439–49). In reintroducing a schism after so much effort had gone into eliminating the earlier one, the conciliarists at Basel made a fatal mistake, discrediting conciliarism in the process. The small, radical and unrepresentative remnant continued to sit at Basel until 1449, claiming that it, and not the papal council at Ferrara-Florence, was the legitimate general council, but the advantage had shifted decisively to the papacy.

At the Council of Ferrara-Florence (1438–45), a Byzantine delegation of about 700 members, including the Emperor John VIII, the patriarch of

Constantinople, and 20 Greek bishops, debated in great detail with western theologians about the theological topics dividing them, especially purgatory, indulgences and the authority of the pope. After long, frank debates, compromises were accepted by both sides. On 6 July 1439, all but two Greek prelates accepted a decree of reunion (*Laetentur Caeli*, 'Let the heavens rejoice'). Over the next six years, the Council of Florence achieved union with other groups of eastern Christians, many of them in Muslim-controlled areas: the Armenians, the Copts of Egypt, some Syrian Christian groups, the Chaldeans and the Maronites of Cyprus. The reunions generally did not last because of religious hostilities and political conditions in the eastern Mediterranean. The most significant reunion, that with the Greek Orthodox Church, collapsed almost as soon as it was announced in Constantinople. Western military aid to the Byzantines was delayed and, when the armies arrived, they were defeated by the Turks at Varna in 1444. Religious differences contributed most to the failure of reunion. Because of their bitter experience of the crusades and conquest by the Latins in 1204, the people and the lower clergy of the Byzantine Empire were anti-Latin and repudiated the reunion, even if it meant conquest by the Turks. But in the west the prestige of the papacy was much enhanced by the apparent success of reunion at Ferrara-Florence.

Pope Eugenius had triumphed over the Council of Basel and over the theories of the conciliarists. In addition to achieving reunion with the Greek Orthodox and other eastern Christians, which won the approval of public opinion, he owed part of his success to his own skilful diplomacy within Christendom. He made or accepted separate arrangements with important European rulers. For instance, King Charles VII of France issued the Pragmatic Sanction of Bourges (1438), which curtailed papal rights in the church of France in favour of royal control. Eugenius accepted the arrangement because there was little he could do, but also because royal control of the church in France made the king less likely to support the conciliarists. Eugenius also negotiated an agreement with Austria, though he died before it was signed in 1448. When many rulers of Europe had settled individually with the popes, they no longer needed the threat of councils to pressure them. Conciliarism as a significant movement collapsed, although its ideas continued to have supporters. In 1460, Pope Pius II (1458–64), a former conciliarist, issued the bull *Execrabilis*, which means 'Damnable', condemning the view that councils were superior to popes and forbidding appeals from papal decisions to a 'future council'. Nonetheless, the appeal to a future council remained a common tactic of papal opponents well into the sixteenth century.

By the second half of the fifteenth century, the papacy had survived the Great Schism. It had reasserted the language and rituals of papal supremacy against the claims of conciliarism. But even though its theoretical basis was restored, it was a changed institution. After almost 150 years of criticising, debating and theorising about reform, little substantive reform had actually occurred. To be sure, some local reform movements within particular regions and religious orders had achieved modest success, but the universal church was reformed neither in its head nor in its members.

Between 1430 and 1530, the popes were mostly aristocratic Italians who lived a life befitting their social class. The Italian Renaissance was in full bloom. The Renaissance (Italian *Rinascimento*, meaning 'rebirth') was a literary, intellectual and artistic movement based on renewed interest in classical culture. The Renaissance popes, often men of taste, were patrons of the arts, and builders of some of the structures so admired in Rome by modern tourists. Saint Peter's Basilica and the Sistine Chapel, with its famous fresco painted on the ceiling by Michelangelo (1475-1564), are but two examples. But the Renaissance popes were also preoccupied with the intricacies of Italian politics. Italy remained divided into several aggressive city-states and kingdoms. The popes were deeply enmeshed in the diplomacy and warfare that maintained a balance of power to prevent the victory of any of the contenders. They were also devoted to the enrichment of their relatives: traditional nepotism was refined to a high art. It is significant that no pope from Celestine V (1294-6) to Pius V (1566-72) was declared a saint by his successors. The pope was still the head of the universal church, but in most places local rulers had severely limited his exercise of power. Only in Italy and Germany, which were so divided politically, were the popes able to exercise a considerable measure of the control that had become traditional during the Avignonese period. Beneath the glitter of papal ceremony and the strong statements of papal theory, the leadership of western Christianity had already passed into the hands of lay rulers in the century before the Protestant Reformation.

II. Road to reformation?

When we describe the church during the era of crises in the fourteenth and fifteenth centuries, we need to avoid the strong (and common) temptation to read backward from 1517 – the year Martin Luther posted his 95 theses, forever changing the direction of the church – to try to find the 'causes' of the Protestant Reformation. Unlike those alive at the time, we have the advantage of hindsight. We know that after a generation of religious strife (1517-55), medieval Christendom was permanently divided into several major denominations (Catholic, Lutheran, Calvinist and Anglican) and numerous smaller groups (such as the Anabaptists). We also know that all those groups drew on the religious heritage of the Middle Ages, though none of them, not even the Catholics, maintained that heritage entirely intact. We know that by 1600 the forces of religious change had remade Christianity everywhere in western Europe, though it was not the same remaking among Catholics, Lutherans, Calvinists, Anglicans and Anabaptists.

We should also assert that none of this was inevitable; that any part of that history could have gone in a different direction. And we must avoid the common 'biological' analogy, applied to many periods of history, which prefers to see every human institution in terms of 'germination', 'flowering' and 'decay'. In spite of the crisis and calamity reported in Chapter 19 and above, the so-called 'late medieval' church was hardly in decay. Historian Eamon Duffy uses a range of evidence – from written documents like wills and memoirs to objects such as rood screens and stained glass windows, even graffiti – to show that every aspect of religious life prior to the Reformation was pious and immensely popular, with members from the nobility and peasantry all taking part. According to Duffy, the late medieval church also maintained its essentially 'corporate' nature, in spite of arguments from some historians that Christianity was becoming more 'individualised'. People knew they were part of something larger than themselves, and they willingly participated in it: attending masses; celebrating feasts; observing fasts; venerating relics; undertaking pilgrimages. In spite of these good arguments, the tradition persists that the 'decline' of the late medieval church somehow 'led to' the Reformation. Such traditions die hard. Perhaps the best we can do is keep in mind that in 1400 or 1500, no contemporary could have predicted what was to happen in the century following 1517. So let us take our eyes off the future for the moment, and evaluate the later medieval church on its own terms.

Fourteenth- and fifteenth-century Europe teemed with reforming zeal and religious commitment. Bishops, religious orders, local rulers, and laymen and laywomen were active in efforts to bring about changes that were almost always described as 'reforms'. But the efforts at reform were generally piecemeal and were often stubbornly resisted by vested interests. For instance, many religious orders had movements to reverse earlier relaxations of the rules on such matters as the possession of private property, diet, clothing and prayer. The reformers were called 'observant' because they observed the details of their order's original rule. The Franciscans had the first observant movement, and similar groups arose within the Cistercians, the Benedictines, some regular canons, and other religious orders during the fifteenth century. The observant groups produced some of the most active preachers and zealous advocates of reform, such as the Franciscans Bernardino of Siena (1380–1444) and John of Capistrano (1386–1456), the Dominican Vincent Ferrer (1350–1419), and even Martin Luther (1483–1546), who was a member of the observant group of the Augustinian Hermits. But as was typical of fourteenth- and fifteenth-century local reforms, the results of efforts to reform religious orders were rarely complete. In practice, the rise of 'observantism' within a religious order generally led to a split, sometimes quite bitter, between the observant group and those who refused to return to the full observance of their order's original rule. The occasional successes of local and regional reforms could not hide the fact that significant reform of the entire church 'in head and members' had not been achieved. Expectations of reform were raised and crushed, frustration grew, radical ideas were given wide circulation, and the shortcomings of the clergy were broadcast for all to see.

It is important to understand the meaning(s) of the term 'reform' in about 1500. There was great variety in the details of proposed reforms, but they virtually always centred on changes in the church's bureaucracy, finances and specific practices. Since belief was not an area that most late fifteenth-century people thought needed reform, a person in 1500 would rarely have called for changes in well-established religious beliefs. Unhappiness with the institution of the church did not translate into tolerance for those who differed from the official church on important points of belief.

There were heretics in the fourteenth and fifteenth centuries. Two of the most influential were John Wycliff in England and Jan Hus in Bohemia (the modern-day Czech Republic), both of whom reflected the popular anticlericalism and religious zeal of their times.

John Wycliff (1324–84) was a university teacher at Oxford. He believed in the infallibility and primacy of Scripture. For him, Scripture was eternal, conceived in the mind of God before it had ever been written down by humans. Therefore, it took precedent over any doctrine or teaching coming from the papacy. Pushing these ideas even further, he argued that the 'real' Church had always existed, and did not come into existence with the incarnation of Jesus. The result of such an argument rendered the nominal church, with its popes and bureaucrats and expenses, meaningless. Wycliffe opposed the doctrine of transubstantiation (that the substance of the bread and wine was transformed in the eucharistic sacrament), and argued instead that the bread and wine remained just that, bread and wine. He stressed the poverty of the early church, and used Scripture as a means of criticising the opulent church of his own day. He believed abuses in the Church should be forcibly corrected by secular powers. He believed that only the predestined made up the true church, but only God knew who they were – and clergy were not necessarily part of this group. One can imagine that Wycliffe did not find many supporters at the papal curia, or among the clergy. But Wycliffe was merely expressing ideas, albeit in a more scholarly fashion, that were already in the air. The English translation of the Bible that bears his name (historians argue about how much of it he did himself), came into circulation in 1382. In 1384, Wycliffe died, but he continued to have followers well into the sixteenth century.

While Wycliffe was at Oxford, he enjoyed protection based on academic freedom, as well as protection from the royal family, in particular John of

Gaunt. Upon his death, he himself had never been excommunicated, but in 1377 Pope Gregory XI had condemned his ideas, as did Oxford theologians in 1382. Wycliffe and his students were driven out of Oxford on the order of Archbishop William Courtenay. Adherents to Wycliffe's teachings, called Lollards, were persecuted almost from the start. There was a strand of Lollardy in the Peasants' Revolt in 1381 – or so the authorities maintained – even though Wycliffe himself opposed the revolt. In general, the nobility grew to oppose Lollardy, seeing it as an equal threat to themselves as to the church. In 1401, parliament passed the law *De heretico comburendo* ('Concerning the burning of heretics'), which prohibited the translating or owning of a translated Bible, and authorised burning heretics at the stake. In spite of this, artisans and members of the middling class, and even some knights and nobles, continued to be drawn to Lollardy. In 1413, the knight John Oldcastle, a close friend of King Henry V (and presumably the basis for Shakespeare's character Falstaff) was tried for Lollardy and imprisoned in the Tower of London. An insurrection was organised to free Oldcastle, but he was recaptured, and eventually executed. In 1415, the Council of Constance declared Wycliffe a heretic, 31 years after his death. They decreed that his books should be burned, and that his remains should be exhumed, burned and the ashes cast into the river. Yet Lollardy held on, even through numerous prosecutions over the years, and eventually blended with the new Protestantism of the sixteenth century.

Wycliffe's ideas found their way to Bohemia, where they were well received. Jan Hus (*c.*1369–1415) was a priest and university teacher who adopted many of Wycliffe's teachings, especially on the primacy of Scripture and ecclesiology (the organisation and function of the church). For example, he taught that the papacy was not an institution of divine origin. Hus's teachings and the spread of Wyliffe's ideas in Bohemia took place in the context of the Great Schism and growing anticlericalism, but also in the context of growing Czech nationalism. One can see the combined effect of these in the controversy over '**utraquism**'. Utraquism (from the Latin *sub utraque specie*, 'in both kinds') maintained that the Eucharist should be administered 'in both kinds', bread *and* wine, to everyone in the congregation, even laypeople. Church practice at the time only allowed the wine to priests. The idea of administering the eucharistic wine to the laity started in Prague in 1414. In June of 1415, the Council of Constance prohibited the practice, which only made the Hussites want to practise it all the more. In July of 1415, the Council condemned Jan Hus and burned him at the stake. (See Figure 20.) In an unexpected turn, at least from the Council's point of view, their stance on utraquism and the execution of Hus conflated in the minds of the Czechs, turned Hus into a martyr, further aroused nationalist sentiment in Bohemia, and turned nobles and commoners alike into ardent supporters of Hus's cause.

Figure 20 Jan Hus
The top register of this printed image shows the archbishops of Pisa and Milan – identified by their coats of arms (*wappen*) – 'degrading' Jan Hus at the Council of Constance (1414–18). The lower register shows armed knights leading Hus away to be burned at the stake for heresy.

Some of the Hussites became more radical. A Hussite league was formed that defended Hussite teaching, essentially blocking the doctrinal authority of the church. The more radical Hussites rejected long-held traditions like the intercession of the saints, the power of relics and the elaborate liturgy. By 1419, King Wenceslas decreed the suppression of utraquism, essentially suppressing the Hussites. A more radical branch of the Hussites, the Taborites (centred in the Bohemian city of Tábor) saw the suppression of the lay chalice as persecution, and a sign that the millennium of Christ was near at hand. Violence broke out between Hussites and Catholics. In 1420, Pope Martin V declared a crusade against the Hussites. Various crusades, civil wars and public violence continued off and on until the Taborites' final defeat in 1434, but Hussitism held on in various forms, and prosecution of heretics continued until the Protestant Reformation.

In spite of Wycliffites and Hussites, the vast majority of western Europeans, even bitter critics of all things ecclesiastical, accepted the faith of the church as true. The popes were criticised for their bureaucracy, their taxes and their worldliness, but not for their teaching. There was no widespread call for reform of doctrine.

One striking aspect of the church in 1500 was the growth of separation between religious institutions and religious fervour. The failure of reform and the persistence of criticism led to a widespread loss of confidence in the major institutions of Christianity, including the papacy, the religious orders, the university theologians, the canon law and the church courts. All of them continued to function, but were subject to a withering barrage of criticism. Such a loss of confidence was not, however, accompanied by a decline of religious fervour in the general sense. Quite the contrary, there was an intense interest in religion, indeed a religious revival had begun in some places in the late fourteenth century and flourished in the fifteenth. Intense piety could be accompanied by anticlericalism: many people ardently practised Christianity while disliking the clergy because of their wealth, legal privileges and moral failings.

Traditional pious practices were, if anything, intensified in the fourteenth and fifteenth centuries. Intellectuals could criticise as they wished, but pilgrimages, the cult of the saints, the veneration of relics and the search for indulgences flourished. For instance, Frederick the Wise of Saxony (1463–1525), who became Luther's protector, was an avid relic collector. His holdings in 1520 included 19,013 relics, which promised an indulgence of almost 2,000,000 days remission of punishment in purgatory to those who visited them on All Saints Day (1 November). The mass and the Eucharist still remained central to religious practice. For example, the exceptionally pious Lady Margaret Beaufort (1443–1509), the mother of King Henry VII of England, heard mass six times every day. Her grandson King Henry VIII was said to hear mass three times a day when he was hunting and five times a day when he was not. Alongside such traditional pious practices, popular preachers encouraged new devotions or the intensification of older ones, such as praying the rosary, devotion to Christ's five wounds through special prayers and masses, and reverence to Jesus's Holy Name, which believers thought could heal body and soul, protect against Satan and deliver God's grace. People with varying degrees of wealth gave religiously motivated gifts during life or at death, though it is significant that in some places more gifts in wills were directed to practical good works, such as hospitals, schools and relief of the poor, and away from the traditional religious orders.

III. Monastic life

The vast, but not tightly organised structure of religious houses and orders, which had developed over more than a thousand years, survived remarkably intact. In many but not all places, the number of monks, friars and nuns was well below the historic highs of the pre-plague period. Some religious houses maintained a high level of fervour, others were scenes of scandalous disorder, but it is fair to say that most were middling places, neither exceptionally fervent nor exceptionally lax. Because of their numbers, endowed wealth and legal privileges, the religious remained a formidable force in society. The secular clergy were also numerous, though divided among themselves by income, education and social standing. In the fifteenth century there were many young men entering the ranks of the secular clergy, indeed in some places too many for them to be usefully employed. Although the regular and secular clergy were criticised for their wealth, their legal privileges and their failures to live up to their own ideals, they found recruits and kept their legal immunities.

The traditional yearning to find ways to live a more perfect spiritual life continued to bubble to the surface. New expressions of religious life jostled with the older ones. Alongside the traditional life of monks, nuns and canons, which was organised around permanent vows, institutions with endowments, legal privileges and special clothing, there was a proliferation of new – we might call them experimental – ways to live a fervent religious life. Some pious men and women consciously chose *not* to enter a structured religious order, but to lead a pious life more or less in the world. One stream of opinion asserted that it was possible to be a good Christian and to live in the world – an idea that would have seemed questionable a few centuries earlier. It is no accident that beginning in the thirteenth century a few lay people, even married lay men and women, took their place alongside monks, nuns and bishops as saints.

In a movement that became quite visible in the thirteenth and continued into the fifteenth century, individual mystics who claimed some direct contact with God attracted followers, imitators, admirers and critics. The mystics were sometimes ordained clergy or in religious houses, notably the Dominican friar Meister Eckhart (*c*.1260–*c*.1327), or the anchoress Julian of Norwich (*c*.1342–*c*.1416). Many mystics were lay people, especially women, who did not live in monasteries but lived as hermits, anchorites or even as married persons. Some of these female mystics, like the Dominican Catherine of Siena (1347–80), who described her experience as a 'mystical marriage' with Jesus, commanded respect for their piety and wisdom. As noted in Chapter 19, Pope Gregory XI returned to Rome from Avignon, in part because of Catherine's pleas. Other female mystics, like the eccentric Margery Kempe (*c*.1373–*c*.1438), could experience misunderstanding and trouble. Margery's autobiography is considered by some to be the first in the English language. In it she tells of her celibate marriage with her husband (after bearing 14 children), and the many pilgrimages she undertook to Rome, Jerusalem and Santiago de Compostela. Margery believed she had been given the 'gift of tears'; she was so joyous about Christ's sacrifice for the redemption of humanity that she wept constantly. This outward show of piety was admired by some, but was a nuisance for others. On several of her pilgrimages, Margery found herself abandoned by her fellow travellers because they could not stand her incessant weeping.

Some people sought to live in the space between religious individualism and strict regular communities. For centuries Christians had banded together for religious purposes, a tendency that had led to the network of religious houses that covered Europe. Some of the pious in the later fourteenth and fifteenth centuries formed loosely organised voluntary associations, such as confraternities and religious guilds. One of the most significant of such pious movements was the *Devotio moderna*, the 'Modern Devotion', which arose in the late fourteenth century in the Netherlands under the inspiration of Geert Groote (1340–84). The followers of the *Devotio moderna* were not vocal critics of the contemporary church, though their choices and concerns shed much light on what some highly spiritual people found troubling in the church of their day. They did not oppose ritual or traditional piety – they were very devoted to the Eucharist – but they stressed inward conversion, contemplation, simplicity and pious reading, and subtly devalued the external acts of religion. The movement attracted followers from the clergy and the laity. Some priests among them became canons of an order centred at Windesheim in the Netherlands, but most followers of the Modern Devotion decidedly did not want to found another religious order. The lay members of the Modern Devotion gathered together voluntarily in single-sex communities, which were not traditional convents or monasteries. Instead, they lived in ordinary city houses. They took no vows and wore no special religious clothing. They did not want the great wealth (and great distraction) of traditionally endowed monasteries, nor did they aspire to what they regarded as the unseemly hucksterism of the begging friars. They pooled income and lived together on their own resources. They earned their living by their own labour; the men often copied and sold religious books and the women did needlework and made lace for sale. They took no formal vow of poverty, though they lived in simplicity. The members were free to leave, and some did so to join religious orders, to be ordained clergy or to marry.

The tension between exceptional piety and membership in the wider church had in the past occasionally led to heresy, but the Modern Devotion was quite orthodox. The followers of the *Devotio moderna* had their own religious practices within their residences, including group prayers and sermons by members who might be lay people. However, they remained members of their local parish where they went to mass and fulfilled their other religious obligations. In late medieval society where law and custom made a sharp distinction between lay people and clergy, the *Devotio moderna* welcomed both lay people and clergy into its circles. In their pursuit of a personal religious life, they composed or translated pious works in the vernacular for use by their humbler members and by outsiders.

To modern eyes, the brothers, sisters and canons of the *Devotio moderna* do not seem very threatening. But their quiet insistence that the true Christian life could be lived 'in the world', without the traditional rules and structures of monasticism, was symptomatic of the widespread desire for an intense personal religious life and a simultaneous distrust of traditional religious institutions. They had critics, especially among the friars, who regarded them as potential rivals. However, they were religiously orthodox, humble, hard working and obedient to church and civic authorities. They received acceptance and support in many Dutch and German cities. They had their counterparts in other places in Europe, as some intensely pious people sought fulfilment at the margins of the church's institutions, which at least by implication they found inadequate.

IV. Humanism

Criticism of contemporary religion came from other perspectives as well. The humanist movement, which began in Italy in the fourteenth century and had spread among intellectuals and lay elites in northern Europe by the later fifteenth century, was critical of many contemporary religious practices. Humanism, which is admittedly difficult to define and is understood in a number of ways in our society, was centred on a new educational ideal which was carried out by the study of literature, history and ethics, based on the rich heritage of ancient Rome and Greece. The humanists valued not only the Greek and Latin classics, but also the New Testament and the fathers of the church. The northern, often German, humanists were especially interested in religious matters. When humanists compared the contemporary church to the idealised church of the New Testament and the fathers, it fared poorly.

Humanist criticism fed into the general religious discontent in the fifteenth century, especially among the educated elite.

One of the most famous humanist writers was Erasmus (1469–1536), a Dutchman who had studied in a school of the Modern Devotion. He did not remember his early educational experience with any affection, but he was probably influenced by the values of simplicity and inwardness in religion. Erasmus wrote a great deal in polished Latin and gained a European reputation among intellectuals and the educated elite. He was one of the first authors to take full advantage of the recent invention of printing to reach larger audiences than anyone before him. Erasmus was a complex figure, but he represents important tendencies among the educated people of the late fifteenth and sixteenth centuries. He was a brilliant scholar of Latin and Greek, but also a witty, interesting and, when he wished to be, biting satirist. He was much concerned with the church, of which he approved very little, although he sought reform rather than revolution.

Intellectuals had always understood Christianity differently from the great mass of people. For instance, in the thirteenth century the Dominican theologian Thomas Aquinas and a south Italian peasant might as well have practised different religions. But most medieval intellectuals did not repudiate the religion of the peasants. They generally thought that sincerity of belief compensated for ignorance and that peasants in their own way could be pleasing to God. But the humanists often loathed the popular piety of their day as vulgar, superstitious and wrong-headed. Many of them, with Erasmus in the lead, were not shy about saying so. In a torrent of books, pamphlets and letters, Erasmus ridiculed much that he saw as objectionable in late medieval Catholicism. He had the usual targets – rich monks, arrogant bishops and cardinals, superstitious lay people, hair-splitting theologians, and hypocrites – but his literary skill made him very effective and influential among the humanistically educated of Europe. Erasmus lambasted pilgrimages, bleeding eucharistic hosts, fake relics, begging friars, fat monks, and all the external features of contemporary religion. He recommended a more spiritual, inward, simple, morally oriented and biblical religion. Pietists, such as the members of *Devotio moderna*, might have regarded a man like Erasmus as proud, sceptical and irreligious. A humanist, such as Erasmus, might have regarded members of *Devotio moderna* as overly pious, credulous and puritanical. But both in their way undermined confidence in the traditional rituals and practices of the late medieval church. Sebastian Brandt (1457–1521), a contemporary of Erasmus, took all parties in this conflict to task in his wildly popular, illustrated work *Das Narrenschiff* ('Ship of Fools'). Published in 1494, this allegory of a ship with fools as passengers and fools at the helm, pokes fun at simple pietists, snooty intellectuals and everyone in between. Its short satiric poems and vivid woodcut illustrations made it more accessible to a wider audience.

V. The state and religion

Pious movements and religious critics had been frequent in the central and late Middle Ages. But their impact was magnified in the decades around 1500 by two developments, the consolidation of the state and the invention of printing. Bureaucratic, centralised governments had been developing in some regions of western Europe since the twelfth century. As they succeeded in asserting their power within their territories, the effectiveness and independence of a universal church headed by the pope slowly waned. The growth of states had not been without setbacks, but in the late fifteenth century strong monarchies emerged in several places, including England, France, the Iberian Peninsula and Sweden. In other places, such as Italy, Germany and the Swiss confederation, strong principalities and city-states were striving to consolidate control of their territories, including the local churches. The growth in effectiveness of such secular states was accompanied by an increase in antipapal sentiment, since papal activity stood in the way of state power. North of the Alps, the popes and their bureaucrats were often regarded as foreigners (they were overwhelmingly Italian) who interfered in local affairs and took a great deal of money out of the country. The Italian churchmen often dismissed the northerners as barbarians.

In many places the two decades on either side of 1500 saw a dramatic increase in the dominance of the state over the church. The popes of the second half of the fifteenth century appeared more and more as Italian princes, or as kings of a small papal state, relying heavily on their central Italian territories for income and concerned to protect those territories, however high the cost. Elsewhere in Europe, rulers had been influential in church finances and personnel decisions for generations, but in earlier times they had exercised their control indirectly through pressure, diplomacy and private agreements with the papacy. In the fifteenth century, many rulers no longer felt the need to hide their power and intervened openly in the church of their territory. Some rulers saw it as their right and their duty to take initiatives in religious matters. The widespread dissatisfaction with the church strengthened the hand of rulers, who found support among their people for religious interventions. It is significant that not all church reformers or clergy opposed an increase in governmental control. They would not accept a ruler's intervention in matters of belief but they knew from frustrating experience that practical reforms were often slowed or prevented by the procedures and delays inherent in the canon law, including costly appeals to the pope. But if a strong king, prince or city council intervened to reform something like a nunnery or a hospital, the matter often moved to a rapid conclusion that was satisfactory to the reformers. Rulers asserted their authority over the church in many ways, including the support of limited reform within their realms.

The primary example of royal reform took place in the church in Spain, which Cardinal Franscisco Ximenez de Cisneros (1436–1517) reformed with the active support of King Ferdinand of Aragon (1452–1516) and Queen Isabella of Castile (1451–1504). In 1478, Ferdinand and Isabella received papal authorisation to create the government-controlled Spanish Inquisition, which carried out the rulers' policies of unifying a diverse society by rooting out Jews, Muslim, heretics and critics, with no interference from the pope. Yet sometimes, as in France, kings asserted their royal power without much reform. In 1516, the pope agreed to the Concordat of Bologna (1516), which gave the French king effective power to appoint clergy to 10 archbishoprics, 82 bishoprics, 527 monasteries and numerous other religious institutions within his realm. It is well known that the Protestant Reformation intensified the subordination of the church to the state, but that process had begun much earlier.

VI. Printing

Finally, we should not ignore the printing press as another powerful force in the fifteenth-century church. It increased pious reading, criticism and calls for reform. Earlier reformers were limited because they had to rely on handwritten manuscripts and public sermons to spread their ideas. In the 1450s, Johannes Gutenburg of Mainz invented the technology that made it possible to print from moveable type. As the printing press spread across Europe in the late fifteenth and early sixteenth centuries, it made possible the rapid dissemination of all sorts of ideas, including a vast range of ideas about reform.

Because late fifteenth-century European society was intensely interested in religion, one of the steadiest markets for printed materials was the consumer demand for religious books, including Bibles, collections of sermons, mystics' writings, saints' lives and books of hours.

Martin Luther (1483–1546), a skilled writer in Latin and German, saw his ideas receive a publicity that no earlier reformer could have imagined. For instance, from 1517 to 1520, 370 editions of Luther's works appeared, often brief and lively pamphlets or single sheets, which sold perhaps 300,000 copies. This helps to explain his ability to mobilise so much of German public opinion to what many of his readers and hearers understood as an anti-papal and anti-Italian movement.

Whether contemporaries knew it or not, great changes would come to the church in the early sixteenth century. The situation was quite unclear and the direction of those changes could not have been foreseen. Traditional religious institutions and practices were discredited in some circles and eagerly cultivated in others. The papacy defended a traditional view of its power, which princes were generally willing to accept even as they drained papal claims of much of their reality. Some intellectuals imagined a unified church without a pope. Ambitious rulers who were quite orthodox in their belief were intent on controlling the church in their territories, limiting the practical powers of the papal bureaucracy. A discordant chorus of voices called for 'reform' of the church as institution, though they did not agree on what the nature or extent of that reform should be. At the same time, nobles and peasants alike expressed popular piety in the form of masses, pilgrimages, religious feasts and fasts, praying the rosary, and other corporate and individual celebrations of the faith.

This was the context into which a friar and theologian named Martin Luther challenged opponents to a debate about indulgences in October of 1517 – a debate that became the catalyst for massive religious change.

Suggested reading

Companion website
www.routledge.com/cw/lynch

20.1   The Pragmatic Sanction of Bourges
'The Pragmatic Sanction', in Frederic Austing Ogg, ed., *A Source Book of Mediæval History: Documents Illustrative of European Life and Institutions From The German Invasions to The Renaissance* (New York: American Book Company, 1908), 395–397.

20.2   Concerning the burning of heretics (1401)
Excerpts from 'De Heretico Comburendo', in Guy Carleton Lee, ed., *Source-book of English History* (New York: Henry Holt and Company, 1901), 214–217.

20.3   Saint Catherine of Sienna Exorcising a Possessed Woman
Rendering by Phillip C. Adamo of Girolamo di Benvenuto (1470–1524), 'Saint Catherine of Sienna Exorcising a Possessed Woman', *c.* 1500–1510, at the Denver Art Museum, Denver, Colorado.

Primary sources

Catherine of Siena: The Dialogue, translated by Suzanne Noffke and Giuliana Cavallini, Classics of Western Spirituality (Mahwah, New Jersey, 1980)

Erasmus of Rotterdam, *Collected Works of Erasmus*, 84 vols (Toronto, 1974-)

Erasmus of Rotterdam, *The Erasmus Reader*, edited by Erika Rummel (Toronto, 1990)

Fudge, Thomas A., editor, *The Crusade against Heretics in Bohemia, 1418–1437: Sources and Documents for the Hussite Crusades* (Aldershot, Hampshire, 2002)

Kempe, Margery, *The Book of Margery Kempe: A New Translation, Contexts, Criticism*, translated and edited by Lynn Staley (New York, 2000)

Peter of Mldonovice, *John Hus at the Council of Constance*, translated from the Latin and the Czech with notes and introduction by Matthew Spinka, Records of civilization, sources and studies, no. 73 (New York, 1965)

Petroff, Elizabeth A., editor, *Medieval Women's Visionary Literature* (New York and Oxford, 1986)

Van Engen, John, *Devotio Moderna: Basic Writings* (New York, 1988)

Modern scholarship

Bainton, Roland, *Erasmus of Christendom* (New York, 1969)

Duffy, Eamon, *The Stripping of the Altars: Traditional Religion in England, 1400–1580* (New Haven, 1992)

Füssel, Stephan, *Gutenberg and the Impact of Printing*, translated by Douglas Martin (Burlington, Vermont, 2005)

Gardners, Edmund, *Catherine of Siena* (1907), edited, annotated and reissued by Jon M. Sweeney under the title *The Road to Siena: The Essential Biography of St. Catherine* (Brewster, Massachusetts, 2009)

Huizinga, Johann, *Erasmus of Rotterdam* (London, 1924)

Kaminsky, Howard, *A History of the Hussite Revolution* (Berkeley, 1967)

Kittelson, James M., *Luther the Reformer: The Story of the Man and His Career* (Minneapolis, Minnesota, 1986)

Kroll, Jerome, and Bernard Bachrach, *The Mystic Mind: The Psychology of Medieval Mystics and Ascetics* (New York and London, 2005)

Lambert, Malcom, *Medieval Heresy: Popular Movements from the Gregorian Reform to the Reformation* (Cambridge, Massachusetts, 1992), pp. 225–389

McFarlane, K.B., *John Wycliffe and the Beginnings of English Non-conformity* (London, 1952)

Mitchell, Marea, *The Book of Margery Kempe: Scholarship, Community, and Criticism* (New York, 2005)

Phillips, Margaret Mann, *Erasmus and the Northern Renaissance*, revised edition (Woodbridge, Suffolk, 1981)

Rex, Richard, *The Lollards* (Houndmills, Basingstoke, 2002)

Spitz, Lewis W., *The Religious Renaissance of the German Humanists* (Cambridge, Massachusetts, 1963)

Stump, Phillip H., *The reforms of the Council of Constance, 1414–1418* (Leiden and New York, 1994)

Tierney, Brian, *Foundations of Conciliar Theory* (Cambridge, 1955)

Van Engen, John, *Sisters and Brothers of the Common Life: The Devotio Moderna and the World of the Later Middle Ages*, The Middle Ages Series (Philadelphia, 2008)

Note

1 This translation is adapted slightly from Henry Scowcroft Bettenson, *Documents of the Christian Church* (Oxford, 1967) p. 135.

21

Epilogue

I. The medieval church as construct

In simplest terms, a 'construct' is an idea or ideal of something that may not exist, or may never have existed, in exactly the way we think we understand it. 'Liberty' and 'femininity' and 'family' are all constructs, as is 'the medieval church'.

There were, of course, real churches in the Middle Ages: stone buildings with carved sculptures and stained glass, in which bishops governed, preachers preached and the laity worshipped. These were hardly just 'ideas'. But our ideas about 'the Church', or 'the Medieval Church' – what the sculptures and stained glass meant, how and why the bishops governed as they did, the impact of medieval sermons, and how the laity understood the church's rituals – all of this comprises a construct, probably several constructs. Since we were not there at the time of the medieval church's existence, this is perhaps the best we can hope for: an idea of what the past might have been like. Of course, we can insist that a good construct be based on the historical evidence, and that historians (and readers of history books) try to keep their biases in check. This is not always an easy thing to accomplish, as we can see if we look at past histories of the medieval church.

The earliest Christians were themselves constructing the idea of the church, in an effort to win acceptance, or at least tolerance from non-Christians. These so-called 'apologists' (from a Greek word *apologia*, meaning 'in defence of') constructed arguments to justify and defend the faith against the arguments of its critics. We saw this in Chapter 4, when Tertullian (*c*.160–*c*.225) argued that the number of Christians was growing, on account of God's favour toward them, even as the number of pagans declined. Yet we also saw Tertullian's construct of a growing Christian church 'deconstructed' in the light of demographic evidence provided by modern historians Ralph Novak and Robin Lane Fox.[1] Eusebius of Caesarea (*c*.260–339) was another early apologist. His *Preparation for the Gospel* argued for the superiority of Christianity over pagan religion and philosophy. While the apologists constructed arguments in defence of the church, many through the ages have constructed arguments opposing the church. One might expect negative constructions of the medieval church during movements such as the Renaissance or the Reformation. Petrarch's image of the church's 'Babylonian captivity' during the Avignon papacy was picked up by Martin Luther and other reformers. Later intellectual movements, such as the Enlightenment, also saw negative constructs of the medieval church. The English historian Edward Gibbon (1737–94), in his monumental work, *The History of the Decline and Fall of the Roman Empire*, argued that Christianity had been one of the main causes of Rome's decline. Enlightenment thinkers, like Gibbon, emphasised reason over faith, and often found religion to be little more than superstition. Gibbon's indictment of the medieval church is summed up in his famous description of the Middle Ages as 'the triumph of barbarism and religion'.[2]

Sectarian constructs of the medieval church continued into our own time, whether from the pro-medieval (Catholic) or anti-medieval (Protestant) camps. The early twentieth century saw a very public debate between the British historian G. G. Coulton (1858–1947) and Francis Aidan Gasquet (1846–1929), a Benedictine monk and historian. Coulton discredited Gasquet for his sloppy scholarship (and rightly so), but Coulton's writings also took on the tone of anti-Catholic polemics. More recent scholars have attempted to take sectarian concerns out of the mix, but this can reduce the medieval church to so much social or political history, with little concern for the very real beliefs people held. For example, a book published in 1996 has five noted economists attempting to interpret the medieval church as an economic construct, a response to historical contingency based on 'supply and demand'.[3]

Theories broadly lumped together under the heading of 'post-modernism' have made us acutely aware of how historians over the ages have constructed views of the medieval church, and how such constructs perhaps reveal more about the historians than about their subject. Surely the book you now hold in your hands is no different.

The title of this book, *The Medieval Church: A Brief History*, is perhaps most honest in its use of the word 'brief'. This is not just a problem with titles, but with textbooks in general: they cannot (and indeed are not intended to) cover everything. In the preface to the first edition, Lynch acknowledged that he 'had to be selective in [his] choice of topics'. He tried to remedy his selectivity by suggesting readings by which students might fill in the gaps. I would like to take that a step further by proposing a way of thinking about the medieval church, based on the history you have read here.

When historians think about history (and when they think about how they think about it), they call it historiography. This kind of thinking includes consideration of the sources and why they were chosen; the methods by which the history was constructed; and how the completed history might be better or worse from the histories that have gone before. In addition to these criteria, historiography should also include some discussion of the relevance of the topic(s) under examination. This must be undertaken with caution. Studying history for its own sake, while valid, can lead to escapism, while insisting that every aspect of history have a one-to-one, cause-and-effect correlation to today, can lead to presentism. Determining relevance is also the moment where our own biases most often get in the way. The relevance of an event may be different depending on one's point of view. Of course, we must try to understand the past on its own terms, but this is not so easy when the people whom we are studying lived so long ago and far away. It is tempting to make claims like 'medieval people were just like us' or, conversely, 'medieval people were downright strange', partly because there is a hint of truth in such claims. But these notions can also rob historical agents of their uniqueness and individuality.

Readers who have made it this far will have noticed some recurring themes in the history of the medieval church, the kind of big questions that make the study of history, especially the history of religion, resonate in our own times: what is the nature of God? How should God be worshipped? How does religion spread? How does a group of believers (a church) ensure unity? How does a church keep beliefs from becoming diluted in a diverse society? What role should the state play in religion? How does a church manage or control the belief and behaviour of its adherents? If you have read the previous chapters even somewhat carefully, specific examples of these issues from the history of the medieval church should now be popping into your head.

For good historical thinking, we need to consider these recurring themes in particular contexts. Even the context of 'the European Middle Ages', the overarching context of this book, was not monolithic, but changed over time. The somewhat arbitrary periods of the 'early', 'central' and 'late' Middle Ages help us start to consider context, but there is even more temporal subtlety within those periods – which do not begin to address spatial, geographic contexts. And the medieval context (once we narrow it down) was also different from our own. As an easy example, the question of God creating the universe and everything in it was much different for medieval people than it is for us, living in a time and place after the Scientific Revolution, and having the benefit of writings by Darwin, Einstein and others. From our vantage point, do we dismiss the medieval belief in creation as simplistic and superstitious? Do we call our contemporaries 'medieval' (in the current derogatory sense of this word), when they espouse 'creationism' or 'intelligent design'? Even before scientists took to offering evidential proofs concerning the origins of the universe, the Dominican friar Thomas Aquinas (1225–74) and his Franciscan contemporary Bonaventure (1221–74) attempted, through the force of reason alone, to prove that God's creation of the eternal universe was at least logically possible. These were medieval people, but they were hardly simplistic in their thinking.

The constructs historians devise are often the product of the historian's own context. The feminist movements of the 1960s and 1970s have led to more interest in the role of women in church history. Other social movements have led historians to examine the medieval church from the ground up, with studies on popular religion, and on those people whom the church tradition- ally marginalised. There are even new interpretations of 'heresy', not as a threat to authoritarian orthodoxy, but as its counterpart – the opposite side of the same coin, believers seeking God on different paths. But even these attempts to broaden the scope of what we define as 'medieval church history' are in themselves constructs, fraught with their own assumptions and biases, that can lead us to binary modes of thinking: paganism vs Christianity; heresy vs orthodoxy; women vs men; mainstream vs 'other'; elite vs popular; the exceptional example vs the commonplace. Such constructs can lead to reduc- tionist tendencies; they over-simplify matters that are in fact extremely com- plex. For example, while the traditional narrative of heresy pits the institution of the orthodox church against the Cathar heretics of the thirteenth and fourteenth centuries, the inquisitor's records of Jacques Fournier (*c.*1280– 1342) reveal more nuanced, 'live-and-let-live' relationships between Cathars and Catholics in the Montaillou region of southern France.[4] Hence between the extremes of persecution and acceptance, we see a range of attitudes where once we saw only binary constructs.

In addition to binaries, historians also struggle with conflation of complex ideas and processes. A good example of this is the construct of 'christianisa- tion'. Historian John Van Engen traces this term to the nineteenth century, and the struggle among historians on how to construct the medieval church:

> Disputing how to treat religion—as beneath notice or a sacred subject—itself became a key part of European history in the nineteenth century. Looking back upon Europe's long religious history, in anger or in nostalgia, historians and pundits attempted to grasp its complexity and movement in a single word, even as they had already effectively reduced its social history to something called 'feudalism' (also a new term). They hit upon the term 'christianisation,' and meant by it the creation of a broad cultural and religious matrix, not just the forming of a church.[5]

In this very textbook, we have seen how this term has persisted. In Chapter 4, we read how 'great obstacles stood in the way of Christianisation', in Chapter 8 of 'superficial Christianisation', and in Chapter 9 of 'the process of Christianisation'. Even in our attempt to offer a more nuanced reading of the medieval church, conflated terms like 'Christianisation' are hard to shed.

When historical constructs contain so many pitfalls, what is the student of history to do? This is especially tricky for students of the medieval church. How can a student with a more secular leaning approach this topic with an open mind? How can a student of faith approach the topic critically? As Van Engen put it: 'In a postmodern, post-Christian, post-Vatican II world, can the medieval church provoke anything but eccentric interest? Offer up anything but hooks for romantics, or polemicists, or reactionaries?'[6]

First, as Lynch suggested, we must read more widely and more deeply, recognising the limitations of textbooks, and branching out to the more specialised monographs on specific topics – books that have the luxury of presenting their subjects more thoroughly. Even in this wider and deeper reading, we must approach the scholarship on the medieval church with a critical eye. If humans are forever doomed to see the world through their own lens, then we must at least be aware of that shortcoming, and vigilant in keeping this reality in the forefront of our thoughts, whether we read medieval church history, or history in general.

Notes

1 Ralph Martin Novak, *Christianity and the Roman Empire: Background Texts* (Harrisburg, Pennsylvania, 2001), p. 103; Robin Lane Fox, *Pagans and Christians* (New York, 1989) p. 592.
2 Edward Gibbon, *The History of the Decline and Fall of the Roman Empire*, David Womersley, editor, 3 vols (London and New York, 1994), vol. 3, ch. 71, p. 1068.
3 See Robert Burton Ekelund, Robert D. Tollison, Gary M. Anderson, Robert F. Hébert and Audrey B. Davidson, *In Sacred Trust: The Medieval Church as an Economic Firm* (Oxford, 1996).
4 See Emmanuel Le Roy Ladurie, *Montaillou: The Promised Land of Error* (New York, 1978).
5 John Van Engen, 'The Future of Medieval Church History', *Church History*, vol. 71, no. 3 (Sep., 2002), pp. 495-6.
6 Van Engen, 'The Future of Medieval Church History', p. 495.

Index

Note: page references in *italics* refer to illustrations or maps